International Adoption

International Adoption

*Global Inequalities and the
Circulation of Children*

EDITED BY

*Diana Marre and
Laura Briggs*

New York University Press

NEW YORK AND LONDON

NEW YORK UNIVERSITY PRESS
New York and London
www.nyupress.org

Library of Congress Cataloging-in-Publication Data
International adoption : global inequalities and the circulation of
children / edited by Diana Marre and Laura Briggs.
p. cm.
Includes index.
ISBN-13: 978-0-8147-9101-1 (cl : alk. paper)
ISBN-10: 0-8147-9101-8 (cl : alk. paper)
ISBN-13: 978-0-8147-9102-8 (pb : alk. paper)
ISBN-10: 0-8147-9102-6 (pb : alk. paper)
1. Intercountry adoption. I. Marre, Diana. II. Briggs, Laura, 1964–
HV875.5.I573 2009
362.734—dc22   2008045878

New York University Press books are printed on acid-free paper,
and their binding materials are chosen for strength and durability.
We strive to use environmentally responsible suppliers and materials
to the greatest extent possible in publishing our books.

Manufactured in the United States of America

c 10 9 8 7 6 5 4 3 2 1
p 10 9 8 7 6 5 4 3 2 1

Contents

Acknowledgments

Diana Marre thanks CIIMU, especially its current director, Carmen Gómez-Granell, and the former chair of the Department of Anthropology at the University of Barcelona, Joan Bestard-Camps, for supporting the first International Forum on Childhood and Family, "On Philias and Phobias: From Biological to Cultural Kinship. Adoption, Homoparentality, and Other Ways to Construct Families," held from 29 September through 3 October 2006 at the Institute of Childhood and Urban World (CIIMU) and the University of Barcelona, Spain, where most of the authors involved in this project met, discussed their work, and decided to collaborate on a volume about the circulation of children. She is also indebted to the Spanish Ministry of Science and Innovation, which financed a research project on transnational adoption in Spain (SEJ2006-5286/SOCI) and provided her with a shared space to discuss and work on this book. Laura Briggs thanks the Tanner Humanities Center at the University of Utah for research support and the Department of Women's Studies at the University of Arizona for time off that facilitated work on this book, and is grateful to the people who read drafts, especially Peter Selman, Karen Dubinsky, and Kathryn Stockton. Finally, we extend our appreciation to Grey Osterud, without whose editorial assistance this book would not have been possible, as well as to Jennifer Hammer and Eric Zinner at New York University Press.

Introduction
The Circulation of Children

Laura Briggs and Diana Marre

In the early twenty-first century, many concerned observers suggest, we are entering a brave new world in reproduction, with medical technologies sundering genetics, gestation, and parenting, the globalization of adoption, and unprecedented waves of migration separating parents and children. This is true. Yet, at the same time, we are contending with the legacies of the past, including the best and the worst of the twentieth century. From the "Great War" that convulsed Europe in 1914 through the civil and international conflicts that have engulfed many regions of the world almost continuously since then, wars, refugee crises, ethnic cleansing, and movements to defend human rights have all marked adoption. As anthropologist Pauline Turner Strong wrote about the adoption of Native children by non-Native parents in North America, "adoption across political and cultural borders may simultaneously be an act of violence and an act of love, an excruciating rupture and a generous incorporation, and an appropriation of valued resources and a constitution of personal ties" (2001: 471). Adoption opens a window onto the relations between nations, inequalities between rich and poor within nations, the history of race and racialization since the end of slavery in Europe's colonies and the United States, and relationships between indigenous and non-indigenous groups in the Americas and Australia. Transnational adoption emerged out of war. Only recently has it become, rather than an occasional practice, a significant way of forming a family for those who cannot have children. Even this new form of transnational adoption has been marked by the geographies of unequal power, as children move from poorer countries and families to wealthier ones—and the forces that make a country rich and powerful are above all historical. In this sense, transnational adoption has been shaped by the forces of colonialism, the Cold War, and globalization.

Adoption has become a reflection of the horror and the generosity of our recent history in part because in the twentieth century we came to see children as innocent and particularly vulnerable to victimization, in contrast to earlier periods when they were regarded as like miniature adults (Ariès 1962, Zelizer 1985). Pediatrics as a distinct medical specialty emerged at the beginning of the twentieth century; the Swedish feminist Ellen Key published a book proposing new attitudes towards children in 1909; the Polish-Jewish physician Janus Korczak wrote about the idea of "children's rights" in 1910; and a group of physicians from Argentina, Uruguay, and Brazil initiated a series of American Child Congresses in 1916 (Therborn 1996). Adoption was transformed over the twentieth century from an institution of labor similar to apprenticeship, or a form of inheritance involving the appointment of a legal heir, by the uneven emergence of this new notion of childhood.[1] To this way of thinking, children are not little adults, smaller and less skilled workers, funnier and cuter participants in all human relationships, but rather occupants of a distinct stage of life—innocent, in need of special protection, and deserving shelter from life's harshness.

Fostering War Refugees in Europe

After the First World War, this notion of childhood was deployed quite effectively to feed refugees, in a project that formed a precursor to transnational adoption. The Fight the Famine Council—an organization that later became Save the Children—was founded in England in response to news reports of hungry children in Germany and Austria subsisting on cabbage, of six-year-olds the size of two-year-olds, when the Allied powers were blockading Austria and Germany in order to force them to accept the terms of the Treaty of Versailles. One of the group's founding members, Eglantyne Jebb, was arrested for handing out a leaflet showing a starving Austrian baby with the heading "Our Blockade Has Caused This." The Famine Council sent relief funds from England to a host of unpopular places and peoples during the interwar years: Germany and Austria (as well as France and Belgium), refugees from the Armenian genocide, and

Soviet Russia. In 1924, the group persuaded the League of Nations to issue a Declaration of Children's Rights (Therborn 1996). In the United States, the American Friends Service Committee, a Quaker group, developed a child-feeding program in response to the crisis.[2]

Although many commentators have dated the history of transnational adoption to the post–World War II period, when the resumption of immigration made U.S. citizens' adoption of foreign children possible, Europeans met the human rights disasters of the 1930s and forties by fostering and adopting children in trouble, including those victimized by the Nazis and by Franco.[3] Civilians have never really been protected from war, but the horrors of "modern warfare" that deliberately targeted civilian populations still had the capacity to shock: the bombs dropped on the Basque city of Guernica by Franco's forces and the German Luftwaffe, the Blitzkrieg against London, the Allied firebombing of Dresden, the atomic bombs dropped by the United States on Hiroshima and Nagasaki, and the Holocaust, the extermination campaign against Jews and others judged racially inferior or politically or socially undesirable conducted by the Nazis. In response to this targeting of civilians, groups across Europe organized to rescue the victims, especially the children. Young people from Guernica were sent to foster and adoptive homes in Mexico, Scandinavia, the Soviet Union, and Belgium. Almost 4,000 children were evacuated from Bilbao, in the Basque region of Spain, to Britain.[4]

The British *kindertransport* brought 10,000 unaccompanied, mostly Jewish refugee children from Germany and German-occupied Austria and Czechoslovakia, while others were relocated to foster and adoptive homes in Holland and Belgium. Swedes took in Danish children after the Nazi occupation there, and an estimated 70,000 Finnish children were evacuated to Sweden to escape Finland's war with Russia. Britain evacuated children from London to rural areas, and an estimated 13,000 were privately evacuated to the United States and Canada. A plan by the Children's Overseas Reception Board to evacuate children to England's overseas Dominions was scrapped after only a few thousand children had been transported, following a tragic incident in which a ship carrying child refugees to Canada, the *City of Benares,* was sunk by a submarine. Across Europe, thousands of Jewish children were hidden in homes, schools, and monasteries to protect them from the Nazis. At the same time, children fathered by German soldiers in occupied areas with "Aryan" mothers were returned to the "fatherland" and adopted there (Altstein and Simon 1992,

Wyman 1968, Laquer 2001, Legarreta 1984, Forbes and Weiss Fagen 1985, 1984, Ressler, Boothby, and Steinbeck 1988, Lovelock 2000, Harris 2000, Slesin 2003).

In the United States, in contrast to these extensive European humanitarian efforts to rescue children during the war, opponents of immigration largely prevented refugees, including children, from entering the country. The 1924 Immigration Restriction Act set strict quotas to minimize the presence of those who, it was said, would degrade the "racial stock" of the U.S. population. Still more devastating, even these restricted quotas were not filled during the war, as the State Department exercised its authority to ban those who were "LPC," liable to become a public charge, i.e., dependent on charitable or government assistance. In 1939, the U.S. Non-Sectarian Committee for Refugee Children was able to persuade its allies in Congress to sponsor hearings on a plan to provide foster and adoptive homes for 20,000 children from Germany and German-occupied areas. Although the committee lined up considerable support from religious leaders, politicians, and child welfare experts, the measure to give visas to unaccompanied children, the Wagner-Rogers bill, was never reported out of committee, defeated by arguments that these children would grow up to take jobs from Americans, anti-Semitism against those whom some called "refu-Jews," and the suspicion that those who opposed fascism were communists. As one person who testified against the bill said, "Of course the communist house would welcome a child" (U.S. Congress 1939: 132). Quietly, being careful to avoid attracting the attention of authorities, some families did bring in unaccompanied Jewish refugee children, the "one thousand," as they were called. About 5,000 British children were also welcomed into U.S. foster homes in 1940.[5]

These initial efforts on behalf of refugee children in the Spanish Civil War and World War II were markedly different from what followed. These were explicitly foster homes, not adoptive families. When possible, children were encouraged to maintain connections with their parents. When parents died or disappeared, as happened to many Jewish children, international social service groups sought other surviving family members to raise the children. Although some foster families objected and many found the separations wrenching, there was little belief that foster parents ought to have rights to, or even contact with children who had spent four or five years with them—some for essentially their whole lives, since they were babes in arms (Slesin 2003, Harris 2000).

Adopting War Orphans and the Progeny of American Soldiers

In the United States, the end of the Second World War brought the uneven and gradual but decisive removal of most legal barriers to immigration, as the nation assumed an increasingly prominent role on the world stage. The human geographer Richard H. Weil linked the interest in overseas adoption at the end of the war with the illegitimate children fathered by men in the U.S. forces occupying Europe and Asia, although "the U.S. military has never developed a policy to deal with foreign adoptions by its personnel" (Falatko 1983, quoted in Weil 1984: 279). The only relevant action was a 1947 order by the Occupation Force that turned over control of local adoptions by U.S. personnel to the German courts (Hochfeld and Valk, quoted in Weil 1984). "The first step [in] formulating appropriate foreign adoption criteria occurred in 1948 when the Displaced Persons Act allowed 4,065 'orphans' (a term which has remained broad enough to include children relinquished by a parent or parents) to enter the country." Among this group were 500 children adopted by U.S. personnel, but how many of them were the progeny of the Occupation Forces is unknown (Weil 1984: 279–82).

As historian Christina Klein has argued, the idea of U.S. Americans adopting children from overseas was part of the "middlebrow imagination" that provided grassroots support for the political transformation of the United States into a world power. She points to Norman Cousins and the *Saturday Review*, where an article about children in Hiroshima orphaned by the atomic bombing prompted an outpouring of offers to "sponsor" a child in an orphanage and urgent questioning about changing U.S. immigration law so that readers could actually adopt the children. Klein argues that these kinds of impulses helped transform the United States from an isolationist nation to one whose citizens could imagine themselves with a somewhat paternalistic responsibility for the rest of the world (2003: 143–90). More formally, the U.S. State Department resettled 1,300 children from Hungary as the Soviet Army waged its bloody battle for Budapest in 1945, as part of Truman's effort to salvage something from the "loss" of Eastern Europe behind the "Iron Curtain" (Lovelock 2000).[6] Another significant group of children was admitted for adoption after the United States supported the anticommunist forces during the civil war in Greece (1946–1949). Liberal groups such as Pearl Buck's Welcome House sought U.S. adoptive parents for "Eurasian" and "Amerasian" children left behind by U.S. and European servicemen in the Philippines, Japan, and China (Buck 1967, Buck and Harris 1966, Conn 1996).

In the United States, though, the largest group advocating the resettlement of children orphaned or displaced by the "small" wars that flared during the Cold War was evangelical Christians (of course, for those who were caught in them, there was nothing small or cold about these wars). A young minister in Youth for Christ, Rev. Bob Pierce, founded World Vision in 1950, an evangelical missionary organization that focused on organizing U.S. Americans to send $5 a month to sponsor a child, beginning in China and then expanding into Korea. Evangelical Protestantism was undergoing a revival during the 1950s as a key ally of a political anticommunism, most famously through another member of Youth for Christ, Billy Graham. Rev. Graham was drawing large crowds with a simple message: the Bible is the literal word of God, and it demands that we act in the world to stop "godless communism" (Bagdikian 1997). Although evangelicals were as politically conservative as the anti-immigrant forces that had blocked transnational adoption to the United States in previous decades, theirs was a universalist faith, insisting that all people were equally God's children. This message inspired U.S. American conservatives, and evangelical anticommunism became powerfully wed to conservative international politics—and both became intimately entwined with transnational adoption.

Bertha and Harry Holt, an Oregon couple, attracted attention for taking Rev. Pierce's plan of sponsoring an orphan one step further and adopting Korean children in the aftermath of the war. Pierce and World Vision had filmed *Lost Sheep*, a documentary full of sad-eyed children in South Korean orphanages that was shown in evangelical churches around the United States, urging viewers to sponsor an orphan. According to their narrative, when Bertha and Harry Holt saw that film one night in Eugene, it changed their lives—and the face of Christian transnational adoption. Through World Vision, the Holts began the arduous mission of legally adopting eight Korean "orphans," most the "Amerasian" progeny of American GIs who had been stationed in Korea, obtaining a special act of Congress to allow visas for the children. Nine children, including one destined for another couple, arrived in Oregon to considerable fanfare. World Vision employed a publicist on their behalf, and photographers and journalists made their arrival into a media circus. A few years later, celebrity couple Roy Rogers and Dale Evans of rodeo, radio, and TV fame, who were also prominent evangelical Christians, adopted a Korean orphan through the Holts' enterprise. The Holts expanded their sphere of church-based child rescue activism to include building orphanages in South Korea and running an adoption service in the United States. Half a century later, Holt International remains one of the largest international adoption agencies in the country (Evans Rogers 1965, Holt and Albus 1956, Holt 1982, Holt, Wisner, and Albus 1992). In significant measure as a result of the Holts' campaign to publicize the plight of Korean children, the Refugee Relief Act of 1953 and another law in 1957 allowed up to 4,000 special visas for children to enter the United States (Hochfeld 1954, Kim et al. 1979, Koh 1982 quoted in Weil 1984: 282). In subsequent years, immigration restriction eased for those entering the United States from Asia; symbolically in 1954, when the McCarren-Walter Act offered ridiculously tiny quotas, and actually in 1965. During these years, smaller but significant numbers of Korean children also began to be adopted to Sweden, Norway, and the United Kingdom (Hübinette 2005, Howell, this volume). When the war in Viet Nam ended in 1975, more than 2,000 children were picked up in Saigon and flown to adoptive families throughout the United States, Canada, and Europe. Many of them were of mixed ancestry, literally embodying the U.S. (and French) war there. Organized by Holt International and a host of other organizations, Operation Babylift (with a name that sounds like a military campaign) was warmly embraced by liberals and conservatives alike as an opportunity to salvage something from the horror of the war. Some witnesses expressed uneasiness, suggesting that children were hurriedly being picked up off the streets of Saigon and packed onto airplanes, without any effort to find their parents, as the city fell to advancing North Vietnamese troops (Warren 2004, Lipman 1996, Dolgin and Franco 2002).[7] Others continue to tell the story of Babylift as a way an individual can make a difference. One of the precipitating events occurred in 1973, when the photographer "Chick" Harrity of the Associated Press took a picture showing a street child sleeping in a cardboard box with her brother by her side on a Saigon street that was published in newspapers around the world. The girl, Tran Thie Het Nhanny, was adopted by Evelyn Heil of Springfield, Ohio, an event that was followed by thousands of Vietnamese children being adopted by American families. In 2005, when Harrity was honored with the White House News Photographers' Association's Lifetime Achievement Award, the awards committee observed "that a picture became instrumental" in promoting the adoption of these children. After an emotional meeting in which Harrity and Nhanny embraced, Harrity added "It was one of those drop-dead moments. It brought home the real aspect of what we do. It can change lives. It certainly changed her life. We can affect the world" (Halstead 2005).[8]

The Korean War marked a change in the nature of efforts on behalf of children in war zones. In contrast to the committees that placed children in foster homes during World War II, Holt and similar agencies understood the goal as adoption, the permanent removal of children from their family, community, and country. Evangelical Protestants were also committed to religious conversion; the children would be raised Christian, whatever the faith of their birth parents. While secular agencies provided no explicit direction about the religious faith in which adopted children would be raised, leaving it up to the adoptive parents represented a real decision to promote or at least allow conversion. In contrast, there was an explicit effort during World War II to preserve the Jewish identity of rescued and hidden children; after the war, if no living relative of a hidden child could be found, international committees sought out a Jewish family to raise the child. Some Catholic institutions and some individual families had baptized Jewish children during the war, but these baptisms were controversial and contested. Those arranging adoptions of Korean children were singularly incurious about the religious background of the children. The programs took for granted that children would be converted religiously, nationally, and socially: they would become little Americans, or Swedes, or Norwegians (see Howell, this volume).

Removing Indigenous Children and Taking Children in "Dirty Wars"

In the 1950s and sixties, many countries in Western Europe and North America expanded their national programs to address poverty, more or less explicitly in answer to the Cold War questions raised by the Soviet Union in particular and socialists in general about whether poverty was better addressed by communism than by capitalism. These programs had contradictory effects on adoption. More people who had been ignored by the state came to its attention; at times they received aid and were subjected to regulation and reform. In the United States, Canada, and Australia, Native children began to be taken into the care of the child welfare system in startling numbers. Although all three countries had had boarding school programs with a curriculum of "civilizing" aboriginal peoples since the nineteenth century, these were contracting, leaving more and more aboriginal children living with their parents on reserves. Efforts to address poverty brought these children to the attention of social workers. The result was what Canadians called the "Sixties Scoop" and Australians called the "Stolen Generation," but most non-Native people in the United States have not yet grappled with: Native children were taken from their families and placed with white families in considerable numbers. In 1969, the Association on American Indian Affairs in the United States calculated the proportion of Native children not living with their families or tribes at as high as one-third in some states (U.S. Congress 1977, Johnson 1983).[9] This period also saw a sharp increase in the number of African American children in foster care, which some in the United States called the "browning of child welfare." The influx of racially minoritized and impoverished children into the child welfare systems put pressure on states to find permanent homes for them, both because temporary homes were seen as bad for children and because state care was hugely expensive. As a result of this increase in children in temporary care, the rise of racially based integration movements, and a spirit of social experimentation, child welfare and adoption systems began to experiment nationally with what the Korea program had initiated internationally: cross-religious and transracial adoptions.

Canada and the United States, through the Adoption Resource Exchange of North America (ARENA) program in the 1970s, organized one of the early transnational adoption programs, initially as a way of placing Native children with white families on both sides of the border. This was the most formal of such adoption exchanges, although not the earliest. In the 1950s, the Congressional hearings on "black market babies" chaired by Senator Estes Kefauver (D-Tenn.) revealed that many private, for-profit adoption exchanges had occurred between the two countries in the forties and earlier (U.S Senate 1955). Canada was both a sending and receiving country for intercountry adoptions from the forties through the seventies, as the United States is now. The United States continues to send children and babies into adoptions to Canada and Europe—mostly to the Netherlands and the United Kingdom—and, especially in the Netherlands, particularly African American children (Balcolm 2007).[10]

At the same time that some Native and African-descended children were becoming more likely to be adopted, rising standards of living on the whole had the opposite effect, reducing the number of white children available for adoption within the United States and Western Europe.

Beginning in the 1960s, fewer "unwed" mothers were placing their babies for adoption as a combination of state supports for parents and rising wages and employment opportunities for women enabled them to keep their children. As soon as single mothers could afford to keep their children, they did. In the United States, this change, together with the legalization of birth control for unmarried women in 1972 and of abortion in 1973, contributed to what some came to call the "white baby famine"—the perception that the only babies available for adoption are Black or Latino children in foster care. Although the growth of private and commercialized adoption in the decades that followed expanded the pool of adoptable white infants, once the Pandora's Box of women being able to control their fertility and support their children on their own wages was opened, there was no return to the relatively high number of adoptable white children available during the 1950s (Solinger 2001, 1992). In Western Europe, where nations did not develop privatized or commercialized adoption systems and the social welfare system was far more extensive, the transformation was even more complete; only small numbers of older children with extensive histories in the child welfare system, usually from families in trouble, are available for adoption domestically.

While the Cold War prompted efforts at alleviating poverty that, at least temporarily, brought greater social equality in some countries, in Latin America it brought fierce civil wars, declared and undeclared, supported with arms and training in intelligence and counterinsurgency by the United States and the Soviet Union. For the superpowers, these became proxy wars, although they were never only that in Latin America. Adoption was a significant propaganda tool in these conflicts. When Castro took power in Cuba in 1959, Cuban exiles in Miami sought to bring Cuban children to the United States. In keeping with other anomalous immigration programs for Cuban exiles after the revolution, Cuban children were admitted without visas, accepted with a simple photocopied letter from a particular Miami priest. There were suspicions that Operation Pedro Pan, as it was called in the United States, not only received these kinds of special favors from the State Department but in fact was actively abetted by the Central Intelligence Agency (CIA). In 1997, political scientist and former Pedro Pan child María de los Angeles Torres sued the CIA under the Freedom of Information Act and received documents that confirmed this suspicion. The CIA was deeply involved with the anti-Castro underground on the island that promoted rumors that Castro was about to "nationalize" children, taking them from parents and sending them elsewhere on the island, or to the Soviet Union. The agency promoted these rumors through Radio Swan, and it was kept apprised of the success of the effort to bring more than 14,000 unaccompanied children to the United States between 1960 and 1962, when the State Department cut off the flow—and stopped parents from reuniting with their children—by halting all flights from Cuba. Wayne Smith, who worked in the U.S. embassy in Cuba in this period, told María de los Angeles Torres that he believed that the goal of the visa waiver program and the rumors that Castro was going to remove children from their families was propaganda. "The idea was to frighten families and . . . strengthen anti-government actions and attitudes. And also it was good propaganda, all these children coming out, fleeing godless communism because the Cuban government might take them away from their parents" (Torres 2003; see also Triay 1998, Conde 1999, Dubinsky 2007, Crespo and Marrawi 2000).[11]

Throughout the Americas, the decades from 1950 through the mid-1990s saw many internal purges of accused communists, opposition members, and many civilians who were essentially innocent bystanders, including the "Dirty War" in Argentina, Chile, and Uruguay, the terror in Stroessner's Paraguay, the civil wars in El Salvador, Guatemala, and Nicaragua, and the bodies by the side of the road under the military junta in Brazil. In these and other countries, taking the children of accused leftists was a tactic of terror, and human rights groups have used these kidnappings and the children's subsequent "adoptions"—including transnational ones—as the focus of criminal prosecutions of those wielding political power during those years.[12] Although many of those who might have otherwise been named as war criminals were protected by retrospective amnesties, kidnapping children and sending them to be raised by other families was the one crime that could be prosecuted, because the children were not returned to their families and the crime continued past the date of the cut-off for pardons (Asociación de Abuelas de la Plaza de Mayo 1995, Arditti 1999, Cortina et al. 2005).

During the Cold War, many Latin American countries began to organize systems to make significant numbers of children available for transnational adoption, based on a model that combined the earlier goal of rescuing refugee children from war zones with the concerns that became prominent in subsequent decades, matching impoverished children with childless couples in other countries. Children "disappeared" for political reasons were also part of this mix, and many well-meaning adopters inadvertently became part of this process of disappearances. After 1989, as the Cold War drew to a close, so too did the era of civil wars and dictator-ships in Latin America, and nation after nation began slowly to return to democratic systems of governance. Transnational adoption, under a cloud of allegations of exploitation, kidnapping, commercialization, and even the adoption of children for organ theft, was gradually reduced to a trickle in most countries by the end of the 1990s in favor of in-country adoption (see Fonseca, Abreu, Leinaweaver, Selman, in this volume).[13] The excep-tion was Guatemala, where the trickle became a flood until 2007; the fu-ture of Guatemalan adoption policy is now uncertain.

Adopting Children "Abandoned" in Post-Communist Countries

The forcible taking of children from indigenous parents and from par-ents accused of political radicalism during "Dirty Wars" are extreme cases of a more general trend. Since the end of the Cold War, most children circulating in adoption are social orphans; they have living parents but have been relinquished by them or taken by the state and declared legally abandoned; they are only legally "orphans." While the primary send-ing countries have shifted, the social character of orphanhood has been reinforced.

As Latin American countries were increasingly "closed" to transna-tional adoption, other nations, particularly in the former Soviet Union and elsewhere in Eastern Europe, "opened," often abruptly. In 1989, with the fall of Nicolae Ceaușescu in Romania, the international press de-tailed the deplorable conditions in Romanian orphanages, where tens of thousands of children were virtually abandoned, victims of Ceaușescu's plans to increase birth rates by outlawing abortion and birth control to build the nation's strength—especially its military—but without the re-sources to care for the children.[14] In 1990, thousands of Europeans and U.S. Americans adopted babies and children from Romania (Selman, this volume). The following year the Romanian government all but halted transnational adoption, saying that the flood of would-be adopters had produced a babies-for-cash market that was resulting in children with no connection with orphanages being "sold" (U.S. Congress 1991).[15] Children from stigmatized ethnic minority groups such as the Rom (Gypsies) were particularly vulnerable. Variations of this story continued to be played out in Eastern Europe: the "opening" of a country to adoption, followed by allegations of commercialization and abuse, sometimes with a period of sharp restriction on transnational adoptions—including the closing of Russia for many adoptions from 2006 to 2008 (see Khabibullina, this volume).

In the wake of the Cold War, China started a transnational adoption program that quickly became one of the largest in the world. That vast and populous country's one-child policy provided significant penalties for those who had a second child, or those whose first child was a girl but longed for a boy. China had no systems that allowed for legal relinquishment, so its transnational adoption program placed abandoned children —those whom some analysts prefer to say were "left where they would be found." Despite a long history of adoption, the country had few mechanisms for adoption by families within China, although this has recently become easier (Volkman 2005a, Evans 2000, Johnson and Klatzin 2004, A. Wolf and Huang 1980, M. Wolf 1985). In 2006, China announced new restrictions on transnational adopters, including their age, educational attainment, and even weight, perhaps in an effort to minimize the number of children adopted overseas and ramp up its domestic adoptions. In the United States and Spain, the two countries with the highest rates of adoption from that nation, adoptive families of children from China are among the most networked and interconnected of all overseas adopting families, producing significant and influential organizations (see Marre and Bestard 2004, Marre 2007, and Volkman, this volume).

The explosion of the Internet provided new opportunities for transnational adoption and transnational adopters, enabling would-be adopters to find agencies, facilitators, and legal intermediaries. In the United States, private adoption came to account for more than half of all adoptions in the 1990s; in Spain, by the late 1990s around 70 percent of transnational adoptions were done independently, with assistance from nongovernmental agents or associations of adoptive parents (Marre 2004, Marre and Gaggiotti forthcoming). Communicating through the Internet, adopters compared experiences, shared tips, and talked with one another about their children's home countries and the challenges of raising them. The ease with which would-be parents met those who might offer them children was a mixed blessing, because it allowed less-than-reputable adoption facilitators, or brokers, to reach potential clients readily.

A series of international treaties, beginning with the Convention on the Rights of the Child of 1989, tried to protect children and families in "sending" countries from exploitation and codified preferences for internal adoption over intercountry adoption. The differences between U.S.

systems—private and for-profit—and the dominant European systems —bureaucratic and state-based—for organizing transnational adoptions became an issue during the negotiations for the most prominent of these treaties, the Hague Convention on Intercountry Adoption of 1993. Ultimately, U.S. negotiators persuaded the group to continue to allow independent adoptions, but under a central authority in each country (Lovelock 2000). For more than a decade, the United States, one of the countries with largest transnational adoption programs (at least in raw numbers, although many European nations, such as Spain and Norway, exceeded it in per capita adoptions), did not come into compliance with the treaty, as it continued to engage extensively in transnational adoptions from Guatemala, which refused to create a central authority, failed to establish workable systems for in-country adoption, and did not develop a system that brought all adoptions before a judge. Although many have seen the Hague and related conventions as providing crucial human rights protections, others have noted that they bring informal adoption practices that have been common for centuries (and historically not always separated by a bright line from legal adoption, in terms of the ways people understand their family relations) particularly among poor people, into conflict with international law (see Fonseca, Schachter, this volume).

The first decade of the new millennium is seeing an unprecedented combination of xenophobia and transnational adoption that may make raising transnationally adopted children more difficult (Yngvesson, this volume). During the World War II period, countries either restricted immigration or took in transnationally displaced children. Now, in contrast, the United States and Western Europe have both increasingly virulent anti-immigrant campaigns (Marre, this volume) and large numbers of transnationally adopted children. Moreover, since both migration and adoption are often viewed as similar in many senses (Legrand, this volume) and are likely to be from former colonies or countries where the receiving country had significant political involvement (Guatemala with the United States, Ethiopia with Italy, Morocco and Latin America with Spain), sometimes the targets of anti-immigrant racism and the adorable babies of transnational adoption come from the same places on different kinds of visas.[16] The issue is interestingly different for Muslims, the religious group that is most often targeted by anti-immigrant movements, because Islamic law does not permit adoption, in the sense of a full legal estrangement from the child's birth parents, but authorizes only a form of guardianship called Kafala, and that privilege is generally reserved for other Muslims (Bargach 2002).[17] Some Islamic children are adopted transnationally, as native-born and immigrant Muslims live in many nations and immigrants, too, adopt (see Ouellette, Marre, this volume).

Transnational Adoption as a Stratified Form of Assisted Reproduction

Beginning in the 1980s, new strategies for making families emerged, including donor insemination (DI), in vitro fertilization (IVF), and gestational surrogacy, in which a woman carries a pregnancy with the intention of relinquishing the newborn to another individual or couple, who generally have some of their gametes involved in the conception of the embryo. Where surrogacy contracts were unlawful, some lesbians and gay men also began openly to use what might be called an "old" reproductive technology: relying on informal relationships, such as a heterosexual friend who became pregnant but felt they could not raise another child, to give them a child (see Cadoret 2002, Cadoret, this volume). Through contractual arrangements, clinics, and sperm banks, or informally, the number of people using these reproductive technologies has exploded, running parallel to and sometimes directly affecting the dynamics of international adoption. During the 1990s, many Western European countries modified their assisted reproduction laws to include all treatments "with donated material, surrogacy or otherwise socially reconstructed forms of parenthood" (Akker 2001: 148). Consequently, in European countries such as Norway, both new reproductive technologies (NRTs) and transnational adoption are considered forms of assisted reproduction. To some extent this is correct; in this period transnational adoption became another way to have a child for parents who were unable or unwilling to do so through "normal" conception. Indeed, in 1990, confronting the changes wrought to parenthood by NRTs, Sandelowski suggested that the meaning of "normal" conception had become unclear (Sandelowski et al. 1990 quoted in Akker 2001: 148). Some studies showed that infertile couples tended to be less favorable in their attitudes toward adoption than fertile couples, perhaps as a result of their experience with and investment in NRTs (Aghanwa et al. 1999, Halman et al. 1992, both quoted in Akker 2001: 149). But NRTs also contributed to the acceptance of adoption by normalizing the idea that reproduction can include more than two people and adding some fuzziness to the binary opposition between "natural" biological reproduction and "unnatural" adoption (compare with Čepaitienė, this volume). As anthropologists Faye Ginsburg and Rayna Rapp point out, "the creation and birth of a baby [through assisted reproduction] may involve as many as five adults contributing everything from genetic material to gestational nurturance to the social life of a family not to mention a cast of thousands in medical laboratories, legal offices, and insurance agencies" (1995: xi). Analogous to the ways in which contraception separated sex from reproduction during the 1950s, in the 1980s NRTs showed that reproduction was possible without sex. It would seem that the locus of "where babies come from" shifted from heterosexual sex to the simple desire to become a parent or to have a child. But the ability to access NRTs was, and is, highly stratified. As happened before with the contraceptive pill, legal and vacuum-aspiration abortion, surgical sterilization, amniocentesis and fetal screening, these technologies are much more difficult for women who are not wealthy to obtain and use. A Spanish adoptive mother with a girl from China told Diana Marre, "adoption is cheaper—and the results are more certain." For middle-class, working-class, and poor women, adoption is often the first choice, for reasons of economy and access.

The categories of people using NRTs and turning to international adoption have changed, too: singles, gay men, and lesbians are far more likely than a generation ago to use reproductive technology, although access to it has been uneven. In the last two decades, most restrictions for lesbian, gay, and bisexual persons in the United States and Canada have fallen away, as reproductive technology has increasingly become available to anyone who can afford it. In Western Europe, however, the picture has been more mixed, and some lesbian couples travel to other countries to find donor sperm—Norwegians going to Denmark, for example, or Italians to Spain (Howell and Melhus 2007). Although reproductive technology is in some ways the opposite of transnational adoption (Čepaitienė, this volume), in other ways it is not: as suggested above, gametes travel across national lines. Even for heterosexuals, one or both partners may need to get a legal adoption in the case of gestational surrogacy, and in the case of donor gametes with IVF, where there is no legal cause for an adoption, there is a sense in which the "parents" are raising another's child. All of this may take place within or across national boundaries (see Gross, this volume).

Falling birth rates in the United States, Canada, and Europe is one factor propelling the rise in transnational adoptions. While the widespread rumors of increasing rates of infertility turned out to be incorrect—there is no evidence that that is the case—it is nevertheless true that large numbers of individuals and couples who want to have children cannot conceive. The major cause is that more women seeking to conceive are older and therefore have impaired fertility. The same social changes that allowed unwed mothers to keep their babies—increasing opportunities for women to earn wages—also resulted in delayed childbearing, as middle-class women sought to become established in a career before having a child. Declining real wages after the 1970s also drove women into the labor force, as more families needed two or more wage-earners (Chandra et al. 2005, Hochschild 1989). Some turned to transnational adoption to remedy this "structural" (i.e., labor force-induced) infertility.

International adoption processes today are not just the result of a war or other kinds of direct violence between or within nations. They are also the product of what anthropologist Shellee Colen has called "stratified reproduction," a transnational system of power relations that enables privileged women to bear and nurture children while disempowering those who are subordinated by reason of class, race, and national origin (1986). Modifying the question posed by Faye Ginsburg and Rayna Rapp (1995: 3) about "who is normatively entitled to refuse childbearing, to be a parent, to be a caretaker, to have other caretakers for their children, to give nurture or to give culture (or both)," after more than a decade of massive levels of transnational adoption, we might ask, who is normatively entitled to expect of others that they will engage in biological reproductive functions for them, while they retain the "right" to be the providers of the child's nurture and culture? The possibility of family formation beyond a certain age, or despite other fertility problems, was enlarged during the 1980s not only because of the development of NRTs but also as a byproduct of wars and economic inequalities that provided children for adoption. These factors allowed the "outsourcing" of such reproductive functions as pregnancy, childbirth, and sometimes the first years of babies' lives to less expensive places and/or mothers—literally, laborers.

From this vantage point, we might ask whether the ways some women are denied access to the means to limit their fertility are a form of "euphemized violence," following anthropologist Ann Anagnost (1995: 34) and Ginsburg and Rapp (1995: 4, 15, n. 2). The Catholic Church's opposition to contraception and Evangelical Protestant pressure to outlaw any form of abortion have been murderous at worst, or at best compelled women to have unwanted children. For example, Argentina legalized voluntary surgical sterilization for women just last year. Nicaragua and El Salvador effectively outlawed even medically necessary procedures after a miscarriage or in the event of an ectopic pregnancy if there were any chance the fetus was still living, as a result of a ban on abortion without an exception to save the life of the mother. But even in Latin America, where access to contraception and abortion has been severely restricted, not all women are affected; it is, rather, working-class, impoverished, and marginalized women who have been condemned to unwanted reproduction by a "seemingly beneficent discourse on morality and the family" (Kertzer 1993, quoted by Ginsburg and Rapp 1995: 4) that results in the "production" of children for the local and international upper and middle class. The Catholic Church encourages women to think about "the best interest of the child" by giving him or her "a better life" in a "good" family through adoption. Thinking in terms of euphemized violence would also help us frame China's one-child policy and its consequences for impoverished rural couples who cannot imagine how they will survive in their old age without a son's income to provide support—and the relative silence surrounding it compared to the international protests of the explicit violence in Tibet. We might similarly note that the demand for childless, unmarried women workers by employers in globalized manufacturing sectors called "Special Economic Zones," *maquiladoras*, or "Export Processing Zones," where labor laws do not apply and where young women frequently live in company-owned barracks, is another way of supplying infants to wealthy women and families, locally and internationally (Johnson and Klatzin 2004, Evans 2000, Hübinette 2005).

Euphemized violence also occurs in wealthy countries and classes. The increasing insecurity of work life until late into adulthood; the salary differentials between women and men—women earn between 17 and 30 percent less than what men do in the EU, and 33 percent less than average male wage in the United States; the lack of policies designed to balance family and work; the failure of heterosexual men to assume half the burden of familial and domestic labor—all conspire to make delaying or "outsourcing" childbearing seem rational or even forced choices. Shellee Colen demonstrates how these "First World" and "Third World" forms of gendered violence work together, following West Indian women who left their own children with kin in the Islands to go to New York looking for well-paid jobs and end up caring for white middle-class children whose working mothers hired them because of their lack of public childcare options, insufficient support to enable them to stay home, and an entrenched sexual division of labor (Colen 1995, 1990, 1989, 1986). Now, the pressure on domestic and child-rearing labor seems to have gone beyond even the point where a nanny can solve it. Many employed women in wealthy countries cannot afford to engage even in pregnancy or childbirth. For example, sociologist Jens Qvortrup stated that 40 percent of German women in academia expect to remain childless (2005: 1), and the last seven permanent positions in a Social Sciences department in a well-known Spanish university were occupied by single men or childless women in their forties, some of whom subsequently decided to adopt internationally. Women who offer children for adoption from Third World countries differ from the West Indian nannies that Colen writes about in that they are not doing it as a job. The only benefit to these women is the avoidance of some other horror. They are doing it because they lack the economic, familial, and/or personal resources to raise a child, they did not have access to contraception, economic hardship forced a male partner to migrate internally or internationally, and a temporary liaison with another man, for economic survival or simple companionship, left them with a child they could not keep. Many are victims of sexual violence; most have other children to support. Whatever the case, adoption does not particularly benefit the mother or her other children, or provide a means to improve her situation. On the contrary, the benefits redound to a long chain of wealthy intermediaries, including governments.

Most recently, some of the partners in transnational adoption have been oddly if unevenly matched in their insecure relationships to their children, as gay and lesbian adopters in the United States, Europe, and elsewhere, with uncertain legal parental rights, acquire children from impoverished communities in the Third World. The question of gay and lesbian adoption has become highly controversial in recent years, with adoption authorities in sending countries such as China withdrawing their qualified willingness to look the other way with gay and lesbian adopters. The ability of gay men and lesbians to adopt seems to be expanding within some countries—a third of the EU countries and South Africa now allow this practice—at the same time that it is contracting elsewhere, as conservative religious groups in the United States struggle to outlaw it. Related questions of gay marriage are similarly in flux, as increasing numbers of places allow it, while others make it more difficult.

The forces impinging on transnational adoption are increasingly contradictory. While demand in the United States, Western Europe, and

Canada continues to grow, including new forms of demand (Collard, this volume), major "sending" countries such as China and Guatemala are scaling back or temporarily halting their international adoption programs. More than ever, we need to recognize the diverse national and transnational forces driving support for and opposition to transnational adoption. Surprisingly, there have been few previous efforts to bring together an international group of scholars or adoption activists together to describe and reflect upon these multiple and diverse strands from their divergent perspectives. This volume initiates a common conversation about adoption.

NOTES

1. This notion of adoption—as a way of organizing children's labor and training—shaped some of the earliest transnational migration of children, which might by some accounts be adoption. The United Kingdom sent about 16,000 child migrants to its largest settler colonies, the United States, Australia, Canada, and New Zealand, between 1618 and 1967; see Bean and Melville 1989, Selman 2008. It also shaped the practice of running "orphan trains" from the East Coast to the Western United States; see Fitzgerald 1992, Gordon 1999. On heirs, see Goody 1969; for adoption of an heir in non-Western cultural contexts, see Waltner 1990.

2. See *A Short History of the Save the Children Foundation*, available online at http://www.oneworld.org/scf/functions/aboutus/history2.html (accessed 28 March 2002); also see United States Congress 1939.

3. The standard source for this post–World War II chronology is Altstein and Simon 1991; see also Weil 1984, Selman 2008, 2002, 1998, Lovelock 2000. The periodization of transnational adoption is a matter of perspective; as long as there have been nation-states, children have been crossing international borders and taking up residence with people who were not their birth parents. The historiographical question is, when did the numbers become large enough, or the conditions sufficiently interesting, to warrant marking it as a phase of transnational adoption that preceded the era of formal, bureaucratic systems? As Volkman (2003) put it, adoption became "visible and vocal" after previously being a taboo topic. This change of attitude followed from the fact that children who physically resembled the adoptive parents were no longer available in some places, and more difficult or costly to locate in others. Also new is the interest shown in this subject by social and cultural anthropologists. The circulation of children was previously seen as a feature of "other" cultures and related to "fictive" kinship, but now it involved legal adoption in these scholars' own societies. As Terrell and Modell have suggested, "apparently what anthropologists find interesting elsewhere may be less interesting, or deeply private, at home" (1994: 157).

4. Some of them remained in Britain after the end of the Civil War and have formed an association: see http://www.basquechildren.org/ (accessed 4 May 2008).

5. "Hoover Backs Bill to Waive Quota Act for Reich Children," *New York Times*, 23 April 1939, 1.

6. Harry S. Truman, "President Truman's Statement and Directive on Displaced Persons," *New York Times*, 23 December 1945.

7. Carroll Bogert and Betsy McKay, "Bringing Baby Back," *Newsweek*, 21 November 1994.

8. Dirck Halstead, "A Surprise from Long Ago and Far Away," *The Digital Journalist*, June 2005; available online at http://convergent.communication.utexas.edu/issue0506/longago.html (accessed 4 May 2008).

9. Anonymous, "Devil's Lake Sioux Resistance," *Indian Family Defense*, Winter 1974; Bertram Hirsch, keynote address at "The Indian Child Welfare Act—The Next Ten Years: Indian Homes for Indian Children," University of California at Los Angeles, 22–24 August 1990.

10. Hari Sreenivasan, "Foreigners Vie to Adopt Black U.S. Babies," *World News Tonight* [broadcast], 5 March 2005; Dawn Davenport, "Born in America, Adopted Abroad," *Christian Science Monitor*, 27 October 2004.

11. "Pedro Pan," interview on *All Things Considered*, National Public Radio, 3 May 2000.

12. María Eugenia Sampallo, the thirty-two-year-old daughter of a couple who was "disappeared" during the Argentine Dirty War, has denounced her adoptive parents—whom she calls "appropriators"—and the member of the army who mediated her adoption in court. For the first time in the Argentinean process of recovering the identity of children who were "appropriated" during the dictatorship, the court ruled in the victim's favor. Indeed, her appropriators and the intermediary were sentenced to eight and ten years in prison respectively. When María Eugenia was asked the reasons for her decision to sue, she answered that "society must not accept that children can be stolen." *La Vanguardia*, 5 April 2008.

13. Spain is an exceptional case. The former colonizer of Latin America continues to be seen favorably by many Latin American child welfare groups. Transnational adoption to Spain began in Latin America, and from the early 1990s until the early 2000s most children adopted internationally in Spain came from Colombia, Peru, Mexico, the Dominican Republic, Brazil, and Bolivia. At present, although the number of transnational adoptions from Latin America to Spain is decreasing, the practice continues from Colombia and Peru and is increasing from Bolivia. In the aftermath of the change of transnational adoption laws in China and the interruption of transnational adoption in Russia, many families in Spain decided to go to Latin America. In a recent meeting with forty of them, Diana Marre asked about the reasons for this decision. Most spoke of a "sweet adoption," meaning that they know the language and spend two months in the

country developing—and allowing the child to develop—an attachment step by step.

14. Jane Perlez, "Romanian 'Orphans': Prisoners of their Cribs," *New York Times*, 25 March 1996; Kate McGeown, "What Happened to Romania's Orphans?" *BBC News*, 8 July 2005.

15. Kathleen Hunt, "The Romanian Baby Bazaar," *New York Times*, 24 March 1991; Carol Lawson, "Doctor Acts to Heal Romania's Wounds of Baby Trafficking," *New York Times*, 3 October 1991; Jane Perlez, "Romania Gives Britons Prison in Baby Case," *New York Times*, 10 October 1994.

16. International immigration and international adoption have also different kinds of benefits and beneficiaries. Estimates suggest that only 10 to 15 percent of the usual cost of an international adoption (US$20,000–30,000) goes to the child's country of origin.

17. In Spain and France (Barraud forthcoming), a certain number of families adopting from Morocco and Algeria have used Kafala as a legal way of harboring children since the late 1980s through early 1990s. Although in France many of these adoptive families have North African origins, some Spanish and/or Catalan families with no previous cultural or religious ties with Muslim countries such as Morocco decided to convert to Islam and to "kafalar" a child—that is, to shelter and raise a child under a Kafala contract. Given the fact that adoption is forbidden by Islamic law, Kafala is used as a substitute for adoption despite the fact that it does not provide for inheritance or locate the child in the new family's lineage.

REFERENCES

Akker, van den, O. B. A. 2001. "Adoption in the Age of Reproductive Technology." *Journal of Reproductive and Infant Psychology* 19, no. 2: 1127–59.

Altstein, Howard, and Rita James Simon. 1992. *Intercountry Adoption: A Multinational Perspective*. New York: Praeger.

Anagnost, Ann. 1995. "A Surfeit of Bodies: Population and the Rationality of the State in Post-Mao China." In *Conceiving the New World Order: The Global Politics of Reproduction*, ed. Faye D. Ginsburg and Rayna Rapp, 22–41. Berkeley: University of California Press.

Arditti, Rita. 1999. *Searching for Life: The Grandmothers of the Plaza de Mayo and the Disappeared Children of Argentina*. Berkeley: University of California Press.

Ariès, Philippe. 1962. *Centuries of Childhood: A Social History of Family Life*, trans. Robert Baldrick. New York: Random House.

Asociación de Abuelas de Plaza de Mayo. 1995. *Filiación, identidad, restitución: 15 años de lucha de Abuelas de Plaza de Mayo*. Buenos Aires: El Bloque Editorial.

Bagdikian, Ben. 1997. *The Media Monopoly*. 5th ed. Boston: Beacon Press.

Balcolm, Karen. 2007. "'Phony Mothers' and Border-Crossing Adoptions: The Montreal-to-New York Black Market in Babies in the 1950s." *Journal of Women's History* 19, no. 1: 107–16.

Bargach, Jamila. 2002. *Orphans of Islam: Family, Abandonment, and Secret Adoption in Morocco.* Oxford, UK: Rowman & Littlefield.

Barraud, Emile. Forthcoming. "Child Adoption in the North African States." Paper to be presented to session on Children's Circulation in and between Contemporary Urban Worlds: Migrations, Adoptions, Fosterages, Travels, Traffics, at the 16th World Congress of the International Unions of Anthropological and Ethnological Scientists in Kunming, China.

Bean, Philip, and Joy Melville. 1989. *Lost Children of the Empire.* London: Unwin Hyman.

Briggs, Laura. 2003. "Mother, Child, Race, Nation: Visual Iconography of Rescue and the Politics of Transnational and Transracial Adoption in the 1950s." *Gender & History* 15, no. 2: 179–200.

———. 2006a. "Adopción transnacional: Robo de criaturas, familias homoparentales y neoliberalismo." Trans. Gloria Elena Bernal. *Debate Feminista* 17, no. 33 (April): 46–68.

———. 2006b. "Making 'American' Families: Transnational Adoption and U.S. Latin America Policy." In *Haunted by Empire: Geographies of Intimacy in North American Empire,* ed. Ann Stoler, 244–65. Durham, NC: Duke University Press.

Buck, Pearl S. 1967. "The Children America Forgot." *Readers Digest* (September): 108–10.

Buck, Pearl S., and Theodore F. Harris. 1966. *For Spacious Skies: Journey in Dialogue.* New York: John Day Company.

Cadoret, Anne. 2002. *Des parents comme les autres: Homosexualité et Parenté.* Paris: Editions Odile Jacob.

Chandra, A., G. M. Martinez, W. D. Mosher, J. C. Abama, and J. Jones. 2005. "Fertility, Family Planning, and Reproductive Health of U.S. Women: Data from the 2002 National Survey of Family Growth." In *Vital Health Statistics* 23: 1–160. Hyattsville, MD: National Center for Health Statistics.

Colen, Shellee. 1986. "With Respect and Feelings: Voices of West Indian Child Care and Domestic Workers in New York City." In *All American Women: Lines That Divide, Ties That Bind,* ed. Johnetta B. Cole, 36–70. New York: Free Press.

———. 1989. "Just a Little Respect: West Indian Domestic Workers in New York City." In *Muchachas No More: Household Workers in Latin America and the Caribbean,* ed. Elsa M. Chaney and Mary Garcia Castro, 171–94. Philadelphia: Temple University Press.

———. 1990. "Housekeeping for the Green Card: West Indian Household Workers, the State, and Stratified Reproduction in New York." In *At Work in Homes:*

Household Workers in World Perspective, ed. Roger Sanjek and Shellee Colen, 89–118. Washington, DC: American Anthropological Association.

Colen, Shellee. 1995. "'Like a Mother to Them': Stratified Reproduction and West Indian Childcare Workers and Employers in New York." In *Conceiving the New World Order: The Global Politics of Reproduction*, ed. Faye D. Ginsberg and Rayna Rapp, 78–102. Berkeley: University of California Press.

Conde, Yvonne. 1999. *Operation Pedro Pan: The Untold Exodus of 14,048 Cuban Children*. New York: Routledge.

Conn, Peter J. 1996. *Pearl S. Buck: A Cultural Biography*. New York: Cambridge University Press.

Cortina, Jon, Sandra Lovo, Edgardo Trejo, and Asociación Pro-Búsqueda de Niñas y Niños Desaparecidos (El Salvador). 2005. *Versión Popular de la Sentencia de la Corte Interamericana de Derechos Humanos en el Caso Hermanas Serrano Cruz*. El Salvador: Asociación Pro-Búsqueda de Niñas y Niños Desaparecidos.

Crespo, Ramón Torreira, and José Buajasán Marrawi. 2000. *Operación Peter Pan: Un Caso De Guerra Psicológica Contra Cuba*. La Habana: Editora Política.

Dolgin, Gail, and Vicente Franco. 2002. "Daughter from Danang." Film. In *American Experience*, Public Broadcasting System. Balcony Releasing.

Dubinsky, Karen. 2007. "Babies without Borders: Rescue, Kidnap, and the Symbolic Child." *Journal of Women's History* 19, no. 1: 142–50.

Evans, Karin. 2000. *The Lost Daughters of China: Abandoned Girls, Their Journey to America, and the Search for a Missing Past*. New York: Putnam.

Evans Rogers, Dale. 1965. *Dearest Debbie (In Ai Lee)*. Westwood, NJ: Revell.

Fitzgerald, Maureen. 1992. "Irish-Catholic Nuns and the Development of New York City's Welfare System, 1840–1900." Ph.D. diss., University of Wisconsin, Madison.

———. 2005. *Habits of Compassion: Irish-Catholic Nuns and the Origins of New York's Welfare System, 1830–1920*. Urbana: University of Illinois Press.

Forbes, Susan S., and Patricia Weiss Fagen. 1984. *Unaccompanied Refugee Children: The Evolution of U.S. Policies—1939 to 1984*. Washington, DC: Refugee Policy Group.

———. 1985. "Unaccompanied Refugee Children: The Evolution of U.S. Policies, 1939–1984." *Migration News* 3: 3–36.

Ginsberg, Faye D., and Rayna Rapp, eds. 1995. *Conceiving the New World Order: The Global Politics of Reproduction*. Berkeley: University of California Press.

Goody, Jack. 1969. "Adoption in Cross-Cultural Perspective." *Comparative Studies in Society and History* 11, no. 1: 55–78.

Gordon, Linda. 1999. *The Great Arizona Orphan Abduction*. Cambridge, MA: Harvard University Press.

Harris, Mark Jonathan, director; book coauthored with Deborah Oppenheimer. 2000. *Into the Arms of Strangers: Stories of the Kindertransport*. Film. Warner Brothers.

Hochschild, Arlie Russell. 1989. *The Second Shift: Working Parents and the Revolution at Home*. New York: Viking.

Holt, Bertha, as told to Dorothy Kaltenbach. 1982. *Created for God's Glory*. Eugene, OR: Holt International Children's Services.

Holt, Bertha, and David Wisner. 1956. *Seed from the East*. New York: Oxford University Press.

Holt, Bertha, with David Wisner, and Harry Albus. 1992. *The Seed from the East Outstretched Arms*. Eugene, OR: Holt International Children's Services.

Howell, Signe, and Diana Marre. 2006. "To Kin a Transnationally Adopted Child in Norway and Spain: The Achievement of Resemblances and Belonging." *Ethnos* 71, no. 3: 293–317.

Howell, Signe, and Marit Melhuus. 2007. "Adoption, Donor Gametes, and Immigration: Disputed Criteria for Identity and Belonging in Contemporary Norway." In *Race, Ethnicity and Nation: Perspectives form Kinship and Genetics*, ed. Peter Wade, 53–72. Oxford, UK: Berghahn Books.

Hübinette, Tobias. 2005. "Comforting an Orphaned Nation: Representations of International Adoption and Adopted Koreans in Korean Popular Culture." Ph.D. dissertation, Stockholm University.

Humphreys, Margaret. 1994. *Empty Cradles*. London: Doubleday.

Johnson, Kay Ann, and Amy Klatzin. 2004. *Wanting a Daughter, Needing a Son: Abandonment, Adoption, and Orphanage Care in China*. Saint Paul, MN: Yeong and Yeong Book Company.

Johnson, Patrick. 1983. *Native Children and the Child Welfare System*. Toronto: Canadian Council on Social Development, in association with James Lorimer and Co.

Key, Ellen. 1909. *The Century of the Child*. New York and London: G. P. Putnam's Sons.

Klein, Christina. 2003. *Cold War Orientalism: Asia in the Middlebrow Imagination, 1945–1961*. Berkeley: University of California Press.

Laquer, Walter. 2001. *Generation Exodus: The Fate of Young Jewish Refugees from Nazi Germany*. Hanover, NH: University Press of New England for Brandeis University Press.

Legarreta, Dorothy. 1984. *The Guernica Generation—Basque Refugee Children of the Spanish Civil War*. Reno: University of Nevada Press.

Lipman, Jana. 1996. "My Lai: Amerasians in Vietnam and the United States." Honors thesis, Brown University.

Lovelock, Kirsten. 2000. "Intercountry Adoption as a Migratory Practice: A Comparative Analysis of Intercountry Adoption and Immigration Policy and Practice in the United States, Canada and New Zealand in the Post W.W. II Period." *International Migration Review* 34, no. 1: 907–49.

Marre, Diana. 2004. "La adopción internacional y las asociaciones de familias adoptantes: Un ejemplo de sociedad civil virtual global." *Scripta Nova: Revista*

Electrónica de Geografía y Ciencias Sociales 8, no. 170, 1–17. Available at http://ec3.ugr.es/in=recs/Geograpnia.htm (accessed 20 July 2008).

Marre, Diana. 2007. "'I want her to learn her language and maintain her culture': Transnational Adoptive Families' Views on 'Cultural Origins.'" In *Race, Ethnicity and Nation: Perspectives form Kinship and Genetics*, ed. Peter Wade, 73–95. Oxford, UK: Berghahn Books.

Marre, Diana, and Joan Bestard, eds. 2004. *La adopción y el acogimiento: Presente y perspectivas*. Barcelona: Ediciones de la Universidad de Barcelona.

———. Forthcoming. "The Family Body: Person, Body, and Resemblance." In *Kinship Matters: European cultures of kinship in the age of biotechnology*, ed. J. Edwards and C. Salazar. Oxford, UK: Berghahn Books.

Marre, Diana, and Hugo Gaggiotti. Forthcoming. "Members, Patients, Parents? Organising around Assisted Reproduction and Transnational Adoption in Catalonia and Spain."

Ortiz, Ana Teresa, and Laura Briggs. 2003. "Crack, Abortion, the Culture of Poverty, and Welfare Cheats: The Making of the 'Healthy White Baby Crisis.'" *Social Text* 76 (vol. 21, no. 3): 39–57.

Qvortrup, Jens. 2005. "Varieties of Childhood." In *Studies in Modern Childhood: Society, Agency, Culture*, ed. Jens Qvortrup, 1–20. New York: Palgrave Macmillan.

Ressler, Everett M., Neil Boothby, and Daniels Steinbeck. 1988. *Unaccompanied Children: Care and Protection in Wars, Natural Disasters, and Refugee Movements*. New York: Oxford University Press.

Selman, Peter. 1998. "Intercountry Adoption in Europe after the Hague Convention." In *Developments in European Social Policy: Convergence and Diversity*, ed. Robert Sykes and Pete Alcock, 147–69. Bristol, UK: Policy Press.

———. 2002. "Intercountry Adoption in the New Millennium: The 'Quiet Migration' Revisited." *Population Research and Policy Review* 21, no. 3: 205–25.

———. 2008. "Intercountry Adoption: Research, Policy and Practice." In *The Child Placement Handbook: Research, Policy and Practice*, ed. G. Schofield and J. Simmonds. London: BAAF.

Slesin, Aviva. 2003. "Secret Lives: Hidden Children and Their Rescuers During World War II." Film.

Solinger, Rickie. 1992. *Wake Up Little Susie: Single Pregnancy and Race before Roe v. Wade*. New York: Routledge.

———. 2001. *Beggars and Choosers: How the Politics of Choice Shapes Adoption, Abortion, and Welfare in the United States*. New York: Hill and Wang.

Terrell, John, and Judith Modell. 1994. "Anthropology and Adoption." *American Anthropologist* 96, no. 1: 155–61.

Therborn, Göran. 1996. "Child Politics: Dimensions and Perspectives." *Childhood* 3, no. 1: 29–44.

Torres, María de los Angeles. 2003. *The Lost Apple: Operation Pedro Pan, Cuban Children in the U.S., and the Promise of a Better Future*. Boston: Beacon Press.

Triay, Victor Andres. 1998. *Fleeing Castro: Operation Pedro Pan and the Cuban Children's Program*. Gainesville: University Press of Florida.

Turner Strong, Pauline. 2001. "To Forget Their Tongue, Their Name, and Their Whole Relation: Captivity, Extra-Tribal Adoption, and the Indian Child Welfare Act." In *Relative Values: Reconfiguring Kinship Studies*, ed. Sarah Franklin and Susan McKinnon, 468–94. Durham, NC: Duke University Press.

United States Congress, Select Committee on Indian Affairs. 1977. *Indian Child Welfare Statistical Survey, July 1976, Appendix G*, 1st Session on S. 1214, To establish standards for the placement of Indian children in foster or adoptive homes, to prevent the breakup of Indian families, and for other purposes. 4 August.

United States Congress, Subcommittee of the Committee on Immigration, United States Senate, and Subcommittee of the Committee on Immigration and Naturalization, House of Representatives. 1939. *Admission of German Refugee Children: Joint Hearings on S.J. Res. 64 and H.J. Res. 168 (Joint Resolutions to Authorize the Admission into the United States of a Limited Number of German Refugee Children)*, 1st Session, April 20–24.

United States Congress, Subcommittee on International Law, Immigration, and Refugees of the Committee on the Judiciary. 1991. *Romanian Adoptions Hearings*, 102d Congress, 1st Session, June 5.

United States Senate, Committee on the Judiciary, Subcommittee to Investigate Juvenile Delinquency. 1955. Hearings on "Interstate Adoption Practices," 84th Congress, 1st Session, July 15, 16.

Volkman, Toby Alice. (2003) 2005a. "Embodying Chinese Culture: Transnational Adoption in North America." *Social Text* 74 (vol. 21, no. 1, Spring 2003): 39–56. Reprinted in *Cultures of Transnational Adoption*, ed. Toby Alice Volkman, 81–115.

——— (ed.). 2005b. *Cultures of Transnational Adoption*. Durham, NC: Duke University Press.

Waltner, Ann. 1990. *Getting an Heir: Adoption and the Construction of Kinship in Late Imperial China*. Honolulu: University of Hawaii Press.

Warren, Andrea. 2004. *Escape from Saigon: A Vietnam War Orphan Becomes an American Boy*. New York: Farrar, Straus and Giroux.

Weil, Richard H. 1984. "International Adoption: The Quiet Migration." *International Migration Review* 18, no. 2: 275–93.

Wolf, Arthur P. 1966. "Childhood Association, Sexual Attraction, and the Incest Taboo. A Chinese Case." *American Anthropologist* (new series) 68, no. 4: 883–98.

———. 1968. "Adopt a Daughter-in-Law, Marry a Sister: A Chinese Solution to the

Problem of the Incest Taboo." *American Anthropologist* (new series) 70, no. 5: 864–74.

Wolf, Arthur P. 2003. "Maternal Sentiments: How Strong Are They?" *Current Anthropology* 44 (Supplement, December): s31–s49.

Wolf, Arthur, and Chieh-shan Huang. 1980. *Marriage and Adoption in China, 1845–1945.* Stanford. CA: Stanford University Press.

Wolf, Margery. 1968. *The House of Lim: A Study of a Chinese Farm Family.* New York: Appleton-Century-Crofts.

———. 1970. "Child Training and the Chinese Family." In *Family and Kinship in Chinese Society,* ed. Maurice Freedman, 35–62. Stanford, CA: Stanford University Press.

———. 1972. *Women and the Family in Rural Taiwan.* Stanford, CA: Stanford University Press.

———. 1985. *Revolution Postponed: Women in Contemporary China.* Stanford, CA: Stanford University Press.

Wyman, David S. 1968. *Paper Walls: America and the Refugee Crisis, 1938–1941.* Amherst: University of Massachusetts Press.

Zelizer, Viviana A. 1985. *Pricing the Priceless Child: The Changing Social Value of Children.* New York: Basic Books.

Part I

||||||||||||||||||||||||||||||||||||||||||||||||||||||

Defining Reproduction
Law, Strangers, Family, Kin

The transnational circulation of children in adoption is a legal institution carefully regulated by international conventions that are intended to guarantee the human rights of the most vulnerable members of society. Yet its advent is intimately related to conflicts that arose from colonialism, international warfare, and civil conflicts, and its current patterns are profoundly shaped by global, racial-ethnic, and class inequalities within and between nation-states. The contemporary European-American system seems to have shifted from the temporary fosterage of children around World War I through the adoption of orphans after World War II and the wars in Korea, Viet Nam, and Latin America to the adoption of children socially defined as "abandoned" in Eastern Europe and Asia. Recently, children from impoverished classes and marginalized racial-ethnic groups have come to the United States and EU countries from both the richest and poorest nations in Latin America, especially Haiti and Brazil, and from Asia, especially China.

Peter Selman analyzes developments in intercountry adoption worldwide at the turn of the twenty-first century. The characteristics of those countries sending and receiving the most children and patterns in the age and sex of children circulating in adoption shows the importance of disparities in wealth and divergent demographic patterns between states. Moreover, the difficulty of obtaining reliable data regarding the countries with the highest rates of intercountry adoptions since 2004 suggests that parts of the system remain opaque and beyond the reach of international conventions.

As new forms of parenthood and family formation emerge in the United States, Canada, and the EU, social anthropologists are at the forefront in analyzing how these processes intersect with transnational adoption and are transforming the meanings of kinship. In this section, Judith Schachter draws attention to the power of the state to define adoption and considers how families whose culture differs from that of the dominant society navigate the system in order to enact alternative definitions of kinship. Schachter juxtaposes the legal form of plenary adoption, in which the adoptee's previous kinship ties are severed, with indigenous forms of adoption and fosterage, which augment rather than erase the child's kin-based identity. Her micro-analysis of a complex Native Hawaiian family in this island state illuminates how indigenous people negotiate the contradictions between colonial legacies and cultural traditions.

Françoise-Romaine Ouellette analyzes three temporal modes in the process of adoption: the length of the process of seeking and placing a child; the child's own development; and the cycle of genealogical transmission. Exploring recent policy developments in Québec, Canada, she shows how new practices and attitudes regarding the closed or open nature of adoption and the right of adoptees to know their origins have called plenary adoption into question. As anthropologists have shown, most societies augment rather than suppress recognition of the child's birth family ties when he or she grows up in another family.

Analyzing interviews with gays and lesbians who are contemplating or embarking on parenthood, Martine Gross explores the relationship between individuals' and couples' desires for children. Do gay and lesbian couples, who can separate biological from social forms of reproduction, understand their children as an outgrowth of their relationship, a "couple project," or is parenting an individual project? In their notions of the couple and the connection between sexuality and attachment, women and men differ quite strikingly. We wonder whether similar patterns prevail in other countries and cultures where the feminist and queer movements may have had greater influence and where lesbians have unimpeded access to assisted reproductive technologies.

Like Judith Schachter, Barbara Yngvesson suggests reconsidering the principle of plenary adoption that is currently enshrined in international conventions and adoption laws in most European-American nations. Examining both the efforts of adoptive families and receiving countries to incorporate internationally adopted children and the movement among some adopted young adults to reunite with their officially nonexistent kin or revisit their counties of origin, she explores how transracial adoptees and their parents wrestle with the complexity of biogenetic and cultural identities in an increasingly global world.

Today, as in the past, not all adoptions are transactions between strangers. Chantal Collard analyzes transnational adoptions of children by their relatives in Québec, where they represent a significant fraction of all international adoptions. Transnational family adoptions remain invisible in most European and American countries, even though approximately half of domestic adoptions and a significant proportion of fosterage relationships are also intrafamilial. Although some sending countries prefer this type of adoption, which parallels and often accompanies international migration, national laws and international conventions are ill-equipped to deal with transnational family adoptions.

Chapter 1

||||||||||||||||||||||||||||||||||||||||||||||||||||||||||||

The Movement of Children for International Adoption

Developments and Trends in Receiving States and States of Origin, 1998–2004

Peter Selman

This chapter explores the implications of developments in intercountry adoption (ICA) worldwide during the early years of the twenty-first century, based on a demographic analysis of trends in numbers and rates in twenty receiving states between 1998 and 2004. The incidence of ICA in states of origin has been estimated using data from these twenty receiving countries. The analysis shows a marked increase in the global number of intercountry adoptions over the seven years, with an estimated *minimum* of 45,000 officially recorded adoptions in the twenty states by 2004, which represents an increase of 42 percent since 1998. Recent growth is most evident in the numbers of children adopted from China and Russia and the numbers going to Spain and Ireland.

Standardization against the number of births indicates that in 2004 the receiving states with the highest adoption ratios were Norway and Spain, while the United Kingdom had the lowest adoption ratio. The highest rates of ICA for states of origin in 2003 were in Eastern Europe and the former Soviet Union, closely followed by South Korea and Guatemala. China and India sent large numbers but had very low rates. The chapter analyzes the social and demographic characteristics of both those countries sending and those countries receiving most children and the age and sex of children received by the United States, France, and EurAdopt agencies[1] for which demographic data is available.

Spain is now the second largest receiving country after the United States in terms of the actual number of international adoptions, and Catalonia has the highest rate per capita (see Tables 1.1 and 1.4). This chapter looks in detail at the nature of intercountry adoption in Spain with special reference to some of the states of origin that currently send most children to Spain. The pattern in Spain will be contrasted with that found in Canada, Italy, France, and the United States, the other four countries that have received 2,000 or more children a year since 1998.

Finally, the chapter offers an overview of the movement of children in the first five years of the twenty-first century and considers changes in the nature of international adoption in the years since the Hague Convention. Regarding prospects for the future, it asks: What does international adoption mean for the children involved? What can we do to ensure that it is practiced only in the best interests of the child?

Patterns of International Adoption in Receiving States

The number of intercountry adoptions has more than doubled in the last twenty years. Table 1.1 shows the estimated numbers over this period for the 14 receiving states included in Saralee Kane's estimates for the 1980s.

TABLE 1.1
*Receiving States with Highest Numbers of Intercountry
Adoptions 1980–2004, by Rank in 2004*

Country	2004	2001	1998	1993–97 (average)	1988	1980–89 (average)
USA	22,884	19,237	15,774	10,070	9,120	7,761
Spain	5,541	3,428	1,487	784	93[a]	19[a]
France	4,079	3,094	3,777	3,216	2,441	1,850
Italy	3,403	1,797	2,233	2,047	2,078	1,006
Canada	1,955	1,874	2,222	1,934	232[b]	109[a]
Netherlands	1,307	1,122	825	640	577	1,153
Sweden	1,109	1,044	928	906	1,074	1,579
Norway	706	713	643	531	566	464
Germany	650	798	922	836	875[c]	189[a]
Switzerland	557	458	456	468	492	616
Denmark	528	631	624	510	523	582
Belgium	470	419	487	183[d]	662	544
Australia	370	289	245	247	516[e]	356
Finland	289	218	181	134	78	40[a]
TOTAL (14 states)	43,848	35,122	30,804	22,799	19,327	16,268

Sources: Kane 1993, Lehland 2000, Selman 2002, 2006.
[a] Underestimate due to incomplete data (Kane 1993).
[b] For 1980–1989, Canadian figures are for Quebec only (Kane 1993).
[c] Estimate based on 4 northern *lander* (Kane 1993).
[d] EurAdopt agencies only.
[e] Figure includes all visas; actual number should be 382 (Rosenwald 2007).

TABLE 1.2
Receiving States: Number of Intercountry Adoptions 1998–2004, by Rank in 1998

Country	1998	1999	2001	2002	2003	2004
USA	15,774	16,363	19,237	20,099	21,616	22,884
France	3,777	3,597	3,094	3,551	3,995	4,079
Italy	2,233	2,177	2,225	2,225	2,772	3,402
Canada	2,222	2,019	1,874	1,926	2,180	1,955
Spain	1,487	2,006	3,428	3,625	3,951	5,541
Sweden	928	1,019	1,044	1,107	1,046	1,109
Germany	922	977	798	884	674	650
Netherlands	825	993	1,122	1,130	1,154	1,307
Norway	643	589	713	747	714	706
Denmark	624	697	631	609	523	528
Belgium	487	450	419	444	430	470
New Zealand	371	356	358	263	278	351
Switzerland	456	312	458	478	656	557
UK	258	391	326	285	300	332
Australia	245	244	289	294	278	370
Finland	181	149	218	246	238	289
Ireland	147	214	179	357	358	398
Luxembourg	60	66	56	47	51	56
Iceland	15	14	17	19	30	28
Cyprus	12	16	10	3	3	3
TOTAL (20 states)	31,667	32,626	36,068	38,339	41,248	45,016

Source: Selman 2006.

The growth has been most spectacular in Spain, but this apparent increase is due in part to a lack of complete data in Kane's analysis (Kane 1993). Tables 1.2 and 1.3 present more complete data for the period 1998 to 2004, based on my own analysis of twenty receiving states, which together probably account for more than 95 percent of all international adoptions during that period (for more detailed analyses of the problems of data, see Selman 2002, 2005b, 2006).

Between 1998 and 2004 the total number of children received by these twenty countries increased from 31,667 to 45,016, or by 42 percent. In Spain, recorded intercountry adoptions doubled between 1998 and 2000 and nearly tripled by 2004. This trend may be linked to the sharp decline in fertility during the 1990s because of deferred childbearing and the consequent increase in infecundity. Other countries showing an above-average increase were Ireland, Italy, the Netherlands, and the United States (see Table 1.3). However, a downturn in numbers in both 2005 and 2006 has affected most countries, in particular the Nordic states, the Netherlands, and Spain (Selman 2008).

The rise in intercountry adoptions must be examined in relation to the demography of the receiving country (Selman 1999, 2000). Table 1.4 shows that Spain is among those countries receiving the most children in relation to its population size and number of live births. In 2004, on both measures, Spain was second to only Norway among the major receiving

TABLE 1.3

Percentage Change in Number of Adoptions 1998–2004 for Selected Receiving States, Ranked by Level of Change

Country	Adoptions 1998	Adoptions 2001	Adoptions 2003	Adoptions 2004	% Change 1998–2004
Spain	1,487	3,428	3,951	5,541	+273.0
Ireland	147	179	341	398	+171.0
Netherlands	825	1,122	1,154	1,307	+58.4
Italy	2,233	1,797	2,772	3,400	+52.3
USA	15,774	19,237	21,616	22,884	+45.1
ALL COUNTRIES	31,667	36,068	41,248	45,016	+41.7
UK	258	326	300	326	+26.0
Sweden	928	1,044	1,046	1,109	+19.5
France	3,777	3,094	3,995	4,079	+ 8.0
Canada	2,222	1,874	2,180	1,955	−12.0
Denmark	624	631	522	527	−16.0

Sources: Selman 2005b, 2006.

TABLE 1.4

Intercountry Adoptions per 100,000 Population (Crude Adoption Rate) and per 1,000 Live Births (Adoption Ratio) in 1998 and 2004

Country	Number of Adoptions 2004	Crude Adoption Rate 2004	Adoption Ratio 2004	Crude Adoption Rate 1998	Adoption Ratio 1998
Norway	706	15.35	12.84	14.6	11.2
Spain[a]	5,541	12.99	12.40	3.8	4.2
Sweden	1,109	12.31	11.67	10.5	10.8
Denmark	528	9.75	8.38	11.8	9.9
Switzerland	557	7.69	8.19	9.4	8.6
Netherlands	1,307	8.05	6.88	5.3	4.6
Italy	3,398	5.86	6.40	3.9	4.4
New Zealand	351	8.80	6.38	8.8	6.4
Ireland	398	9.75	6.32	3.3	2.8
Canada	1,955	6.12	5.96	5.3	6.5
USA	22,884	7.75	5.54	5.8	4.2
France	4,079	6.77	5.48	6.4	5.3
Australia	370	1.86	1.49	1.3	1.0
Germany	506	0.61	0.74	1.1	0.9
UK	326	0.55	0.50	0.4	0.4

Sources: Lehland 2000, Selman 2002, 2006.

[a] In Catalonia in 2004 the level of adoptions was higher than in either Spain or Norway; the rate was 22.9 per 1,000 population, the ratio 17.3 per 1,000 births (Selman 2008).

states. A year later Spain had the same rate as Norway and a higher ratio. The table also puts into perspective the low rates for Australia, Germany (non-relative adoptions), and the United Kingdom, which has a rate of 0.55 per 100,000 population, compared to 13 for Spain and over 15 for Norway. As early as 1977, the adoption ratio in Sweden had reached 20 per 1,000 live births (Andersson 2000: 346).

A Perspective from the States of Origin

It has often been pointed out that adopted children's states of origin, or sending countries, have changed dramatically over time: from the pre-dominance of war-torn and defeated countries after World War II through the long period of adoption from South Korea after the Korean War to the emergence of Latin America as a major source in the 1980s and the recent dominance of China and Russia, with brief periods of high levels from Viet Nam and Romania. Table 1.5 shows the change in rank ordering over the last twenty years. Six of the states of origin featured in the top ten sending countries in Kane's analysis were no longer in the top ten by 2004. Brazil and the Philippines were still in the top twenty, but the number of children travelling from Sri Lanka, Chile, Peru, and El Salvador is now very low. In Brazil, intercountry adoption continues but involves mainly older and special needs children.

If we look at the 2004 data for the five major receiving states shown in Table 1.6, we see that the largest group of internationally adopted children

TABLE 1.5
Countries Sending Most Children for Intercountry Adoption, 1980–2004

1980–1989[a]	1995[b]	Rank	1998[c]	2004[c]
S. Korea	China	1	Russia	China
India	S. Korea	2	China	Russia
Colombia	Russia	3	Viet Nam	Guatemala
Brazil	Viet Nam	4	S. Korea	S. Korea
Sri Lanka	Colombia	5	Colombia	Ukraine
Chile	India	6	Guatemala	Colombia
Philippines	Brazil	7	India	Ethiopia
Guatemala	Guatemala	8	Romania	Haiti
Peru	Romania	9	Brazil	India
El Salvador	Philippines	10	Ethiopia	Kazakhstan

[a] *Source*: Kane 1993, children sent to 13 receiving states.
[b] *Source*: Selman 2002, children sent to 10 receiving states.
[c] *Source*: Selman 2006, children sent to 20 receiving states.

TABLE 1.6
*10 States of Origin Sending Most Children for Adoption to
USA, Spain, France, Italy, and Canada in 2004*

USA[a]	Spain[b]	France[c]	Italy[d]	Canada[e]
China	China	Haiti	Russia	China
Russia	Russia	China	Ukraine	Haiti
Guatemala	Ukraine	Russia	Colombia	Russia
S. Korea	Colombia	Ethiopia	Belarus	S. Korea
Kazakhstan	Ethiopia	Viet Nam	Brazil	USA
Ukraine	India	Colombia	Poland	Philippines
India	Bolivia	Madagascar	Ethiopia	Thailand
Haiti	Nepal	Ukraine	Romania	Colombia
Ethiopia	Bulgaria	Latvia	Bulgaria	India
Colombia	Romania	Brazil	India	Ethiopia
22,884	5,541	4,079	3,998	1,955

Source: Selman 2006.
[a] U.S. State Department.
[b] Instituto Nacional de Estadistica.
[c] Mission de l'Adoption Internationale.
[d] Commissione per le Adozioni Internazionali.
[e] Citizenship and Immigration Canada (CIC).

in the United States, Canada, and Spain came from China. China accounted for 43 percent of all adoptions to Spain in 2004, but sent no children to Italy. Russia features in the top ten for all five countries and is the most important source of children for Italy. Guatemala, South Korea, and Kazakhstan are prominent in the United States but are not present in the top ten for the three European countries. Colombia and Ethiopia feature in the top ten for all five countries. The pattern indicated for the United States was repeated in 2005, but in France Viet Nam emerged as the major source of children and Mali entered the top ten. In Spain, the top five sending countries remained unchanged, but Kazakhstan and Peru replaced Romania and Bulgaria in the top ten.

These variations reflect many complex causes, but raise some interesting questions about the influence of history and cultural links. What is seldom considered is the role of states of origin in determining where their children go and whether some movements are more in the interests of the children who are sent than others. Are Korean children better off in the United States than in Sweden? Why does Korea send no children to the United Kingdom, Italy, and Spain?

The lists presented in Tables 1.5 and 1.6 are dominated by larger countries such as China and Russia, so it is important to consider these numbers in relation to their population size or level of births. Total population is a misleading measure for standardization, as the proportion of a country's population that is under age 5 may vary substantially. I have, therefore, standardized rates in relation to the under-5 population and the number of births. Table 1.7 shows the results for the year 2003 and 2004. Despite the large numbers, the rates or ratios of adoptions from China and India are relatively low, while some Eastern European countries with low absolute numbers have much higher rates. The rates for Romania would have been much higher than any of those listed during the short period in the early 1990s when Romanian adoptions counted for a very high proportion of all international adoptions (Selman 2008). Similarly, in the 1980s the ratio and rate for South Korea would have been very high (Selman 2007).

I have written elsewhere (Selman 1999, 2002, 2004, 2005a) about the paradox that the countries sending most children in recent years have not been the poorest or those with the highest birth rates, despite assumptions that this would be the case. As Table 1.8a shows, four of the top five sending countries have a total fertility rate (TFR) below replacement level. Three of these have rates lower than most of the countries to which they are sending children; of the top five receiving states, only Spain and Italy had total fertility rates below 1.5 in 2004 (see Table 1.8b).

The economic disparities in per capita gross national income (GNI) are vast: in 2004 the range for the receiving countries was $21,000–41,000, but less than $4,000 for all the sending countries other than Korea. However, of the five countries listed, only two had a GNI less than $2,000 and none was below $1,000, in a year (2004) in which UNICEF's *State of the World's Children* gives the average GNI for the fifty least developed nations as $345. Differences in infant mortality rates are also substantial: 4–7 per 1,000 for the receiving states, and up to 30 per 1,000 for the sending states. The emergence of Ethiopia as a major sending country modifies this picture: in 2004 its GNI was only $110 and its TFR was 4.6.

Age and Sex in International Adoption

What differences are there in the ages and sex ratios of children sent for adoption by different countries? Spanish statistics do not currently report the age and sex of children adopted into the country, but I examine data for the countries sending most children to Spain in 2004.

TABLE 1.7
Standardized Adoption Rates and Ratios in States of Origin, 2003
(20 countries sending most children to the 20 states in table 1.2)

Country	Number of Adoptions 2003	Adoption Rate per 10,000 population under age 5	Adoption Ratio (per 1,000 live births) 2003	Adoption Ratio (per 1,000 live births) 2004
Bulgaria	962	31.5	15.5	6.3
Belarus	636	14.9	7.2	7.1
Guatemala	2,673	13.8	6.4	8.1
Russia	7,664	12.5	6.3	7.6
Ukraine	1,958	9.6	4.8	4.8
Haiti	1,055	9.4	4.2	4.6
S. Korea	2,306	7.9	4.1	4.0
Kazakhstan	857	7.5	3.4	3.8
Romania	456	4.0	2.0	1.2
Colombia	1,750	3.7	1.8	1.8
Poland	345	1.85	0.95	1.1
Cambodia	284	1.47	0.65	0.67
China	11,230	1.21	0.60	0.77
Viet Nam	935	1.22	0.57	0.33
Madagascar	390	1.28	0.54	0.46
Thailand	476	0.90	0.44	0.47
Ethiopia	847	0.68	0.28	0.49
Philippines	399	0.41	0.19	0.19
Brazil	477	0.29	0.14	0.14
India	1,172	0.1	0.05	0.04

Source: Selman 2006.

TABLE 1.8A
Social and Demographic Characteristics of 5 States of Origin Sending
Most Children for International Adoption in 2004

States of Origin	Total sent in 2004 (to 20 states)	GNI per capita ($US)	Total Fertility Rate	Infant Mortality Rate
China	13,408	1,290	1.7	26
Russia	9,345	3,410	1.1	17
Guatemala	3,406	2,130	4.5	30
S. Korea	2,238	13,980	1.2	5
Ukraine	1,949	1,260	1.1	14

TABLE 1.8B
Social and Demographic Characteristics of 5 States Receiving
Most Children for International Adoption in 2004

Country	Adoptions 2004	GNI per capita ($US)	Total Fertility Rate	Infant Mortality Rate
USA	22,884	41,400	2.0	7
Spain	5,541	21,210	1.3	4
France	4,079	30,090	1.9	4
Italy	3,402	26,120	1.3	4
Canada	1,955	28,390	1.5	5

Source of demographic and social data: UNICEF 2006.

Everyone knows that most children adopted from China are girls and that this pattern is linked to the high level of abandonment of female infants, which in turn is a consequence of the one-child policy and the traditional preference for sons. What is less often recognized is that there are other countries where girls comprise a clear majority and rather more where a majority of children sent for adoption are boys. Table 1.9 provides recent data on this issue using statistics provided to the Hague Special Commission by France for 2004, the 2004 statistics for EurAdopt agencies, and 2005 data from the United States *Yearbook of Immigration Statistics* (U.S. Department of Homeland Security 2006).

The patterns are similar in all three data sets. Three major states of origin—China, India, and Viet Nam—had a clear majority of girls in the children sent. Children adopted from South Korea were predominantly boys, a pattern that probably reflects a preponderance of females in domestic adoption. Males predominate in adoptions from Colombia and Ethiopia to Europe in 2004, but girls were a majority in those going to the United States in 2005. This difference suggests the need to look in more detail at the patterns of intercountry adoption by both state of origin and receiving state. Few states of origin provide comprehensive data on the sex of children they send for intercountry adoption, but the data provided by Colombia for the Special Commission at The Hague confirms the pattern based on data from receiving countries.

Thanks to the efforts of the Hague Conference, we now have data on

TABLE 1.9

International Adoptions by Sex of Child Placed: Euradopt Agencies 2004, France 2004, USA 2005

| | Receiving State(s) | | | | | | | | |
| | Euradopt 2004 | | | France 2004 | | | USA 2005[a] | | |
State of Origin	F	M	% F	F	M	% F	F	M	% F
China	1,612	96	94	482	9	98	7,545	394	95
India	138	76	65	9	4	69	235	89	73
Viet Nam	11	2	85	230	133	63	382	136	64[b]
Colombia	136	147	48	135	179	43	171	131	57
Ethiopia	118	138	46	160	230	41	234	196	54
Brazil	19	28	40	40	52	44	30	35	46
Russia	30	81	37	176	269	40	2,307	2,345	50
S. Korea	102	156	40	23	50	29	606	998	38

Sources: EurAdopt Statistics 2004, French submission to Hague Special Commission 2005, U.S. Department of Homeland Security 2006.
[a] Breakdown by age and sex not available for USA in 2004.
[b] USA figures for 2003, as only 7 children came from Viet Nam in 2005.

TABLE 1.10

International Adoptions by Age of Child Placed: USA 2005, France 2004,
EurAdopt 2005; Percentage of Children in Each Age Group at Time of Entry

	Receiving State(s)								
	United States 2005			France 2004[a]			EurAdopt 2005		
State of Origin	< 1	1–4	5+	< 1	1–4	5+	< 1	1–4	5+
S. Korea	92	8	1	98	2	0	97	3	0
Guatemala	79	18	3	43	54	3	33	67	0
Viet Nam	57[b]	37	6	78	22	0	46	54	0
Colombia	44	19	36	21	55	23	41	40	19
China	35	63	3	13	86	0.2	27	72	1
Ethiopia	32	26	43	33	31	36	48	37	15
Russia	20	51	29	28	48	25	4	79	17
Haiti	10	48	42	10	73	17	2	71	27
India	8	71	20	0	62	38	8	76	16
Thailand	6	66	28	5	74	21	22	73	5
Philippines	5	41	55	13	75	12	20	71	9
Poland	4	45	51	11	33	56	16	46	38
Brazil	5	22	74	2	27	71	0	39	61

Sources: U.S. Department of Homeland Security, 2006, French submission to Hague Special Commission 2005, EurAdopt Statistics 2005.
[a] Breakdown by age not available for France in 2005.
[b] U.S. figures are for 2006, as only 7 children came from Viet Nam in 2005.

age as well as sex for many receiving states beyond those included in Eur-
Adopt statistics. Table 1.10 shows the age distribution for the United States
in 2005, France in 2004, and the EurAdopt agencies in 2005. The figures
show a wide variation in the ages of children sent by different states of
origin. In some cases this pattern reflects procedural rules about the age
at which children can be adopted; for example, Thailand and the Philippines send few infants for international adoption, while Korea does not
normally allow adoptions over age three. In other cases, the pattern reflects the children who are deemed suitable for overseas as opposed to
domestic adoption. With age, as with sex, there are variations between the
three sets of statistics for some states of origin, such as Ethiopia, which
suggest a need for more detailed analysis looking at factors influencing
age at adoption.

Changing Patterns of International Adoption in States of Origin

This section examines some of the characteristic of states of origin and
the children they send by looking closely at five countries that have very

different trajectories in recent years: Brazil, China, Ethiopia, Cambodia, and Guatemala. In previous papers (Selman 2002, 2004, 2005a) I have looked in more detail at China, India, and Korea.

The history of international adoption and the changing patterns of source countries since World War II have often been noted (Altstein and Simon 1991, Lovelock 2000, van Loon 1990, Weil 1984). Countries that had suffered from wartime destruction sent most children for international adoption in the 1940s and 1950s. Indeed, for 25 years after the Korean War, South Korea provided more than half of all children sent to the United States. Then intercountry adoption grew in South America, but the trend has now been reversed in many Latin American countries. For a brief period, in the early 1990s, Romania was the major source of children. Since the mid-1990s, the picture has been dominated by adoptions from China, Russia, and the former Communist countries of Eastern Europe and central Asia. The most recent change has been the very rapid growth of adoptions from Ethiopia, although the ratio of these adoptions to live births remains relatively low (see Table 1.7).

The five sending countries scrutinized here have strikingly different patterns. Brazil is an example of a Latin American country now sending fewer children for international adoption than during the early 1990s. China is now the major source of children worldwide, as well as in Spain and many other receiving states. Ethiopia has experienced a very rapid rise in the numbers of children sent in recent years. Cambodia and Guatemala are examples of much-criticized states of origin that have in recent years sent children to only a small number of receiving states, but while most of these states have now halted adoptions from Cambodia, the number of children moving from Guatemala to United States continued to increase through 2006.

Brazil

In the 1980s Brazil was the fourth most important sending country in Kane's analysis, sending 7,527 children during the decade to the 13 receiving countries for which she had accurate data. Since then there has been a significant decline in the number of adoptions from Brazil. Official data show that the number of international adoptions fell from 2,100 in 1990 to 630 in 1999. I have been unable to get more recent official figures, but estimates based on children sent to twenty receiving states show that

TABLE 1.11

Adoptions from Brazil 1998–2004, by Rank Order in 2004 of
Countries Receiving 30 or More Children in 1998

Country	1998	1999	2001	2002	2003	2004
Italy	158	205	133	131	228	217
France	143	143	82	91	103	92
USA	103	64	33	26	30	69
Netherlands	50	45	29	20	25	30
Switzerland	76	55	36	36	32	22
Germany	78	43	27	17	8	16
Spain	40	26	11	7	22	18
Norway	35	15	16	24	27	16
TOTAL	714	616	379	358	476	487

Source: Selman 2006, based on data from 20 receiving states. In 2004, Brazil also sent children to Canada, Ireland, Sweden, and the UK.

numbers fell from 616 in 1999 to 358 in 2002 and then rose again to 487 by 2004 (Table 1.11).

Claudia Fonseca (2002) notes the effect of public concern over the negative image of Brazil as a result of sending so many children and a drive to increase in-country adoption, which was successful in relation to infants but less so for older or special needs children. The data on age of children sent (Table 1.10) show that Brazil now sends mainly older children for international adoption. The U.S. State Department advises prospective adoptive parents that the types of children most commonly available to its citizens are single healthy children aged five and above, sibling groups of any number and of all ages, and special needs children of all ages.

China

China is the main source of children going to Spain for adoption. Table 1.12 shows the rapid increase in the number of children sent worldwide by China. At present the Chinese do not publish their own statistics, so these numbers are based on data from the twenty receiving states. Only Italy, Cyprus, Germany, and Luxembourg received no children from China. The number of children sent from China more than doubled between 1998 and 2004, during which time total numbers sent by all states of origin rose by only 42 percent. However, in 2006 the number of children sent to all countries, including Spain, fell sharply (Selman 2008).

TABLE 1.12

Adoptions from China to 16 Receiving States, Ranked by Number Received 1998–2004

Country	1998	1999	2000	2001	2002	2003	2004	TOTAL
USA	4,206	4,101	5,053	4,681	5,053	6,859	7,044	36,997
Spain	196	261	475	941	1,427	1,043	2,389	6,732
Canada	901	697	604	618	771	1,108	1,001	5,700
Netherlands	210	271	457	445	510	566	644	3,260
Sweden	123	123	165	220	316	373	497	1,817
Norway	162	115	126	216	310	298	308	1,535
France	23	57	105	130	210	360	491	1,376
UK	123	149	176	175	111	108	175	1,007
Denmark	97	119	126	134	145	177	164	962
Belgium	61	38	110	95	138	138	205	785
Finland	11	17	24	36	34	35	133	316
Ireland	0	0	16	16	51	56	56	199
Australia	0	0	0	0	39	46	112	197
Iceland	0	0	0	0	10	22	21	53
N. Zealand	2	0	0	2	10	12	14	40
Switzerland	0	1	1	3	0	2	4	11
TOTAL	6,115	5,949	7,438	7,712	9,135	11,203	13,408	60,987

Source: Selman 2006, based on children sent to 16 receiving states in 2004. No children were sent to Cyprus, Germany, Italy, or Luxembourg.

Ethiopia

Until recently the number of children adopted from Ethiopia, like most other African states, was very low, but there has been a dramatic change in the last few years and Ethiopia now features as a major source of children for many countries (see Table 1.6). In 2005 and 2006 Ethiopia was second only to China in the number of children placed with EurAdopt agencies and fourth (after Viet Nam, Haiti, and China) for France. The number of children sent to the United States has also risen: in fiscal year 2006, 732 orphan visas were issued. The growing popularity of adoption from Ethiopia has been attributed to publicity surrounding the adoption of an Ethiopian child by Angelina Jolie in 2004, but the number of children adopted from other African countries such as Liberia has also been rising. Table 1.13 shows the rise in numbers of children sent by Ethiopia between 2001 and 2004. By 2006 the number of children sent worldwide had grown to over 2,000.

Cambodia

Intercountry adoption from Cambodia has for some years been a matter of concern (Selman 2005a). From 1998 to 2002 the most striking feature is that most of the children sent went to two countries, the United States and France. Numbers sent fell sharply in 2003 following growing concerns in those countries, but in the same year 40 applications were approved in the United Kingdom and the number to Italy rose to 29 (Table 1.14). Subsequently the United Kingdom called a halt to adoptions from Cambodia (see Selman 2005a), and no applications were approved in 2005. The U.S. State Department announced a suspension of adoptions

TABLE 1.13

Adoptions from Ethiopia to 17 Receiving States, Ranked by Number Received in 2004

Receiving Country	2001	2002	2003	2004	% Increase 2001–2004
France	234	209	217	390	66
USA	158	105	135	289	83
Spain	0	12	107	220	—
Italy	79	112	47	93	17
Norway	50	44	46	53	6
Netherlands	25	25	39	72	188
Belgium	38	41	52	62	63
Australia	37	36	39	45	21
Switzerland	25	31	58	43	72
Denmark	22	22	40	41	86
Sweden	17	18	21	26	53
Germany	23	16	19	20	−14
TOTAL (20 states)	728	695	847	1,510	107%

Source: Selman 2006, based on children sent to 17 receiving states in 2004. Ethiopia also sent children to Austria (25) and Malta (18).

TABLE 1.14

Intercountry Adoptions from Cambodia 1998–2004, ranked by number sent 1998–2003

Receiving State	1998–2003	1998	2000	2001	2002	2003	2004
USA	1,543	249	402	266	285	124	0
France	1,083	95	169	278	328	60	6
Canada	85	?	21	19	22	23	14
UK	49	2	1	0	6	40[a]	18[a]
Italy	43	0	0	0	14	29	43[b]
Subtotal (5 states)	2,803	346	592	563	655	276	81
% of all	99.3	99.7	99.3	99.6	99.7	96.5	86.2[c]
TOTAL (to 20 states)	2,823	347	596	565	657	286	94

Source: Selman 2006, based on data from 20 receiving states.

[a] UK statistics record approved applications only. Following the suspension of adoptions from Cambodia in 2004, many of these did not result in the entry of children.

[b] The rise in the number of children to Italy 2002–2004 continued in the next two years, reaching 147 in 2006.

[c] The lower percentage attributable to the four named countries was due to the ending of adoptions to the United States and a rise in the number of children sent to Switzerland.

from 2002, and in 2004 none were recorded in published lists. However, the number going to Italy rose to 76 in 2005 and 147 in 2006. A growing number of adoptions was also reported by the Austrian agency Family for You: 7 in 2004 and 41 in 2005. Spain received no children from Cambodia in those years. Cambodia acceded to the Hague Convention in April 2007, although objections have been made by Germany, the Netherlands, and the United Kingdom, and the United States has continued its suspension until the country fully implements the provisions of the protocol.

Guatemala

Table 1.15 shows how the pattern identified for Cambodia seems also to hold for Guatemala, another country where there has been considerable concern—manifested in the two most recent Hague Special Commissions—about controls over the process of intercountry adoption. As with Cambodia, the top three receiving states in 2003 were the United States, France, and the United Kingdom, with very few adoptions to other European countries. In contrast, other adoptions, e.g., from China and Korea, involve a much wider range of countries and those from India are weighted towards the smaller receiving states. Subsequently adoptions from Guatemala to the United States rose further: to 3,840 in 2005 and 4,135 in 2006. Since 2002 Guatemala has taken over from South Korea the position of the third most important source of children for the United States, while the number of children going to other countries remains very low. Adoptions from Guatemala to Spain fell from 90 in 2000 to only 3 in

TABLE 1.15
Adoptions from Guatemala (2003–5) and 4 Other Sending Countries (2003)

	Guatemala			Russia	China	Korea	India
	2005	2004	2003	2003	2003	2003	2003
USA	3,783	3,264	2,328	5,209	6,859	1,790	472
France	>60	72	247	333	360	46	23
UK	21	13	28	33	108	0	24
Italy	13	16	8	380	0	0	121
Spain	0	3	8	1,157	1,043	0	100
Canada	0	0	0	92	1,108	73	70
Subtotal for 6 states	3,817	3,368	2,619	7,204	9,478	909	810
(% of all)	(99)	(99)	(99)	(95)	(84)	(83)	(72)
% to USA	98	96	87	67	61	78	40
TOTAL (to 20 states)	3,840	3,420	2,656	7,632	11,230	2,306	1,118

Source: Selman 2006, based on data from 20 receiving states.

2004, and none were recorded in 2005. In the same period the number of children adopted by EurAdopt agencies fell from 66 to 5.

Statistics collated by the Guatemala government for the Hague Special Commission confirm the dominance of the United States as a receiving state, accounting for 79 percent of all adoptions between 1997 and 2004 and 93 percent in 2004, when the number of adoptions to France fell to 72. At the Hague Special Commission in 2005, Guatemala was well represented, having not attended the previous meeting in 2000, and an action plan was outlined to improve the situation (Hague Conference 2001, 2006). However, critics say that the country has become a "baby farm where adoptions are too easy and prone to corruption" (Llorca 2006). Llorca also noted that "today every 100th baby born in Guatemala grows up as an adopted American" but suggested that the numbers might fall when the United States ratified the Hague Convention.

The current situation is unclear, as a new Guatemalan adoption law went into force on December 31, 2007, that introduces new procedures and prohibits adoptions from non-signatory countries. The United States ratified the convention in December 2007 with effect from April 2008, and in January 2008 the Department of State advised potential adoptive parents and adoption service providers "not to initiate new adoptions from Guatemala because of the great uncertainties surrounding implementation of Guatemala's new adoption law." Meanwhile the UK government has suspended all adoptions from Guatemala.

Conclusion

This chapter provides an overview of trends and patterns in international adoptions, based on data about children sent to twenty receiving states, as a framework for the detailed ethnographic insights offered by subsequent chapters. This final section raises a number of issues pertinent to taking forward our analysis and understanding of this important phenomenon. Given the evidence that the number of children involved reached an all-time high in 2004, and with it the controversy over the ethics of inter-country adoption (Bojorge 2002, Masson 2000b, Smolin 2005a), we must ask: Whose interests are being served by this process? What can be done to counter perceived trends toward a trade in children, which David Smolin (2005b) calls "child laundering"?

Changes in levels of adoptions in both receiving states and states of origin raise questions about how to develop adequate structures to meet the requirements of the Hague Convention in countries experiencing a very rapid increase in a short time, such as Spain as a receiving state and Ethiopia as a state of origin. In Spain about half of international adoptions are handled through the central authorities, but there has been a determined move toward developing authorized mediating agencies. At the 2005 EurAdopt conference held in Barcelona, Spanish authorities asserted the importance of developing more agencies that could meet the demanding standards of EurAdopt membership: from 2002 to 2006, only AAIM (Associacio d'adjuda als infants del mon) has been a member.

We should consider why such changes take place. Why is there such variation in levels of adoptions to different receiving states? How does this relate to the extent of in-country adoption in those states? The United Kingdom had just over 300 international adoptions while Spain had over 5,000, but the United Kingdom had 4,000 adoptions of "looked after" children, while Spain had only 1,000 domestic adoptions, few of which involved special needs children, and large numbers remained in institutional care. However, the United States demonstrates that high rates of international adoption are not incompatible with the development of special needs adoption: in 2002, 10 percent of children in public care were placed for adoption, a total of 53,000, more than double the number of international adoptions (Selman and Mason 2005). Opposition to intercountry adoption by social workers and public authorities have been cited as a reason for low numbers in the United Kingdom (Masson 2000a, Hayes 2005) and Australia (Commonwealth of Australia 2005).

The issue of in-country adoptions in states of origin is even more important. The pattern in Brazil has been reflected in other Latin American countries, but the development of in-country adoption has proved difficult in South Korea (Sarri et al. 2002). The situation in Romania is especially important to consider, bearing in mind arguments that the existence of intercountry adoption tends to discourage this development (Dickens 2002, 2006). Romania has now officially called a halt to ICA, other than by close relatives, a move seen as in part a result of pressures from the EU (Post 2007). That policy may have also been a factor in the fall in adoptions from Bulgaria, which also acceded to the EU in January 2007. However, several of the new member states from former Eastern Europe continue to send children for overseas adoption. For example, Poland sent 387 children in 2004, half of whom went to Italy; many seem to have been sibling groups or older and special needs children.

Finally, the variations in the type of child sent by different countries —from China predominantly females under age 2; from Korea predominantly males under age 1; from Brazil predominantly children aged over 5 or with special needs—raise questions about any generalizations in respect to outcomes of intercountry adoptions. Some of the chapters in this volume offer ethnographic accounts of the situation regarding international adoption in specific countries, examining the cultural factors influencing this process (see also Bowie 2004, Johnson 2004, Volkman 2005). This direction of research is certainly welcome.

NOTE

1. EurAdopt is "an umbrella organisation of non-profit accredited European organisations" (Sterky 2000: 389) that has developed its own code of ethics going beyond the Hague Convention and meets every two years to debate issues of intercountry adoption.

REFERENCES

Altstein, Howard, and Rita J. Simon. 1991. *Intercountry Adoption: A Multinational Perspective.* New York: Praeger.

Andersson, Gunilla. 2000. "Intercountry Adoption in Sweden: The Perspective of the Adoption Centre in Its 30th Year." In *Intercountry Adoption: Developments, Trends and Perspectives,* ed. Peter Selman, 346–67. London: BAAF.

Bojorge, Celica. 2002. "Intercountry Adoptions: In the Best Interests of the Child?" *QUT Law & Justice Journal* 2, no. 2: 266–91.

Bowie, Fiona (ed.). 2004. *Cross-Cultural Approaches to Adoption.* London: Routledge.

Commonwealth of Australia. 2005. *Overseas Adoption in Australia: Report on the Inquiry into Adoption of Children from Overseas.* Canberra: House of Representatives Standing Committee on Family and Human Services.

Dickens, Jonathan. 2002. "The Paradox of Inter-Country Adoption: Analysing Romania's Experience as a Sending Country." *International Journal of Social Welfare* 11: 76–83.

———. 2006. "The Social Policy Context of Inter-Country Adoption." Paper presented at the *Second International Conference on Adoption Research,* University of East Anglia, Norwich, UK, 17–21 July.

Fonseca, Claudia. 2002. "An Unexpected Reversal: Charting the Course of International Adoption in Brazil." *Adoption and Fostering* 26, no. 3: 28–39.

The Hague Conference. 2001. *Report and Conclusions of the Special Commission of November/December 2000 on the Practical Operation of the Adoption Convention.*

———. 2006. *Conclusions and Recommendations of the Second Special Commission of September 2005.* The Hague, Netherlands: Permanent Bureau of The Hague Conference. Both reports are available via the intercountry adoption section of the Hague Conference website: www.hcch.net/index_en.php?act=text.display& tid=45 (accessed 13 May 2008).

Hayes, Peter. 2005. "Deterrents to Intercountry Adoption in Britain." *Family Relations* 49, no. 4: 465–71.

Johnson, Kay A. 2004. *Wanting a Daughter, Needing a Son: Abandonment, Adoption, and Orphanage Care in China.* St. Paul, MN: Yeong and Yeong Book Co.

Kane, Saralee. 1993. "The Movement of Children for International Adoption: An Epidemiological Perspective." *Social Science Journal* 30, no. 4: 323–39.

Lehland, Ketil. 2000. *Crude Adoption Rates for Receiving Countries in 1998.* Oslo, Norway: Adopsjonsforum.

Llorca, Juan Carlos. 2006. "Hague Treaty Likely to Slow Guatemala Adoptions." Associated Press, 29 July.

Lovelock, Kirsten. 2000. "Intercountry Adoption as a Migratory Practice." *International Migration Review* 34, no. 3: 907–49.

Masson, Judith. 2000a. "The 1999 Reform of Intercountry Adoption in the United Kingdom." *Family Law Quarterly* 34, no. 2: 221–38.

———. 2000b. "Intercountry Adoption: A Global Problem or a Global Solution?" *Journal of International Affairs* 55, no. 1: 141–68.

Post, Roelie. 2007. *Romania—For Export Only: The Untold Story of the Romanian "Orphans."* The Netherlands: EuroComment Diffusion.

Rosenwald, Trudy. 2007. "The Devil Is in the Detail: Adoption Statistics as a Post Adoption Service in Australia." *Adoption Australia* (Spring): 18–22.

Sarri, Rosemary C., Yenoak Baik, and Marti Bombyk. 2002. "Goal Displacement and Dependency in South Korean–United States Intercountry Adoption." *Children and Youth Services Review* 20: 87–114.

Selman, Peter. 1999. "The Demography of Intercountry Adoption." In *Mine-Yours-Ours and Theirs: Adoption, Changing Kinship and Family Patterns,* ed. Anne-Lisa Ryvgold, Monica B. Dalen, and Barbro Saetersdal, 230–46. Oslo, Norway: University of Oslo.

———. 2000. "The Demographic History of Intercountry Adoption." In *Intercountry Adoption: Developments, Trends and Perspectives,* ed. Peter Selman, 14–37. London: BAAF.

———. 2002. "Intercountry Adoption in the New Millennium: The 'Quiet Migration' Revisited." *Population Research and Policy Review* 21: 205–25.

———. 2004. "Adoption: A Cure for (Too) Many Ills?" In *Cross-Cultural Approaches to Adoption,* ed. Fiona Bowie, 257–73. London: Routledge.

———. 2005a. "The Quiet Migration in the New Millennium: Trends in Intercountry Adoption 1998–2003." Keynote speech at the 8th Global Consultation on Child Welfare, Manila, Philippines, 10–12 August.

———. 2005b. "Intercountry Adoption 1998–2003: A Demographic Analysis." Paper presented at the First Global Research Conference on Adoption, Copenhagen, Denmark, 9–10 September.

———. 2006. "Trends in Intercountry Adoption 1998–2004: Analysis of Data from 20 Receiving Countries." *Journal of Population Research* 23, no. 2: 183–204.

———. 2007. "Intercountry Adoption in the Twenty-First Century: An Examination of the Rise and Fall of Countries of Origin." In *Proceedings of the First International Korean Adoption Studies Research Symposium*, ed. K. Nelson, E. Kim, and M. Petersen, 55–75. Seoul: International Korean Adoptee Associations.

———. 2008. "From Bucharest to Beijing: Changes in Countries Sending Children for International Adoption 1990 to 2006." In *International Advances in Adoption Research for Practice*, ed. Gretchen Miller Wrobel and Elsbeth Neil. London: John Wiley.

Selman, Peter, and Kathy Mason. 2005. "Alternatives to Adoption for Looked After Children." In *Adoption: Better Choices for Our Children*, Annex C. Edinburgh: Scottish Executive.

Smolin, David M. 2005a. "The Two Faces of Intercountry Adoption: The Significance of the Indian Adoption Scandals." *Seton Hall Law Review* 35: 403–93.

———. 2005b. "Child Laundering: How the Intercountry Adoption System Legitimizes and Incentivizes the Practices of Buying, Trafficking, Kidnapping, and Stealing Children." Express Preprint Series. Working Paper 749.

Sterky, Kerstin. 2000. "Maintaining Standards: The Role of EurAdopt." In *Intercountry Adoption: Developments, Trends and Perspectives*, ed. Peter Selman, 389–404. London: BAAF.

Swedish Intercountry Adoptions Authority (MIA). 2005. *Adoption in Sweden: Policy and Procedures concerning Intercountry Adoption*. Stockholm: MIA.

UNICEF. 2006. *State of the World's Children 2006*. New York: UNICEF.

U.S. Department of Homeland Security. 2006. "Immigrant Orphans Adopted by U.S. Citizens by Gender, Age and Country of Birth, Fiscal Year 2005." *2006 Yearbook of Immigration Statistics*, Table 12.

Van Loon, Hans. 1990. *Report on Intercountry Adoption*. The Hague, Netherlands: The Hague Conference.

Volkman, Toby Alice (ed.). 2005. *Cultures of Transnational Adoption*. Durham, NC: Duke University Press.

Weil, Richard H. 1984. "International Adoptions: The Quiet Migration." *International Migration Review* 18, no. 2: 276–93.

Chapter 2

||||||||||||||||||||||||||||||||||||||||||||||||||||||

International Adoption
Lessons from Hawai'i

Judith Schachter

This chapter starts simply, with a family I know—perhaps even belong to —in Hawai'i.

Fourteen children grew up in that family. Two were biological children brought into the family by the wife, and four were biological children of the husband and wife. Four children were legally adopted, and three "stayed" in the household and considered themselves children of the family. The last was a *hanai* child—adopted according to Hawaiian custom. The patriarch of the family, my friend Sam, showed me fourteen photograph albums, one for each child, all alike.

The situation posed questions for me. Did the fourteen children really belong to the family in the same way? What was the meaning of "adoption" for Sam and his wife, Loretta? Was there a difference between fostering and caring for children? These questions prompt us to think about the evolution and consequences of familiar distinctions among ways of "having children." The distinction between adoption and foster care, in particular, carries a weight of cultural ideology and legal paraphernalia. These are Euro-American distinctions and apply clumsily, or not at all, in other cultures and societies—even in Hawai'i where they carry the force of law. These distinctions, however, guide decisions about and implementation of the movement of children incorporated under *international adoption*.

This chapter focuses on the story of Sam's family and the decisions he made about having children as a way of exploring issues that are pertinent to international adoption. I never met Loretta, who had died seven years before I met Sam, and I know about her role in the family through Sam, his children, and his grandchildren. In those accounts, Sam and Loretta shared a commitment to "taking care" of children, to providing a loving and stable household, and to incorporating children of any origin into the extended family, or *'ohana*. Sam's conversations with me also revealed the close connections between his understandings of Hawaiian "tradition" and his recognition of the opportunities offered by an American legal system. Sam defined himself as a "Native Hawaiian" man, and the way he constructed a family in an American state inform us of the complexities of moving children under circumstances in which notions of parent-child relationships diverge and, often, compete.

The story of Hawai'i, too, is a story of shifting power relationships. From the colonialism of the early nineteenth century to the present struggles for cultural autonomy, Hawai'i illustrates the close connection between imperialist policies and definitions of kinship. Control of the family is a resource in the contest between *haole* ("stranger") and Native Hawaiian; how you have children is key to maintaining cultural and political authority. Considering my Hawaiian family the ethnographic core of a broader analysis, I will delineate the effects on interpretations of kinship of the clash between a law-based culture embodied in American courts and a tradition-based culture embraced by *kama'ainana*—Hawaiians of indigenous ancestry.[1] My data come from over a decade of fieldwork and time spent with social workers, lawyers, and teachers, as well as with individuals who consider themselves to be Native Hawaiian. To this fieldwork material, I add archival sources: key cases in decisions about the placement of children. I have drawn on selected legal opinions from Hawaiian court cases in which the meanings of terms such as child and issue, blood and contract, care and commitment, are debated. These cases not only set precedents for the development of laws of adoption in Hawai'i but also permeate the decisions individuals make about transferring a child according to custom. Legal requirements and the language of the law influence people's perceptions of their options as parents. This is the lesson from Hawai'i that applies to a consideration of international adoption.

My training as a cultural anthropologist holds that a "thick description" or ethnographic account yields insights into the tangled ideologies and intimate personal investments that underlie the construction of kinship in any setting (see Dorow 2006, Volkman 2005, Bowie 2004). Sam's story shows the creative use and subversion of cultural imperialism: how the actions of individuals are formed by and reciprocally form the larger framework in which relationships occur, evolve, and become the substance of overarching decisions about who can do what, when, and how when it comes to having and raising children.

Sam's Family in Hawaiian Context

Fourteen children. What did this really mean, within the family, in terms of the rights and obligations associated with kinship, and in terms of my own analysis of Hawaiian-American relations? Sam's use of the courts for adoption and his embrace of Hawaiian custom in the *hanai* designation carry the legacy of the past, specifically the arrival of *haole* and the introduction of an alternative U.S.-based system for establishing parent-child relationships. The history of law and custom in Hawai'i infuses the accounts I heard and influences the behaviors I observed in a decade of fieldwork. Sam's comments on his family and on the forging of kinship ties testify to the continual intertwining of legal strictures and customary norms. His account demonstrates the reciprocal and dynamic relation between systems, as well as the dent that individual actions make in any hegemony of rule, whether law or custom.

I first met Sam in 1989 at a meeting for senior citizens on the coast of Oahu. He explained my work on adoption to the elderly audience, introducing me instantly to the problem of defining and using terms. I had already talked to the group about my project, to study the impact of North American adoption policy on the practice of "traditional" Hawaiian adoption, or *hanai*. Sam told my project to the seniors in another way, resisting the anthropological terminology I had employed and instead providing a series of stories: a person who raised her granddaughter, an "auntie" who had taken in three sets of siblings, and an army companion who had given Sam and Loretta two children. When I got to know Sam better, after three summer fieldtrips, he invited me to his house in the Hawaiian Homestead community of Waimanalo. There, while we sat in the garage with our soft drinks, he showed me fourteen photograph albums and told the story of how each child entered the family.

Sam's account of family-making leads in several directions for my consideration of international adoption. First, his description of modes of having children points to the significance of terminology and to the denotations and connotations of concepts that frame a discussion of adoption policy and practice. Second, Sam's language reveals both the power of and resistance to official discourse concerning the ways of having children. His story shows how practices can at once sustain and subvert ideologies of kinship. Third, my conversations with Sam demonstrate the link between cultural identities and ways of having children. His self-image as a Native Hawaiian in an American state structured his narratives and his actions. His embrace of Americanness paralleled his pronouncement of Hawaiian values.

Sam's process of family-making is preeminently an indication of the fluidity of identifications in a colonial setting.[2] To take the circumstances of colonial and post-colonial societies into account, we need a more nuanced and culturally relative approach to international adoption. The complexities of practices and interpretations that a close analysis of Hawai'i yields, through the example of Sam, suggest what a more subtle and complete analysis of international adoption would look like.

The colonization of Hawai'i in the early nineteenth century established the framework for the decisions Sam made during the second half of the twentieth century. American missionaries arrived in the Sandwich Islands in the 1820s, a short forty years after the British navigator, Captain Cook, had visited the islands. Europeans unable to comprehend the terms of kinship reported that chaos ruled relationships between women and men and between adults and children. From the perspective of the missionaries, women and men formed transitory liaisons based on sex rather than commitment. Even more distressing to these visitors from New England, children moved from household to household, apparently at will and at whim. Children seemed not to know, or at least not to be raised, by their "own" parents. By 1840, the missionaries had enough influence on the royal family to persuade the king to draft a constitution. Regulation of the family was a primary component. From that time on, the model for the Hawaiian family was the Christian nuclear family, initiated by marriage and continued through biological reproduction.

A legal relationship replaced the presumptively casual connections between men and women. Law also regulated the place of children, preferably with biological parents but, if not, at least legally contracted to another adult. The Hawaiian kingdom had laws of adoption by the mid-nineteenth century, ahead of the United States.[3] Cases that tested the meaning and interpretation of these laws came to the Honolulu Court almost immediately. In those cases, pleas, opinions, and decisions exposed the profound importance of parenthood to assertions of political authority and of cultural identity for the *haole* legal experts and the *kama'ainana* petitioners. The earliest cases involved property and the transmission of property when no will had been written. Later cases delved into the rights and obligations accruing to the relationship between child and parent. The first half of the twentieth century brought attention to the child in Hawaiian courts, in response to the principle of best interests that dominated North

American child placement policy. By the time Sam reviewed his options in the late twentieth century, court cases also mandated the nature of ties between the biological and social parents—specifically, the termination of parental rights and the erasure of contact between "giving" and "taking" parents.

As cases came before them, judges wrote opinions in which they examined and established definitions of such terms as child, issue, blood, and nature. Delving into the meaning of terms, the entailments of custom, and the precedents in law, the judges did work similar to that of anthropologists. The nineteenth-century decisions I examined resemble the debates over terminology and the implications of terms that preoccupy literature on adoption. Court opinions confronted the analytic problems revolving around the "transfer of parenthood" and the "exchange of children" well before anthropologists considered adoption a central and serious topic of inquiry. Not until the 1960s and 1970s did literature focusing on child exchange appear, and then with warnings the Hawaiian judges would have appreciated. In an early edited volume, Vern Carroll warned: "there is great hazard in using the term 'adoption' in descriptive ethnography without indicating carefully what it is (if anything) that is being translated by the term" (1970: 11). By the 1990s, the word adoption acquired a pragmatic universalism to facilitate cross-cultural comparison. But, as Fiona Bowie cautions in her introduction to *Cross-Cultural Approaches to Adoption,* the term is useful only as long as writers convey the distinctive content and meanings of indigenous practices (2004: 6).

Judges could not rest with academic debate, though there is plenty of that in opinions. Judges had to make decisions based on a reading of social kinship, its origins, entailments, and relationship to biological kinship. The content and meanings of adoption evolved in a context of competing interests and interpretations, which continues to be the case today as child circulation moves from the local to the international arena.

The first adoption cases judges heard in Hawai'i's courts were brought by adults who claimed rights to property on the basis of adoptive status in the family.[4] Disputes propelled the definitional task, and judges interpreted legal precedent and customary practice according to their own lights. Adoption would be worthless, stated one judge, if it did not grant a right of inheritance. In his view, the adopted child, like the "blood" child, should continue the family's proprietorship. Another judge concluded that an adopted child's right to inherit depended on the motives of those who adopted, which was a matter of inquiry and evidence. Did the adopting parent intend to have the child become an heir? Decisions in these cases were individualized and varied with the status of the claimant, the persuasiveness of supporting testimony, and the viewpoint of the judge on the import of constructed kinship. Prince Liholiho received the crown lands as a *hanai* child whose parent, witnesses said, intended him to succeed to the throne. A commoner claiming adoptive status in order to inherit land fared less well, and in another case the judge deemed the adoption a matter of whim and caprice.

In the decades after 1840, the term adoption, strictly interpreted, referred to a transfer of parenthood that had the backing of a written contract signed before a judge. By contrast—or so it seemed—*hanai* referred to customary practices in which the transfer rested on an oral agreement between adults. The distinction in discourse, however, was blurred in actuality, inasmuch as adoption and *hanai* were equally ambiguous on the matter of rights and duties accruing to the constructed relationship. Both forms of social parenthood eschewed examination of the material and the psychological consequences of the arrangement for the child.

Best Interests

In Hawai'i, the question of inheritance was settled in 1905. By law, the Territory of Hawai'i granted legal adoptees the right of inheritance, deeming the social arrangement analogous to the blood relationship. Blood, the American courts stated, presumed that a child inherited from an intestate parent. Claims to a legacy on the basis of customary practices were not so easily resolved, and judges in Hawai'i's courts pursued the analysis of intention to determine the "reality" of a parent-child tie. This pursuit evolved into an examination of the child's treatment: had she been cared for, loved, and cherished? Attention to the child and to childhood was bolstered in the early twentieth century by the dominance of the principle of the best interests of the child in North American child welfare policy, which served as a guideline for policies in the territory. While the language of Hawai'i's original adoption law placed the interests of the child over those of the adults, the principle did not become operative until a half-century later when rightful placement, not rights to property, brought disputes to Hawai'i's courts. Although encoded in a *haole* system and imposed by territorial authorities, best interests actually brought legal and customary adoption closer together. The custom of *hanai* implied a special concern for the child, and Native Hawaiian records of Hawai-ian custom emphasize the love and indulgence given the *hanai*, pet of the family (Pukui, Haertig, and Lee 1972). One judge dismissed the claim to adoptive status on the grounds of a lack of love: the child, he said, had been treated like a servant in the household. A contradiction of twenti-eth-century Anglo-American views of childhood and of the meaning of *hanai*, parental refusal to cherish the child voided the social relationship.

With its roots in concepts of feeding, nurturing, and sustaining, *hanai* offered an elegant implementation of best interests. The principle under-lined the (ostensibly) primary purpose of an adoption: to provide a child with security, love, and the continuity of kinship. From that point of view, multiple forms of transferring a child could fulfill the purpose and be covered by the word *adoption*.

The principle of best interests was not so easily implemented, however. "Love" made experts nervous; mere emotion was too vague and too capri-cious to prevent risk to the child, concluded trained professionals in the twentieth century. Best interests brought calculation into placement deci-sions, an antidote to the whim of love. Inquiries and objective measures were established to determine the potential of an adult to be a parent. The effect of measuring qualities was to separate the birth parent from the adoptive parent in terms of capability, character, and class. Paradoxi-cally, the persistence of *hanai* as a practice perpetuated the ideological components of best interests while the form of the arrangement came under suspicion. Perceived as weaker than contract, the oral agreement and exchange of a child between adults who knew one another slid to the margins of legitimate adoption. Personal and imprecise, by the mid-twen-tieth century customary practice appeared to be risky, as missionaries and judges had concluded a century earlier.

Statehood in 1959 confirmed a relationship between indigenous prac-tices and North American interpretations of adoption that had been de-veloping for over a century. Local practices persisted, in the face of inter-pretations enshrined in policy and imposed by a *haole*-run child welfare system. As is generally true, law did not banish custom. Rather, law im-plied a hierarchy among ways of having children that individual actions, like those of Sam and Loretta, contested. In policy, legal adoption served the best interests of the child. By the end of the twentieth century, adop-tion by law starred in North American child welfare policy and in the in-ternational conventions that regulated the movement of children around the world. In practice, other modes of caring continued to serve a child's interests.

Sam and Loretta went to court in the 1960s intending to adopt four children by law. Their case was a strong one because they satisfactorily met the American criteria for parenthood: married, middle class, and stable. The birthparents' rights were terminated, and Sam and Loretta became full, permanent, and acknowledged parents of the children. A generation later, Sam and Loretta took Lihua, the first child of their son, in a classic *hanai* arrangement. For everyone concerned, they became the full, permanent, and acknowledged parents of Lihua. Two modes of having a child existed, by law and according to custom, and Sam and Loretta chose one and then the other on the basis of particular circumstances.

The choices of law and of custom were strategic and pragmatic, and they did not affect the understandings of being a parent that Sam later conveyed to me. Strategically, going to court was necessary because the birthparents had demanded the children back, violating the original agreement. Sam and Loretta drew on the definitiveness of law to resolve a conflict not resolvable in discussion or through consensus. Strategically, *hanai* worked because the son considered it a resource at a time when he and his wife were not able adequately to parent the infant. Sam described the differences to me, proud of his recognition by an American court as the fit parent and equally proud of the sustained *hanai* relationship within his 'ohana (extended family). Law had constructed an unambiguous parent-child relationship. The *hanai* arrangement had established an equally unambiguous relationship between two generations of parents and child.

The distinctions between law and custom came from a "foreign" system, but they proved entirely useful to Sam and Loretta. At the same time, these categorical distinctions did not alter Sam's interpretation of parenthood. As the photograph albums testified, the four adopted children and the *hanai* received the same treatment, along with the three who "stayed" and the six who were born to Sam and Loretta. Although missionaries might have viewed Sam's assortment of reproductive strategies as indicating the casual quality of Hawai'ians' relationships and judges might deem it capricious, for Sam the assortment expressed the constituents of kinship. For Sam, care, concern, and cherishing were aspects of being a parent in every case. Sam might have called these feelings *aloha*—as he did when he related his sense of parenthood to his identity as a Native Hawaiian.

The existence of clearly defined categories of having children opened a range of choice for Sam. *Adoption, fosterage, hanai,* and *caring for* each established parenthood, in forms that differed in origin but not in their realization of his interpretation of kinship. The actions Sam took in the context he occupied reveal the opportunities categorical distinctions can provide, the connection between modes of being a parent and assertions of cultural identity, and, finally, the resource that alternative systems can be for the design of practices and ideologies that comprise a new geography of kinship (see Volkman 2005: 19).

Reflections on International Adoption

My work on adoption and fosterage concentrates on the United States and reflects my anthropological training in kinship theory. Extending the inquiry to Hawai'i and to residents of an American state who preserve indigenous traditions deepened my theoretical frameworks. The intersection of custom and law perceived by the individuals I knew, especially Sam and his family, shed light on the problems raised by transferring children from culture to culture in international adoption. The stories Sam told me reveal both the possibilities and the difficulties that an intersection of law and custom in the global arena prompts. I point to Hawai'i, then, not because children from that state are transferred around the world, but because issues raised there about how individuals simultaneously respect customary child-transfer and acknowledge the weight of law are directly pertinent to the global circulation in the twenty-first century. Sam and Loretta, according to Sam, maintained legal adoption and *hanai* as equivalent routes to having children. Yet the very coexistence of legal adoption and customary adoption produces a precarious balance, in which custom may fade, attain the inappropriate rigidity of law, or expand to include almost any instance of child transfer.

The coexistence of law and custom characterizes debates over and regulations of the transfer of children from culture to culture and nation to nation. The example I bring from Hawai'i indicates how intimately these issues affect interpretations of kinship, family, and parenthood. It also indicates the importance for policies and outcomes of the circulation of children of the diverse decisions individuals who adopt and who relinquish children make. In the end, my work in Hawai'i displays both the pliability of interpretations of kinship and the power of ideologies of kinship. This paradox contains an important truth about the role of practice for altering hegemonic notions of kinship, personhood, and identity.

I develop this idea by focusing on three points: (1) the continuing and imperialistic force of an "as-if-begotten" model for parent-child relationships; (2) the ambiguous role of choice in adoption; and (3) the narrowing of meanings and, consequently, the restriction of practices of transferring children. Adoption in an international arena exposes the cultural imperialism that determines relationships within and across societies, while also demonstrating the impact of individual decisions on the meanings given to kinship.

The example of Hawai'i displays the persistence of an "as-if-begotten" model in various manifestations. In the nineteenth century, strangers brought new ideas of family and relatedness to the indigenous population of the islands. These ideas, coded in law, intersected with the understandings of kinship embraced by Native Hawaiians. For the *haole*, relationships constructed by individuals at will appeared random, casual, and transient and, ultimately, dangerous to the civil order. In an effort to ensure permanence, the law instantiated contract for relationships between women and men and nature for the relationship between parent and child. While the logic of contract upheld one relationship, the symbolism of blood upheld the other. Where blood represents solidarity and enduring ties, birth accords both primary rights and essential aspects of identity—an ideology distinct to European and American culture. The ideology informed the decisions made by judges in the Hawaiian Islands well before the principle of "as-if-begotten" was articulated. Comparisons between biological issue and adopted child run through court cases, establishing the priority of the first as the measuring rod for the second mode of forming a parent-child relationship.

Explicit if not instructive, the principle of "as-if-begotten" dominated American and European laws of adoption in the twentieth century. Only at the end of the century did the phrase drop out of discourse on adoption and, too, become problematic in law. Considered inappropriate to the diversity of families created through adoption—especially international adoption—the model persists in adoption practices and in prescriptions for adoptive families. The principle is as strong today as ever, albeit in new guises. "As-if-begotten" underlies the practice of introducing a child into the adoptive family's extended kinship network in order to provide roots that replicate genealogical connections. It equally frames the practice at the other end of the continuum, of immersing an adopted

child in the culture of her or his birth family. Finally, this model generates the continuing perception of risk to children who are brought up by
other than a biological parent. In these guises, "as-if-begotten" remains
thoroughly a part of international adoption and a powerful manifestation of the imperialism of Euro-American interpretations of family and
kinship.

The imposition of this ideology also results in a disparagement of alternative understandings of transferring a child from biological to social
parent. These alternatives bring up the notion of choice, the second point
of my conclusion.

We have rightly grown sensitive to the powerful roles played by poverty
and political oppression on the global circulation of children. At the same
time, and consequently, we have shied away from the notion of choice in
the movement of children. In doing so we reinforce attributions of vulnerability, denying the possibilities that adoption offers its participants. In
Sam's case, his assumption of parenthood had a counterpart in the choice
another person made to relinquish parenthood. Both participated in a
transaction, one giving and the other receiving a child. Both had agency
in the decision to transfer parenthood. I do not mean to discount differences in circumstances but rather to emphasize the *agency* with which
individuals respond to circumstances. Over time and throughout the
world, individuals have demonstrated this agency through a negotiation
of parenthood.

The framework of choice has recently fallen out of favor in adoption
discourse. Among other reasons, the word seems to impose American
notions of individualism and autonomy and to misrepresent the conditions under which adoption often occurs. Yet for participants, experts,
and scholars, adoption preeminently represents choice, and this fact is
signaled by the substitution of constructed kinship for the familiar notion
of genealogical kinship. The growth of international adoption proclaims
the victory of socially constructed over biologically determined kinship.
International adoption also illustrates the limits, and the condemnation,
of choice in practices of exchanging children.

Contemporary adoption laws and practices narrow the options open
to individuals deliberating the assumption of parenthood. International
adoption returns us to a situation that is similar to the question posed
by nineteenth-century missionaries: how to ensure the security of a child
who is "circulated" from one adult to another. The very question bespeaks
a model of security that is dependent on a belief in biological bonds and,

lacking nature, in its replacement by contract. A plurality of forms of caring for children continues to trouble the gatekeepers and experts on childhood. Consequently, the spread of international adoption has coincided with an extension of laws regulating the movement of children. While I am not arguing against controls over the movement of children, I am suggesting that such control must not be limited to a legal structure that has its origins in Euro-American assumptions about security, identity, and kinship. To claim, as the missionaries did, that the exchange of children among adults cannot be good for the child is to narrow our view of the responsibility taken—and the love given—when adults enter a transaction in parenthood.

Sam recognized both the virtues and the limitations of the distinctions that proceeded from an imposition of North American law on adoption practices in Hawai'i. The virtues were strategic: law offered an option that, for him, existed as an alternative to and not a replacement for customary practice. The limitations stemmed from associated expectations about the behaviors and the emotions that cement a parent-child relationship. Sam chose among the options his context provided for becoming a parent at the same time that he resisted the ideologies of parenting attached to those options. Like others I encountered, Sam relished the array of practices for making kin that *hanai* epitomized. In relishing the diversity of practices, he made a space for negotiating the meaning of kinship that challenged the power of law and the force of custom.

Sam's approaches to parenthood connect to his perceptions of himself as a Native Hawaiian in an American state. His movement between an American system of child welfare and Native Hawaiian kinship practices contributed to his formation of an identity in the colonial setting of late twentieth-century Hawai'i. Becoming and being a parent was a crucial aspect of Sam's ongoing juxtaposition in the construction of his identity of Native Hawaiian roots and the values represented by an American regime. Identity, or in its active mode, identification, has for some years preoccupied adoption literature.[5] Analyses have focused on the adopted individual and, recently, especially on the transracial, transcultural, and transnational adoptee. Based on my fieldwork, I suggest that we pay equal attention to the roles that adoption plays in the identity-forming processes of adults in the transaction.

Sam's story presents a view of adoption and identity that emphasizes the link between ways of having children and the conjoining of diverse sources of identity. The process in which Sam engaged pertains to contemporary adoption, which is marked by the confrontation of cultures and the recurrence, in new guises, of the shifting power relationships that characterized the history of family and kinship in Hawai'i. As his description of *hanai* evinced, Sam self-consciously constructed an identity as Native Hawaiian. He bolstered this view of himself in an autobiographical memoir he gave me, entitled *Life Story of a Native Hawaiian*. His sister reiterated the identification in the words she used about Sam and Loretta: "they would have taken in any child." She referred, as Sam did more elaborately, to the persistence of the incorporative and welcoming *'ohana*, in which entry created kinship. Yet at the same time Sam fully and insistently proclaimed his identity as the citizen of an American state. His account of *hanai* revealed the components of his Hawaiian identity, and his description of legal adoption displayed the elements of his American identity. Diverse modes of having children gave Sam a means of carrying on the complex task of managing "multiple points of identification" (Yngvesson 2002).

The restriction of practices under a national or international code for the movement of children may deny or limit the options Sam had to make a family. A global restriction might also eliminate assertions of cultural identity that are associated with making kin. The Hague Convention on Intercountry Adoption begins with an open-ended goal: "Recognizing that the child, for the full and harmonious development of his or her personality, should grow up in a family environment, in an atmosphere of happiness, love and understanding . . ." (1993, Preamble). The rest of the document narrows the means of accomplishing that goal to adoption, when a birthparent or family cannot raise the child. The ensuing description of the arrangement indicates that the primary model is based on Euro-American law. The regulations proposed in the Hague Convention construct adoption as a contractual agreement drawn between entities which, whether person or institution, possess full knowledge of the terms of the arrangement. Information is confidential, provided to the participants only with the approval of a central authority. Birthparent and adoptive parent are anonymous to one another, and the child's past becomes the province of the adoptive parents. Social bonds between the adults engaged in the transfer are nonexistent. The child, the wording goes, has been "freed" for adoption.

The term "adoptable" refers to this status of being freed (see Howell, this volume). Moreover, the term shifts inadvertently from available to desirable: an adoptable child is a child someone wants, not "any child" (to quote Sam's sister) who needs a family environment. The slippage of adoptable in the direction of desirable occurs as well in recent Federal Guidelines in the United States, for instance in the change from "special needs" to "special" as a way of ensuring the child's adoptability.[6] The opposite term, unadoptable, rarely appears in policy documents. The effect of "unadoptable" would be to prevent a class of children from acquiring the conditions for happiness, love, and understanding.

I am quite sure Sam would have found the term "adoptable" strange and disturbing, given its suggestion that children can be classified according to traits, features, or circumstances. Whether he went to court or adopted according to custom, Sam concentrated on the interests of the children, and his interpretations of those interests underline the problematic implications of the Hague Convention. These implications stem from the assumptions about family the regulations perpetuate and the equation of clear and permanent with contracted and jural in the transfer of a child. The customary arrangement through which Sam and Loretta took Lihua into the family was as clear and permanent as the cases they took to court.

Sam and Loretta would have taken in any child. For them, as Sam conveyed to me, the action resonated with Hawaiian values of generosity and care. A child who needed a family was adoptable by virtue of that fact alone, and in his view nurture and sustenance would naturally be provided. The cultural significance of "to feed," the etymological root of *hanai*, naturalized the relationship. Referring to the tradition he considered Hawaiian, Sam subsumed the informed consent and signed contract of legal adoption under the rubric of *aloha*: caring for, sustaining, and cherishing. According to tradition, the expression of *aloha* included the birth parents, independent of their presence in the social network of adoptive family and child. For Sam *aloha* represented the bond between the adults who exchanged a child, whether they knew one another, as in Hawaiian customary adoption, or were unknown to one another, as in American legal adoption. Despite its watering-down in tourist brochures and colloquial discourse, *aloha* remains core to assertions of Hawaiian identity. The concept is also core to an understanding of kinship in which persons become kin by being incorporated into a social network. In adoption, the child is incorporated into and belongs to an ʻohana.

Considering my ethnographic example, I conclude that *belonging* may be a better concept than *permanence* for guiding the circulation of children, locally as well as internationally. Both the Hague Convention and

North American child placement policy cite permanence as the most important factor in ensuring the child's happiness and ability to thrive. In the convention and in various federal guidelines, permanence reflects a particular view of parent-child ties: the enduring solidarity that is, at its basis, modeled on Euro-American interpretations of kinship. Now, as in nineteenth-century Hawai'i, when social parenthood replaces biological parenthood, contract replaces the bonds of blood. The language of both the Hague Convention and the law makes it clear that contract is viewed as protecting the child from the whimsical instability that love and generosity represent, even years after judges, policy makers, and social workers inserted those dimensions into placement decisions. The concept of permanence effectively eliminates practices of caring for children that do not involve contract, written agreements, or a dyadic relationship between child and adult. These practices have sustained generations of children throughout the world, and we exclude them at our peril. The concept of belonging, by contrast, acknowledges the many ways in which children can be and are taken in, with full security and love.

Sam and Loretta incorporated fourteen children into their 'ohana. Law and custom, along with biological birth, brought the children into a community of kin, sustained by generosity and by love. As Sam and Loretta displayed in practice and Sam described to me, the construction of parenthood promised a certainty of belonging but not a unitary source of belonging—not the one-dimensional attachment based on a nuclear family model but the solidarity promised by diverse nodes of affiliation. Sam and Loretta's children were embedded in a community of kin represented by the 'ohana and the Hawaiian nation. Belonging connects the core of kinship with the conception of nationhood.

Until we acknowledge the range of ways in which children can be cared for safely and permanently, we conserve a system in which hegemonic ideologies of kinship reinforce vulnerability. These ideologies eliminate the vital practices that allow many peoples of the world to sustain, in safety, a generation of children. The perpetuation of hegemonic ideologies of kinship through adoption convention and law deprives individuals from extending the making of kin to the making of community, on a global scale. The example Sam and Loretta provide, of bringing children into the 'ohana through affiliation and aloha, shows the ways in which dimensions of belonging can transcend the cultural and national boundaries that still frame our interpretation of the movement of peoples.

ACKNOWLEDGMENTS

As always, Albrecht Funk deserves special appreciation.
Judith Schachter formerly published under the surname Modell.

NOTES

1. Several terms are used for the indigenous peoples of Hawai'i, with varying denotations and connotations. The terms also have consequences for the distribution of rights and privileges. I have chosen to use *kama'ainana*, indigenous to a place. Talking with me, Sam used the term "Native Hawaiian," perhaps to avoid reference to the controversial terminology associated with recent sovereignty movements. Sam's term accords with the language in official state documents.

2. Under the control of Americans, politically and economically in the nineteenth century, then formally as a territory and a state in the twentieth century, Hawaii can justifiably be considered a colony of the United State; see Merry 2000.

3. The 1855 Massachusetts law is said to be the first adoption law in the United States; see Modell [Schachter] 1994.

4. The situation in Hawai'i was complicated by the fact that land was privatized in the same period that an adoption law was passed. The Great Mahele of 1848 divided land among the monarchy, the chiefs, and the commoners; see Kame'eleihiwa 1992.

5. From the early work of Betty Jean Lifton to recent examinations of identity formation in transnational, transcultural, and transracial adoptions, adoptee identity has been a major theme in the literature; see Volkman 2005, Dorow 2006, Howell 2006.

6. See United States Government, *Adoption and Safe Families Act*, 1997.

REFERENCES

Bowie, Fiona. 2004. "Adoption and the Circulation of Children." In *Cross-Cultural Approaches to Adoption,* ed. Fiona Bowie, 3–20. New York: Routledge.

Carroll, Vern (ed.). 1970. "Introduction: What Does 'Adoption' Mean?" In *Adoption in Eastern Oceania,* ed. Vern Carroll, 3–17. Honolulu: University of Hawaii.

Dorow, Sara K. 2006. *Transnational Adoption: A Cultural Economy of Race, Gender and Kinship.* New York: New York University Press.

Hague Convention on Protection of Children and Cooperation in Respect of Inter-country Adoption 1993. The Hague Conference on Private International Law, May 1993.

Hawaii State Bar Association. 2001. *Hawaiian Adoption Manual*. 3rd ed.

Howell, Signe. 2006. *The Kinning of Foreigners: Transnational Adoption in a Global Perspective*. New York: Berghahn Books.

Kame'eleihiwa, Lilikala. 1992. *Native Land and Foreign Desires*. Honolulu: Bishop Museum Press.

Merry, Sally. 2000. *Colonizing Hawaii: The Cultural Power of Law*. Princeton, NJ: Princeton University Press.

Modell, Judith Schachter. 1994. *Kinship with Strangers: Adoption and Interpretations of Kinship in American Culture*. Berkeley: University of California Press.

Pukui, M., E. W. Haertig, and C. Lee. 1972. *Nana I Ke Kumu (Look to the Source)*. Honolulu: Queen Lili'uokalani Children's Center.

United States Government. 1997. *Adoption and Safe Families Act*. P.L. 105-89.

Volkman, Toby Alice (ed.). 2005. "Introduction: New Geographies of Kinship." In *Cultures of Transnational Adoption*, ed. Toby Alice Volkman, 1–22. Durham, NC: Duke University Press.

Yngvesson, Barbara. 2002. "Placing the 'Gift Child' in Transnational Adoption." *Law and Society Review* 36, no. 2: 227–56.

Chapter 3

IIIIIIIIIIIIIIIIIIIIIIIIIIIIIIIIIIIIIIIIIIIIIIIIIIIIII

The Social Temporalities of Adoption and the Limits of Plenary Adoption

Françoise-Romaine Ouellette

The social dynamics of adoption in Québec have been shaped by important issues regarding both its legal regulation and the development of children's identity, and the recent development of adoption policy in Québec contributes to a better understanding of adoption politics and practices in other societies. Québec ranks among the Western societies posting the highest ratios of foreign adoptions to births per annum and to overall population size. International adoptions averaged 805 per year between 1990 and 2004. In spite of subsequent decreases (to 496 in 2007), they still account for the large majority of all adoptions in Québec. The number of domestic adoptions is low, but has been rising recently because of policies to move children from foster care to adoption. Significantly, adoption is now defined as a child protection measure rather than a kinship institution.

In Québec, as in the United States and many European countries, the only legal form of adoption is plenary adoption, which entails the complete dissolution of the child's original kinship ties.[1] The child becomes not only a full member of the adoptive family, as if born into it, but also a legal stranger to his or her birth parents and other birth relatives. This transformation of identity is too often thought of as the inevitable and most desirable effect of adoption. Yet plenary adoption cannot always provide transnationally adopted children with an identity and kinship affiliation consistent with their personal histories and their particular needs and interests. Plenary adoption need not be the only option, however. Indeed, it is not always the rule everywhere. In France and Belgium, courts sometimes authorize a "simple" adoption, which gives the child an additional family without entirely erasing the original one. In some international adoptees' birth countries, legal adoption grants parental rights to the adoptive parents but does not annul the child's previous kinship ties. Anthropologists have shown that the circulation of children that is customary in most societies is not antithetical to the open recognition of their birth families.

Over the past thirty years, a series of challenges concerning the legitimate circulation of children has arisen that is especially acute in the transnational context. In sociological terms, these social struggles that have emerged around adoption constitute a clearly delineated social field (Bourdieu 1980: 113–20).[2] The members of the adoption triad—biological parents, adoptive parents, adoptee—play only minor roles in this field's dynamics, compared to the other private and institutional agents moving into position around them (Ouellette 1996, 2005). In Québec, officials wield the greatest influence since legislation strongly opposes private transactions in order to enforce the clean break implied by plenary adoption. The Director of Youth Protection is in charge of the entire process in all domestic adoptions[3] and is solely responsible for the psychological assessment of adoptive parents in many international adoptions as well. The Secrétariat à l'adoption internationale (SAI) coordinates all international adoption initiatives. Nonprofit agencies operate as accredited intermediaries between adopters and the countries of origin, while adoptive parents' associations generate mutual aid networks and lobby policymakers. Professionals in government agencies or in private practice provide assessment, as well as medical and psychosocial follow-up for the families involved. In the sending countries, orphanage directors, civil servants, and judges can either smooth or block access to adoptable children. Researchers influence attitudes and decisions on contested issues in adoption policy.

All these different agents must collaborate on promoting the interests of children, but their particular interests give rise to divergent views and even confrontations. Their differential access to resources for defending their respective positions shapes struggles over adoption practice and policy. The principal stakes for which they invest their time, energy, and material, political, or symbolic capital are articulated to the three temporal dimensions of adoption explored in this chapter. First, the length of the legal and administrative process of intercountry adoption triggered the struggles for power and legitimacy that birthed the field. Second, the child's development gradually became a major clinical and ethical concern, prompting governmental adoption and youth protection services to overhaul their practices and giving rise to new types of influential expertise. Third, genealogical transmission has recently produced new practices and attitudes with regard to the symbolic issue of identity and the right of adoptees to know their origins.

Length of the Legal and Administrative Process

An adoption becomes final at the end of an administrative and legal process that may take years. Applicants are anxious to have the process move along as quickly as possible. However, government officials who are required to ensure the legality of the proceedings impose time-consuming constraints. This source of tension between applicants and institutional stakeholders was one of the main factors shaping Québec's adoption field in the 1980s and 1990s. The prolonged duration and myriad uncertainties of the process were a particularly serious problem for international adoptions, in part because the practice was just developing and regulations had to be devised, tested, and modified.

International adoption networks developed quickly when adoptable children born in Québec became scarce after the profound societal changes of the 1960s. Adoptive parents provided others with contacts in their children's country of origin, and nonprofit associations began to operate as intermediaries. However, international adoption was recognized as a well-founded practice that should enjoy public support only after considerable debate. Until 1979, the Québec government confined itself to approving the issuance of Canadian immigration visas for children adopted abroad and conducting the psychosocial assessment required by some countries of origin. The associations that assisted adopters in foreign countries worked in a vacuum as far as rules were concerned, especially since few countries of origin had suitable legal frameworks. The success of an adoption depended on personalized relationships of trust and a great deal of resourcefulness, opening the door for violations of various kinds. Some adopters came back to Canada with a child lacking proper papers and applied to legitimize the child's civil status after the fact. The Youth Protection Act of 1979 led to the formation of the SAI, which in 1982 was given the task of supervising intercountry adoptions.

At its inception, SAI favored a rules-based, control-oriented approach to limit the all too real risks of child abuse and trafficking. It significantly reduced the room for initiative and autonomy previously enjoyed by adopters and voluntary agencies. Those individuals and groups challenged the rules that SAI was seeking to impose, demanding that it provide practical support for international adoption and recognize them as its partners. Discontent centered on the unduly long wait for psychosocial assessment, which became mandatory in 1979. The waiting lists in some social service centers stretched from four to seven years because of the shortage of resources. Each assessment took a great deal of time, and the criteria used were neither clear nor consistent. Organizations with contacts with foreign orphanages and expertise in international adoption were hamstrung. Some courts refused to recognize foreign adoption judgments that did not convey the same effects as plenary adoption, which definitively terminates the child's previous kinship ties. The pressure became intense after 1986, with the passage of a law officially restricting international adoption to those countries that practiced plenary adoption. After lively debate by a parliamentary commission,[4] the legislation was amended to provide for converting simple adoptions granted abroad into plenary adoptions. At the same time, other rules and requirements were strengthened. SAI alone controlled contacts with officials in the countries of origin, but it could generate very few adoption proposals in comparison to private organizations. Adopters who managed to receive a child proposal from abroad through personal contacts or a licensed agency were usually unable to accept the proposal, submit it to SAI, and gain court approval within the prescribed time because they were still awaiting psychosocial assessment. An estimated 1500 adoptive applicants were left waiting in social service centers.

Starting in 1988, the government yielded to the pressures from adoptive parents' associations and agencies and unofficially relaxed the requirements. SAI gave post facto approval for certain procedures undertaken abroad by private individuals or agencies. A few social service centers agreed to delegate their assessment work to professionals in private practice when adopters on their waiting list received a child proposal. In 1989, the Minister of Health and Social Services appointed an advisory committee comprised of SAI and social service center representatives, as well as representatives of adoptive parents' associations and licensed international adoption agencies. That committee's recommendations were instrumental in the drafting of new legislation that finally eased the tensions between these groups.

New legislation concerning adoption and amending the Civil Code of Québec, the Code of Civil Procedure, and the Youth Protection Act took effect on September 24, 1990.[5] It accelerated international adoptions by making provisions to shorten psychosocial assessment waiting lists and the time required for adoption procedures in countries of origin. It promoted adoption through licensed agencies and clarified their role and responsibilities. However, it also authorized adoption through private contacts and eliminated the requirement for court approval of adoptions; adopters must simply have SAI verify that normal procedures were followed. The legislation allowed private social workers and psychologists to assess prospective adopters relative to standardized criteria that were divulged to applicants. Rather than favoring strict mediation by the child welfare state, as in domestic adoptions, the policy erected a fairly flexible framework for private initiatives. The child's interest was set in a perspective that encompassed the interests of the future adoptive parents, including faster procedures and easier interchanges with sending countries. Newly accredited organizations and dozens of evaluators in private practice aided hundreds of new adopters. Although the time spent waiting for a child proposal varies considerably, depending on the country of origin and the intermediary involved, most international adoptions now take place without long delays.

The decision of Québec lawmakers to authorize international adoption through private contacts drew its share of criticism. It gave adopters back the freedom they demanded at just about the same time that the international community reached consensus on the Hague International Convention on Protection of Children and Co-operation in Respect of Intercountry Adoption, which was intended to tighten state control and supervision in order to protect children's rights and interests. Without entirely prohibiting independent adoptions, it definitely favors recourse to licensed agencies. Those countries that allowed a more liberal approach had to qualify their positions. Although Québec already adhered to the main tenets of the Hague Convention, it took ten years to enact an implementing statute that reinstated certain limitations it required. Legislation that was passed in 2004 and took effect in 2006 obliges all adopters to go through an accredited intermediary, except in exceptional cases such as family adoptions. This prohibition on independent adoption has aroused only isolated protests; the vast majority of adopters prefer going through licensed agencies. Adoptive parents' associations are now more concerned with issues pertaining to the adjustment of adopted children and access to post-adoption services.

The length of the international adoption process no longer seems to be a serious concern. The smooth transfer of children from foreign countries always calls for a major financial investment, and costs have risen as controls have been tightened. Still, the opposition between the interests of adopters on the one hand and of governmental and child protection agencies on the other has eased significantly. At the same time, the diverging interests of countries of origin and receiving countries have become clearer. Receiving countries and their licensed agencies are actively seeking new countries to which they can refer adopters. Is this solely to meet the children's needs, or in response to the shutdown of some countries and intensifying pressure from potential adopters? How much weight does this pressure carry in curtailing implementation of appropriate legislation and social services in the countries of origin? Is sufficient emphasis placed on promoting the adoption of children who are least likely to receive adequate care in their own country, especially older or disabled children?

A basic issue remains unanswered: When certain countries of origin have granted adoptions without terminating kinship ties, is it fair or desirable to convert those arrangements into plenary adoptions once the children have settled in the receiving countries? The Hague Convention authorizes conversion into plenary adoption only if formal consent to the legal effects of this adoption was given knowingly. But does the person giving consent really have a choice? Receiving countries impose the adoption scheme they prefer without seriously considering the possibility of adapting it to reflect the situation in birth countries with different laws and cultural practices.

The Temporal Dimension of Child Development

By providing a new family for children, adoption helps them along the road to adulthood. In this sense, it contributes to their development and may remedy or compensate for certain developmental delays. The attention that health experts pay to this temporal dimension of adoption has been instrumental in changing Québec's youth protection interventions, which are now designed to see that children placed in extended foster care become eligible for adoption. It has also introduced new possibilities for working with families with children adopted internationally by underlining the special challenges confronting those families. These innovative practices raise important questions about the impact of plenary adoption on a child's identity.

"Mixed bank" programs, which recruit prospective adopters to foster abused and neglected children before they are released for adoption, involves harmonizing two separate initiatives: the life project designed for a child, and the parental project of applicants.[6] The idea of a foster care-adoption continuum breaks with the traditional conception of adoption as a new birth and involves adopters in an experience of shared parenthood, since the birth parents retain parental authority while the child is being fostered. This feature sets the mixed bank scheme apart from closed adoption. Still, mixed bank adoption ultimately severs the child's former kin connections in order to create the impermeable family boundaries that are socially normative, without regard for significant variations in the situations involved.

Other initiatives focus on prevention and support, offering coaching, counseling, and training for adoptive parents and their internationally adopted children, especially in the post-adoption stage. Until recently, adoptive parents' groups had failed to recognize the adjustment problems experienced by some adoptive families. Now experts in pediatrics, mental health, social work, and psychology provide adopters with direct services in local community centers, hospitals, or private clinics and through meetings arranged by licensed adoption agencies or adoption associations.[7] Professionals help guide children with health, attachment, or developmental issues and support adults shaken by the experience. Expanded post-adoption services that are more accessible and supported by the public health and social service network are among the key demands that emanate from adoptive parents and adoption professionals.

This orientation toward children's psychosocial development raises questions about the preparation and supervision of adopters. Since experience shows that adoptive parents are not always capable of meeting the challenges of international adoption unaided, would it be justifiable to require preliminary training in addition to assessment of their child-rearing capacities? Could authorities require training to which the future parents of biological children are not subject? A related issue is the universal right to health and social services that are accessible and free of charge. Does the specific nature of certain adoption-related problems warrant public spending to provide special services for adopted children and their parents?

Transmission Time for Key Markers of Identity

Plenary adoption integrates adopted children into their new families by giving them the same rights they would enjoy if the adoptive parents were their birth parents. But it also severs kinship ties, alienating the children from their birth families. Since adoption radically alters the adoptee's filiation, it involves the transmission of key markers of identity over time: name, kinship ties (such as siblings and grandparents), language, and nationality, as well as social, ethnic, and cultural affiliations. As with other aspects of a family's cultural or religious heritage transmitted from one generation to the next, the heirs may accept or refuse these reference marks of identity, but must nevertheless relate to them in order to build self.

Plenary adoption allows adopted children only one intergenerational pathway: through their adoptive family. This approach was long bolstered by secrecy within the family, the confidentiality of adoption records, and the ban on direct contact between birth and adoptive parents. Not all aspects of this approach still apply. Most adoptions no longer take place under cover of complete anonymity. The International Convention on the Rights of the Child recognizes that children have the right to know their parents, to be reared by them whenever possible, to maintain a personal relationship with them unless it is contrary to the child's interests and, as far as possible, to enjoy continuity in their ethnic, religious, cultural, and linguistic affiliations. Theoretically, the search for the children's best interests should take account of these rights of the child. Pursuing this goal entails keeping an intergenerational channel open to the birth family. What might this look like in practice for international adoptions?

The right of children to know their origins supposes explicit recognition of a place for the birth parents in their life trajectory. The differences in the appearance of foreign-born adoptees and their adoptive parents often make it difficult to deny their origins. Yet the conditions surrounding most international adoptions continue to foster the tendency to see adoption as the beginning of a new history that eclipses the past. Administrative practices in some countries of origin thwart efforts to learn about the circumstances of the child's birth and abandonment, somewhat like the situation prevailing in Québec fifty years ago. The People's Republic of China, for instance, provides only minimal information about the child, who is always said to have been "found": the child's date of birth, the name given at the orphanage, and her weight, height, and medical condition. The information about her personal history is so stereotypical that adoptive parents can scarcely give it credence. Countries that maintain reliable records and provide them to adoptive parents remain the exception. Some adoptive parents make direct contact with the birth family, but not all of them agree to sustain it.[8]

Adoptive parents, who are often ambivalent about knowing their child's antecedents, have precious little information with which to build a memory of the kinship network from which the child came. A few emphasize the child's belonging to their family and his or her Québec identity, seeing these as the child's only referents for the foreseeable future. Most, however, attempt to provide the child with some knowledge and appreciation of his or her origins. The centerpiece of that memory is their own journey to the child's birth country, the problems they encountered there, the things they liked, and the contrast between living conditions there and in Québec, featuring photographs and videos they themselves recorded. Since most adoptive parents are highly educated and well informed, they explore the country's food, music, history, and spiritual values. Several adoptive parents' associations established in the 1990s encourage members to gather information about their child's country of origin, take part in cultural activities organized by immigrants from that country; and introduce their child to linguistic, culinary, or artistic practices that will help him or her appreciate the birth country. Some support family trips to the country of origin or host delegations from foreign orphanages. This interchange gives people who adopted children from the same country and especially from the same orphanage the sense that their children are linked by a common origin.

This effort to create an appreciation of origins for internationally adopted children is distinctive because the point of reference is a country and its culture, not a family. In providing this type of identity marker for their child, adoptive parents bypass the child's biological parents, out of necessity or more or less conscious choice, and avoid having to question the exclusivity of the child's adoptive relationship. Recognition of the child's origins is redefined as integration into a receiving society that advocates some degree of multiculturalism. The familial dimension of the child's origins remains shrouded in silence (Ouellette and Méthot 2003, Ouellette 2003).

Challenges to Closed Adoption

Much of the difficulty in acknowledging the origins of adopted children lies in the legal framework and impediments to relational interchange between the birth and adoptive families. Restoring this transmission channel could require reform of the adoption rules. Proposals for open adoption and for simple adoption that would not necessarily require severance of the child's original kinship ties rethink adoption with an eye to continuity.

An adoption is labeled "open" when it includes some direct contact between birth and adoptive parents. Rather than relying solely on professional intermediaries for an anonymous transfer, they seek to know the other family in order to make an enlightened decision and to enable the child to know his or her origins. In practice, the openness of the adoption varies considerably, from contact limited to the initial placement to long-term direct communication (Demick and Warner 1988, Goubau 2000). While open adoption is not recognized under Québec law, youth center workers are often asked to facilitate it. Generally speaking, they tread very cautiously, reassuring adopters that they can refuse to honor contact arrangements later. Other Canadian provinces recognize the legal merits of open adoption (Goubau 2000). In the United States, open adoption is frequent, and some private adoption agencies lean toward making it the rule. Agreements providing for continued contact are sometimes made at the time of the adoption judgment, but the courts are still reluctant to bind severance to a contact agreement (Hollinger 2000). This seeming paradox attests to the limits of the reigning adoption model. Some analysts feel that open adoption is more indicative of the value that the adults involved place on information than of their willingness to create links centered on the child (Modell 2001). Still, experts contend that contacts can make a positive contribution to development of the child's identity (Campbell, Silverman, and Patti 1991, Gritter 1997, Silverstein and Roszia 1999). Continuity would be particularly helpful for older children, sparing them another loss of filiation. In some cases, it may be the only way to protect the interests of the child to be adopted without eliminating significant kinship ties. The issue of open adoption is rarely raised in case of international adoption, even when the child's antecedents are not kept confidential. The adoptive parents meet the biological parents more through unexpected circumstances than because they wanted to meet them, except when they are already related.

These considerations are grounds for reviewing the legislative mandate for adoption necessarily involving severance rather than continuity at a time when individuals are increasingly asked to weave the threads of their personal history into a composite fabric of identity. When an unconditional adoption connection is necessary, should that automatically preclude maintaining prior ties? In what circumstances can it be said that the interests of the child lie in breaking all connections with his or her birth family as a social and symbolic source of identity and belonging? Even when ties to the birth parents are severed, should the child become a stranger to his or her entire kin group?

At this time, most Québec adoption stakeholders are not thinking of challenging recognition of plenary adoption, although some were ready to do so in the 1980s before generalization of the practice of converting foreign adoptions without severance of ties into plenary adoptions. Adoption could be modified to render it more inclusive. The simple adoption model used by such European countries as France and Belgium creates a new filiation in addition to the existing one instead of replacing it. International adoptees often come from countries where adoption does not break previous ties. Contrary to often-expressed fears, the effects of additive filiation could be handled so as not to disadvantage the child by comparison with a child adopted under the plenary scheme. Nor would it necessarily entail contact privileges for the birth parents, unless the court ordered them.

From the 1970s on, movements in several Western countries clamored for an end to the secrecy surrounding adoptees and their biological parents and for access to information enabling them to find one another. As a result of those demands, several countries unlocked their adoption records. Upon reaching the age of fourteen, adoptees in Québec can ask for their sociobiological antecedents and be informed of the identity of their birth parents if the parents consent. Adoptees born in Québec are entitled to a summary of their record, and a psychosocial worker can accompany them to a reunion. International adoptees' access to similar services was only recently recognized as warranting concerted effort by the parties concerned. In Québec, information about the origin of internationally adopted children is divided among various stakeholders, and not all of it is preserved under the same conditions. Some documents are in the hands of the adoptive parents, who are not legally required to divulge them to their adopted child. Others are kept by the youth center or the SAI and are automatically treated as confidential. The records of licensed agencies, which contain details on the exchanges between applicants, agency and contacts in child's birth country, may prove useful to trace a child or locate the birth parents. Finally, Canadian and Québec immigration services and Canadian embassies abroad hold documents gathered to issue a visa for the child's entry into the country and others pertaining to the preliminary medical examination carried out in the country of origin. The dispersal of information among numerous agencies hampers implementation of the Hague Convention, which requires signatories to conserve this information and make it accessible to adoptees where permitted by their legislation.

Until recently, the SAI received the bulk of requests for information and tried to follow them up, but had no official mandate to do this and could not require collaboration from the youth centers, licensed agencies, or other stakeholders. Adoptees had to knock on many doors and often failed to obtain the services to which they were apparently entitled. Some searched through unofficial channels. This situation prompted an SAI initiative to develop better services. The necessary legislative amendments were worked out in 2002 by the Comité sur la recherche d'antécédents sociobiologiques et les retrouvailles internationales (RASRI) in response to the recognition that the right to know one's origins belongs to the child, not the adoptive parents. Those amendments are included in the legislation enacted in 2004, which gives force of law to the Hague Convention in Québec.

SAI is the sole designated point of contact for international adoptees in search of their origins. It oversees the preservation not only of the adoption records it constituted but also of the records of the licensed agencies, which are required to forward those files to SAI within two years following the completion or dissolution of adoption procedures. It can obtain information from public agencies in Québec and abroad, such as youth centers and immigration services, in order to complete its own information and identify or locate the parties targeted by requests for sociobiological background information and reunions. Where necessary, it relies on licensed agencies that liaise with adoption stakeholders in the birth country and may supply helpful facts about its kinship culture. When information is provided to the adoptee, psychosocial support can be provided by a youth center or community organization. While each of these social agents previously enjoyed relative freedom to manage information about adoptees' origins, SAI's service distribution model requires them to release the information they hold.

For persons adopted in Québec, access to the information in their confidential adoption records means primarily the lifting of secrecy about the identity of their biological mother, provided that she consents. In international adoptions, the identity of the biological parents is often no secret to adoptees and their adoptive family. Many birth countries do not require that adoption records be kept confidential and provide adoptive parents with their child's original birth certificate. Adoptive parents sometimes obtain specific information from the orphanage, foster family, or local authorities. In sum, preserving and disclosing international adoption records is less a matter of lifting the secrecy about a child's origins than a matter of the keys they may provide to open the door for possible reunion, such as the birth mother's location. Those records are better protected from possible loss than if they were kept by the adoptive families (Ouellette and Mossière 2004).

Now that SAI is officially mandated to centralize records and requests for information, the issue is to determine how far the state can go in using its own resources to facilitate information searches in foreign countries and to support adoptees' interest in traveling to their birth country. The international reunions occurring elsewhere illuminate the challenges posed by reunions from the standpoint of the adoptees themselves, such as problems relating to loss of their original citizenship, access to necessary documents and authorizations, and living expenses while abroad. Another issue is to clarify the means of implementing collaboration with countries of origin that do not have the same confidentiality rules, especially when it comes to locating individuals and seeking their consent to reunions. Will Québec's legislative restrictions, which do not allow biological siblings to seek reunion, serve as guidelines for cooperation agreements with countries whose laws do not include such restrictions?

Conclusion

This chapter identifies some of the main adoption-related social issues that have arisen in Québec since the 1980s and examines the relational dynamics among the stakeholders in three temporal dimensions of adoption in order to underline the limits of plenary adoption, especially in intercountry contexts.

The time frame for the administrative and legal processing of adoptions is clearly the major concern in discussions of institutionalized practices and proposed modifications. This issue points most directly to the issues of legality of the procedures, protection of children and their rights, and the broader policy question of dividing responsibilities among the state, public- and private-sector practitioners, voluntary groups, and families. Those issues are also central to international discussions about intercountry adoption and regulations. The future of adoption plays out largely at this level, and we can expect the concern for preventing risk to drive the growing formalization of adoption practices. Independent private initiatives seem out of order, for even with the best of intentions they opened the door to abuses. This trend is commendable, for children are better protected. Still, the institutionalization and growing standardization of practices have in no way divorced the social environment of adoption from an impersonal market logic. Adjusting the offer of children to the fluctuating demand of exclusive rights on these children from Western adopters is one of the chief driving forces in the field of adoption, even if this is often left unsaid.

The temporal dimension of the child's development refocuses the main rationale for adoption and forces us to concentrate on issues of protection, health, and welfare. Québec's mixed bank adoption programs, which create a continuum between fostering and adoption, subordinate adoption decisions to the imperatives of child development. Nevertheless, the decisions made from the vantage point of specialists in health and psychology are applied within a legal framework that lacks the flexibility of clinical judgments. The child's urgent need for a family does not necessarily imply the need for an exclusive new filiation. Indeed, plenary adoption involves consequences that have not been thought through. The child's development is the time frame of greatest interest to adopters. Parents who have adopted children from a foreign county are surprised to discover the relatively high incidence of adopted children suffering from severe or chronic health problems, attachment disorders, or developmental delays. There has never been a greater demand for counseling, training, and support services by specialized practitioners. Although still few in number, these professionals are influential new agents in the field of adoption.

The change in filiation resulting from plenary adoption disrupts the intergenerational transmission of key reference marks of identity: genealogical position, name, ethnicity, and cultural and linguistic affiliation. Adoptive families are mindful of these issues, as the practice of valorizing the birth culture of internationally adopted children shows. Still, like many professionals in this field, they hold onto the idea that adoption resembles a new birth. The legal framework for plenary adoption should not be construed as self-evident and unalterable. We should test plenary adoption against the situations actually experienced so as to consider more open adoptions or simple adoptions that do not entirely sever birth connections.

The closed and plenary model is also challenged when adoptees search for their origins. The new service organization model recently introduced in Québec for international adoptees comes at just the right time. Many adoptees are entering adolescence or adulthood and will take a high-profile place on Québec's adoption scene in the future. No doubt they will raise other issues that will call into question our customary mindsets and attitudes about adoption.

For example, some young adoptees encountered during a recent research project[9] have reconnected with members of their birth families in Haiti, the Dominican Republic, the Philippines, Viet Nam, and other places (Ouellette and Saint-Pierre 2008). Some want to go live in their birth countries and work in international cooperation; others want to sponsor a brother or sister with a view to immigration. However, still others have no desire to renew contact with their birth country, even though they sometimes say they are not interested in being rooted here more than elsewhere. They have plural identities and affiliations. How can our society best metabolize such plural identities, which also occur in immigration networks and blended families, without overriding them? Adoption issues are connected with overarching societal questions regarding cultural pluralism. It is important to factor them into our thinking and generate dialogue about this institution. Adoption holds too much potential to become a mere tool for managing social problems.

NOTES

1. The adoption situation in Québec has several points of resemblance with the situations in Europe's civil law countries and in several birth countries of internationally adopted children, but is also strongly marked by North American views of the family and child protection.

2. Bourdieu's sociological concept of field is based on a metaphor relating a sector of social life to a field both of forces (fusion and fission) and of struggles. The structure of a given field gradually becomes autonomous and then is transformed or remains more or less unchanged owing to the alliances, competitions, and confrontation taking place there.

3. The DYP has sole authority to place children. Special consent can be granted to a person designated by the biological parents only if that person is a close relative.

4. The Regroupement des organismes et associations de parents en adoption internationale (ROAPAI) was temporarily in operation at that time.

5. Before this legislation took effect, the Civil Code of Québec included the following provisions governing adoption of a child domiciled outside Québec: all persons domiciled in Québec and wishing to adopt a child domiciled outside Québec shall first apply to the Director of Youth Protection by registering with the social service center (CSS) for their region (s. 614.1 CCQ); they shall undergo assessment by a CSS social worker; they must proceed through the Minister of Health and Social Services or a body certified by that government department (s. 614.1 CCQ); the adoption project shall be approved by the Youth Division before any foreign adoption can follow through (s. 614.2 CCQ); and once the child arrives in Québec, the Youth Division shall recognize the adoption judgment pronounced in the foreign country involved (s. 622.1 CCQ). See MSS 1994.

6. See ACJQ 1999, Ouellette, Méthot, and Paquette 2003, Goubau and Ouellette 2006.

7. For example, a few CLSCs provide pre- and post-adoption training and counseling; Hôpital Ste-Justine's International Health Clinic provides pediatric consultation; and several psychologists and social workers have taken the "Adopteparentalité" training provided by social worker Johanne Lemieux. See the widely circulated study by Chicoine, Germain, and Lemieux 2003.

8. Direct contact is not the norm, but neither is it exceptional; see Ouellette and Méthot 1999. In some cases, biological siblings adopted into different families stay in touch.

9. This comparative study, a collaborative undertaking directed by Françoise-Romaine Ouellette, with Chantal Collard (anthropology, Concordia University) and Carmen Lavallée (law, Université de Sherbrooke), is titled *Les ajustements du droit aux nouvelles réalités de l'adoption internationale* and was funded by the Fonds québécois de recherche sur la société et la culture. See Ouellette, Collard, Lavallée, et al. 2005.

REFERENCES

Association des Centres Jeunesse du Québec (ACJQ). 1999. *Guide de pratique en matière d'adoption d'un enfant domicilié au Québec*. Montréal: ACJQ.

Bourdieu, Pierre. 1980. *Questions de sociologie*. Paris: Éditions de Minuit.

Campbell, Lee H., Phyllis R. Silverman, and Patricia B. Patti. 1991. "Reunions between Adoptees and Birth Parents: The Adoptee's Experience." *Social Work* 36: 329–35.

Chicoine, Jean-François, Patricia Germain, and Johanne Lemieux. 2003. *L'enfant adopté dans le monde (en quinze chapitres et demi)*. Montréal: Hôpital Sainte-Justine.

Demick, Jack, and Seymour Warner. 1988. "Open and Closed Adoption: A Developmental Conceptualization." *Family Process* 27, no. 2: 229–49.

Goubau, Dominique. 2000. "Open Adoption in Canada." In *Parents de sang, parents adoptifs: Approches juridiques et anthropologiques de l'adoption—France, Europe, USA, Canada*, ed. Agnès Fine and Claire Neirinck, 63–85. Paris: Maison des Sciences de l'Homme and Librairie Générale de Droit et de Jurisprudence, coll. Droit et société no 29.

———. 1994. "L'adoption d'un enfant contre la volonté de ses parents." *Les Cahiers de Droit* 35, no 2: 151–72.

Goubau, Dominique, and Françoise-Romaine Ouellette. 2006. "L'adoption et le difficile équilibre des droits et des intérêts: Le cas du programme québécois de la 'Banque Mixte.'" *Revue de droit de McGill* 2: 1–26.

Gritter, James L. 1997. *The Spirit of Open Adoption*. Washington, DC: Child Welfare League of America.

Hollinger, Joan H. 2000. "L'adoption ouverte aux États-Unis." In *Parents de sang, parents adoptifs: Approches juridiques et anthropologiques de l'adoption—France, Europe, USA, Canada*, ed. Agnès Fine and Claire Neirinck, 45–61. Paris: Maison des Sciences de l'Homme and Librairie Générale de Droit et de Jurisprudence, coll. Droit et société no 29.

Modell, Judith Schachter. 2001. "Open Adoption: Extending Families, Exchanging Facts." In *New Directions in Anthropological Kinship*, ed. Linda Stone, 236–63. Lanham, MD: Rowman and Littlefield.

Ministère de la Santé et des Services Sociaux (MSSS), Direction de l'adaptation sociale. 1994. *L'adoption un projet de vie*. Montréal: Gouvernement du Québec.

Ouellette, Françoise-Romaine. 1996. *L'adoption: Les acteurs et les enjeux autour de l'enfant*. Québec: Institut québécois de recherche sur la culture and Presses de l'Université Laval.

———. 2003. "L'enfant adopté et la question de sa filiation." *Prisme* 41: 28–41.

———. 2005. "Le champ de l'adoption, ses acteurs et ses enjeux." *Revue de droit, Université de Sherbrooke* 35, no. 2: 376–405.

Ouellette, Françoise-Romaine, Chantal Collard, Carmen Lavallée, et al. 2005. *Les ajustements du droit aux nouvelles réalités de l'adoption internationale*. Rapport au Fonds québécois de recherche sur la société et la culture. Montréal: Institut national de la recherche scientifique Urbanisation, culture et société.

Ouellette, Françoise-Romaine, and Caroline Méthot. 2003. "Les références identitaires des enfants adoptés à l'étranger: Entre rupture et continuité." *Nouvelles pratiques sociales* 16, no. 1: 132–47.

Ouellette, Françoise-Romaine, Caroline Méthot, and Julie Paquette. 2003. "L'adoption, projet parental et projet de vie pour l'enfant: L'exemple de la 'banque mixte' au Québec." *Informations Sociales* 107: 66–75.

Ouellette, Françoise-Romaine, and Géraldine Mossière. 2004. "La circulation des informations sur les origines des adoptés internationaux." In *Comprendre la famille*, ed. Carl Lacharité and Gilles Pronovost, 153–72. Sainte-Foy: Presses de l'Université du Québec.

Ouellette, Françoise-Romaine, and Julie Saint-Pierre. 2008. "La quête des origines en adoption internationale." *Informations sociales* 146: 84–91.

Silverstein, Deborah N., and Sharon K. Roszia. 1999. "Openness: A Critical Component of Special Needs Adoption." *Child Welfare* 78, no. 5: 637–51.

Chapter 4

IIIIIIIIIIIIIIIIIIIIIIIIIIIIIIIIIIIIIIIIIIIIIIIIIIIIII

The Desire for Parenthood among Lesbians and Gay Men

Martine Gross
Translated by Léo Thiers-Vidal

Studying the desire to have children among gay men and lesbians can teach us more about the desire for children among men and women in general. This chapter explores how gay men and lesbians in France articulate conjugality and biological and social parenthood, as well as the possible innovations introduced by gay and lesbian parented families and the social roles of men and women in relation to children.

The study of gay and lesbian parental projects as a miniature social laboratory allows us to analyze the common and divergent points in the expression of the desire for children among men and women. The gay and lesbian parental project detaches and isolates the desire for children from the heterosexual desire for the parent of the other sex. In what ways are conjugality and the desire for children then articulated? Do adults desire a child to represent the future of the same-sex couple's love, as the symbolic culmination of the couple's relationship, or do adults individually desire a child independently of the couple's life? Or is it a combination of both a couple's and an individual's desire?

In most cases of hetero-parenting, when the couple is not affected by infertility, these elements overlap: the child is the product of the couple's procreative sexuality in such a way that even if each adult has an individual desire to transmit his or her genetic heritage, the desire for children can be experienced by one or both of the adults as a common parental project.

The modalities chosen by lesbians and gay men to become parents involve several issues:

- The articulation between conjugality and parenthood, for lesbians and for gay men;
- The articulation between biological and social parenthood, for lesbians and for gay men;
- The tension between two tendencies: the persistence of an essentialist ideology valuing biological mothers and fathers over non-biological parents, and the fundamental innovation—an equivalent social role, on the same level for each sex, in their relation with children.

My analysis builds on two surveys conducted at two different periods: a questionnaire-based survey conducted in 2001 with 285 members of the Association of Gay and Lesbian Parents and Future Parents (APGL); and a qualitative survey performed in 2002–2003 based on directed but open-ended interviews with about 60 gay fathers, lesbian mothers, or gay men and lesbians who wanted to become parents.

Two Asymmetries

First, we must take note of the fundamental legal fact that men and women in France are not equal when they want to become parents, whether giving birth or adopting. After centuries when women had no legal control of their bodies, they have gained the right to control their reproduction, to have "a child when I want to, if I want to." They are free to abort or to procreate. Carrying a child and giving birth automatically gives them the status of legal mother (Iacub 2004). They can relinquish motherhood and legally erase delivery itself, treating it as if it did not take place, under the legal fiction called "secret delivery" or "delivery under X." In sum, motherhood rhymes with naturalness. For a man to become a father, he must know which woman has given birth to his child so as to be able to declare his will to be a father. Fatherhood, detached from motherhood, is somehow unnatural.

Gay men and lesbians face this asymmetry. While lesbians cannot receive donor insemination (DI) in France, they can go to neighboring countries such as Belgium or Spain to benefit from insemination by an unknown donor. Or they can go to the Netherlands for a DI that allows the child to know the identity of the genitor when he or she turns sixteen. They can ask a friend to help them conceive a child without playing any role in the child's upbringing, benefiting from a known donor. They can apply to adopt. They can also choose co-parenthood: get in touch with a gay man and his companion or with a straight man in order to co-parent a child they conceive together.

Men do not have as many choices as women. They can neither benefit from insemination nor carry a child. In order to become a father, they will have to go through a woman or adopt. Adoption is not impossible, but remains difficult: couples are preferred to singles, and it is probably more difficult for single men than single women to adopt. Have men integrated this difficulty, as do some separated fathers who, believing that it is difficult to obtain primary custody of their children (Neyrand 2001), do not even ask for it because they are convinced their request will not be granted? French bioethics laws of July 1994 make it impossible to utilize surrogate motherhood. Benefiting from it abroad is very complex and probably explains why so few men reach for this solution. Most men (85 percent) of the APGL wishing to become parents seek co-parenting arrangements, while less than half (40 percent) of the women choose this family configuration.

Another asymmetry is the legal difference in the parental positions of the actors founding a family depending on whether they do or do not fit within the exclusive filiation model of French family law, which requires "a father, a mother and not one more." Those who do not fit within this legal framework, such as a mother's or a father's partner, do not have any legal parental status. If they behave as parents, they qualify themselves as "social parents" but have no legal rights or obligations applying to the parent-child relation. The social parent may be excluded because he or she is the same sex as the legal parent, or because the child already has a father and a mother. In this respect, they are in the same position as the spouses of divorced hetero-parents.

Articulating Conjugality and Parenthood

The 2001 questionnaire given to members of the APGL showed that 82 percent of women and 67 percent of men live with a partner. Women who responded to the APGL survey were also more likely to have been living with a partner for more than five years (69 percent of women and 41 percent of men).

These findings regarding gender differences can be compared to other surveys on the sexuality of the French population (Spira, Bajos, and ACSF

TABLE 4.1
Duration of Same-Sex Couple Relationship by Sex

Duration	Women % (n)	Men % (n)
< 2 years	7 (14)	20 (11)
2–5 years	24 (51)	39 (21)
> 5 years	69 (144)	41 (22)
TOTAL	(209)	(54)

Source: APGL Survey 2001.

Group 1993, Bozon, Leridon, Riandez, and ACSF Group 1993, Jaspard 1997, Bajos, Bozon et al. 1998, Simon et al. 1972). Studies of people's first sexual relationship show that girls more often associate sexuality with love and even lasting relationships (Bozon 2001), while boys consider it as a way to learn about sexuality. According to Michèle Ferrand (2004), this initial misunderstanding is played out during heterosexual encounters: in general, men look mainly for a sexual partner, while women continue looking for a stable affective relationship. Ferrand also notes that the way a person describes his or her homosexuality differs according to gender. Women generally say they prefer conjugality as a way to manage their love and sex life. They prefer a lasting relationship based on psychological and emotional support to a relationship that is merely erotic. Men, on the contrary, say they value the erotic dimension of their relationship (Schiltz 1999). While such oppositions can never be absolute, they represent some differences in *tendency* that are relevant to our study. This female preference for the relational and conjugal dimension and this male preference for the sexual dimension seem to be confirmed by the APGL survey data: women are more likely to be in a relationship and for a longer time.

Men wishing to become parents or who already are parents are often those who are in a relationship, although this is true even more often of women (67 percent of men and 81 percent of women). (See Table 4.1) In 1995, more than half of respondents to surveys on gay male lifestyles declared that they had a stable relationship with a man (Schiltz 1999). The men who belong to the APGL are more likely to be in a stable relationship than gay men in general. In this research, I have studied the conjugal and individual dimensions of the parental project of gay men and lesbians in a relationship. To be in a relationship when elaborating or realizing such a project appears to be a necessary but insufficient condition for the project's conjugal dimension. A person can be in a relationship and still elaborate an individual parental project.

As indicators of the project's conjugal dimension, I have looked for specific expressions situating the child as an extension of the couple—that is, the couple as indispensable condition of the realization of a desire which can precede the couple's formation; and the partner's positioning as a parent.

Men

Men's parental projects, which may take the form of adoption, co-parenting, or surrogate motherhood, are more often projects of one of the members of the couple. Sometimes, two individual projects coexist.

For example, Alain and Fabien each had a project of his own. According to Alain: "I had this project before meeting him, and it only grew stronger when I met him years ago because he's very close to children. . . . Recently, he filed an [adoption] agreement request. For the time being, nothing's sure, but what I have in mind is that each one of us continues his journey until, if all goes fine, full adoption. Furthermore, he dreams of only one thing, a little girl, so it would be perfect and then, we fuse." Fabien, his partner, had a co-parenting project: "I have forever wished to have one or more children. This desire already existed before the discovery, if I can use that word, of my homosexuality. . . . It wasn't a couple project; it clearly wasn't a couple project."

The quantitative survey confirms this tendency. (See Tables 4.2 and 4.3.) Half of men who answered the question "If you are the partner of a legal father or mother and the project to have a child has been elaborated in a lesbian/gay parenting context, how did you relate to that project?" said that they support the project but do not consider themselves a parent. On the other hand, more male partners of a would-be father responding to the question "As a partner of a gay or lesbian future parent, how do you relate to the project of having a child?" position themselves as a future

TABLE 4.2

If you are the partner of a legal father or mother, how did you relate to that project?

Response	Women % (n)	Men % (n)
As a parent	79 (54)	43 (6)
As associated with the project without being a parent myself	16 (11)	50 (7)
I was unwilling or opposed	4 (3)	7 (1)
TOTAL	(68)	(14)

Source: APGL Survey 2001.

TABLE 4.3

As a partner of a gay or lesbian future parent, how do you relate to the project of having a child?

Response	Women % (n)	Men % (n)
As a future parent	85 (94)	59 (10)
As associated with the project without being a parent myself	13 (14)	35 (6)
I was unwilling or opposed	3 (3)	6 (1)
TOTAL	(111)	(17)

Source: APGL Survey 2001.

parent (59 percent against 43 percent of male partners of men who are already fathers). This difference may indicate that representations are becoming less rigid. Rigid gender role assignments do inhibit gay men and lesbians who are not legal parents from considering themselves parents.

Nevertheless, defining oneself as a parent or future parent when expressing a parental project does not say anything about the concrete reality of daily life with a child. The term "parent" has numerous significations: legal status, blood bond, affective bond through the daily practice of parental functions. The fact that the project is expressed as being an individual and not a couple project does not say anything about the parent-child relations that are created once the child is present. The child's presence situates both men in a couple in the daily practice of parental functions. Emmanuel Gratton (2005) notes that often the partner's involvement ends up equal to or even surpasses the project initiator's involvement.

Women

The desire for children is often clearly expressed as a couple project: the child is the symbol of love. This expression of a conjugal project is encouraged by Belgian clinics (Baetens, Ponjaert, Van Sterteghem, and Devroey 1996). Nathalie, who adopted Antoinette, lamented: "It's unfair, it's frustrating. The child is the materialization of our love. And we can not [have one]. Moreover, it's unfair not to be able to have a child, whether the couple is homosexual or heterosexual." Jeanne and Clothilde had a co-parenting project. When asked, "was it your couple's project or that of Clothilde?" Jeanne replied: "It was both of us. It was the couple. The desire is born in the couple. Before, we didn't have any desire for children."

The same-sex partners of legal mothers, more often than those of legal fathers, position themselves as second parents and define themselves as mothers of a child with whom they have no legal or biological link. Brigitte and Clarisse are co-parents of a child that Brigitte conceived through DI. Clarisse explained, "we were in favor of two mums." Speaking about films shot during the child's birth: "when one sees me, it's clearly the mum; and then, of course, one sees her [Brigitte] breastfeeding." Carla and Marie-Laure illustrated this position in the media. Marie-Laure's children, born through DI, bore the names of both women from birth. They first took measures so that Carla could adopt Marie-Laure's children. Then they took measures so that Carla's acquired parental rights were transferred back to Marie-Laure, since she had to relinquish her parental authority in order to conform to the adoption law. Carla and Marie-Laure's children have two mothers, not only at home but also legally, both by filiation and regarding parental rights.

In sum, men more often elaborate individual projects. Their partners participate in parental functions when the child is present but do not position themselves as a second father. Women more often elaborate couple projects. The child is not a natural product of the couple but its symbolic materialization. Mothers' partners quite often position themselves as a second parent.

We can also note the weight of gender representations on this different articulation of conjugality and parenthood. To be a mother reinscribes a lesbian into womanhood; she is rendered a "women like the others" (Hayden 1995). Moreover, since women often privilege couple relations, they perhaps more easily combine the parental and the conjugal dimensions. Fatherhood not only does not have this function for gay men; it does not make them "a man like the others." On the contrary, it can even designate them as "monstrous" people suspected of pedophilia. Moreover, men more often think in terms of a separation between the sexual dimension and the conjugal one. These factors may explain why it is more difficult for them to combine the parental and the conjugal dimensions.

When we consider the position of social parents as well as the articulation of conjugality and parenthood, it is important to take into consideration that is not the same to have two parents—for example, a lesbian couple who benefits from DI or adoption—as it is to have several parents—for example, co-parenting, where as many as four adults can be involved in a parental project. I distinguish between bi-parental configurations, in which two people raise children within a couple; and multi-parental configurations, in which more than two people behave as parents, for example, co-parenting between a gay and a lesbian parent where their respective partners are active as social parents. Let us now consider how the articulation of conjugality and parenthood relates, or does not relate, to the decision to found a bi- or multi-parental family configuration.

Choosing a Two-Parent Unit

When gay and lesbian parents are asked about their motives to adopt, to benefit from DI or surrogacy, or to co-parent, all mention that they carefully considered each of the alternatives and discarded those which did not conform to their beliefs about the child's best interest or their understandings of parenthood or family. Men choosing bi-parenthood believe it materializes a certain representation of fatherhood: the relation with the child is fundamental, as expressed in the daily, full-time, concrete care for the child. Women choosing bi-parenthood believe that it materializes family as an extension of the couple, rather than motherhood per se. On the other hand, when they choose co-parenting their discourses resemble one another: men and women want to give their child both "a father and a mother." Beyond these similar discourses, however, co-parenting leads to tensions, sometimes even major conflicts, between men's and women's representations of what it means to be a father or to be a mother.

Men

The specificity of paternal identity is less clear today than it was before. No one knows anymore exactly what a father is or what the male parental function entails, as Françoise Hurstel (1996) and Geneviève Delaisi (1981) contend. Being genetically related does not suffice for defining paternal identity. During the 1960s, fathers were criticized for not taking care of their children and for privileging their career, and the authority and constraint associated with fathers' parenting style were criticized as inadequate child-rearing methods. The French law of 4 June 1970 substituted shared parental authority between the mother and the father for paternal power (*puissance*), contributing to the equalization of paternal and maternal functions and privileging a representation of the "good parent" as involved in the parental relationship rather than merely representing or wielding authority (Ferrand 2004). According to Christine Castelain-Meunier, fathers believe that "the importance of the affective bond with the child is what characterizes, in their eyes, contemporary fatherhood" (2002: 82).

Gay men who choose to be fathers through adoption or surrogacy —that is, without having to share parental functions with a mother— often say that they want to act as fathers without any constraints. They determinedly are "new fathers"; they define their role foremost through a relational paternity with the child and consider themselves as capable as women to take care of children. They initially considered co-parenting and discarded it as incompatible with the bond they wish to develop with their child. Some express very clearly that they do not want to depend on a woman to gain access to their child. They do not want to be fathers only every other weekend and during short school holidays, the situation they see among many divorced heterosexual fathers. They wish to be full-time fathers and take their paternity entirely upon themselves.

This desire for sole paternity does not imply that women will be excluded from the child's environment, as men who are fathers to a child or children without a mother generally have recourse to motherly and grandmotherly figures within their family, their friendship networks or, if needed, the professional sector.

Women

All the women in APGL who chose to adopt, to benefit from DI or from a known donor who will not be present in the child's daily life, also considered co-parenting. Unlike men, they do not evoke any particular fear of being limited in their relationship with the child, as if these relations were naturally secured. This concealed aspect of co-parenting can lead to insoluble conflicts. The women decided against co-parenting because of the risk of weakening the couple through the introduction of a third person in the relationship. They said that "it is already complicated enough as it is. We are a non-traditional family; being more than two will add difficulties." They do not wish to dissociate the parental from the conjugal dimension.

They are not indifferent to social discourse that states that the best interest of the child would lie in having a father and a mother. In order to resolve this tension between "not making the situation more complicated" and "the demand for a paternal figure in the child's life," some women choose to use a known donor. This option is not without risk, as informal agreements about the child have no legal standing. If a known donor legally recognizes his child, he may demand to exercise his parental rights.

Nathalie and her partner opted for adoption. She explained why they did not choose co-parenthood with a known donor or male friend: "It's already difficult to build a relationship with someone that lasts a long time. So, sharing a child's rearing for twenty years with a friend, in a friendship and not a romantic relationship, one would have to find the right person" (quoted in Cadoret 2002: 130). Marie-Laure explained that she and Carla "considered having a child with a known donor. We thought it normal that, as the father was someone we knew, he would be present in the child's life. We were open for a discussion with him on the role he would have had. . . . When taking all these steps, we wondered what exactly our desire for a child was and we realized that it was a desire within the couple, so we then positioned ourselves more like a couple facing difficulties having children, and who have recourse to technology to remedy this problem." Carla elaborated: "Having thought about it, we realized that we wouldn't really have known how to integrate someone external and it would be difficult to raise a child with three people" (quoted in Dubreuil 1998: 236).

Choosing Co-Parenthood

Men and women seem on the surface to articulate similar discourses concerning co-parenting: it gives a child both a father and a mother, a model of gender alterity. This discourse makes them feel less guilty for transgressing social norms as it complies with representations transmitted by the media, psychologists, and social discourse. It partially answers questions concerning what will be mirrored back to the child in school and in general outside the family. Notwithstanding what one may wish, we should keep in mind that men and women are not equal when choosing and that they face representations of fatherhood and motherhood that are in conflict, even within hetero-parental families.

Men

Co-parenting is often the only available option for gay men to become fathers. To have recourse to a surrogate mother is exceptionally rare. Most men surveyed consider it unimaginable. Representations of a child deprived of a mother and of a mother who chooses to give away the child to whom she gave birth are very guilt-ridden. Few men opt for adoption because it is such a difficult process. A man has to hide his homosexuality to obtain an agreement from most French departmental administrative units. In January 2008, the European Court of Human Rights condemned France for discriminating, so agreements will be less easily refused for this explicit motive. On the other hand, if someone has obtained an agreement with disclosure of his or her homosexuality, it will be an obstacle to further international adoption. No country will give a child to an openly homosexual person. Furthermore, few countries will give a child to a single man. Co-parenting has two advantages. It is not constrained by any social control, thanks to its "naturalness": a man and a woman may procreate however they want to and can become parents without having to ask permission from society. It also eases men's and women's feelings of guilt about putting a child in an unusual situation. The representation of "good fatherhood" privileging spending time with children is also influential, although it may not be explicit at the time of the project's elaboration.

Women

Women's choice to co-parent is not determined by the difficulty of becoming a mother without sharing parenthood with a father. Women can benefit from DI or choose adoption. Some wish to experience pregnancy. When they decide against DI, they say that they want to give the child a father. If today's good father is close to his children, the bad mother still is the one who loves them too much, who risks fusion, or does not love them enough, one who abandons them emotionally. The necessary presence of a mother is seldom stated explicitly in social discourse, as it seems self-evident. But the absence of a father is pointed to as the cause of many evils, including juvenile delinquency. A child whose father is absent would be in danger of emotional problems as he or she would be at risk of fusion with the mother. These discourses pervade pop psychology: the father is the one who separates the child from excessive mothering (Naouri 2004); society's evils are due to fathers becoming mother-like (Schneider 2004) and to mothers' exercising excessive power now that fathers no longer exercise paternal "might" (*puissance*). Even if these fathers and mothers do not recognize themselves in these images, which are socially constructed conceptions of the maternal and paternal functions, can they entirely escape them? How can they not be affected by these discourses? Some gay men and lesbians did give weight to these representations of a fusional mother and a distancing father who expresses the law; they choose co-parenting and were all too willing to play out a fusional mother who has difficulty separating herself from her newborn.

Janine admitted: "Frankly, during the first four months, yes, I can say, I was fusional with her. So adapting to day care, starting to work again when Zoé was 3, 3½ months old, has been very tough. I also wanted to organize some adaptation to her father, for him to take her for a few hours. He told me: 'but I am her father, she does not need any adaptation.' Maybe I was the one who needed to adapt to this. But he did not understand at all. I could not; it was beyond my possibilities. Moreover, he told me frankly, 'just pump her milk and bring her over for the night,' but that was out of the question for me, really, that hurt too much. I don't like these breast pumps, and in the evening Zoé nursed every two hours. I also woke up at night and I had my breasts full of milk before she even woke up—we were quite in sync for that. And it's true that if I could not breastfeed her, I would not know what to do and it was very painful. And he could not understand that. When you breastfeed your child, you need to have the baby close to you, because it really causes great suffering!"

Some mothers realized that giving the child a father implies giving up a little bit of the parental role, changing one's register and giving the child to its father now and then. Claudine found this difficult: "You have generous ideas in the beginning, you want to give a father to your child. But you then realize that you have to give your child to the father and that that is different. It hurts." A man on the APGL mailing list said: "I have the feeling, more and more clearly, that the main obstacle to materializing or maintaining a co-parenting project is to be found in that maternal instinct which makes the mother balk at letting the toddler be with the father, and fear that one day she will have to let him be the guardian. Put simply, I tend to think that mothers consider that fathers are not 'really' capable of providing security and education to their children."

Tensions between "New" Fathers and "Traditional" Mothers

The development of new representations of fatherhood culminates with gay fathers. The journey from the moment they become conscious of their homosexuality until the moment that, despite these difficulties, they become fathers leads them, perhaps more than other men, to consider fatherhood as an essentially relational issue.

As a man on the APGL email list put it: "A gay man who wants children theoretically does not want a situation where he would be the third wheel of the coach. When that is the case, he has to question his desire for children. Less complicated leisure pursuits exist, with less suffering. You never hear [whether] these men [really exist]. I can't stop myself from considering them retarded (oops, forgive the non-non-judgment), or unconscious people who do not distinguish a pet from a child. If it is only about taking the child on an outing every two weeks to show him or her to his own mother or someone else, and feeling inflated and important because of the idea of being a Father, I find that a bit ridiculous."

Claudine explained what happened in her co-parenting project: "You can talk about the project for months, but the reality is something different. Afterwards, there are tensions, limits. . . . For example, we agreed on shared custody with a period of progressive evolution. I thought of such an evolution as being spread over five years, Marc over five weeks! But we had not rendered this explicit in writing. . . . I think we did not want to stop the project for this reason. Anyway, whatever the custody time allotted to each parent, the mother will always consider that it's not enough, and the father that she has always too much. We tried ten different rhythms over two years and, each time, I felt he has the child too much, and he says that it's not enough!"

These examples illustrate the inevitable tensions between those fathers who position their fatherhood as a relationship that can only grow through actual time spent with the child, and mothers whose representations of motherhood are positioned on the same register: time spent with the child, in bodily and relational experience. If fathers are "new," mothers are still quite "traditional." Men and women do not give the same meaning to fatherhood. When women want to give a father to their child, they seem to want to give the idea of a father rather than conditions allowing a father-child relationship to grow and potentially rival their own relationship with the child. They say: "I want my child to know who his father is"; "she needs to have a paternal figure." But this paternal figure is shaped by representations transmitted via the media: the father represents authority and acts out the law.

Women are critical of mothering fathers. Disappointed that they do not position themselves as a third person dictating law, these mothers do not want a "father hen." Christine Castelain-Meunier (2002: 94) depicts this situation in hetero-parenting families: "Men are often solicited in a contradictory manner: around a role women expect and contest; around the experience of a new role, which they dread as they fear losing old privileges related to their specific relations with the child." She notes "that the image of a usurper is transmitted by a current of pediatric medicine (Aldo Naouri), by psychoanalytic representations concerning the father role—referring to the law (Freud) and depending on the way the father is introduced by the mother (Lacan)—and seals up or limits the ways fathers can inhabit their fatherhood. They thus find themselves locked up in stereotypes reducing them to a 'sub-mother' or rendering them dependent on the place created by mothers." When fatherhood and motherhood are detached from the conjugal heterosexual interaction, the definition of functions and roles that are not assigned sexually is questioned. Paternal and maternal functions become family functions, not confused with actual people.

Another element makes these tensions even more acute: the competition between conjugal parenting and hetero-parenting. Lesbians have often elaborated a parental couple project. The absence of a legal status for the co-parenting partner is even more painful as she can only position herself as a "third" parent and not a "second" one. Following the first months after birth, the mother will try to reassure her partner about her place in the child's life, even more as in daily life it is the female couple who takes care of the child. The father, who is already impatient during pregnancy, experiences this as being discarded. In some cases, when the father and the mother finally manage to come to an agreement, the mother's relationship with her partner comes undone.

The difficulties encountered during the first months or year of co-parenting generally are eased over time. Adjustments and compromises are found. But this situation illustrates the tension between the persistence of an essentialist conception of men's and women's family roles and an innovation in gender relations toward greater equality for each gender's parenting role. The essentialist representation active within co-parenting contributes to the maintenance of hierarchy: mothers, because they have given birth, have the power to designate which other parent they wish to have on their side, their partner or the father. Two hierarchies are possible: the mother, her partner, the father, and his partner; or the mother, the father, the mother's partner, and the father's partner. Women's control of their motherhood makes them, as Marcela Iacub put it, the "main protagonists of the new gendered order of reproduction" (2002: 246). Procreation historically positioned women under men's domination. They have now conquered this domain, but if they remove men from the bond with the child, they risk restoring inequalities and remaining the only repositories of parental responsibility. Besides this inverted hierarchy of the sexes, egalitarian values concerning each sex's role within co-parenting progressively are instituted. These egalitarian values translate into the increasingly frequent establishment of shared custody.

A woman on the APGL mailing list explained: "As far as maternal instinct and fathers' capacity to raise children are concerned, you should avoid generalizing: there are women (ourselves included) who do not feel invested with capacities superior to men concerning this register. We have brought up this subject with the boys; we intend to start shared custody from the first weeks onwards (at the end of the first month)." Some women say that they will do their best to let men have a proper father's place, and some men say that they trust mothers or lesbian couples to share parenting equitably. Agreements establishing parameters are being drafted and signed between the co-parenting father and mother.

Conclusion

The data from the 2001 survey conducted with APGL members and the interviews conducted in 2003 show that gay men and lesbians do not articulate their parental projects and conjugality in the same ways. Women more often consider parenting a couple project. Given the importance accorded to the biological dimension by French family law and by popular cultural representations, two tendencies confront one another concerning gender relations and parenting: a tendency that renders fathers dependent on mothers to gain access to fatherhood; and a tendency toward equality of maternal and paternal roles and functions.

ACKNOWLEDGMENTS

This essay was originally published under the title "Désir d'enfant chez les gays et les lesbiennes" in *Terrain* 46 (March 2006) and is reprinted in revised form courtesy of MSH Editions, Maison des Sciences de l'Homme, Paris. The English translation is by Léo Thiers-Vidal.

REFERENCES

Bajos, Nathalie, Michel Bozon, Alexis Ferrand, Alain Giami, and Alfred Spira (eds.). 1998. *La sexualité au temps du sida*. Paris: PUF.

Baetens, Patricia, Ingrid Ponjaert, A. C. Van Sterteghem, and P. Devroey. 1996. "PMA et nouvelles formes de familles: Une étude sur les inséminations artificielles de femmes seules et homosexuelles." *Thérapie Familiale* (Geneva) 171: 51–60.

Bozon, Michel. 2001. "Sexualité et genre." In *Masculin-Féminin: Questions pour les sciences de l'homme*, ed. Jacqueline Laufer, Catherine Marry, and Margaret Maruani, 169–86. Paris: PUF.

Bozon, Michel, H. Leridon, B. Riandez, and Groupe ACSF. 1993. "Les comportements sexuels en France: D'un rapport à l'autre." *Population et Sociétés* 276 (February): 1–4.

Cadoret, Anne. 2002. *Des parents comme les autres*. Paris: Odile Jacob.

Castelain-Meunier, Christine. 2002. *La place des hommes et les métamorphoses de la famille*. Paris: PUF.

Delaisi de Parseval, Geneviève. 1981. *La part du père*. Paris: Seuil.

Dubreuil, Eric. 1998. *Des parents de même sexe*. Paris: Odile Jacob.

Ferrand, Michèle. 2004. *Féminin, masculin*. Paris: La découverte, collection Repères.

Gratton, Emmanuel. 2005. "Les déclinaisons de la paternité gaye." In *Homoparentalités: État des lieux*, ed. Martine Gross, 281–90. Ramonville: Eres.

Gross, Martine. 2005. *L'homoparentalité: Que sais-je?* Paris: PUF.

Hayden, Corrine. 1995. "Gender, Genetics, and Generation: Reformulating Biology in Lesbian Kinship." *Cultural Anthropology* 10, no. 1: 52.

Hurstel, Françoise. 1996. *La déchirure paternelle*. Paris: PUF.

Iacub, Marcela. 2004. *L'empire du ventre*. Paris: Fayard.

———. 2002. *Le crime était presque sexuel*. Paris: EPEL.

Jaspard, Maryse. 1997. *La sexualité en France*. Paris: La découverte.

Naouri, Aldo. 2004. *Les pères et les mères*. Paris: Odile Jacob.

Neyrand, Gérard. (1994) 2001. *L'enfant face à la séparation des parents: Une solution, la résidence alternée*. 3rd ed. Paris: La découverte.

Schiltz, Marie-Ange. 1999. "Un ordinaire insolite le couple homosexuel." *Actes de la Recherche en Sciences Sociales* 128 (June): 30–43.

Schneider, Michel. 2004. *Big Mother: Psychopathologie de la France politique*. Paris: Odile Jacob.

Simon, Pierre, Jean Gondonneau, Lucien Mironer, Anne-Marie Dourlen-Rollier. 1972. *Rapport sur le comportement sexuel des Français*. Paris: Julliard et Charron.

Spira, Alfred, Nathalie Bajos, and Groupe ACSF. 1993. *Les comportements sexuels en France*. Paris: La documentation française.

Chapter 5

IIIIIIIIIIIIIIIIIIIIIIIIIIIIIIIIIIIIIIIIIIIIIIIIIIIII

Refiguring Kinship in the Space of Adoption

Barbara Yngvesson

In May 2006, while visiting Stockholm to present my research on transnational adoption in Sweden,[1] I spent time with several adopted adults whom I had interviewed over the course of the previous eight years regarding trips they had made to visit their birth countries and in some cases their birth families. Since my last visit, a number of these adoptees had given birth to children of their own, an event that carries a powerful emotional charge for a parent who was herself "abandoned" by her mother at birth or shortly thereafter. Two young women, one in her late twenties and the other in her mid-thirties, had five-week-old daughters. One was living with her *sambo*, an unmarried partner with legal standing in Sweden, while the other was married to the father of her child. I spoke with each of them about the experience of pregnancy and giving birth.

Katarina, who was born in Chile in the early 1980s, explained that she had felt no desire to have children until she reunited with her birthmother in 2004. This reunion, which began with an awkward encounter in the hotel in southern Chile where Katarina, her boyfriend, and her adoptive mother were staying, ended with a visit to the house where her birthmother lived with her husband and children. Katarina described a powerful moment when her feelings about giving birth changed. Holding an album with pictures from the trip, she showed me a picture of her birthmother with her left arm around Katarina's shoulders and her right hand on her abdomen. Katarina explained that her birthmother had whispered an endearment to her and touched Katarina's chest, then her abdomen, and held her close. She said, "At that moment, I thought, 'Of course I can have a child.'" On her return to Sweden, she "unexpectedly" became pregnant.

During our interview in a park, jiggling her daughter in an elaborate baby carriage, Katarina told me that as her pregnancy progressed she decided to deliver by a voluntary caesarian. Caesarians are less common in Sweden than in the United States and are seldom performed without a medical reason. Staff at the health care center tried to dissuade her, but she remained firm. Moreover, she decided not to nurse her baby but to bottle-feed the child, and described the baby to other adopted adults at a meeting a few days later as "*ett flask barn*," a bottle child. To me, Katarina expressed her disappointment that this baby had not made her feel connected either to her adoptive family or to her birth family. "I feel as though my mother would prefer to have a grandchild that is her [biogenetic] daughter's baby. I know this is only an idea in my mind, that it is not the way she feels. But that is the way I feel. And my birthmother doesn't know me at all, so the baby doesn't connect me to her, either."

I visited the second woman, Birgitta, who was adopted from Ethiopia in the early 1970s, a few days later. As we talked, her daughter slept, snuggly wrapped in a swaddling cloth that Birgitta had wound carefully around her own body. She told me about her last trip to Addis, together with her husband, Peter, a few months before her baby was born, to visit the hospital where her own mother had died giving birth to her. She described her fear as she gave birth to her baby in Stockholm, that she, too, might not survive, and her elation when she realized that her daughter had been born and she was alive.

These two stories illuminate the work involved in creating kinship (Carsten 2001), regardless of whether the kinship is biogenetic or adoptive. Katarina became interested in pregnancy following a meeting when her birthmother's gestures seemed to affirm Katarina's connection to her by birth. When Katarina herself became pregnant, however, she opted for a form of delivery and of feeding her child that is evocative of her relationship with her adoptive mother, who neither gave birth to her nor was able to nurse her. Although this effort to "connect" with her two mothers had not succeeded, Katarina accepted the fact that connection requires work; it is not a biogenetic given. She planned to return to Chile with her daughter when the baby was old enough. For Birgitta, visiting the hospital where her mother had died in childbirth while she herself was carrying a child was a way of realizing kinship. Linking her birthmother and her future child created connections through which she herself was able to take her place in the world. The "given" child (Birgitta) and the child to whom she subsequently gave birth are metaphorically and materially joined in this moment. The presence of the baby's father contributed to making this family, just as the historical connection of Sweden to Ethiopia was enacted in Birgitta's return and transformed by her giving birth to a Swedish-Ethiopian child.

These narratives suggest the power of idiomatic discourses of biogenetic connection in practices of adoptive kinship, even as they point to the kinds of work that are involved in producing new forms of relatedness. In both cases, the stark contrast of blood as versus law that underpins distinctions between biogenetic and adoptive kinship is blurred, even as the power of blood is acknowledged, if only in adoptees' struggles to rework its conventional meanings.

"Being Biological" or "Like Them"

In this chapter, I examine what Laurel Kendall describes as "the plasticity as well as the potency of idiomatic kinship" in the context of transnational adoption (2005: 177). This form of adoption began in the 1950s as falling birth rates in the overdeveloped world and a scarcity of children available for domestic adoption created an opening for children in the so-called developing world to become resources for individuals and couples who wanted to become parents and were unable to bear a child. Transnational adoption was conceptualized as simultaneously solving the adults' desire for a child and a child's need for a family, but in both cases the solution —"a family"—was the same.

The Hague Convention on Intercountry Adoption (1993), like domestic adoption laws in many Euro-American nations, is premised on an exclusivist concept that William Duncan describes as the "clean-break model" of adoptive kinship. This approach underpins plenary adoptions that involve "the complete integration of the child into the adoptive family and the severance of ties with the biological family" (1993: 51; see also Hollinger 1993). The erasure of biogenetic kinship and the construction of an adoptive family in its place produces what Judith Schachter Modell (1994) has termed "as-if-begotten" families. In the United States the adoptive family is secured in its "as if" status by a policy of secrecy, sealing hospital records of the birthmother's delivery and the original registration of the child's birth and amending the birth certificate so that the adoptive mother is recorded as the only mother.

In Sweden, where adoptees are guaranteed access to their adoption records once they reach the age of eighteen, domestic adoptions, which were common before the 1960s, tend to be invisible, and recent research describes the tensions and silences surrounding the familial origins of the adopted child (Matwejeff 2004, Landerholm 2003). In Sweden, as in the United States, the concept of blood ties (*blodsband*) is a powerful signifier of belonging. Because Swedish welfare policy provides broad support for mothers and children, including generous maternity and paternity leaves, free health care, and free education, as well as ready access to contraception and legal abortion, few domestically born children are placed for adoption. When social workers deem it in the best interests of a child to be removed from the care of the birthmother, current practice discourages termination of parental rights, and children are typically placed in foster care and the foster mother is expected to encourage the ongoing relationship of birth parents and child. Even when a birth mother requests that her child be adopted, social workers may try to dissuade her (Barth 1992: 40–41).

In both Sweden and the United States, transnational adoptions complicate the project of producing an "as-if-begotten" family, since in many of these adoptions the difference between adoptive parent and child is obvious. Since the late 1950s, the majority of adopted children have originated in Asia, Latin America, Africa, and Eastern Europe. As a brochure available in the mid-1990s from the Swedish government's Committee for International Adoptions (NIA) and aimed at adoptive parents points out: "Our adopted children today most often have an appearance that differs from the common Nordic appearance. . . . Adoption means that the child with its [different] appearance will trumpet out [*basonera ut*] for those around it the fact that continues to be so sensitive: that the couple cannot have a biological child" (NIA n.d.: 21–22, freely translated). Transnational adoptions intensify the tensions between a "natural" family and an adoptive family and point to the connection between blood ties and a racialized national identity in Euro-American countries.[2] In this sense, they operate as a form of biopower, creating a "biological-type caesura" (the as-if child, the as-if citizen) that produces "what appears to be a biological domain" (Foucault 1997: 255) in the families and nations where they are placed. At the same time, the figure of the adoptee complicates this image of national identity.

In Sweden, transnational adoption both contributed to and provided a potential for intervention into growing racial tensions surrounding immigrant populations in the 1970s and 1980s. These tensions developed as the postwar economic boom came to a close in Western Europe and programs for bringing in foreign workers were terminated, ending a process by which Sweden was gradually becoming a multiethnic, multicultural nation. Over the next three decades, refugees from Allende's Chile, Kurdish nationalists, Somalis, and Bosnians replaced so-called economic migrants from the Middle East, generating "the 'sudden' phase of the emergence of multiethnic Sweden" (Caldwell 2006: 56). As increasing numbers of non-European refugees sought asylum in Sweden in the 1970s and 1980s, creating "a media-induced moral panic" with images of Sweden as threatened by an " 'invasion' or 'uncontrolled flood' of refugees" (Pred 2000: 43), the adoptee came to embody Swedes' positive vision of their country as a multicultural nation.

The figure of the adoptee was imagined as radically different from the Swedish on the outside, but as *helsvensk*, completely Swedish, on the inside. In a series of articles in the journal published by the Adoption Centre, Sweden's major adoption organization, "the adopted child," who was described as coming from a "wildly different" culture in Asia or Africa to "perhaps the first family the child has ever had," was contrasted to "the immigrant child," whose difference was maintained by the child's "family situation and home life," which was presumed to remain "Turkish"—the stereotypical immigrant of the mid-twentieth century in Sweden—after the family settled in Stockholm or Göteborg (Kats 1975: 124).

The assumption that the adopted child could become "completely Swedish" (Andersson 1991: 2) was unsettled as the first generation of adoptees began to mature. Adopted adults describe their experiences of racism in school and their dawning perception that they were different and might be mistaken for immigrants. Sara Nordin, who was adopted from Ethiopia in 1969, explained this transition:

> My thoughts about that kind of thing began when I was about fourteen or fifteen, because there were lots of race problems in school. It was a school with lots of immigrants. . . . There was lots of fighting. I got into a strange situation, because I became almost an immigrant although I felt myself to be very Swedish (*jättesvensk*). The immigrants thought I was like them, and my Swedish friends thought I was like them. I couldn't really decide myself where I belonged. . . . Then I began to think about all of this, but they were pretty depressing thoughts. It wasn't fun.

Another adult adoptee, who was born in South Korea, describes her con-
flicted relationship to immigrants as she was growing up in a Stockholm
suburb in the 1970s:

> I believe that it is definitely easier to be adopted from South Korea than
> from Ethiopia, for example. A Korean appearance is not connected with
> refugees. . . . Everyone who sees me understands that I am adopted, or a
> voluntary immigrant who works and does her part. That can feel really
> nice, because otherwise one is standing in a sense outside. I feel uncom-
> fortable in the proximity of immigrants, which I think is because they in
> some sense unsettle the picture I have formed of myself as Swedish. They
> remind me that I, too, am a kind of immigrant, even though I feel that I
> am not, because I don't want to see things that way. Today I can handle it.
> It was worse ten years ago, when immigrants first began coming to Skel-
> lefteå. (von Melen 1998: 163)

Adoptive parents and senior staff of Adoption Centre express similar
concerns. What happens, asked Madeleine Kats, a psychologist and former chair of the board of Adoption Centre, "if our family gets a child
who isn't like us and who doesn't become like us—a child who doesn't
just look different but in fact *is* different and will always be so?" Kats asks
that parents rethink "*on what terms* we adopt" (1990: 9). Research into
the adaptation of Swedish adoptees in the 1980s cautioned that an overly
energetic effort to "Swedishize" the adopted child (*att försvenska barnet*)
might backfire (Cederblad 1984, Cederblad et al. 1994), citing literature
on domestic adoptions in England (Triseliotis 1973) that emphasized the
importance of integrating past with present in an adopted child's life.

This debate about the identity of the adoptee and his or her belonging
in the adoptive nation made clear certain prevailing assumptions about
the adopted child and his or her recalcitrant "nature." As Marilyn Strathern has analyzed the logic of Euro-American conceptions of identity, persons are assumed to possess properties that constitute them "as a unitary
social entity" (1988: 157–58). "Any interference with this one-to-one relationship is regarded as the intrusion of an 'other.'" Just as the individual
is assumed to be the owner of his or her own person, society is conceptualized as owning the properties—persons—that intrinsically constitute
it (1988: 137). The transferal of a child from one owner to another, from
one family or nation to another, unsettles the relationship of product to

producer—of a nation to its citizens, a parent to its child, or a person to his or her nature. In commodity thinking, separation from this ground of belonging must produce an alienated subject, one inevitably pulled back to where it *really* belongs (Yngvesson and Coutin 2006).

Debates between representatives of sending and receiving nations at the Hague Conference on Intercountry Adoption in the early 1990s were informed by these competing understandings of the child's identity. The child was represented as a natural "resource" of the sending nation (Carlson 1994), and the final draft of the 1993 Hague Convention included provisions that transnational adoption was to be a last option for abandoned children, following efforts to reunite them with their birth family, or place them with an adoptive family in their birth nation. Transnational adoption was preferable only to orphanage care.

This approach to the rights of the abandoned child built on the 1989 UN Convention on the Rights of the Child, which specifies the child's right to a name, a family, and national belonging but does not limit these rights to the child's birth family or nation (Article 8). In the 1993 Hague Convention, tensions between sending and receiving nations surrounding this issue were finessed by a series of conflicting stipulations: Article 4 calls for "termination of the legal relationship between the child and his or her family of origin" and Article 18 for a change in the permanent residence of the child; but Article 16 mandates "due consideration [to] the child's . . . ethnic, religious and cultural background" in placement decisions, and Article 30 calls for preservation of information concerning the child's origin. At the same time, the Hague Convention endorsed certain legal fictions on which adoption is premised: the "orphan" status of the child; voluntary and "irrevocable" relinquishment by birth parents; and adoption as producing a clean break from the past. In this way, the adoptable child was constructed as freestanding, as "part of a[n anonymous] store on which others draw" (Strathern 1997: 302; see also Yngvesson 2002). The idea of legally producing a freestanding child from one whose "natural" properties were shaped by his or her birth parents is a dimension of the same commodity logic that posits a singular identity, either completely Swedish or completely Asian, African, or Latin American. Legal policy presumes that a child's adoptability requires the cancellation of one identity and its replacement by another. The experiences of adoptees and adoptive families in the 1970s and 1980s suggested that legal cancellation did not produce a blank slate from which the transformation of the adoptee into a completely Swedish person could be effected, but that the history of the adopted child left traces that would haunt the adoptive family and adoptive nation.

My research on transnational adoption began when Sweden, long an active promoter of international protections of children's rights, was beginning to rethink its adoption policies in light of the Hague Convention. Central to this rethinking was the question of the adopted child's connection to its culture and ultimately its family of origin, increasing attention to "roots" trips and "heritage" tours, and growing insistence among psychologists and social workers on the importance of integrating the birthmother into the child's adoptive history (Cederblad et al. 1994, Stjerna 1976). Ingrid Stjerna, a Stockholm social worker with more than three decades of experience with transnational adoption, argues that "there is no such thing as a motherless child—even if she is dead, she is important." This fact should compel the adoptive parents to recognize that an adopted child "is not really *your* child." I understand this declaration to mean not that the adopted child belongs to the biogenetic parent, but that his or her identity is produced in the passage from one place and parent to another and that this history shapes the nature of the child. Stjerna recognizes that accepting the birthmother is one of the most challenging tasks confronting adoptive parents. She describes the typical attitude: "Background and country and decorations and songs, all that is fine: but the mother, no."[3]

In a small but steadily increasing number of cases, the integration of the birthmother into the adoptive family may move beyond coming to terms with her existential reality to meeting her and other members of the birth family and forging an ongoing relationship with legally nonexistent kin, including siblings, cousins, and grandparents as well. In some cases these meetings have evolved into regular visits. Interviews with adopted adults and their adoptive parents, both in Sweden and in the United States, confirm Stjerna's experience regarding this issue. Amanda Fredriksson, who was adopted from Ethiopia in the 1970s and has made several return visits to spend time with her extended birth family, explained that for her Swedish family, particularly her Swedish mother, these journeys became a charged topic. The third time she went, her mother asked: "'Why do you want to go there again? What is so good about it?'" Only after the fourth journey did her mother explain that she had assumed that the first trip back, when she was a teenager and was accompanied by her adoptive parents, would be the only one. When she returned again after five years, her mother told her that she "was afraid that I would become transfixed by my feelings and by Ethiopia. But I told her that I can't be transfixed by it. It is a reality I live in. It isn't that I create something that doesn't exist."

The reality that adoptees live in is shaped in part by experiences of racism that situate them as outsiders in Sweden. These experiences include being identified with immigrants, whose increasing isolation in segregated housing developments marks the boundaries of civil society in Sweden (Rojas 1995, Pred 2000, Caldwell 2006), and explicit slurs that link them to abject categories such as the *neger* or *chingchong* (von Melen 1998: 67).[4] Blood ties are a central consideration in assumptions about family in Sweden. As Sara Nordin noted: "When one comes here [to Sweden], one is a little lonely in this whole situation, but there [in Ethiopia]—it is a little hard to put words to it—there is so much surrounding one, and so many things happening. To be adopted or to have been abandoned, it's no big thing there. But here in our society it's huge." Amanda Fredriksson added: "Friends and contacts we have there, there are many who live in big families, there are cousins and neighbors, and many of them are not related by blood. So they say: 'Jaha, that one there is also my brother, though not my real brother.' But here, people are really careful about: 'And who are you like, and who is yours?'—so that one is reminded the whole time that one actually is not biological. There, one has people, even if one isn't family, one is like them. But here, one is like very few."

The contrast between the categories "related by blood" and "being biological," on the one hand, and "not related by blood" but "like them," on the other, with the ambiguous meanings of "likeness" as abandoned and adopted or as color, *neger*, suggest the plasticity and potency of blood and its capacity for reproducing biological kinship while at the same time encapsulating other meanings.[5] Here, as in the stories of Katarina and Birgitta, biogenetic kinship is both realized and complicated through what begins as a search for, or return to origins.[6]

A parallel example is provided by Deann Borshay Liem's autoethnographic film, *First Person Plural* (2000), in which Liem recounts her effort to trace the family she had been part of in Korea before she was put on a plane to an adoptive family in the United States in the mid-1960s. Liem, whose Korean name was Kang Ok Jin, had been placed temporarily in an orphanage near her home by her mother after her birth father's death and was sent to the United States by the orphanage director, without her mother's final consent to the adoption, in place of another child, Cha Jung Hee, who was unexpectedly removed from the orphanage just before she was due to leave for the United States Eight-year-old Liem arrived in the United States with Cha Jung Hee's history and name and with documents that identified her as an orphan. Once she was able to explain that she was not an orphan and had a family in Korea, her adoptive parents told her that this was a common fantasy of adopted children. So she eventually forgot her previous family, forgot the Korean language, and seemed to integrate fully into her family and school in California. Many years later, plagued by nightmares and suffering from depression, she went back to her adoption file and discovered pictures of two different eight-year-olds, each with the name Cha Jung Hee, but only one of which was a picture of the child who became Deann Borshay.

Liem wrote to the orphanage and several weeks later received a letter from her brother in Korea confirming her identity as Kang Ok Jin and telling her that she had a mother and two sisters in Korea. Liem traveled to meet them and eventually arranged the trip with her adoptive parents to visit her birth family that is recorded in her film. The film focuses on Liem's struggle to reconcile her dreams and memories of Korea and of the mother and siblings she left behind with the reality of the relationship she has established with her adoptive parents. It is clear throughout the meeting between the two families that in spite of a powerful emotional connection, especially between Liem and her birthmother and between Liem and the older of her two sisters, the differences are not easily bridged. Indeed, the visit seems to facilitate greater intimacy with her adoptive mother. At the end of the film, Liem voices not only her sense that her "real" mother is her adoptive mother but also her conviction that only by realizing that her birthmother is "not my mother" will she be able to develop a relationship with her.

Here, a successful search for a birthmother "realizes" the adoptive mother, while transforming an imagined kinship with the biogenetic parent in such a way that a different kind of relationship can be established with her. In another case, Kim Hyo Jin, a Korean child who was adopted at eight years of age by a family in New Jersey and became Jaclyn Campbell Aronson, returned to meet her birthmother when she was twenty-two. Aronson, who has a close relationship with her adoptive mother, regards her birthmother as the parent of Kim Hyo Jin, "the little girl who never got a chance to grow up past eight and a half years" (1997: 30). Aronson continues to maintain a relationship with this former parent, based both on her provision of economic support and on her memories of the Korean child who continues to be symbolically within her; but the relationship is enabled by the strength of her connection to her adoptive family and their support for the complex and painful ties she maintains with Korea.

"Bright Star"

I have focused to this point on the ways that a relationship understood as based on blood is realized through and becomes a way of figuring an adoptive relationship, particularly in the context of parent-child relations. But the plasticity of idiomatic kinship in transnational adoption manifests itself in quite different ways as well. In Sweden, as in other receiving nations, adult adoptees have formed informal support networks and more formal organizations, typically based on national origins. In Stockholm, two of the most active groups are the Association of Adopted Koreans (AKF) and the Association of Adopted Ethiopians and Eritreans (AEF). The AEF was established in the mid-1990s and has provided a kind of safety net for its members. One woman who has been active in the organization from the beginning said that the meetings, which take place at an Ethiopian restaurant in Stockholm, provide a space where "one doesn't need to explain, present, and tell, but one can just be part of it. Plus one can hear other experiences and can see variations on the same theme." Some members' interest is principally in Ethiopia, while others are more concerned with the problem of being black in Sweden. Daniel Rosenlind, its organizer, explained:

> When I think about "black" I think that I have more in common with people from Colombia. And then I think that there are different kinds of black, with different status. I think about black Americans, for example. They are cool, they are Americans. There are many whites that look up to them, young people, for example, Turkish young people. But if one is from Gambia, for example, it isn't nearly so cool. If you are from the West Indies, it can also be pretty cool. You might have dreadlocks. There is a scale distinguishing different kinds of black. But at the same time, I feel that I have quite a lot in common with all blacks.

In this case, an organization that developed on the basis of its members' national identification as coming from Ethiopia became a vehicle for establishing kinship with others who identify as black in Sweden. At the same time, as a third member of the organization, Mikael Järnlo, related after one of their monthly meetings, the commonality of each member's birth in Ethiopia and sense of kinship with other blacks in Sweden is complicated by regional differences of "Swedishness": for example, he is easily identified by his accent as coming from Skåne in southern Sweden, while others are clearly from Stockholm, or further north. In this sense, the "black" is fragmented by the "Swedish" in unexpected ways in the life of Ethiopian adoptees, even as the Swedish is transformed by their presence.

AEF has been active in a more global arena through its connections to "Bright Star," an organization established in Addis Ababa by Gizachev Ayka, that seeks to teach Ethiopian adoptees about their birth country and assist them in reuniting with their birth families. Ayka is the brother of eight children who were adopted abroad before he was born. In a recent article in a quarterly journal published by Sweden's Committee on International Adoptions (MIA), Ayka explains that as he was growing up, his parents talked about his birth siblings and showed him their photos. He suggests that because Ethiopians whose children are adopted abroad are poor and have been told that sending their children overseas will give them a better life, when children who have been adopted return (as seven of his adopted brothers and sisters have done), their parents "want to know that they did the right thing for the child. They expect to be rewarded. It is a cultural question. . . . It is hard for the adoptees. After they have met their families and feel happy about the reunion, the next step is that they must help their family" (quoted in Sammarco 2003: 6, freely translated).

Järnlo, who praises Ayka's commitment to helping adopted adults interested in visiting Ethiopia, expresses reservations about some of his goals and about Ethiopian nationalism more generally. Järnlo describes how quickly he was accepted as Ethiopian the first time he visited the country: "Just the fact that one has chosen to make contact with them and shows one's interest, they think it is so great, and then they think, 'Well, you are of course Ethiopian and you should learn to speak the language and you should marry an Ethiopian woman.'" But Järnlo added that while he felt that he was Ethiopian, that didn't change the fact that he was "first and foremost Swedish." He was particularly cautious about the idea that adopted adults should feel a responsibility to support their birth families: "To have been abandoned and then to expect that you will help the abandoning parents, that is a lot to expect from an adoptee." Other

Ethiopian-born adoptees express differing opinions about sending remittances to birth families. One member of AEF, who has made regular trips back to visit her large extended family in Ethiopia, is comfortable making occasional contributions for a particular project, such as replacing a roof. But this woman worries that another member of AEF had become "a kind of bank" for her birth family.

The links established by Swedish-Ethiopian adoptees with one another and with birth families in Ethiopia is one of the ways idiomatic kinship —as *blodsband* in Sweden and as national belonging in Ethiopia—is both affirmed and transformed in transnational adoption. Perhaps the most striking example of this simultaneous affirmation and transformation of national belonging can be found among Korean-born adoptees, whose active engagement on the Internet and in large transnational gatherings in Washington, D.C., Seoul, and elsewhere has linked adoptees from Europe, North America, Australia, and New Zealand into a powerful global movement that is raising questions about the nature of kinship, biological ties, and national belonging. As Eleana Kim (2005: 58–60) suggests, this movement is both an effect of a Korean state project to constitute a "global family of Korea," in which adoptees are now seen as significant participants, and a consequence of the efforts of some adopted Koreans to dissociate themselves from Korea's global family based on their shared experience of exile.

The refiguring of kinship in the space of transnational adoption involves creating relatedness at various levels: constituting the relationship of parent to child, constituting kinship among adoptees from a particular sending nation who are living in a particular receiving nation, building links among adoptees who are classified as "black" in predominantly "white" receiving nations, and reconstituting links between legally orphaned adults and legally nonexistent family members who were left behind, as well as the more encompassing transnational projects created by adopted Koreans. This refiguring reaches back to rework the past and forward to construct the future, as well as stretching across the national borders that transnational adoption has both secured and unsettled over the past half-century. It incorporates familiar dichotomies of Euro-American idiomatic kinship—"nature" versus "nurture," "blood" versus "law," "biogenetic" versus "adoptive" families—and reworks them in ways that have the potential to create new forms of consciousness as well as to transform everyday practices of relatedness.

ACKNOWLEDGMENTS

The research on which this article is based was funded by two grants from the National Science Foundation (#SES-9113894 and #SBR-9511937) and by faculty development grants from Hampshire College.

NOTES

1. Spanning the period 1995–2004, the research included two phases. First, with a base in Adoption Centre (AC) in Stockholm, Sweden, I interviewed staff members, attended conferences with local adoption professionals in Bolivia, Chile, Colombia, Ecuador, India, and Hong Kong, accompanied them on visits to institutions for children in Asia and Latin America, and interviewed those involved in placing children for international adoption. In the second phase, I attended events organized by adopted adults in Sweden, read memoirs and watched videos they made about their experiences, and interviewed adopted young adults between the ages of 16 and 30 who were born in Chile, Colombia, Ethiopia, India, and Korea about growing up adopted in Sweden and/or returning to visit their birth country or birth family.

2. "Transnational," "international," or "intercountry" adoption has been identified as transracial adoption only within the past decade or so. The terminology distinguishes domestic transracial adoptions in nations such as the United States, where transracial conventionally referred to the adoption of African American children by white parents and has long been controversial, from seemingly less fraught placements across national boundaries. In Sweden, the idea that transnational adoption constitutes a form of transracial adoption is still resisted by many adoptive parents, as well as by agency officials.

3. Stjerna was addressing a group of coworkers who were visiting the Adoption Centre from the Russian Federation in August 1999; quoted in Yngvesson 2005: 43. She has repeatedly pushed adoptive parents on this issue, both verbally and in print; see Stjerna 1976.

4. Anna von Melen points to the hierarchy of value implied by these categories, in which *neger* is the most abject, while *chingchong* is more accepted. Adoptees from Latin America, many of whom are light skinned, have the least difficulties with racism in Sweden.

5. See Stuart Hall's discussion of "the trace of something which still retains its roots in one meaning while it is, as it were, moving to another, encapsulating another" (1997: 50, citing Jacques Derrida's *Writing and Difference*).

6. See Yngvesson and Coutin 2006 for a critique of the concept of "return" in adoption discourse.

REFERENCES

Andersson, Gunilla. 1991. "Intercountry Adoption in Sweden: The Experience of 25 Years and 32,000 Placements." Sundbyberg, Sweden: Adoption Centre.

Aronson, Jaclyn C. 1997. "'Not My Homeland': A Critique of the Current Culture of Korean International Adoption." Senior thesis, Hampshire College, Amherst, MA.

Barth, Richard P. 1992. "Child Welfare Services in the United States and Sweden: Different Assumptions, Laws and Outcomes." *Scandinavian Journal of Social Welfare* 1: 36–42.

Caldwell, Christopher. 2006. "Islam on the Outskirts of the Welfare State." *New York Times Magazine*, 5 February, 54–59.

Carlson, Richard. 1994. "The Emerging Law of Intercountry Adoptions: An Analysis of the Hague Conference on Intercountry Adoption." *Tulsa Law Journal* 30: 243–304.

Carsten, Janet. 2000. "'Knowing Where You've Come From': Ruptures and Continuities of Time and Kinship in Narratives of Adoption Reunions." *Journal of the Royal Anthropological Institute* 6, no. 4: 687–703.

———. 2001. "Substantivism, Antisubstantivism, and Anti-antisubstantivism." In *Relative Values: Reconfiguring Kinship Studies*, ed. Sarah Franklin and Susan McKinnon, 29–53. Durham, NC: Duke University Press.

Cederblad, Marianne. 1984. "Följde sin pappa som en skugga" (Followed his father like a shadow). Originally published in *Att Adoptera* 3, 1983; reprinted in *Ur Att Adoptera Åren 1979–1983*: 31–34.

Cederblad, Marianne, M. Irhammar, A. M. Mercke, and E. Norlander. 1994. *Identitet och anpassning hos utlandsfödda adopterade ungdomar* (Nr. 4). Lund, Sweden: Forskning om barn och familj, Avdelning för barn och ungdomspsykiatri, Lunds universitet.

Duncan, William. 1993. "Regulating Inter-Country Adoption: An International Perspective." In *Frontiers of Family Law*, ed. Andrew Bainham and David S. Pearl, 46–61. London: John Wiley and Sons.

Foucault, Michel. 1997. *"Society Must Be Defended": Lectures at the Collége de France, 1975–1976*. New York: Picador.

The Hague Convention. 1993. The Hague Conference on Private International Law, Final Act of the Seventeenth Session, May 29, 1993, 32 I.L.M. 1134.

Hall, Stuart. 1997. "Old and New Identities, Old and New Ethnicities." In *Culture, Globalization, and the World-System*, ed. Anthony D. King, 41–68. Minneapolis: University of Minnesota Press.

Hollinger, Joan H. 1993. "Adoption Law." *The Future of Children* 3: 43–61.

Kats, Madeleine. 1975. "Är adoptivbarn invandrarbarn?" (Are adopted children immigrant children?). *Att Adoptera* 6, no. 2: 124.

Kats, Madeleine. 1990. *Adoptiv barn växer upp* (*Adopted children grow up*). Stockholm, Sweden: Bonniers.

Kendall, Laurel. 2005. "Birth Mothers and Imaginary Lives." In *Cultures of Transnational Adoption*, ed. Toby Alice Volkman, 162–81. Durham, NC: Duke University Press.

Kim, Eleana. 2005. "Wedding Citizenship and Culture: Korean Adoptees and the Global Family of Korea." In *Cultures of Transnational Adoption*, ed. Toby Alice Volkman, 49–80. Durham, NC: Duke University Press.

Landerholm, Lotta. 2003. *Adopterad: Lämnad. Vald. Och Sen?* Stockholm: Alfabeta Anamma.

Liem, Deann Borshay. 2000. *First Person Plural*. Ho-He-Kus, NJ: Mu Films.

Matwejeff, Susanna. 2004. *Svenskfödda adopterades sökprocess* (Swedish-born adoptees' search process). Linköping, Sweden: Institutionen för beteendevetenskap, Linköpings Universitet.

Modell, Judith Schachter. 1994. *Kinship with Strangers: Adoption and Interpretations of Kinship in American Culture*. Berkeley: University of California Press.

Nämnd för Internationela Adoptioner (NIA). n.d. *Gruppsamtal om adoption*. Stockholm, Sweden: Statens Nämnd för internationella adoptionsfrågor.

Pred, Allan. 2000. *Even in Sweden*. Berkeley: University of California Press.

Rojas, Mauricio. 1995. *Sveriges oälksade barn: Att vara svensk men ändå inte* (*Sweden's unloved children: To be Swedish but yet not Swedish*). Stockholm: Brombergs.

Sammarco, Lovisa. 2003. "The Bright Star—en kulturbrygga." *NIA informerar* 2: 6–7.

Strathern, Marilyn. 1997. "Partners and Consumers: Making Relations Visible." In *The Logic of the Gift: Toward an Ethic of Generosity*, ed. Alan D. Schrift, 292–311. New York: Routledge.

———. 1988. *The Gender of the Gift*. Berkeley: University of California Press.

Stjerna, Ingrid. 1976. "Biologiska mamman—ett hot? (The biological mother—a threat?)" *Att Adoptera* 7, no. 3: 100–101.

Triseliotis, John. 1973. *In Search of Origins*. London: Routledge and Kegan Paul.

United Nations. 1989. *United Nations Convention on the Rights of the Child*. G.A. Res. 44/25, U.N. GAOR, 61st plenary meeting, Annex at art. 21.

von Melen, Anna. 1998. *Samtal med vuxna adopterade* (*Conversations with adult adoptees*). Stockholm: Rabén Prisma.

Yngvesson, Barbara. 2002. "Placing the 'Gift Child' in Transnational Adoption." *Law & Society Review* 36, no. 2:227–56.

———. 2005. "Going 'Home': Adoption, Loss of Bearings, and the Mythology of Roots." In *Cultures of Transnational Adoption*, ed. Toby Alice Volkman, 25–48. Durham, NC: Duke University Press.

Yngvesson, Barbara, and Susan Coutin. 2006. "Backed by Papers: Undoing Persons, Histories, and Return." *American Ethnologist* 33, no. 2: 177–90.

Chapter 6

||||||||||||||||||||||||||||||||||||||||||||||||||||||

The Transnational Adoption of a Related Child in Québec, Canada

Chantal Collard

"In a conventional American adoption, the birth family and the adoptive family are not kin; they do not know one another" (Modell 1994: 3). This view of adoption is widely shared, even though about half of national adoptions in Western countries are intrafamilial—that is, between close relatives. In Québec, "adoptions familles" are thought to be of a different kind altogether than non-family adoptions. Nevertheless, some intercountry adoptions are also family adoptions. In countries with a high immigration rate, such as Canada, recent immigrants often want to adopt children from their country of origin, despite geographical distances among kingroup members. Transnational family adoptions represented 5.2 percent to 7.2 percent of all international adoptions in Québec between 1990 and 2004 (Government of Québec 2004b). This new phenomenon is part of the growing diversification in the types of intercountry adoption, which over its brief legal history has come to serve a wide variety of different goals with varying levels of success (Selman 2004: 257).

What happens in the globalized world of transnational adoptions when adoptees and their adoptive parents are not strangers, but are related before the transfer of the child, usually to one adoptive parent through consanguinity and to the other through marriage? Which countries or cultures favor this type of adoption? How are these requests processed by various legal channels? Who is involved in deciding and organizing the transfer of the child within the same immediate or extended family? Ultimately, how is kinship being legally reformulated? This essay addresses these issues through a case study of intercountry family adoptions in Québec. It explores why some sending countries more than others favor this type of adoption and documents the age and sex distribution of adoptees.

Finally, I argue that the provincial, national, and international laws concerning adoption are particularly ill-equipped to deal with transnational family adoptions, especially—and ironically—when it comes to issues of kinship and filiation.

The circulation of children among kin-group members through fosterage or adoption is well documented by anthropologists studying non-Western societies (Lallemand 1993, Leblic 2004, Bowie, 2004). In the West, transnational adoption of a related child is a more recent phenomenon tied to globalization. In a brilliant article, Esther Goody (1982) wrote about the cultural misunderstandings that resulted from the transnational circulation of children from Ghana to England, which the Ghanaian birth parents understood as long-term, long-distance fosterage and the British adoptive parents saw as plenary adoption. Some of the tensions she described exist today between birth parents and adoptive parents who are kin; though they have a common cultural background, they may not share the same objectives as far as the appropriation of the child is concerned.

Anthropologists have shown how interracial transnational adoptions contribute to shaping the public discourse on pluralistic societies. Toby Volkman has argued that "Over the past ten years, transnational adoption has become both visible and vocal and that contemporary practice of transnational adoption provokes new ways of imagining race, kinship, and culture in North America" (2003: 29). While I agree with her conclusions regarding the pluralizing effects of transracial intercountry adoptions on Western societies, I find that transnational family adoptions, though few in number compared to conventional "stranger" adoptions, constitute a pull in the opposite direction. Whatever their initial goals might be, transnational family adoptions contribute to the maintenance of previous racial, kinship, and cultural boundaries and to the growth of diasporic communities. In the complex field of international adoptions, several different trends are at work simultaneously.

Though rarely studied by anthropologists, transnational family adoptions are a well-known challenge for government officials in the immigration and adoption bureaucracies who have to make decisions regarding these requests on a regular basis. The evaluation process requires an understanding of complex family dynamics and adoption policies in many different countries that many find daunting. Regulations and practices are constantly evolving in both sending and receiving countries. The intentions of biological and adoptive parents involved in family adoptions are diverse and may be divergent. These motives include the informal circulation of children among kin (fostering), finding substitute parents for orphans, and providing humanitarian aid for children living in poverty, affected by armed conflict, and/or experiencing epidemics (for instance, the AIDS epidemic in Haiti and some African countries). Transnational family adoptions fulfill parents' desire to adopt a child who is of their "own blood." Clearly, transnational family adoption does not constitute a homogenous phenomenon but rather a multifaceted one.

International and National Conventions and Laws Regarding Family Adoptions

Transnational family adoptions, like all intercountry adoptions, fall under the provisions of international regulations. At first glance, the adoption of a related child seems especially well suited to answer current concerns of the International Convention regarding continuity and the maintenance of a child's family identity. Article 8 of the United Nations Convention on the Rights of the Child (1989) recognizes "the right of the child to preserve his or her identity, including nationality, name and family relations, as recognized by law without unlawful interference." Canada has ratified that convention, as have most countries with the exception of the United States and Somalia. Article 29 of The Hague Convention on Protection of Children and Co-operation in Respect of Intercountry Adoption (1993), which strongly opposes private adoptions in order to prevent the trafficking of children, recognizes the inevitable contact between birth and adoptive parents in family adoptions and gives them the right to arrange the adoption without recourse to an accredited adoption agency. Yet the convention requires that the adoptive parents of transnational family adoptions be evaluated, arguing that shared kinship does not automatically make an adoptive parent a "fit" parent.

At the national level, family adoption or family sponsorship without adoption is generally favored by the immigration laws of receiving countries. However, firm boundaries are established when it comes to the degrees of kinship that permit the sponsorship of a family member. Restrictive immigration laws contribute to the number of transnational family adoptions reported. In Canada, to qualify for family sponsorship without adoption, a child must be the brother, sister, nephew, niece, or grandchild of the sponsor; in addition, he or she must be an orphan, under the age of eighteen, and not married or in a common-law relationship. Children who are not documented double orphans must be adopted in order to immigrate to Canada (Government of Canada 2007). As is well known, many children put up for non-family adoption are not orphans either, and several researchers have questioned the myth of the adoptee as an orphan (Hoellgaard 1998, Gailey 2000, Yngvesson 2000, Collard 2005).

The definition of kinship enshrined in Canadian immigration law is too restrictive for many applicants, whose cultures recognize more extended kin relationships. Oddly, the same definition is applied to transnational as to national family adoptions.[1] Some prospective adoptive parents attempt to circumvent this difficulty by using classificatory kinship terminology, claiming that in their country of origin they would fall under the provisions of the Canadian immigration law for sponsorship. One man argued, for example, "In my country I call his father, who belongs to the same lineage as me, 'my brother'; therefore this child is my 'nephew.'"[2] But this cultural argument has not been accepted by Canadian immigration authorities.

Family Adoptions According to Countries of Origin

In Québec, children adopted by relatives between 1990 and 2004 came from some fifty-five different countries. As Table 6.1 shows, most of these children come from only a few countries: 31.3 percent from Haiti, 11.4 percent from India, 10.6 percent from the Philippines, and 5.5 percent from the Democratic Republic of Congo. Family adoptions from African countries soared in 2000. Given the political instability in many African nations and the high prevalence of AIDS, which has decimated families and left many children orphaned, this trend is bound to accelerate in the coming years.

If we compare the statistics regarding the countries of origin of adoptees (between 1990 and 2004) with those pertaining to the sending countries of immigrants to Québec (between 1996 and 2002 only), we see that the countries most likely to be involved in family adoptions—Haiti, India, and the Philippines—are not necessarily the principal sending countries of immigrants to Québec. Between 1996 and 2002, Haitians comprised the fifth largest group of immigrants to Québec, having sent 6,330 individuals; India was seventh with 4,390 immigrants, and the Philippines eighth with 3,435 immigrants. France and China, the main sending countries for immigrants to Quebec, are only occasionally involved in family

TABLE 6.1
Number and Percentage of Family Adoptions
According to Countries or Regions, 1990–2004

Country or region	Number (%)
Haiti	148 (31.3)
India	54 (11.4)
Philippines	50 (10.6)
Democratic Republic of Congo	26 (5.5)
Caribbean region (except Haïti)	38
West Africa	32
South America	20
Viet Nam	18
Middle East	16
Eastern Europe	14
Central and Southern Africa (except Democratic Republic of Congo)	14
Asia (except China)	14
China	12
United States	10
East Africa	5
Western Europe	4
TOTAL	473

Source: Secrétariat à l'adoption internationale, Ministère de la Santé et des Services sociaux, Gouvernement du Québec.

adoption. Countries where Islam is the dominant religion, such as Algeria and Morocco, which rank third and fourth among countries sending immigrants to Québec, prohibit adoption; Shari'a laws allow only *kafala*, guardianship.

The greater number of transnational family adoptions from Haiti, India, and the Philippines is influenced by the kinship cultures of these countries of origin as reflected in their respective national adoption legislation. In the Philippines an adopted child is often stigmatized, so the adoption is often kept secret and the child is presented to the community as the adoptive parents' biological child (Umali 2005). This policy of secrecy was also prevalent in Europe and North America not long ago. Today in Filipino society a child who is related to the adoptive parents has a much higher status than an unrelated child. This culture of kinship puts strong pressure on biological parents to give up a child to a close relative who is infertile and living in the country or abroad, and even sometimes to conceive a child with that purpose in mind. Filipino adoption law contains a clause favoring transnational family adoptions over conventional ones; indeed, as many as four degrees of kinship qualify for this kind of adoption.

The Indian state is reconsidering its religiously based policies favoring family adoption. Child adoption within the family was codified in accordance with Hindu family law.[3] The primary concern in these cases was the interests of the childless adoptive parents. Family adoption was promoted to perpetuate the family name and lineage. Adoptive sons were seen as providing security in old age and played vital roles in funeral rituals. Adoption was influenced by patriarchal values: male children were preferred to provide a "son for the sonless." "The adoption of an unrelated child is now more widely accepted" (Damodaran and Mehta 2000: 406–7). However, some Indians are still reluctant to adopt non-relatives. Sayeed Unisa (2005) found that of the 332 infertile women participating in her study in Delhi, only 10 percent had adopted, and they had done so informally by taking in the child of a close family member. These women considered it futile to adopt an unrelated child, for they believed they would not gain the same love or security in old age as from a related child.

In Haiti, the adoption of a related child is customary, because blood ties are very important and it is a family obligation to "share" children with infertile family members. The 1974 adoption law, which is still in effect, states that only infertile couples can adopt without dispensation. Traditionally an infertile couple would ask a relative blessed with many children to relinquish one for adoption (Collard 2004, 2005). Today Haitian authorities continue to support this practice at the national and international level and strongly favor transnational family adoptions, provided that they are in the best interest of the child.[4] Given the strikingly high levels of child poverty in the country, Haitian authorities can be very liberal in their procedures. Fosterage within Haiti is widespread and has become transnational along with the Haitian diaspora (Collard 2004). As in many cultures where fosterage is practiced, to be a "good parent" in Haiti does not require the birth parents to look after the child themselves, but rather to make the best arrangements for the child's future in terms of schooling and employment opportunities. The same cultural forces behind the adoption or fosterage of a child of the same kinship group are also present in many African countries.

Although the Hague Convention gives the country of origin the authority to decide on a child's "adoptability," officials at the Secrétariat à l'adoption internationale (SAI) in Québec can contest the legitimacy of foreign procedures if they do not believe the family adoption is in the best interest of the child "as they understand it." They are now rejecting many requests involving children from the Philippines or India, which they see as serving the interests of the parents rather than those of the children. The dominant view is that it is always best for a child to remain with the biological parents; only when they are destitute do these officials see adoption as in the child's best interest.

Distribution According to Sex, Age, and Kin Relationships

Family adoptions occupy a niche of their own and do not seem to be in competition with non-family intercountry adoptions. In all cases where the adoptive parents could be contacted through informal networks, they said that the children would not have been adopted otherwise, as they were placed with family members and not living in an orphanage in their country of origin. This picture is confirmed by the SAI files; many adoptive families are neither wealthy nor childless, yet they are willing to take in additional related children.[5] In quite a few cases, however, it can be inferred from the dossiers that the adoptive parents' infertility is the primary motive for adoption, as no "children of their own" are listed.

The age of the child in family adoptions varies widely. As Table 6.2 shows, they range from babies of three months to eighteen-year-olds. The sex ratio is quite skewed; many more girls than boys are adopted. Even

TABLE 6.2
Age and Sex of Related Children Adopted 1990–2004

Year	Total	Male Children %	Female Children %	Oldest Child	Youngest Child
1990	37	38	62	16 years, Viet Nam	1 year, Haiti
1991	32	38	62	15 years, Myanmar	3 years, India
1992	26	42	58	14 years, India	4 months, Taiwan
1993	20	25	75	14 years, Philippines	3 months, Taiwan
1994	12	25	75	16 years, India	11 months, India
1995	15	37	33	16 years	1 year, India
1996	21	39	61	unknown	2 years, Philippines
1997	23	39	61	16 years, Haiti	3 years, Haiti
1998	31	42	58	18 years, Zaire	3 months, Haiti
1999	46	46	54	17 years, Cambodia	1 year, Viet Nam
2000	54	n/a	n/a	n/a	n/a
2001	56	37	63	19 years, Philippines	2 years, Haiti
2002	32	34	66	19 years, Haiti	9 months, Philippines
2003	39	21	79	19 years, Democratic Republic of Congo	3 months, Taiwan

Source: Secrétariat à l'adoption internationale, Ministère de la Santé et des Services sociaux, Gouvernement du Québec.

TABLE 6.3

Kinship Relation between Adoptive Parents and Adoptee
Prior to the Adoption, 1990–2004

Year	sibling	child	cousin	nephew/ niece	grandchild	distant cousin	stepchild	unknown
1990	1	1	1	31		1		2
1991			1	30				1
1992			1	24		1		
1993				17		2		1
1994				11		1		
1995			2	9	1	1		2
1996			1	16	2			2
1997			1	16	1			5
1998				21			4	6
1999	3		3	34	1	1		4
2000			(data for 2000 not available)					
2001			5	42	5	2		2
2002			1	26	2	1		2
2003				28	2	3		6

Source: Secrétariat à l'adoption internationale, Ministère de la Santé et des Services sociaux, Gouvernement du Québec.

within the kin-group, the perception of the usefulness of giving out or taking in a child is differentiated along gender lines. However, the gender imbalance is still less pronounced than in non-family transnational adoptions.[6]

Table 6.3 shows that the family connections listed most often in the SAI files are those of uncle/aunt and nephew/niece. In ethnographic interviews with adoptive parents, we found that a few of these relationships are classificatory—that is, they reflect lineage affiliations rather than consanguineal relationships. The man who called all male lineage members of his own generation "brother" and their sons his "nephews" was claiming this type of kinship.

Contact between Relatives Prior to a Family Adoption

The individuals involved in transnational family adoptions may have known each other quite well prior to the transfer of the child. The adoptive parents may have contributed to the costs of schooling for the child in their country of origin, for example. But in other cases the parties involved may have been aware of one another's existence through mutual kin connections, but not been particularly close or even engaged in a face-to-face relationship. The one constant in my interviews is the larger kin-group's involvement in the process and the presence of relatives who act as mediators between the biological and adoptive parents. Traditional and non-traditional practices must work together to facilitate transnational family adoptions. Only someone who knows the cultural dynamics in both countries involved can fully appreciate the strategic engagement that is required to make the transfer within the family possible and relatively conflict free.

Three cases illustrate the range of possibilities and the delicacy of the process. Consider, first, a single adoptive mother of Haitian origin without biological children. She told the researcher that she always wanted to have a big family, planned for it, and decided to adopt mostly girls from her extended family in Haiti. At the time of the interview she had adopted three children: in 1999, two four-year-old girls, who were the daughters of two of her cousins, and in 2000, one eleven-year-old boy, who is her own half-brother. In 2003 she adopted three other unrelated girls known to her extended family, who were all around the age of four. She described the context of the first three adoptions: "It was my grandmother who had the photos. My grandmother was their aunt. My mother was their cousin. I saw the children. I asked if their parents would agree to give them for adoption. But first it was Cindy, the youngest. She lived in Haiti. She [my grandmother] had spoken to her mother and she said yes. Next, I received another letter. The parents said that there was another cousin as well. She did not live far, therefore the two girls often played together. Her parents had also consented to give her for adoption. So I did the paperwork for both of them. As for the boy, he is my half-brother. Before he died my father asked me to take him." Interestingly, this adoptive mother claimed that by giving a picture to her aunt, the birth mother of the first girl announced her willingness to relinquish her for adoption. The second girl is a first-degree biological cousin of the first. Despite the informant's assertion that the extended family's rationale for offering these female cousins for adoption together was that the two little girls often played together, we must assume that poverty was also at play. The woman had met her half-brother a couple of times before the adoption. After her father died, though the birth mother was still alive, the child was sent to live with the sister of his biological mother for a year. The adoptive mother mentioned with much satisfaction that this boy looks like her. She emphasized that she had been very explicit with his biological mother that this was a plenary adoption and not fosterage. While the boy was still young she wanted to ensure that all ties to the biological mother were cut in order for her to be the only guardian and to establish the child's place in his adoptive family.

Another set of adoptive parents have different cultural backgrounds: the wife is of Polish origin, and the husband comes from the Democratic Republic of Congo. They lost a son at birth and have a fifteen-year-old biological daughter, but were unable to conceive again. They decided on a family adoption, and the adoptive father was especially emphatic with the researcher that he would never have adopted an unrelated child. He explained the process of adopting his nephew: "I had said to my older brother with whom we have regular contact that we wanted to adopt a child. And he said to me, 'listen, there is a boy.' He asked me, 'a girl or a boy?' And I told him a boy. He said, 'our little sister has a boy that you will take.' He took charge of the rest himself, until the child left his parents' home to go to the sister's home [the aunt's residence] . . . The boy was eight years old." This child was the youngest boy among the descendents of all the father's siblings. Once the adoption was decided upon, the boy was sent to live with an aunt in the capital while waiting for the adoption to be formally concluded. In this case, as in the first case, during a liminal period between the decision to give up the child and the actual placement in the adoptive home the child was sent to live with another relative elsewhere in the country of origin.

National as well as international laws take for granted the Western view that a child has only one mother and one father who have exclusive rights to the child and that only birth parents can relinquish a child for adoption or lose their parental rights. Yet in many societies, a child belongs to a group that is larger than the nuclear family, such as an extended family or a lineage. Isabelle Leblic (2004) asked: when a child circulates within a classificatory kinship group that multiplies the number of "mothers" and "fathers," should this be considered an adoption, since the child does not change his or her larger family affiliation? In the second case, the adoptive father, a sophisticated cultural broker himself, commented that in his culture of origin (Pende), the child would have called his adoptive mother, the wife of his maternal uncle, by the term "mother" prior to the adoption, but that he himself would have been called "uncle" and not "father." He mentioned that he saw this adoptive child as a way for his daughter to understand his cultural background. The adoptive father's motives included not only the desire to have a son related to him by blood but also the chance to reconnect with his culture and family of origin.

In the third case, the adoptive parents are a couple from the Democratic Republic of Congo who arrived in Canada as political refugees in 2003. They have three biological children. Before coming to Canada they took in two war orphans whose parents had disappeared; only oral testimonies, rather than official certificates, documented these births and deaths. The immigration law regarding family sponsorships did not allow this couple to include these children as family, as they were not close kin as the law defines it. The African adoption had been informal, so the couple had to adopt the children to be allowed to bring them to Canada. The legal requirement that parents and children be of different generations created additional complications. The adoptive mother is only twenty-three; the daughter is now fourteen, and the second child is a boy of five. Although the daughter was more closely affiliated with the wife prior to the adoption in terms of kinship, because of the mandatory age difference between adoptive parents and children, she had to be adopted as a relative by the husband. This type of blended family is not unusual in countries affected by HIV/AIDS and war.

The Inadequacy of Legislation for Family Adoptions

Recently, the Province of Québec revised the law to conform to the conventions on the protection of children in international adoptions. "An Act to Implement the Convention on Protection of Children and Co-operation in Respect of Intercountry Adoption" (R.S.Q. c. M-35.1.3) went into effect on February 1, 2006. Most significantly, all international adoptions in Québec must now be done through a certified body, ending the independent private adoptions that had been possible since 1990. Yet family adoptions are considered extraordinary cases and can still be done privately (*Arrêté ministériel* 2005-019). It is also possible to adopt privately on the basis of "possession d'état," if the adoptive parent has assumed responsibility for the child's care, supervision, and education for a period of six consecutive months within the past two years in the child's country of origin.[7] To qualify for a family adoption, the child must be a brother, sister, nephew, niece, grandchild, cousin, half-brother, or half-sister of the adoptive parent or their spouse, including a common-law spouse after three years of cohabitation. The fact that the category "cousin" is not specified in terms of degree gives SAI agents flexibility when processing adoption requests.

The law allows the adoption of siblings and half-siblings because it was designed to complement immigration and family sponsorship laws.

According to regulations, all adoptions are kept confidential and a new birth certificate is produced for the child. This practice is applied to family adoptions, even though the Convention on the Rights of the Child says that the child has a right to its identity and family relations. The Hague Convention recognizes only plenary adoptions, even in the case of intrafamily adoptions. As Françoise-Romaine Ouellette (1996) has argued, adoption is seen mostly as a measure for the protection of the minor, and the symbolic inscription of the child in a family genealogy is only of secondary concern. This viewpoint ignores the very real meanings of kinship that are at play in family adoption. In the process of rewriting the child's birth certificate, an aunt or a half-sibling of the child can become its mother. How are other members of the family inscribed in this new genealogy? If my half-sister is now my mother, is my full brother who has not been adopted by my half-sister now a half-uncle, an ex-brother, or still a brother?

The paradox of recognizing the importance of genetic and social links to kin prior to adoption while rendering them distant and anonymous by removing a child's previous genealogical affiliation upon adoption is puzzling. But, as Marilyn Strathern (2005) has argued, notions of the embodied and distributed person sit uncomfortably with legal personhood. Ouellette (2005) adds that in societies where the rights of parents and the economic and normative checks on families are multiple and complex, it is important to define precisely which persons are known as father(s) and mother(s) of the child. Those who have vested parental authority can legitimately receive family allowance, tax credits, and other advantages normally reserved only for parents. Western societies do not recognize more than one set of parents (Cadoret 1995).

Conclusion

The applicants who make the most use of transnational family adoptions come from cultures with a strong emphasis on blood ties that favor fosterage and the circulation of children on a large scale, especially in times of crisis. The age range of the children involved in family adoptions is much wider than in non-family adoptions. While it is generally assumed that biological parents, or even biological mothers alone, make the decision to relinquish children for adoption, in fact a whole network of kin is involved in family adoptions. What these relatives or governments agents consider in the "best interest" of the child is culturally determined. Officials in receiving countries can impose their own values when approving family adoptions, even if the right to decide on the adoptability of a child is the legal purview of the country of origin. Research is needed to evaluate how children fare and to hear their side of the story.

Finally, although adoption in Western countries is a legal institution concerned with filiation as well as the welfare of the child, in practice the genealogical aspect is treated as secondary, and very little consideration is given to symbolic filiation and kinship. Family recomposition after adoption rather than the continuity of the child's kinship ties is the norm. As Bob Simpson (1998) has pointed out, family recomposition is not new, but its scope, frequency, and acceptance is striking (see also Strathern 2005). Even more than the continuity of the child's origins and the addition of kin through multiple parenthood, the adoption of a related child is inscribed in a logic of family blending in which all of the elementary relations of kinship—filiation, genetics, and alliance—are drawn in and reshuffled.

ACKNOWLEDGMENTS

This work was carried out within the framework of a research project directed by Françoise-Romaine Ouellette with Chantal Collard and Carmen Lavallée participating as co-researchers. This project was done in partnership with the Secrétariat à l'adoption internationale and the Association des centres jeunesse du Québec and financed by Action concertée pour le soutien et la promotion de la recherche sur la famille et les responsabilités parentales, Fonds québécois de recherche sur la société et la culture.

All translations from French and Haitian Creole are by the author.

NOTES

1. In Québec, the following kin qualify for adoption by special consent: a grandparent of the child and/or their legal (married) spouse; an uncle or aunt of the child and/or their legal (married) spouse; a brother or sister of the child and/or their legal (married) spouse; the legal (married) spouse of one of the parents of the child; and the common-law spouse of one of the parents of the child, if they have lived together for at least three years.

2. It is possible that adoptive parents were using classificatory kinship terminology to their advantage, fearing that more distant consanguineal kin would not be considered by government officials.

3. The *Hindu Adoption and Maintenance Act* of 1956 and the *Guardians and Wards Act* of 1890, which was modified in 1961, continue to apply.

4. Interviews conducted in Port-au-Prince, Haiti, 2001.

5. In order to respect the confidentiality of the adoption dossiers, an SAI employee compiled the data for the researcher.

6. There are few transnational family adoptions from China, though it provides many girls in intercountry adoption.

7. Order respecting the adoption without a certified body of a child domiciled outside Québec by a person domiciled in Québec, R.Q. c. P-34.1, r.o.02.

REFERENCES

Bowie, Fiona (ed.). 2004. *Cross-Cultural Approaches to Adoption*. London: Routledge.

Cadoret, Anne. 1995. *Parenté plurielle: Anthropologie du placement familial*. Paris: L'Harmattan.

Collard, Chantal. 2004. "La politique du fosterage et de l'adoption internationale en Haiti." In *L'adoption: Des pratiques de filiation différentes*, ed. Isabelle Leblic, 239–68. Clermont-Ferrand, France: Presses Universitaires Blaise Pascal.

———. 2005. "Triste terrain de jeu." *Gradhiva,* special issue on Haiti, 1: 209–24.

Collard, Chantal, Carmen Lavallée, and Françoise-Romaine Ouellette. 2006. "Quelques enjeux normatifs des nouvelles réalités de l'adoption internationale." *Enfances, Familles, Générations* 5 (August). Évolution des normes juridiques et nouvelles formes de régulation de la famille, ed. Alain Roy. Electronic document, http:///www.erudit.org/revue/efg/v/n5/index.html (accessed April 12, 2007).

Damodoran, Andal, and Nilima Mehta. 2000. "Child Adoption in India: An Overview." In *Intercountry Adoption: Development, Trends and Perspectives*, ed. Peter Selman, 405–18. London: British Agencies for Adoption and Fostering.

Gailey, Christine. 2000. "Race, Class, and Gender in Intercountry Adoption in the U.S.A." In *International Perspectives on Intercountry Adoption*, ed. Peter Selman, 298–303. London: Skyline House.

Goody, Esther. 1982. *Parenthood and Social Reproduction: Fostering and Occupational Roles in West Africa*. Cambridge: Cambridge University Press.

Government of Canada. 1992. *Convention internationale relative aux droits de l'enfant*. Rés. A.G. 44/25 Annexe (1). Ottawa: R.T. du Canada.

———. Citizenship and Immigration Canada. 2007. Document on sponsorship: http://www.cic.gc.ca/english/information/applications/family.asp. Document on the immigration process in international adoption: http://www.cic.gc.ca/English/immigrate/adoption/index.asp.

Government of Québec. 2004a. Secrétariat à l'adoption internationale, Ministry of Health and Social Services. See http://www.msss.gouv.qc.ca/adoption/_fr/index.html.

———. 2004b. *An Act to Implement the Convention on Protection of Children and Co-operation in Respect of Intercountry Adoption.* L.Q., c.3. R.S.Q. c. M-35.1.3.

———. 2005. *Arrêté Ministériel.* R.Q. c. P-34.1, r.0.02.

Hoelgaard, Suzanne. 1998. "Cultural Determinants of Adoption Policy: A Columbian Case Study." *International Journal of Law, Policy, and the Family* 12, no. 1: 202–41.

Lallemand, Suzanne. 1993. *La Circulation des Enfants en Société Traditionnelle: Prêt, Don, Échange.* Paris: L'Harmattan.

Leblic, Isabelle (ed.). 2004. *L'Adoption: Des Pratiques de Filiation Différentes.* Clermont-Ferrand, France: Presses Universitaires Blaise Pascal.

Modell, Judith. 1994. *Kinship with Strangers: Adoption and Interpretation of Kinship in American Culture.* Berkeley: University of California Press.

Ouellette, Françoise-Romaine. 1996. *L'adoption: Les acteurs et les enjeux autour de l'enfant.* Laval, Québec: Presses de l'Université Laval.

———. 2005. "L'adoption devrait-elle toujours rompre la filiation d'origine?" In *Familles en mouvance: Quels enjeux éthiques?* ed. Françoise-Romaine Ouellette, Renée Joyal, and Roch Hurtubise, 103–20. Sainte-Foy: Presses de l'Université Laval/IQRC.

Selman, Peter. 2004. "Adoption: A Cure for (Too) Many Ills." In *Cross-Cultural Approaches to Adoption,* ed. Fiona Bowie, 257–73. London: Routledge.

Simpson, Bob. 1998. *Changing Families: An Ethnographic Approach to Divorce and Separation.* Oxford, UK: Berg.

Strathern, Marilyn. 2005. *Relatives Are Always a Surprise: Kinship, Law and the Unexpected.* Cambridge: Cambridge University Press.

Umali, Violeda. 2005. "Understanding the Stigma of Child Adoption in the Philippines." Paper presented at the Conference on Reproductive Disruptions: Childlessness, Adoption and Other Reproductive Complexities, University of Michigan, Ann Arbor, May 19–25, 2005.

Unisa, Sayeed. 2005. "Adoption among Infertile Women in a Patriarchal Society: Evidence from India." Paper presented at the Conference on Reproductive Disruptions: Childlessness, Adoption and Other Reproductive Complexities, University of Michigan, Ann Arbor, May 19–25, 2005.

United Nations. 1993. *Convention on Protection of Children and Co-operation in Respect of Intercountry Adoption.* Geneva: UNHR.

———. 1989. *Convention on the Rights of the Child.* Geneva: UNHR.

———. 1997. *Convention sur la protection des enfants et la coopération en matière d'adoption internationale.* Geneva: UNHR.

Volkman, Toby Alice. (2003) 2005. "Embodying Chinese Culture: Transnational Adoption in North America." *Social Text* 74 (vol. 22, no. 1): 29–56. Reprinted in *Cultures of Transnational Adoption*, ed. Toby Alice Volkman, 81–115. Durham, NC: Duke University Press.

Yngvesson, Barbara. 2000. "'Un nino de cualquier color': Race and Nation in Intercountry Adoption." In *Globalizing Institutions: Case Studies in Regulation and Innovation*, ed. Jane Jensen and Boaventura de Sousa Santos, 247–305. Aldershot, UK: Ashgate.

Part II

||||||||||||||||||||||||||||||||||||||||||||||||||||||

Perspectives from Sending Countries

A comprehensive understanding of transnational adoption necessarily includes the perspectives of sending countries, especially the kin-groups and communities that children leave behind. The case studies that follow attend to the voices and viewpoints of the many parties involved in transnational adoptions in Brazil, Peru, Russia, and Lithuania, which send significant numbers of "abandoned" children to Europe and the United States. Very few of these children are actually orphans. Most are social orphans: they have living parents who are, for various reasons beyond their control, deemed unable to care for them and lose their legal rights. Any account of transnational adoption must reckon with this reality. The coercion involved in the surrender of children extends from the impoverished and disempowered single mothers who bear and try to raise them to the relatively underdeveloped nation-states that are unable to fund social policies supporting disadvantaged families.

Brazil was one of the world's primary sources of internationally adopted children from the early 1980s until the mid-1990s, when it became enveloped in controversy over allegations of the abuse of adoptive children and their birth mothers. Police investigations and Parliamentary inquiries led to significant changes in public policy. Domingos Abreu scrutinizes the many actors involved, from private intermediaries such as philanthropic orphanages, lawyers, and clergy, to public institutions for "abandoned" children and birth parents. Drawing on fieldwork conducted in the province of Ceará and in France, where many Brazilian children were adopted, Abreu charts the complex tensions involved in international adoption. What motivated the unauthorized intermediaries who were responsible for the great majority of both domestic and intercountry adoptions? What were the symbolic and material rewards of this work for them? How did state regulation play into their practices?

Claudia Fonseca looks at changing Brazilian policies toward international adoption as they developed through the complex interweaving of local and transnational influences. She suggests that adoption lies at the crux of children's rights and class discrimination, two emergent themes in human rights debates. Controversies over the "export trade" in children have recently fueled a shift toward facilitating domestic adoption. Much as domestic violence against women was once naturalized as a conflict outside the state's authority, so adoption has been presented as a humanitarian issue involving, at most, a child's "right" to a family. Fonseca joins other contributors in pointing out that the dominant model of plenary adoption may be singularly ill-suited to promoting the best interests of the child.

Lilia Khabibullina's study of international adoption from Russia, which is a major source of children for Western Europeans and North Americans, represents one of the first examinations of public attitudes and policies in this post-communist state. In Russia, as in Brazil, cases of child trafficking and abuse involving foreign adoptive parents and adoption agencies recently captured media attention. Consequently, Russia made international adoption more difficult. Public discourses tend to position adopted children as objects of market transactions, which they see as imposed by Western capitalist countries. While nationalists worry about "losing genofund," the genetic resources that represent the country's potential wealth of talent, social democrats are concerned that children are becoming commodified. The fear that children who disappear across borders are being raped and murdered by abusive adoptive patents or maimed and dismembered so their organs can be utilized by the rich for transplants is a telling metaphor for the unequal power relations that shape adoption internationally.

The transnational influences of biomedical discourse also figure centrally in Jessaca B. Leinaweaver's study of international adoption from Peru. Although adoption is typically contrasted to biological forms of reproduction, local and global understandings of biology and adoption are deeply intertwined in practice. Scrutinizing the processes that deem children legally adoptable and that certify some parents as fit and condemn others as unfit, Leinaweaver shows that international discourses surrounding children's rights are bolstered by globalized discourses about biomedicine as officials utilize normative notions of mental health and malnutrition in order to deem birth parents guilty of neglect or incapacity. Adoptive parents, too, are deeply enmeshed in the biomedical in their previous failed attempts at assisted reproduction and the medical examinations and tests required of them. The discourse of nation is also shaped by biomedicine, as North Americans and Europeans calculate health risks when choosing a country from which to adopt.

Auksuolė Čepaitienė compares Lithuanian discourses related to adoption with those surrounding assisted reproduction technologies (ART). Drawing on ethnographic research in Lithuania, she explores how people negotiate their evaluation of infertility solutions. Individuals use the words "genes" and "inheritance" very loosely, and sometimes in contradictory ways, in thinking about the relative advantages and disadvantages of ART or adoption. The idea that children have particular inborn characteristics is widely held in Lithuania. Although both ART and adoption make the child a member of the kin-group in the eyes of society, people's concept of inborn properties leads to a perception that children who are adopted or conceived through ART are external to the adoptive family. Adopting those whose parents have been deemed unfit is regarded as especially risky, although sending those same children into international adoption is, paradoxically, regarded as a regrettable loss of precious genes by the nation.

||||||||||||||||||||||||||||||||||||||||||||||||||||||||||

Chapter 7

Baby-Bearing Storks
Brazilian Intermediaries in the Adoption Process

Domingos Abreu

International adoption is a relatively new phenomenon. Although there are traces of the intercountry transfer of children from previous epochs, the large-scale institutionalization of these practices occurred during the second half of the twentieth century, following tragic incidents such as the wars in Korea, Viet Nam, and Biafra (Modell 1994). Middle-class European and North American couples with infertility saw the adoption of orphaned children overseas as a humanitarian gesture as well as a solution to their personal problems. However, as intercountry adoption spread beyond the war zones, sending countries began to react against what appeared to many as the untoward exploitation of their misery. The debate on intercountry adoption oscillated back and forth between the advocacy of "child saving" and the condemnation of "child trafficking" (see, for example, Triseliotis 2000).

From the early 1980s until the mid-1990s, Brazil was among the world's primary sources of children for international adoption (Kane 1993). A highly polemical debate brought on numerous police investigations and Commissions of Parliamentary Inquiry designed to clarify the legality of intercountry adoptions, as well as the diverse forms of abuse linked to them. Little was actually revealed, however, about the variety of actors involved in the process, who range from private intermediaries, such as philanthropic institutions and orphanages, lawyers, and clerical agents, through public institutions for "abandoned" children to birth parents.

This chapter, based on fieldwork I conducted in Brazil, especially in the state of Ceará, and in France (see Abreu 1994, 2002, 2003), presents a systematic analysis of the role of private intermediaries, exploring various tensions involved in the field of international adoption that, from the viewpoint of local agents, are often obscured by stereotypic images. I ask, in particular, what motivates the unauthorized intermediaries who were responsible for the great majority of domestic adoptions, as well as many international adoptions before 1985. What are the symbolic and material rewards they hope for? How does state regulation play into their practices? Focusing especially on the clashing opinions that structure the debate and the social conflicts that underlie them, I suggest a rethinking of "the traffic in children" that has justified many of the state's interventions.

Inspired by Bourdieu, who criticizes both rational choice theory, which sees all behavior as determined by conscious aiming at explicitly stated goals, and mechanical economism, which recognizes nothing but material interest and the deliberate search for the maximization of profit (Bourdieu and Wacquant 1992: 118), I bring out the symbolic aspect of the exchange system:

> Practices may have principles other than mechanical causes or conscious ends, and may obey an economic logic without obeying strictly economic interests: there exists an economy of practice. . . . If we do not recognize that the economy described by economic theory is but a particular case of a wider universe of economies, that is to say, fields in conflict that are different in terms of what's at stake, of what valuables are being produced, and of the different sorts of capital at play, then we will not be able to understand its forms, its contents, and its specific points of application. (Bourdieu 1980: 85–86)

This line of inquiry is designed to complement a Maussian approach that centers the relationships involved in any system of exchange. As anthropologists studying different forms of child circulation throughout the globe have pointed out, the transfer of a child from one household to another involves an exchange between adults who may see the transaction as anything from an altruistic gift to a strategic investment (Mauss 1950, Lallemand 1993, Massard 1983, 1988, Fonseca 2001). To take commerce in its strictly monetary sense as the sole point of interest in the study of international adoption would impoverish our analysis. Rather, the adoption of a child is imbedded in a social space of personal relations marked by competition and dispute. A child may be considered not only for its mercantile value but also for what it symbolizes as a "priceless" valuable, or an untransferable good; a child may be seen as a blessing or a burden, depending on the logic of the agents in conflict. I outline these differing logics by describing the different intermediating agents involved in the adoptive market.

Storks and Their Charitable Missions

One of the central figures in the placement of Brazilian children in substitute homes was—and still is—the person known as a *cegonha*, stork. This category of intermediaries is generally composed of women belonging to the middle and upper classes who spend part of their time trying to find children who are available for adoption, as well as people who want to adopt children (Costa 1988: 101). These activities all take place completely outside Brazilian law.

The storks build a network of relations with professional health workers, including doctors, nurses, and social workers, who let them know when a woman says she cannot keep her child. They develop another network with women in lower-income neighborhoods who might know of pregnant girls who, at the outset of pregnancy, express a desire to give the baby away. These lower-level intermediaries are often drawn from occupations that bring them into frequent contact with upper-class Brazilian women: maids, manicurists, cleaning ladies, etc. Living in the working-class neighborhoods where most mothers who relinquish children reside, they are in a good position to furnish useful information. Another channel is developed through the stork's personal friends, whose live-in maids get pregnant and are forced by their employers to choose between their baby and their job.[1] Storks also have connections with religious groups; some nuns and priests in Christian churches, as well as spiritist centers,[2] refer women to them. Some intermediaries engage in charitable activities with lower-income populations, where they encounter pregnant women willing to give up their children.

Many storks claim to be motivated by the desire to provide an alternative to abortion. I heard intermediaries tell how they fell into this "ministry" (as women linked to religious groups tend to label their activity) by "saving a child" from abortion. A typical tale goes:

> You see, I'm a spiritist. Once, during a spirit session, I received a message about an abortion. The spirit which had possessed me pleaded, "Little

mother, don't have an abortion." When I came back to normal, I saw a woman in the group sobbing and sobbing. She was pregnant and was just about to have an abortion. She said, "I was going in tomorrow for the abortion." So I said, "Don't you worry. I'll help you. Go ahead with your pregnancy and I'll find you parents for it." She said, "OK, I'll call you every month." Every month she called me. And she handed the child over to me as soon as it was born.

That was the first child. From then on, it's as though one led to another. And these pregnant girls . . . from the moment they look me up until the moment they give birth, I'm always with them. Some of them decide to stay with the child after its birth. We furnish milk for a certain period, and some basic foodstuffs so that they'll be able to nurse.

The stork's work is shrouded in mystery because her activities are frequently illegal. This intermediary has no official mandate to substitute for, or compete with state services, so she is constantly in danger of breaching the law. The very act of asking a pregnant woman whether she wants to keep her child is perilously close to being illegal. Even though the stork insists she was sought out by the woman, it is impossible to be sure whose interests she is serving. When the pregnant girl is a domestic servant, for example, is the stork aiming to please her, or her employer? How can we be sure she exerted no pressure? After the child's birth, it is not unusual for the mother, who has begun nursing her baby, to doubt her decision, or even change her mind. The stork is then in a difficult situation since she has already promised the child to a couple. What sort of pressure might the stork exert on the mother for her to follow through on her original intentions?

Interviews with the professional team at the state adoption service indicate that the great majority of women who decide to relinquish their children do not change their minds after the child's birth. However, they can always cite exceptions to the rule. Some of these exceptional cases end up in court, where birth families are not always favored. A state employee gave the following account:

There are occasional conflicts between adoptive mothers and biological mothers, to see who stays with the child. These are rare, but they do occur. Usually, it's the adoptive mother who keeps the child. You know, there's a tendency for the judge to decide to leave the child where it is. Lots of times the biological parents just give up, because the court process just drags on and they end up letting things ride. Sometimes the court will try to arrange a sort of compromise between them, so their problem won't go to court. The child stays with the adoptive parents and the birth mother will have occasional visiting rights. Really, the normal procedure is to leave the child where it is.

In this situation, the adoptive family often wins the case and the adoption is confirmed. This still happens today, despite the legal principle announced in the 1990 Children's Code that priority should be given to the tie between a child and its biological family.

Another element whose legality is ambiguous is the financial aid given by storks to the expecting mothers for prenatal or postnatal care. How can we distinguish between the provision of financial assistance and the purchase of a child? The words of a birth mother suggest the complexity of this issue:

This woman wanted to adopt a baby, for a friend of hers, and so she asked me if I was really going to give my baby away, and I said yes. She told me, "What I want is a little girl. . . . If your child is a girl, are you going to give her up?" And I said, "Yes, because my employer won't accept me in her house with a baby," so I told [the stork] all about my predicament. She was a nurse. She asked if I wanted to have my tubes tied. I said yes, that I didn't want any more kids. I couldn't raise them. So I had my tubes tied. She fixed everything. She even made an appointment to do an ultrasound. She paid for everything because she wanted to be sure it was a girl. When she found out, she went wild with joy. She helped during the prenatal period. Every month I went to the doctor to know how my baby was getting on. She was so nice to me. She paid 150 for my [sterilization] surgery. . . . She did all sorts of things for me. She paid my taxi, sent me things during the lying-in period. She sent food, milk, porridge—things for me to be strong and healthy. She gave me money, too. After the baby's birth, until I was entirely recovered, she sent things, and a little money. That lasted for three months. Because of the Cesarean and the sterilization, it took me three months to get well.

I heard many narratives of birth mothers telling how they were helped during pregnancy. Some of them claim they felt so obligated by the stork's kindness that they would find it nearly impossible to go back on the decision to give their child away.

The question of money and goods furnished to birth mothers, either by the stork or directly by the adoptive mother, has been discussed by Costa (1988: 141–44) in her study of adoption in the Brazilian state of Parana. She explains that, among middle-class people, an "adoption ethic" presents the mediation of adoptions as an act of charity. The child is seen as priceless, so there is no question of paying either the mother or the intermediary for it. This situation exists, however, only on the theoretical level. On the practical level, it is very difficult to separate the purchase of a child from the financial aid furnished a poverty-stricken mother.

Several times, I heard my upper-class informants saying that, considering the birth mother's financial misery, they simply couldn't refuse to help with "a bit of money" and "some food." These situations appeared particularly common in the case of adoption by Brazilian nationals. Intermediaries involved in intercountry adoption said "you'd have to be crazy" to give money for a child who is destined to a foreign couple because everyone would think the child was being bought. I know of cases where foreign couples gave money to the intermediaries to be passed on to their child's birth mother (Abreu 1994). However, in most of these instances, the storks refused this gesture, suggesting that the money go to a charitable association instead.

Storks do deal with money, but they are careful to present any financial transaction in euphemistic terms so as not to contaminate what in their vision is the "priceless child" circulating within the same network (see Zelizer 1985). Abuses do exist in domestic as well as intercountry adoption. Financial donations to birth mothers, however, are rarely perceived either by the storks or the birth mothers as payment for the child. This fact does not mean that storks are not rewarded for their efforts, since almost always a sort of symbolic value is reaped from the transaction. It is not correct to reduce the adoption market to its purely financial dimension. There are other values that circulate within this sphere, different ways of accumulating capital and of exchanging goods. The major sort of value circulating between the stork and her clientele is prestige. The mediators of these transactions discover a rich symbolic vein that can be exploited beyond any market calculations.

By mediating international adoption, women may accumulate a good amount of symbolic and social capital (Bourdieu 1980). They do so by preventing the occurrence of the "crime" of abortion and "saving an abandoned child" from misery. The mediators are frequently the first (beyond the birth mother's family) to see the child. When, as is often claimed, the child is undernourished or in poor health, the stork may even take the child home and bring in doctors and other necessary support. The stork acquires prestige among her friends, as well as among the adoptive parents.

Storks Flying over National Borders

The storks linked to intercountry adoption have certain additional particularities. Some make frequent trips abroad to check up on their "protégés," "godchildren," "sons and daughters," or "compatriots," as they call the youngsters who passed through their hands. They are received by the adoptive parents with pomp, festivities, and a whole series of honors worthy of someone who opened the door to parenthood. For years afterwards, they receive visits, letters, telephone calls, photos, birthday presents, and New Year's greetings from adoptive parents. As the adoptees grow up, their adoptive parents encourage them to see the stork as a sort of Brazilian grandmother.

I had the opportunity to observe some encounters between Brazilian mediators and adoptive parents in France and Switzerland. The Swiss experience was most impressive since it took place in a castle and was organized by a couple of Swiss nobles who were part of the group of adoptive parents. The organizers of the party invited everyone in France, Italy, Switzerland, and Germany who had adopted a child through a certain stork. There were hundreds of children, most of them dark-skinned or of African descent, and hundreds of adoptive parents from diverse localities, speaking different languages. Children's laughter and a general festive commotion echoed through the castle corridors. Awaiting the Brazilian mediator's arrival, the lights were turned off, everyone hid, and silence descended on the scene. As the stork walked into the central parlor, the party exploded into life with lights, colored balloons, and the adopted children running in from every corner, screaming with glee and hugging the dazed elderly woman. The adoptive parents appeared next with waves of flash cameras to record the scene. Tears flowed in abundance. The champagne was opened, and everyone commented on the extreme "joy" they felt in receiving this woman.

As the day came to an end, the stork received small gifts and heard a long line of success stories about each of her "protégés," with details on their activities ranging from sports to school. The older children played soccer in the castle gardens while the younger ones, folded in their mothers' skirts, listened to tales about the difficulties of their adoption in Brazil —"problems with the judge," early illnesses because of malnutrition—and the "happy ending" signified by the adoption. After the feast, the older Swiss adopted children gave a short recital of songs in honor of the stork, finishing with a chorus of shouts, in heavily accented Portuguese, of the word for "thanks": *obrigado.*

The next day, I spoke with the stork, who told me that all her efforts "had been worth it." Despite all the prejudices she'd had to put up with from Brazilians, she had no regrets; days like the one she'd just been through made up for it all. "Did you see," she asked excitedly, "A real castle! Isn't this all marvelous?" And then came the inevitable question: "What do you think would have happened to these children if they had stayed in Brazil?" When I visited this woman some years later in Brazil, I saw posted on the walls of her bedroom and study a collage of snapshots of the various children she had helped to place, including photographs taken at this gathering.

We cannot understand what motivates these storks if we limit our analysis to purely financial considerations. The prestige, the accumulation of noteworthy relations with Europeans (even Swiss nobles!), the admiration received from Brazilian friends and neighbors for having helped to save so many children are all subtle and powerful mechanisms of reward in this symbolic economy.

The salvationist appeal of the process is enormous. The varied steps of the stork's job are all of dubious legality: locating pregnant girls who are unable to keep their babies, convincing the woman not to have an abortion, certifying that the child will be given up, picking it up at the maternity ward, and keeping it in her house, while ignoring the fact that children can only be transferred from their biological parents to another adult through judicial mandate. The intermediary knowingly takes risks, but she perseveres because she believes in her "mission."

Interviews with storks linked to religious groups illustrate the force of this ideology. These people who, despite the new Children's Code that expressly forbids much of this activity, arrange "ready adoptions" for Brazilians received me with certain reservations. Nonetheless, despite their worries that I might be a scandal-mongering journalist or even a police agent investigating irregular activities, they said they had no fear because they knew that "God was protecting their work." One woman, after having described a series of ways to disguise illegal adoptions, abruptly stopped and issued the challenge: "Now if you want to arrest me, go ahead and do it." Although she recognized that her work was riddled with irregularities and false declarations which might easily be construed as crimes, this mediator expressed pride in her ability to arrange successful adoptions.

The Stork's Nest: Privately Run Nurseries

Mediators who run their own private orphanages constitute a variation on the stork theme. For many years these orphanages, which we will call nurseries, were tacitly tolerated by government agencies. Some even had formed partnerships with the state, receiving help from the Children's Bureau at the district or state level. During the late 1970s and early 1980s, it was not unusual for upper-class ladies, or even nuns and priests linked to religious congregations, to maintain nurseries. This type of stork was responsible for the great majority of adoptions carried out in Brazil during the first half of the 1980s. Moreover, with their own nurseries, and enjoying partnerships with public authorities, these people were better equipped than independent storks to conduct intercountry adoptions.

Owners of nurseries enjoyed considerable popularity in the neighborhoods where they were located. Money brought in from foreign adoptive parents helped to finance local charities. Birth mothers with difficult-to-place children appreciated the establishment's good reputation. The placement of certain children—especially those who were visibly of African descent or had special needs—was a serious problem among Brazilian adopters, and most birth mothers were well aware of this fact.

The willingness of foreigners to take children who, in Brazil, would probably not be accepted into an upper-class family impressed all concerned. The first reports on intercountry adoption in Brazil frequently mentioned that these children were being "saved" by "unprejudiced" parents in other countries. The international stork reaped symbolic benefits from these infant salvage operations. Denouncing Brazilian "prejudice" against children with special needs made the mediator appear to be superior to her compatriots in refraining from invidious value judgments.

Occasionally, a stork gave into the temptation of adopting one of the children she had taken in. The storks who had become adoptive mothers gained additional prestige among their peers, as though they incarnated the "infant salvation mission" other adoptive mothers had undertaken.

These adoptions would be paraded as a sign of "good faith" on the part of storks when anyone spoke of "trafficking in babies." Those mediators who adopted children were practically guaranteed a reputation as "honest" and "disinterested," especially if she already had biological children. The search for adequate adoptive parents for the children under their protection gained new legitimacy. Even if the storks did not readily offer this information to the researcher, adoptive parents availing themselves of the mediator's services consistently referred to this fact.

With the advent of widespread criticism of intercountry adoption, international storks began to disappear.[3] Storks gave up mediating connections between Brazilian children and foreign adopters when they could no longer count on the symbolic benefits. The rewards of prestige, honor, and recognition began to diminish when concerns about "the traffic in children" and "the sale of babies" began to circulate in the stork's social circles. One mediator explains why she ceased her activities: "Look, I had a nursery. There were people from all over the world who came to adopt children through me and it was all beautiful, straight up front." Speaking of traffic in children, she said: "I have a certain name" to protect "and I don't need these cases of 'selling children.' There were a lot of things wrong . . . there were some lawyers . . ." After a long silence, she continued: "those who had no scruples . . . I don't doubt it. There were lawyers charging five thousand dollars for an adoption. I think that's absurd!"

> In my case, it wasn't like that. We only charged what it cost us to maintain the nursery. This business of high prices . . . we never did that. We did it for love . . . to give a home to these children. It's a shame people couldn't understand. It was all for free. When you see the children . . . They were lucky. They still send me pictures and letters. It was a lovely endeavor.
>
> In the beginning, lots of people helped. Later, there were all those stories about traffic and people began to be afraid. I found out the federal police was investigating my nursery. There were always some fellows hanging around on our block. . . . It lasted about two months. It was awful. I had no reason to worry. But you can't put the feathers back after the chicken's been plucked.
>
> The director of the federal police came to talk with me afterwards. He apologized. He said my work was all perfectly legal, but you can't fix things like that. I'd had it. I closed the nursery and gave the kids over to the [state] nursery. It was a real shame.

Some mediators linked to the Catholic Church, especially nuns, continued to operate nurseries until the mid-1990s, ignoring all the denunciations made against the traffic or sale of children. Their nurseries were closed down only after the police intervened. These cases are particularly interesting from a sociological point of view, since the prestige and honor—the "feathers" that the previous stork spoke of—had already been plucked and the recognition had backfired, giving these women a bad reputation. The symbolic benefits they reaped from these transactions might be better understood within a "field of religious forces" (Bourdieu 1971). The benefits and prestige at stake are vastly different from those governed by the philanthropic rationality of upper-class storks. The "suffering" and "persecution" that accompany devotion to the "noble cause" produce symbolic religious results, appreciated only within the social milieu where sacrifice makes sense and confers "salvation" or even "sainthood."[4]

An eighty-year-old nun, the Mother Superior of a prestigious congregation, told me of the suffering and humiliation she and other sisters had undergone and how they bore it "for the love of the children" and "by the grace of God." She kept her nursery and international adoption service functioning until 1995, despite police harassment and even criticism from the congregation's lay leadership. She lost nearly all support among the city's moneyed classes, and even the couples who had adopted children from her began to doubt the legality of the adoptions she had arranged. For her, the "hardest blow" came when her own congregation asked her to stop mediating adoptions because her activities were giving the religious order a bad name. She said she was very old and lacked energy to continue fighting, but she knew that "God sees everything" and that one day "her children" would thank her.

Birds of a Feather . . .

Although woman who acted as intermediaries viewed their mission as governed by a morality that was above the state's laws and bureaucracy, the predominantly male lawyers who specialized in adoption had embarked on the practice because of the high demand and good clientele, and they prided themselves on knowing all the possible loopholes in existing legislation.

Before the rise in intercountry adoption, lawyers had only occasional connections to adoption. Following an age-old tradition known as "adoption Brazilian-style," most adoptive parents would simply go the registrar's office and take out a birth certificate for their ward as though he or she were their own natal offspring. Barring an express denouncement, judges would turn a blind eye to such illegal procedures, and some even dared to defend the practice openly. Intercountry adoption put a new twist on things, as receiving countries invariably required full legal documentation on children entering the country. As the number of prospective foreign adopters rose during the mid-1980s, so too did the number of lawyers, happy to mediate a transaction that would pay fees that were exceedingly attractive by Brazilian standards.

Lawyers could work with public institutions, but they seldom chose to do so. Bureaucracy complicated contacts with the children in public orphanages. Technically, the lawyer had to get official permission each time he visited a child, and each step—whether soliciting special privileges for the child, or trying to expedite the process of having the child legally declared to have been abandoned—came under close scrutiny. But, most of all, lawyers did not go through the state-run orphanages because the adoptable children were elsewhere. Explaining that they preferred the more personalized treatment they received from *cegonhas*, most birth mothers sought out the neighborhood nurseries and charitable organizations rather than leave their children at the state institution.

During the 1980s, the majority of lawyers involved in the adoption process worked through private nurseries. Granted, the material conditions in these establishments were not up to the level of state institutions: the hygiene may not have been up to muster, nor the caregivers well paid. But the personal relations with the *cegonha* dispensed with a good part of the bureaucracy, permitting greater flexibility and even legal sleights of hand.

Lawyers interviewed today remember the golden age of intercountry adoption during the 1980s as a time when "it was best not to have a [birth] mother." For an international adoption dossier to move along quickly, it was best that the judge presiding over the case consider the child a "foundling" (*exposto*), abandoned by its parents in a public locale or on a private doorstep. With the stork's complicity, lawyers would present witnesses to testify to the effect that the child had been discovered on the steps of the local church or at a friend's back door, as though it were of entirely unknown origin. This tactic is reflected in the 1987 statistics on international adoption in Ceará kept by the federal police. Of the 217 adoption proceedings, almost half (103, or 47 percent) involved children who were found to be abandoned in a public locale; one third (73) were relinquished directly by the mother; almost one fifth (40, or 19 percent) had been in a private nursery; and only one had been in a state-run orphanage at the time the adoption proceedings began.

Many judges admit they were aware of irregularities, but saw them much as they saw "Brazilian-style" adoptions—as a sort of necessary evil that, in the long run, would work out best for the child. However, as intercountry adoption received increasing attention in the media, the situation began to take on a different tenor. Brazil's 1990 Children's Code was specifically designed to hem in intercountry transactions. Children were to be maintained in their original families when at all possible; barring this possibility, they were to be placed in a local substitute family. The adoption of Brazilian children by foreign nationals was to be a last resort. In order to guarantee respect for the child's interests, public defense lawyers were to supervise each intercountry adoption, conducting a search for the birth parents when necessary.

The 1990 legislation did not, however, bring about immediate changes. Lawyers found new loopholes. As one informant told me, the new regulations meant mostly that "it was best to bring the (birth) mother along":

> Starting in 1990 or 1991, but especially from 1992 on, it was necessary to get the mother's authorization. The judge would be afraid of getting into trouble by approving the adoption of child without its parents' permission, so I would take the mother in to see the judge. She would say, "I want my son to go this lawyer and his wife." That made it hard for the judge to give the child to another Brazilian family. And, that way, I was covered. A social worker could go to the mother's home and ask her. If the police got on my heels, I'd tell them, "Go ask the mother if she didn't give me her child". It was all safe.

For a short while, judges continued to facilitate adoptions and turn their backs on irregularities, as they had done previously.

The 1990s brought new forms of control. As a result of police and Parliamentary investigations of international adoption, politicians lost votes, court officials were suspended, judges dismissed, and lawyers sentenced to jail (although it is not clear whether or not they ever served time). Between 1992 and 1994, no fewer than seventeen lawyers in the state of Ceará were indicted by the police inquest.[5]

In 1993, the state of Ceará, following directives of the 1990 Children's Code, formed a Judiciary Commission for International Adoption composed of local dignitaries, which filtered all requests by potential adopters from overseas. The commission's tacit mission was to eliminate not only the need for, but the very possibility of paid intermediaries operating in the adoption field. Significantly, international adoption dropped dramatically, from 223 in 1993 to 54 in 1994. Among the lawyers I interviewed, many protested indignantly, as did the *cegonhas*, that they had always acted for the children's benefit and their activities had been misunderstood or distorted by investigating commissions. However, when conditions were no longer auspicious, they quickly switched to new specialties. We might surmise that they benefited less than their female counterparts from the symbolic laurels of international adoption. Associated, through their male identity and profession, with finance and business, they derived little from the maternal or child-saving connotations of their mediating activities. Faced with scandal and the loss of reputation, they were quick to abandon the adoption field to the state services.

The unauthorized intermediaries in international adoption working in northeast Brazil cannot be neatly categorized as "honest" or "illegal," "altruistic" or "greedy." In the fact, the mutual dependence of *cegonhas* and lawyers reveals that these two seemingly contrasting categories—one motivated by altruistic generosity, the other by financial gain—are complementary. Furthermore, lawyers often claimed to be motivated by humanitarian intentions, while upper-class charity workers also reaped considerable benefits that enhanced their own economic and political status.

Ironically, professionals from the state adoption services flatly condemn the self-serving involvement of *cegonhas* in times past, while they themselves continue to enjoy many of the non-material benefits of this activity: making frequent trips abroad to check up on their previous wards, receiving small gifts, gratitude, and photos. This retrospective reflection on the role of unofficial go-betweens in the process of international adoption indicates that we should consider the adoption market as a system involving not only purely commercial aspects but also symbolic values of considerable social and political consequence. While recognizing the many laudable innovations in the field of adoption, I suggest that there are many continuities between the dynamics of the past and those of the present. We might learn a good deal about child activists militating in the child's best interest, legislators shoring up loopholes, as well as psychologists and social workers involved in "helping" childless couples and "supporting" birth mothers, by framing our analyses in terms of the material and symbolic values linked to the adoption market.

NOTES

1. More than half the birth mothers in Brazil are classified as maids; see Abreu 2002.

2. Spiritism centers on communication with the spirits of the dead through mediums and on the spiritual healing of physical illnesses. It flourished during the twentieth century, especially among the middle classes. It has elements in common with Holiness movements and with Christian Science. See Hess 1991, 1994. One popular spiritist group, Kardeicism, is widely known for its charitable activities.

3. Condemnation of intercountry adoption varies from one part of the country to another. In certain cities, it is now practically impossible to find private mediators for intercountry adoption, but in others, particularly in the North, the practice continues to be relatively common.

4. Saint Paul aptly captured the spirit of this religious culture when he stated that God's wisdom may look like humanity's folly.

5. *Folha de São Paulo*, 30 August 1994.

REFERENCES

Abreu, Domingos. 1994. "Adoption et aide humanitaire: Stérilité biologique, fécondité sociale et parenté symbolique." Diplome d'Etudes Approfondus de Sociologie et Sciences Sociales (master's thesis), Université Lumière-Lyon 2.
———. 2002. *No bico da cegonha*. Rio de Janeiro: Relume Dumará.
———. 2003. "Récits et Représentations d'adoption internationale: Les logiques du dom et de la dette." In *Littérature Orale: Paroles vivantes et mouvantes*, ed. J. B. Martin, 139–156. Lyon: Presses Universitaires de Lyon.
Bourdieu, Pierre. 1971. "Genèse et structure du champ religieux." *Revue Française de Sociologie* 12, no. 3: 295–334.
———. 1980. *Le sens pratique*. Paris: Minuit.
Bourdieu, Pierre, and Loïc J. D. Wacquant. 1992. *An Invitation to Reflexive Sociology*. Chicago: University of Chicago Press.
Costa, Cecília. 1988. "Os 'filhos do coração': Adoção em camadas médias brasileiras." Doutorado em Antropologia Social (Ph.D. diss. in Social Anthropology). Rio de Janeiro: Museu Nacional, Universidade Federal do Rio de Janeiro.

Fonseca, C. 2001. "La Circulation des Enfants Pauvres au Bresil: Une pratique locale dans un monde globalisé." *Anthropologie et Sociétés* 24, no. 3: 24–43.

Hess, David J. 1991. *Spirits and Scientists: Ideology, Spiritism, and Brazilian Culture.* University Park: Pennsylvania State University.

———. 1994. *Samba in the Night: Spiritism in Brazil.* New York: Columbia University Press.

Kane, Saralee. 1993. "The Movement of Children for International Adoption: An Epidemiologic Perspective." *Social Science Journal* 30, no. 4: 323–39.

Lallemand, S. 1993. *La circulation des enfants en société tradicionell—Prêt, don, échange.* Paris: Harmattan.

Massard, J. 1983. "Le don d'enfant dans la société malaise." *L'Homme* 23, no. 3: 35–62.

———. 1988. "Engendrer ou adopter: Deux vision concurrentes de la parenté chez les malais péninsulaires." *Anthropologie et Société* 12, no. 2: 102–28.

Mauss, Marcel. 1950. *Sociologie et anthropologie.* Paris: PUF.

Modell, Judith Schachter. 1994. *Kinship with Strangers: Adoption and Interpretations of Kinship in American Culture.* Berkeley: University of California Press.

Triseliotis, John. 2000. "Intercountry Adoption: Global Trade or Global Gift?" *Adoption and Fosterage* 24, no. 2: 45–54.

Zelizer, Viviana. 1985. *Pricing the Priceless Child: The Changing Social Value of Children.* New York: Basic Books.

Chapter 8

IIIIIIIIIIIIIIIIIIIIIIIIIIIIIIIIIIIIIIIIIIIIIIIIIIII

Transnational Connections and Dissenting Views
The Evolution of Child Placement Policies in Brazil

Claudia Fonseca

This chapter examines the complex interweaving of local and transnational influences in the evolution of child placement policies in Brazil over the past twenty years. Inspired by the work of other scholars (Ginsburg and Rapp 1995, Yngvesson 2000), the analysis in this chapter is founded on the premise that child placement is a profoundly political question involving contrasting discourses and practices regarding kinship, family, and "the best interests of a child." A decade ago, Judith Schachter Modell, in a path-breaking study of disputes between Native Hawaiian families and the state child welfare system, came to the conclusion that fosterage, particularly when governed by decision-makers who do not share the original family's worldview, is a highly politicized mode of childcare. Pointing out that fosterage involves "the distribution and not just the 'production' of children" (Modell 1998: 157), she underlined the need to redefine the very notion of reproduction, "so as not simply to equate the word with 'having a child,' but rather to recognize its meaning as 'raising a generation'" (169). Following her lead, we extend Modell's mode of inquiry to the question of legal adoption and to a social context in which people are divided not so much by ethnic differences as by class disparities. In light of profound social and political cleavages in Brazil visible in the unequal status of birth mothers and adoptive parents, we suggest that fosterage may be preferable to the complete and irrevocable rupture of kinship ties implied in plenary adoption.

Tracing the production of adoptable children in Brazil led me through an intricate network of forces, including various and often opposing attitudes, operating through local, national, and international institutions. Rather than focus on one node of the network, I have chosen to analyze the multiple intersecting forces involved. I frame the development of child placement policies and practices in Brazil in three phases. With the description of a recent television program portraying the role of avaricious foreign adopters in the "traffic" in children, the analysis centers first on highly negative images regarding intercountry adoption in the national media. Although today such images are relatively rare, they were common during the 1980s and early 1990s and exercised considerable influence on national policy. Next I consider certain elements of Brazilian judicial policy, shaped by international discourses on the rights of the child, that made an idealized form of plenary adoption the top priority in child placement during the 1990s. Finally, I consider a more recent phase in which national NGOs, with distinctly international connections, have played a major role in publicly airing alternatives to adoption, confronting generally conservative local adopters as their major adversaries. These crosswinds of debate and swings in national child placement policy cannot be easily explained, much less predicted. They are neither, as some would have it, a result of the "global forces of imperialism" nor, as others would have it, the victory of enlightened individuals battling for social justice within Brazil. Rather, they are the outcome of an intricate interplay between public opinion, specific interest groups, and personal agency that all involve dissenting views and transnational connections.

This project began with ethnographic research among the families of shantytowns and working-class neighborhoods of Porto Alegre in southern Brazil where, during the 1980s, I first encountered women whose children had been officially given in adoption (Fonseca 2003, 2004).[1] Since then, following the route of the "native anthropologist" in Brazil (Peirano 1992), I have branched out into other locales. Given entrance to activities in various juvenile courts, residential homes and orphanages, associations for adoptive parents, and NGOs involved in child rights, I have coordinated a research team of university students that provides consultancy services in various NGOs and government services, as well as conducting academic field and archival studies.[2] Through this sort of "multi-sited" ethnography (Marcus 1998), which is particularly well adapted to the analysis of long-term changes, I bring into focus transnational influences during the past two decades of Brazilian child placement policies.

An Accent on North-South Divisions

In July 2001, Brazil's leading television channel broadcast an hour-long program on the international traffic in children for adoption. In the two opening scenes, viewers see fragments of an anonymous, purportedly European reporter's videotape in which impoverished women attempt to sell their infants. One mother, explaining simply that she has four other children to take care of, appears ready to relinquish the toddler in her arms for a mere bagatelle (R$150, around US$70). Another woman, visibly a mother-to-be, drives a harder bargain; speaking in terms of U.S. dollars, she insinuates that the price—$1,000—is insultingly low for the child she is about to bear.

Between these shocking images of a mother who gives little value to her child and of a woman who cynically manipulates this value, the spectator hardly has time to catch her breath before the camera moves on to a new subject: the venal intermediaries involved in intercountry adoption. For the next fifty minutes, viewers are presented with lawyers, judges, a nun, and an ex-priest, located in different parts of Brazil, who are accused of illegally facilitating the intercountry adoption of Brazilian children, many of them for personal gain. The obviously foreign accent of the two church figures helps to firm conviction that the major threat to these poverty-stricken families comes from overseas.

In Brazil, as in many other sending countries, media coverage generally depicts foreign intervention in the adoption process as predatory. Newscasters in the United States and Western Europe tend to dwell on "child-saving" images: stark halls in sordid, Third World orphanages, filled with dirty cribs and usually dark-skinned toddlers stretching out their arms, as though begging for a charitable soul to adopt them. In sending countries, the media favor stories about "infant snatching," the "baby trade," and "trafficking in orphans." During the 1980s, stories about babies mysteriously disappearing from maternity wards were published in Brazil side by side with articles on unscrupulous lawyers who reap untoward gains from foreign adoptive parents (Abreu 2002). Indignation over purported abuses linked to the early phases of intercountry adoption proved contagious. In October 1993, a French deputy in the European Parliament, in his general condemnation of the traffic in children, estimated that, out of four thousand Brazilian children adopted in Italy, only a thousand still survived; the rest were supposedly dead—victims of abuse, or killed and their organs harvested for transplants.[3] The following month, the BBC fired the debate, presenting a low-level Argentine diplomat who claimed to possess evidence of atrocities involving Brazilian children. Police and adoption services throughout the country began to investigate "denunciations that Brazilian children with physical deficiencies were being adopted in other countries to have their organs torn out."[4] By September 1994, when the newspaper reported on a new book titled *O Mercado Humano* (*The Human Market*) (Berlinguer and Garrafa 1996), panic was at its peak. Speaking of adoption "for the dismantling of children," the author pointed out that, while a child could be acquired through intercountry adoption for approximately US$8,000, a single kidney could be sold for US$40,000 to US$50,000. At this point government officials began to wonder about the enormous number of missing children in Brazil.[5] The adoption of older and physically or mentally impaired youngsters became especially suspicious. A Pernambuco judge who suspended all intercountry adoption in 1994 admitted he had no absolute proof of the alleged atrocities against Brazilian adoptees, but noted a "strange fact" that could be indicative of abuse: of fourteen children adopted abroad under his supervision that year, five were over eight years old, and two were somehow deficient.[6]

A massive wave of legal investigations of any judge, lawyer, or charity worker who had served as go-between in an intercountry adoption began in the late 1980s. Public opinion underwent an about-face from praising these agents as "child savers" to condemning them as "child traffickers" (see Abreu 2002). As more and more state officials began to see involvement in intercountry adoption as a political liability, these programs were suspended altogether in some regions. In sum, *official* intercountry adoptions were curbed along with the *illegal* smuggling of youngsters.

Certainly, there was an element of genuine social reform involved in the reformulation of adoption policy. During the 1980s, the Brazilian political scene went through important changes. Emerging from twenty years of military dictatorship, the country tolerated a myriad of social movements: workers' strikes, invasions of housing projects, marches for land reform, and church-led neighborhood associations. A rising number of university-educated professionals, including social workers and community health agents, as well as a technologically more efficient state bureaucracy, created a demand for greater intervention in people's domestic affairs. The writing of a new constitution, completed in 1988, mobilized thousands of activists aiming at social reforms who then turned their attention specifically to the subject of children. The 1990 federal Children's Code, which put strict limits on intercountry adoption, was partially responsible for the drop in outgoing children. In many states of the federation, public placement services suspended or slowed down their activities for a year or more so as to "restructure" their services in conformity with the new legislation.

During the 1980s, Brazil was classified as the world's fourth largest source of adopted children (Kane 1993), and until the mid-1990s intercountry adoption outstripped local adoption in many regions of Brazil. The turning point came around 1993, as the number of intercountry adoptions went into steady decline, dropping from over 2000 per annum to just over 400 at the decade's close (Fonseca 2002a; see also Selman, this volume). Several other sending countries followed a similar course. In response to the scandals involving intercountry adoption, national and international regulations were modified to put "national adoptions first." Article 31 of the Brazilian Children's Code states that adoption by foreigners should be considered an exceptional measure, following the Hague directive that intercountry adoption should occur only "if the child cannot be placed in a foster or an adoptive family or cannot in any suitable manner be cared for in the child's country of origin" (Hague Convention: article 21, item b). Gradually, as the legislation began to take effect, adoption scandals in the media died down. The question remains: Had all the abuses of power been curbed? Or were there still elements of dire inequality that no longer encountered an outlet for scandal?

Child Circulation in Brazil from Birth Families' Point of View

The images projected in the media of birth mothers oppressed by poverty into a numb sort of abdication or, worse, cynical manipulation of their motherhood, stand in contrast to the narratives I heard during fieldwork from women who had given a child to be raised by others.

Elsewhere (Fonseca 2004), I have described the plight of Eliane, a young black woman who, unmarried and living with her mother when she became pregnant for a third time, was forced by circumstances to give her child away. Having searched among relatives and acquaintances for her future child's adoptive parents, her choice fell upon the baby's paternal aunt, a woman who, after years of trying to get pregnant, had recently lost a stillborn child. Eliane recalls in detail the tearful respect with which the potential mother treated her: "She said, 'Look Eliane, we don't want to force you.' She gave me liberty to do what I wanted." After weeks of soul-searching and mutual support, the decision was made. Six years later, living with a steady companion, who is a reasonably prosperous junk dealer, and four of her five children, Eliane keeps discreet tabs on the lad through occasional visits to his home. However, she insists, the child has no idea she's his mother: "When I go there, he calls me 'Auntie.'"

Other stories I heard were variations on the theme. Iara, whom I met at the small factory where she works as a seamstress, had fallen unexpectedly pregnant from her first boyfriend who, shortly after learning of his impending paternity, simply disappeared. Barely out of adolescence at the time, she was living from hand to mouth, with no nearby relatives to help her out. She turned to a slightly better-off neighbor who had agreed to be her daughter's godmother (*comadre*). "I told her, 'I'm really hard up. I don't know where to leave the child. Each day, I leave her in a different place.'" The godmother offered to take the child until Iara managed to pull her life together. When Iara asked for her daughter back almost a year later, she met with resistance. "They'd become attached to her. My comadre cried so hard, it broke my heart. Out of pity, I decided to leave the little girl a little longer. And so she stayed on and on." A few years later, having found a stable position, Iara, now with two younger children (both boys), tried once again to call the daughter back. However, this time facing the resistance of her own daughter, she reasoned, "Now that she's nearly grown, what good would it do, to bring her back? To hang around here in the favela, when I know that, there, she has every comfort she needs?"

In Brazil, unlike Europe or North America, poor families clustered in vast shantytowns and housing settlements cannot be considered marginal. Since the colonial period, working-class people have relied on alternative social institutions, including kinship networks and the informal sector of the economy, to keep them going. Their strategies for seeing to the welfare of their children and guaranteeing the survival of new generations include the circulation of children. Through this practice, documented by historians and social scientists in diverse parts of Brazil, parents passing through difficult times share the economic burdens involved in raising a child with a series of informally chosen, and generally unpaid, foster parents (Cardoso 1984, Fonseca 2003, 2004, Hecht 1998, Goldstein 1997, Kuznesof 1998). The outcome of these arrangements, especially when children are placed with non-relatives, is not always predictable. Many women, after a period of "shared motherhood," end up bringing their children home. Others contend with the resistance of their child's caretaker who, after years of affective ties and financial outlay, considers she has earned rights to exclusive motherhood. Some of the women I met during my early field-work, before the new Children's Code, had used the state orphanage as a sort of boarding school, a stop-off in the various placements of their chil-dren, only to learn that their child had been irretrievably lost to an adop-tive family. Significantly, none of the women I met in over fifteen years of research ever admitted to having "abandoned," much less bartered, her child. Many who, like Eliane or Iara, had "given away" a son or daughter spoke with wrenching concern of the care they invested in choosing their child's adoptive parents.

When looking at children taken from impoverished families to be raised in middle-class homes, whether in Brazil or abroad, we are deal-ing with delicate issues of class *and* cultural difference. The concept of class brings home the fact that we are not dealing with folk-like cultural repertoires of equal political weight (Colen 1995). In Brazil, the poor are undeniably "Western," although their way of looking at the world appears to have little in common with that of dominant groups. The political di-mension of cultural difference becomes glaringly apparent when we con-sider that many of the gatekeepers, particularly lawmakers, are from the national elite and may or may not share values in common with people to whom laws are applied. We turn now to a consideration of judicial practices to assess where local authorities have looked for inspiration—at home or abroad—to forge new child welfare policies.

The Judicial Thrust Toward a Rigid Form of Legal, Plenary Adoption

After the enactment of the 1990 Children's Code, the Brazilian judiciary, acting through specialized courts in the major townships (*Juizados de In-fância e de Juventude*), became the key agents of official childcare policy. Although many services, including shelters for abused and abandoned children, were to be decentralized and taken over by municipal rather than state authorities, all child placements were to be registered, super-vised and articulated through the juvenile courts. This period, with its renewed emphasis on child rights, brought many welcome changes. Anx-ious to dissociate themselves from the previous decade's scandals, juvenile authorities now concentrated their efforts on adoption by *local* families.

Together with this thrust, however, came policy orientations that bear examination.

The rise in popularity of legal adoption increased pressure on state authorities to expedite the "freeing" of children for adoption. In Brazil, as elsewhere, the great majority of people who lose their children to adoption do not actively seek this solution. Most children have been made available through a court order (*destituição do pátrio poder*) that unilaterally strips parents of their rights. Aware that many people had lost their parental rights because of miserable living conditions, legislators wrote into the 1990 Children's Code a clause stating that "The lack or scarcity of material resources shall not be sufficient motive for the loss or suspension of *pátrio poder*" (art. 23). Nonetheless, the law did not prevent the stigmatization of poor families.

Addressing this issue, Andrea Cardarello (1998) conducted a study in the state-run children's homes in Porto Alegre comparing reasons for admission in 1985 with those in 1994. In 1985, 42 percent of the 350 children admitted entered the institution because of "socio-economic problems," and fully 81 percent of the classifications such as "street beggars," "family disintegration," and health problems concerning the child or its parents were, in the institution's orientation manual, explicitly linked to poverty. Ten years later, in 1994, nearly three-fourths of the children were admitted for reasons that pointed to the malefic influence of their parents or guardians: "abandonment," "ill treatment," "negligence," "abuse." Over time, there was a clear shift toward categories that underline the original family's moral fault, with few, if any, mitigating considerations. Interviews with the professionals responsible for admitting the children suggested, however, that this change was not necessarily due to an actual shift in behavior. One social worker explained that some of the clerks "mark 'negligence' when, in fact, it's an 'assistance' case. They confuse the two terms. It just depends on who fills in the form." In written reports, elaborated by the institution's administrators, there were persistent complaints, in both 1985 and 1994, that, because of inadequate social policies for the population at large, the major clients of the children's homes continued to be poverty-stricken families. Cardarello concludes that entrance categories took a turn for the worse precisely because, after the enactment of the Children's Code, it was no longer admissible to institutionalize children simply because of their parents' utter poverty. Childcare professionals discovered "parental neglect" as the flip side of "child rights," and, once classified under these accusatory labels, institutionalized youngsters moved one step closer to becoming candidates for adoption.

At the same time, the Children's Code created pressure for a shift from "ready adoptions," in which informal transfers of children are subsequently made official in court and the children accumulate filial identities, to plenary adoptions, mediated exclusively by state juvenile authorities, in which a child's adoptive identity precludes any trace of his or her original family. Some efforts were invested in "family preservation" and the evaluation of the biological families' capacity to "reintegrate" their children. But once the child was declared available for adoption, the idea of sharing any information with the birth mother about her child's adoptive family, or vice versa, was never entertained. Images of child traffic loomed large over this scenario, reinforcing the assumption that birth mothers were either feeble or mercenary: that they should be protected against pressures from candidates to adoptive parenthood, or, on the contrary, that adoptive parents should be protected against the venal demands of their child's biological family. Even the most progressive of professionals and academics ignored the existence of open adoptions (Grotevant and McRoy 1998) and labored under the impression that no-contact, plenary adoption was "the only form of adoption that exists in developed countries."

Perhaps the most disturbing element of this period was the policy of casting aspersions on a wide array of options for childcare that fell outside the polarity of birth family versus adoptive family. Because of my research on traditional forms of child circulation as well as state-sponsored childcare systems, I had long been curious about official programs concerning foster families. From the early 1990s on, I was repeatedly told that foster programs no longer existed; they were clearly not up to the standards of the new Children's Code. Ironically, it was from a colleague at the other end of Brazil, Domingos Abreu, that I first heard about Porto Alegre's "Substitute Homes," a foster care program that had served as a model for other states during the 1970s and 1980s. An investigation of this program by an anthropology graduate student revealed interesting details. In 2003, Pilar Uriarte (2005) was able to find only a dozen or so of these (now aged) foster mothers still raising children placed by the state. The monthly meetings and training courses for foster mothers and the children's privileged access to doctors, medicine, and psychotherapy had all been stopped after the passage of the Children's Code.

The reason for the program's demise is set out clearly by a judicial sentence of 1992. A juvenile court judge, responding to a request to authorize the official guardianship of a child who had been living for years with his foster mother, responded with a resounding "no": "Human beings were not made to live in institutions, nor in 'patched-up' families, but in groups that can be seen as" families (Uriarte 2005: 121). This decree represents the judge's translation of the Children's Code's directives. The document places a distinct emphasis on a child's need for a family, the preferred space for its development and protection. When its "natural" family is unable to furnish a suitable milieu, the child is to be placed in a "substitute" family. Although the code allows for the possibility of different child placement options and recommends financial assistance for substitute families, this alternative has rarely figured in public discussion. Of all possible alternatives for children in long-term institutional care, adoption received unambiguous priority during the 1990s. The judge's decision expresses the prevailing attitude: "Utopian or not, the Children's Code does not merit this destructive interpretation"—that is, including foster families in the category of "substitute families." "To do so would be a true step backward" (Uriarte 2005: 121).

Before the passage of the Children's Code, there were a few foster care initiatives in different parts of Brazil. Church-related philanthropies were trying out small residential homes run by full-time "social parents." The Swiss-based International Children's Villages had set up houses in a dozen or more Brazilian cities. However, by the 1990s, these alternatives to institutional care were little more than tolerated as a distant runner-up to idealized adoptive families. Public authorities all but ignored the option of home-based foster care. In December 2003, in all of Brazil, I could find only some half-dozen publicly run programs, involving around 50 foster families and no more than 100 children. Considering that estimates for the same period put the number of institutionalized children in Brazil at nearly 100,000 (Silva 2004), we must conclude that foster care was statistically insignificant. In 1997, the authors of a worldwide survey of foster care systems explained that they were unable to include Brazil among their case studies because the country simply had no cultural or legal precedents in the realm of foster care (Colton and Williams 1997). This erroneous statement is symptomatic of how the tradition of child circulation was totally silenced during the 1990s, creating the impression that adoption was the *only* possible alternative for children who could not be raised in their original families. Official rhetoric posed the issue in either/or terms, obscuring alternative policies as well as the political nature of the different options.

Tense Undercurrents to a Seeming Consensus

Brazilian authorities, while greatly inspired by the national Children's Code, were also highly responsive to international debates on the rights of the child. From these debates, however, certain opinions carried over more easily than others. For example, the report from the 2000 meeting of the Hague Convention's Special Committee points out that certain sending countries practice only "simple" adoption while most receiving countries require all adoptions to be "full" and plenary. Contesting the automatic conversion of the former to the latter, delegates to the Commission pointed out that "a simple adoption may sometimes be entered into, not because this is the only alternative available, but because the birth parents do not wish to sever all legal ties with the child. Reservations were expressed in respect of any system which treats conversion as an automatic process. Such an approach ran the risk of 'disenfranchising' the birth parents, by giving the adoption effects beyond those for which the consent was given" (Report 2000, art. 78). Similar comments have not emerged in Brazilian national debate, where the voices of birth mothers, coming from society's most powerless sectors, have been routinely left out, not so much by design—channels for participation do exist in some places—but for lack of attentive listeners. Even in the UN report, the reservations as to the wishes of birth parents are all but lost amidst the much more lengthy passages aimed at eliminating private entrepreneurs' financial gain and regulating financial charges, concerns that adoptive parents consistently take to heart.

Observers have repeatedly called attention to the contrasting evolution of adoption patterns in sending and receiving countries: "While adoption in the West is gradually moving away from the notion of sealed records and a complete break with the past, in the international market the trend is still toward the freeing of infants for placement overseas by severing all links with their natal family (and countries)" (Bowie 2004: 14). These observations are a provocative reminder that, rather than thinking of two parallel lines of development, we might well ask about the link between one pattern and the other. Following this line of analysis, Barbara Yngvesson (2003, 2004) points out the generally conservative, traditionalist, and patriarchal tone of family-based policies in the field of intercountry adoption. In reference to the 1993 International Hague Conference on the Protection of Children and Co-operation in Respect of Intercountry Adoption, she observes that while representatives from sending countries generally endorsed local solutions for children in need, those from receiving countries considered intercountry adoption preferable to many local solutions which might include foster homes and institutional care. "This position is . . . of a piece with the assumption that a permanent, self-contained (nuclear) family environment is the best environment for any child. Such an assumption tends to undermine the potential of temporary institutional care or of foster placement, since neither fits the definition of a self-contained family" (2004: 216). The net result of the "mutual education" process (Yngvesson 2004: 215) that takes place in international conferences is not so much a massive increase of intercountry adoptions as it is an exaggerated enthusiasm for plenary adoption as a "cure for (too) many ills" (Selman 2004).

NGOs and the Diversification of Child Placement Policies

Although before the elaboration of the Children's Code, a considerable number of private citizens, including lawyers, society ladies, charity workers, and church officials openly served as intermediaries in the adoption process (see Abreu, this volume), foreign adoption agencies such as Holt International were never active in Brazil.[7] Nonetheless, certain international groups engaged in child welfare have long exerted an influence, broadening institutional alternatives.

One particularly active association that has come to exercise leadership in the field of child welfare in recent years with the government's bid to decentralize the administration of social programs and its increasing reliance on non-governmental organizations (see Pantaleón 2002) is Terra dos Homens. A brief review of this NGO's involvement in child placement issues highlights the interplay of local and global influences. During the 1960s, humanitarian concern was channeled toward placing orphans of the Algerian war in European adoptive homes. During the mid-1970s, however, policy planners began to favor long-term development projects rather than emergency aid in response to their recognition that, as the French branch of the organization states on its website, children's fate depends above all on the social conditions in which their parents live.[8] By 1989, the organization had officially renounced any involvement in intercountry adoption.

The coordinator of the Brazilian branch of Terre des Hommes, active in the association since 1983, recounts the evolution of its policy in

Brazil from the supervision of intercountry adoptions in the 1980s to the insistence on national adoption during the 1990s. The organization also shifted its priorities to favor the adoption of difficult-to-place children: older, dark-skinned, and physically or mentally disabled youngsters. It is not entirely clear where the initial impetus for change came from. While granting that the European-based NGO gave crucial financial support to their different programs, my Brazilian interviewee implied that local officials produced a major policy change at the Swiss headquarters, and not vice versa. This organization, like most other NGOs active in childcare, was enmeshed in the transnational exchange of ideas and personnel.

At the turn of the millennium, these NGOs began to spearhead a policy change away from adoption and toward other forms of child placement. While most juvenile courts were still giving priority to adoption campaigns, NGOs linked to child rights began concentrating their efforts more and more on what Brazilians call *convivência familiar*, which can be loosely translated as "family living" or "family-based models" of childcare. The term itself is central to the 1990 Brazilian Children's Code, but the way it is used has changed markedly. Instead of justifying vigorous campaigns in favor of *adoption*, today the notion is applied to programs designed to help maintain children in their *original families* with the possibility of temporary care in *foster families*. Starting in 2003, international organizations of all kinds, including UNICEF, have joined hands with Brazilian academics and activists to promote four major conferences on alternatives to plenary adoption (Fonseca 2004). This policy shift remains incomplete. Fosterage is conceived only as a temporary measure. If, after receiving benefits and guidance, the birth family is unable to reassume responsibility at the end of a year, the child becomes eligible for adoption. These fosterage programs resemble those of North American adoption agencies (Leifsen 2004, 2006, Hoelgaard 1998) which are active in other Latin American countries: at the same time that they provide humanitarian relief to poor families, they help expedite the freeing of children for adoption. Other possible state-sponsored measures, tried with varying success in Europe and North America, might also be tried in Brazil: long-term fosterage, intra-family fosterage, subsidized adoptions, fostadopt programs, and open adoption. However, policies aimed at giving more heed to birth parents, facilitating adoption for lower-income families, and divesting adoption of its "as-if" aura have nowhere entered into Brazilian policy debate.

Pressures from Candidates to Adoptive Parenthood

To understand the formidable challenges facing new perspectives on childcare, we should consider a final interest group that exerts a steady influence on official policy: adoptive parents. In October 2005, around 200 people gathered in the Porto Alegre cultural center in response to an appeal broadcast in the media for volunteer "godparents," people ready to establish "affective bonds" with an institutionalized child or adolescent, receiving him or her in their home on a regular basis for weekends and holidays. The sponsor of the event was *"Amigos de Lucas,"* a local NGO in a nationwide network of *"Grupos de Apoio à Adoção"* (Adoption Support Groups) initiated by Terra dos Homens.

Amigos de Lucas takes a broad approach to the problems of institutionalized children, insisting on the now globally disseminated philosophy that adoption is aimed not at "finding a child for a family, but rather at finding a family for a child." In monthly meetings with prospective adopters, the organizers do their best to combat typical stereotypes: the ideal of a white infant, generally female, in perfect health, received soon after birth, just "as if" she or he had been born to the adoptive family. The NGO's name, "Friends of Lucas," was coined by its founders to describe the children whom their own son, a physically impaired child adopted when he was well past infancy, had left behind in the state residential home—those youngsters who, because they were dark-skinned, older, or suffered physical or emotional handicaps, were considered "unadoptable." Since 2002, this NGO, working in close cooperation with local juvenile authorities, has inaugurated a program of foster families intended to mediate on-going contact between the child and its original family and of "affective godparenthood" to enable institutionalized children to find sponsors for life beyond the orphanage. Those who responded to the public appeal for godparents ranged in age from university students to retirees, with women slightly outnumbering men. There was only one hitch: during the question and answer period, it became evident that people had come looking, not for a godchild, but for an adoptive son or daughter. Many had already entered their names on the waiting list at the juvenile court's adoption service but, tired of what they consider long waits and excessive red tape, they were seeking another channel to parenthood. The event's organizers were exasperated. They had encountered the same attitude while screening candidates for foster parenthood. These staunch, middle-class citizens wanted nothing of an arrangement that would leave them competing with other caretakers; they correlate commitment with exclusivity and were willing to take on full responsibility for a child.

During the 1990s, the judiciary conducted media campaigns to promote adoption, yet it did *not* increase. Indeed, studies suggest that intracountry adoption may even have declined.[9] Ironically, the decline may be due to the very forces that were designed to better organize legal procedures. Numerous public policies emerged during the 1990s (*bolsa família, bolsa escola, bolsa alimentação*) designed to help lower-income families maintain their offspring. Rather than summarily withdraw a child from its poverty-stricken home, social workers could try out home-based alternatives. A child might only become legally adoptable when he or she was older and less appealing to potential adopters.

The difficult dialogue I observed in Porto Alegre between NGOs and candidates for adoptive parenthood reminded me of an event I attended as a panelist in 2004 in Spain, one of Europe's most dynamic receiving countries (see Marre and Bestard 2004). This small seminar was organized by a local NGO bent on promoting discussion on various questions of adoption and childcare. A dozen specialists, several brought in from abroad, spoke to a packed auditorium filled with adoptive parents and would-be parents. Despite the varied positions of the participants, general debate seemed to underline attitudes prevalent among a certain group of adopting parents. Intercountry adoption was seen as a necessary evil, a process in which European couples, finding it difficult to adopt a child in their own country, were forced to face inefficient and corrupt Third World bureaucracies. Local authorities from the state child welfare service were repeatedly reproved for not making more children available for adoption. The general mood was that the state should remove children from "unfit" parents as quickly as possible, giving the youngsters the benefit of "real" —read, adoptive—families. Although one or two of the speakers brought up positive elements of foster care, this alternative was quickly cast aside during discussion. Most commentaries revolved around the problem of integrating newborn infants into the family. Less idealized forms of adoption, such as simple adoption, or the adoption of older or handicapped children, were scarcely addressed. Nowhere in the public debate was there any mention of the adopted children's birth parents or any questioning of the "clean break" model of plenary adoption (see Cadoret 2004).

Dissenting opinions were confined to the discreet audience of coffee-break clutches. There, I heard one young woman who had recently adopted a little girl from Haiti recounting with great emotion her two-hour encounter, arranged by the orphanage, with the child's birthmother. Although unsure as to whether or not her letters were getting through, she continued to mail this woman pictures of the little girl whose destiny they shared between them. Were she to make a suggestion to policy makers, she confided, it would be to facilitate contact. This sort of comment did not surface during the general debate. The prevailing opinion, even among experts, was that "shared motherhood," such as that described in many non-Western societies, was a utopian dream, and that "open adoption" in which, as in Haiti, birth and adoptive parents may meet under careful supervision, "would never work" in European adoptive families.[10] Ideas like those we observed in the meeting with European adoptive parents strike a chord among Brazilian adopters, and, more consequentially, among national policy makers. These perspectives make sense to the "consumers" of adoptable children—that is, adoptive parents who are almost always "foreign" in terms of nationality or class to the child's original milieu.

Final Considerations

The problem of adoption lies at the crux of children's rights and class discrimination, two emergent themes in human rights debates in Brazil. Despite this fact, intranational adoption has, until very recently, been passed over by activists. Child activists may well protest that, on the contrary, adoption has long been under scrutiny. The furor over *intercountry* adoption in Brazil, as well as many other Third World countries, did become a *cause célèbre* of innumerable politicians and activists from the 1980s on. The glaring inequality between sending and receiving families concerned in international adoption was experienced by sending countries as an affront to their national honor. Curiously enough, the same inequality implied in intranational adoptions, with the abrogation of some parents' rights in favor of the prerogatives of others, did not automatically become a problem.

It would be simplistic to suppose that inequality in the adoption field pertains only to relations between First and Third World countries. Shellee Colen (1995) reminds us that families should not be studied in isolation; they should be situated within a wider context that involves asymmetrical power relations of class as well as nationality. While in the first phase of the recent evolution of child placement in Brazil the accent was on the apparent antagonism between sending countries in the South and receiving countries in the North, the second phase highlighted Brazilian judicial authorities who, in their bid to faithfully apply international child rights principles, ended up silencing local dynamics of childcare. Finally, a new transnational influence, articulated through certain NGOs, has been designed to bring families to center stage in the hope of preventing them from becoming mere "birth" families. Ironically, the conservative adversaries of these NGOs are proving to be Brazilian, as well as foreign nationals, generally from the better-off sectors of society, clamoring for proprietary interests over the children they wish to adopt.

I close with the suggestion that it does little good to overcome stereotypes about rapacious, baby-stealing foreigners if we continue to formulate our policies in the shadow of another grotesque stereotype, that of abusive or money-grubbing birth mothers. Nonetheless, it is just such a stereotype that appears to justify the "clean break" model of plenary adoption. Here, questions of social justice concern not so much *who* takes the child in but rather *on what terms* the transfer takes place. Debates formulated in terms of simple dichotomies—foreigners versus nationals, or adoptive versus birth families—may well be diverting attention away from more pressing issues, delaying a critical reform of the child placement system as a whole in which issues of inequality and class discrimination *within* the country will finally be taken into account.

NOTES

1. In 1981–1983, I studied a squatter settlement where approximately half of the mothers I interviewed had placed a child with another family or at the state institution. From 1986 to 1988, a second field project in a less miserable, working-class neighborhood showed that about half the adult women had, at some time, taken in to raise a child who was not their own. In 1993, we videotaped interviews during fieldwork in various low-income neighborhoods in Porto Alegre; see Fonseca, Cardarello, Godolphim, and Rosa.

2. Núcleo de Antropologia e Cidadania (NACI), Programa de Pós-Graduação em Antropologia Social, Universidade Federal do Rio Grande do Sul. This research team involves both undergraduate and graduate students.

3. Leon Schwartzemberg's statements were reported on in local and national papers in Brazil. See, for example, *Zero Hora* (Porto Alegre), 6 October 1993, 45.

4. *Folha de Sao Paulo*, 13 August 1994.

5. *Folha de Sao Paulo,* 3 August 1994.
6. *Folha de Sao Paulo,* 30 August 1994.
7. For contrasting examples of Ecuador and Guatemala, see Leifsen 2006 and Briggs 2007.
8. Information gathered from the organization's website, http://www.terredes hommes.asso.fr/faq.htm (accessed 6 May 2008).
9. See, for example, *Folha de São Paulo,* 27 March 2004; Caderno and Cotidiano 2004.
10. For European examples that contradict this generalization, see Yngvesson 2000, Cadoret 1995.

REFERENCES

Abreu, Domingo. 2002. *No Bico da Cegonha: Histórias de adoção e da adoção internacional no Brasil.* Rio de Janeiro: Relume Dumará.

Berlinguer, Giovanni, and Volnei Garrafa. 1996. *O Mercado Humano: Estudo bioético da compra e venda de partes do corpo.* Brasília: Editora Universidade de Brasília.

Bowie, Fiona. 2004. "Adoption and the Circulation of Children: A Comparative Perspective." In *Cross-Cultural Approaches to Adoption,* ed. Fiona Bowie, 3–20. New York: Routledge.

Briggs, Laura. 2007. "Body Snatchers and Homeless Waifs: Contesting Reproduction and Negotiating U.S. Foreign Policy in Transnational Adoption." Paper presented at the University of Michigan, 1 November.

Cadoret, Anne. 1995. *Parenté Plurielle: Anthropologie du placement familial.* Paris: Harmattan.

———. 2004. "Pluriparentesco y família de referencia." In *La adopción y el acogimiento: Presente y perspectives,* ed. Diana Marre and Joan Bestard, 273–82. Barcelona: Universitat de Barcelona.

Cardarello, Andrea D. L. 1998. "A transformação de internamento 'assistencial' em internamento por 'negligência': Tirando a cidadania dos pais para dá-la às crianças." *Ensaios FEE* 19, no. 2: 306–30.

Cardoso, Ruth. 1984. "Creating Kinship: The Fostering of Children in Favela Families in Brazil." In *Kinship Ideology and Practice in Latin America,* ed. Raymond T. Smith, 196–203. Chapel Hill: University of North Carolina Press.

Colen, Shellee. 1995. "'Like a Mother to Them': Stratified Reproduction and West Indian Childcare Workers and Employers in New York." In *Conceiving the New World Order: The Global Politics of Reproduction,* ed. Faye D. Ginsburg and Rayna Rapp, 78–102. Berkeley: University of California Press.

Colton, M. J., and Margaret Williams. 1997. *The World of Foster Care: An International Sourcebook on Foster Family Care Systems.* Brookfield, VT: Arena.

Fonseca, Claudia. 2002a. "An Unexpected Reversal: Charting the Course of International Adoption in Brazil." *Adoption and Fostering Journal* 26, no. 3: 28–39.

———. 2002b. "The Politics of Adoption: Child Rights in the Brazilian Setting." *Law & Policy* 24, no. 3: 199–227.

———. 2003. "Patterns of Shared Parenthood among the Brazilian Poor." *Social Text* (special issue on "Transnational Adoption," ed. Toby Volkman and Cindi Katz) 21, no. 1: 111–27.

———. 2004. "The Circulation of Children in a Brazilian Working-Class Neighborhood: A Local Practice in a Globalized World." In *Cross-Cultural Approaches to Adoption,* ed. Fiona Bowie, 165–81. London: Routledge.

Fonseca, Claudia, Andrea Cardarello, Nuno Godolphim, and Rogério Rosa. 1994. "Ciranda, Cirandinha: Histórias de circulação de crianças em grupos populares." Video produced by PPGAS UFRGS, Laboratório de Antropologia Social.

Ginsburg, Faye D., and Rayna Rapp (eds.). 1995. *Conceiving the New World Order: The Global Politics of Reproduction.* Berkeley: University of California Press.

Goldstein, Donna. 1997. "Nothing Bad Intended: Child Discipline, Punishment, and Survival in a Shantytown in Rio De Janeiro, Brazil." In *Small Wars: The Cultural Politics of Childhood,* ed. Nancy Scheper-Hughes and Carolyn Sargent, 389–415. Berkeley: University of California Press.

Grotevant, Harold D. and Ruth G. McRoy. 1998. *Openness in Adoption: Exploring Family Connections.* London: Sage.

The Hague. 2000. *Report and Conclusions of the Special Commission on the Practical Operation of the Hague Convention of 29 May 1993 on Protection of Children and Co-operation in Respect of Intercountry Adoption.* 28 November–1 December.

Hecht, Tobias. 1998. *At Home in the Street: Street Children of Northeast Brazil.* Cambridge: Cambridge University Press.

Hoelgaard, Suzanne. 1998. "Cultural Determinants of Adoption Policy: A Colombian Case Study." *International Journal of Law, Policy, and the Family* 12, no. 1: 202–401.

Kane, Saralee. 1993. "The Movement of Children for International Adoption: An Epidemiologic Perspective." *Social Science Journal* 30, no. 4: 323–39.

Kuznesof, Elizabeth Anne. 1998. "The Puzzling Contradictions of Child Labor, Unemployment, and Education in Brazil." *Journal of Family History* 23, no. 3: 225–39.

Leifsen, Esben. 2004. "Person, Relation and Value: The Economy of Circulating Ecuadorian Children in International Adoption." In *Cross-Cultural Approaches to Adoption,* ed. Fiona Bowie, 182–96. London: Routledge.

———. 2006. "Moralities and Politics of Belonging: Governing Female Reproduction in 20th Century Quito." Ph.D. diss., Social Anthropology, University of Oslo, Norway.

Marcus, George. 1998. *Ethnography through Thick and Thin.* Princeton, NJ: Princeton University Press.

Marre, Diana, and Joan Bestard (eds.). 2004. *La adoptción y el acogimiento: Presente y perspectives.* Barcelona: Universitat de Barcelona, Estudis d'ántropologia Social i Cultural, 13.

Modell, Judith Schachter. 1994. *Kinship with Strangers: Adoption and Interpretations of Kinship in American Culture.* Berkeley: University of California Press.

———. 1998. "Rights to the Children: Foster Care and Social Reproduction in Hawai'i." In *Reproducing Reproduction: Kinship, Power, and Technological Innovation,* ed. Sarah Franklin and Helena Ragoné, 156–72. Philadelphia: University of Pennsylvania Press.

Pantaleón, Jorge. 2002. "Antropologia, desenvolvimento e organizações nãogovernamentais na América Latina." In *Antropologia, Impérios e Estados Nacionais,* ed. Benoît de l'Estoile, Federico Neiburg, Lygia Sigaud, 235–51. Rio de Janeiro: Relume Dumará.

Peirano, Mariza. 1992. *Uma antropologia no plural: Três experiências contemporâneas.* Brasilia: Editora UnB.

Selman, Peter. 2004. "Adoption: A Cure for (Too) Many Ills?" In *Cross-Cultural Approaches to Adoption,* ed. Fiona Bowie, 257–73. London: Routledge.

da Silva, Enid Rocha Andrade (ed.). 2004. *O Direito à Convivência Familiar e Comunitária: Os Abrigos para Crianças e Adolescentes no Brasil.* Brasília: Instituto de Pesquisas em Educação Aplicada.

Uriarte Bálsamo, Pilar. 2005. *Substituindo famílias: Continuidades e rupturas na prática de acolhimento familiar intermediada pelo estado em Porto Alegre, 1946/2003.* M.A. thesis, Anthropology, Universidade Federal do Rio Grande do Sul.

Yngvesson, Barbara. 2000. "'Un niño de cualquier color': Race and Nation in Intercountry Adoption." In *Globalizing Institutions: Case Studies in Regulation and Innovation,* ed. Jane Jensen and Boaventura de Souza Santos, 247–305. Aldershot, UK: Ashgate.

———. 2003. "Going 'Home': Adoption, Loss of Bearings, and the Mythology of Roots." *Social Text* (special issue on "Transnational Adoption," ed. Toby Volkman and Cindi Katz) 21, no. 1: 7–28.

———. 2004. "National Bodies and the Body of the Child: 'Completing' Families through International Adoption." In *Cross-Cultural Approaches to Adoption,* ed. Fiona Bowie, 211–26. London: Routledge.

Chapter 9

||||||||||||||||||||||||||||||||||||||||||||||||||||||||||

International Adoption in Russia
"Market," "Children for Organs," and "Precious" or "Bad" Genes

Lilia Khabibullina

From the point of view of international adopters, Russia is a significant sending country. Yet the foreign adoption of Russian children has seldom been studied and the Russian context remains unknown, as is true of many sending countries. Children adopted from Russia to Western Europe and the United States are invisible because of their European looks; indeed, the popularity of Russian children might be explained in part by the "racial" preferences of adoptive parents. Within Russia, however, international adoption is controversial, and the rules and regulations governing the practice have been made stricter as a consequence of several notorious violations of Russian law. Cases of child abuse, murder, rape, forgery of legal documents, and child trafficking have been associated with international adoption; in some cases foreign adoptive parents and representatives of adoption agencies were involved. Children in transnational adoption are frequently seen as objects of commodification, available for a price that only wealthy parents can afford. In receiving countries, market transactions are often hidden under a rhetoric of "the gift" (Modell 2002, Fonseca 2004, Leifsen 2004) and discourses about "saving" children. Russians resist market terminology, regarding it as imposed by the West. National media discourse is framed by a rhetoric of "losing genofund"—the valuable genetic information embodied in the whole population of the nation.[1]

International adoptions from Russia began in 1991 during *perestroika*, as a result of the opening of the "Iron Curtain" and the difficult economic situation. Increasing numbers of children were abandoned because of poor economic conditions. During 1991–1992, 578 of 25,000 abandoned children were adopted by foreigners (Sargeant 1996). According to statistics kept by the Russian Ministry of Education and Science, which deals with both international and domestic adoptions, the number of international adoptions rose from 5,647 in 1998 to 9,419 in 2004. More Russian "orphans" were adopted by foreign citizens than by Russian nationals that year (59 percent versus 41 percent).[2] This fact aroused serious concern among Russian authorities. According to the most recent statistics from May 2006, the proportion of adoptions by Russian nationals has increased and that by foreigners has decreased.[3] The rise in intranational adoptions was prompted primarily by stricter regulations on international adoptions, along with several moratoriums in 2005. Still, the number of children in state care is higher than the number of adoptions by Russian nationals and foreign citizens. According to 2006 statistics, Russia has 800,000 children without parental care, 68 percent of whom are in foster homes. The other 32 percent, more than 260,000 children, are in orphanages. Russian children adopted abroad go to the United States (26 percent), Spain (17 percent), and Italy (8 percent), followed by a variety of other countries.[4]

Scandals Involving the Abuse of Children Adopted Internationally

In Russia, the image of adoption in general and international adoption in particular is quite negative. Heated debates appeared in the Russian media after notorious cases of child abuse, mostly in the United States. Strict new measures were introduced after two-year-old David Polreis was beaten to death by his adoptive American mother, Rene Polreis, in 1996. Between 2000 and 2005, two or three murders of adopted children were discussed in the media each year, involving eight boys and four girls ranging in age from one to eight years. Small children were beaten, thrown, or dropped, or adoptive parents claimed that they died accidentally; the parents were convicted only of negligent homicide or involuntary manslaughter. In a notorious case, six-year-old Viktor Matthey was kept in an unheated basement room and severely beaten. His parents were sentenced to 27 years in prison for confining Viktor, inflicting excessive corporal punishment, and failing to provide medical care for him. Liam Thompson, aged three, was placed in a tub of scalding water, burned, and then not given medical care; his parents received 15 years in prison. Dennis (Uritski) Merrymen was starved to death. The accused parents often defended themselves by arguing that, rather than being harmed while in their care, their adopted children had preexisting medical conditions. All of these cases were prosecuted in the United States because the adopted children were U.S. citizens.[5] There were several cases of rape and child trafficking in 2005. In Pennsylvania, adoptive father Matthew Alan Mancuso was convicted of incest and the rape of his twelve-year-old daughter adopted from Russia. He had placed photos of the adopted girl on pornographic websites and raped her repeatedly.[6] The Verbitzkaya case concerned the selling of children born by underage girls and the forgery of documents in a so-called surrogate mother program.[7] In January 2006, "child traffickers" were discovered in Russia associated with an adoption agency; Alexei Geiko, the subject of the notorious Pavlis case involving organ donation, was adopted through this agency.[8]

Although most of these cases occurred in the United States, where the majority of Russian adoptees go, an important case of child trafficking involved Italy, where between 7 and 9 percent go. Nadezhda Fratti, a former resident of Russia and also a citizen of Italy, represented the Italian adoption agency Arcobaleno and helped Italians get children faster and more efficiently in exchange for considerable sums of money. The legal prosecution of this case took many years and was conducted in Russia, since Fratti had dual citizenship. Initially she was acquitted because of lack of evidence, but she was finally convicted in 2001. In 2005 there was a case of child abuse by Italian adoptive parents: Kirill Pushkin was beaten on the plane, arousing international attention. He was taken to a Russian hospital and his adoptive parents had to go to court. In the end, though, Kirill was returned to his adoptive parents.[9]

The demand for Russian children in the international adoption market has stimulated many projects that aim to promote national adoption, fostering, and assistance for children. The Ministry of Education and Science offers detailed information and support for Russian prospective parents. An extensive website offers legal information and the necessary forms, as well as a history of adoption and an explanation of the differences between fosterage and adoption. The site includes a data bank of children available for adoption that can be sorted by criteria such as sex, age, location, sets of siblings, and availability for adoption or fosterage. In a section for sharing experiences, several relinquishment stories contrast intranational and international adoptions. Others tell of children who were relinquished for international adoption without the knowledge of their parents, who had left them in orphanages temporarily. Some biological mothers seem incapable of taking care of children because of bad economic conditions and lack of governmental support. The conflict between poverty and wealth pervades debates about adoption.

Although in Spain adoptions from Russia and Ukraine are presented as chaotic, or even illegal (Marre 2008), the Russian media present international adoption as a highly formalized legal process that is violated by foreign adoptive parents and intermediaries. The majority of articles on international adoption describe cases of abuse and murder in legal terminology. For the Fratti case of child trafficking, for example, the headlines in *Newsru* read: "More than 600 Russian children were illegally adopted to Italy"; "In Volgograd they will judge criminals who sold Russian orphans."[10]

The articles focus primarily on Americans' murder of Russian children and violations of Russian law. Headlines proclaim: "U.S. woman faces capital punishment for killing Russian boy";[11] "American family starves to death an 8-year-old boy adopted in Russia."[12] Sometimes the term "death" is used more neutrally: "Russian prosecutors request information from U.S. on death of adopted girl."[13] Usually the term "murder" or "killing" is emphasized: "Russian orphan killed in U.S. adopted illegally";[14] "Russian girl killed in U.S. was adopted legally."[15] The dichotomy between legal and illegal adoptions is highlighted by the Russian media. After discovering that a child has been killed, Russian officials tried to find out whether the adoption agency had a valid accreditation; if there were intermediaries; if bribes were involved; and if the interests of Russian parents were protected. Debates about the legality of the adoption were central in the Pavlis and Hilt cases; Nina Hilt's adoption was presented as legal by I. Belasheva and as illegal in *MosNews*.[16]

International Adoption Promoting as a Market in Children

International adoption is presented as "a gray market" (Modell 2002: 147) surrounded by bribes, intermediaries, and noncompliance with the law. Yet Russian law is presented as solid rather than malleable. The interests of the child are rarely mentioned in public debate. Instead, the interests of the state are central. The state's laws are being violated: "Foreign adoption agencies often break Russian laws—prosecutor";[17] "Prosecutor's Office comes to grips with child adoption legislation abuse."[18] The interests of Russian potential parents are also presented as violated. The media refer specifically to the right of local parents to adopt guaranteed by the Hague Convention; for example, recently a case of vacations abroad for orphans was suspected of violating Russian foster parents' right of first choice.[19]

The exchange of money and the application of market terminology is a contested issue. As Viviana Zelizer says: "Pricing the priceless child therefore became a complex task, creating confusion in legal thought and practice, controversy in the insurance business, and uncertainty in the 'exchange' of adoptive children. New sentimental criteria were established to determine the monetary worth of child life" (1994: 210). Margaret Jane Radin's radical idea of a domino effect might be applied to the Russian context: as soon as a price is attached to a child, one domino falls, and then another, until nothing is left standing. The knowledge of the price contaminates the adoption experience, even if a price was not paid but only known. Commodification seems to "fail to treat children as persons, to make them all realize that they have a definite commercial value, and that this is all their value amounts to, even if their parents did not choose to sell them or did not obtain them by purchase" (Radin 1996: 100). Esben Leifsen argues that both the rhetoric of the "gift" and "commodification" usually coexist in the process of adoption. In international adoption, "The child could be given up by its birthparents or relatives involuntarily and in despair, or be given away voluntarily motivated by hopes for a better future for the child, or simply out of indifference. It could be handed over by temporal caregivers in an act of altruism, objectified and even commodified in the process by bureaucrats and agencies' representatives, and received by the adoptive parents as a desired gift" (2004: 192).

Russians' negative attitudes toward market terminology developed under socialism, and the media began to apply commercial terms to international adoptions in the 1990s during the transition to a market economy. In the earliest article, called "Children for export," journalist J. Nikolaeva used market language and identified a minimum price ($4,000) that U.S. citizens paid to adopt.[20] The phrase "children for export" recurs in later debates.[21] The Russian media is sharply critical of the market in children, describing it with such negative adjectives as "disgusting."

An article titled "Russia's Orphans Sold to the Highest Bidders" published in *MosNews* during the Pavlis scandal elaborated:

> [The] Pavlis case is playing into the hands of small dealers of Russia's not so much most monstrous, but rather most unpleasant market—*the child trade market*. This market's turnover is easy to imagine. The adoption industry in the United States is a market of $3.5–$4 billion annually. In the United States an adoption costs $4,000–$30,000 plus unlimited sums spent on the so-called adoption agency: the costs can reach $15,000–$150,000. As for international adoption, the NAIC states the average amounts that foster parents have to spend. In the United States official costs make up about $1,000. The rest—$7,000–$25,000—you can pay to a licensed adoption agent. Another option that U.S. adoption websites call "additional expenses on individual child search" is to pay the money straight to someone in Guatemala or Russia who helps you find a child.[22]

Despite his own discomfort with the market, Butrin describes the logic of foreign adoption in business terms. He refers to the Pavlis case as a "cheap deal": instead of using expensive adoption agencies, Pavlis "turned to private assistance" and got two children that "cost them $11,000. This was clear dumping; usually to adopt a single Russian child costs $10,000–15,000." Butrin's main argument is "that Russian parents are deprived of their rights to be the first in the adoption of Russian-born kids and have to wait on waiting lists, while those who can buy—buy." Adoption in Russia is "free of charge: the state doesn't sell parentless children; you only have to pay the necessary charges defined by the law." Russian law specifically forbids profiting from adoptions, although adoptive parents from abroad are seldom aware of this fact.

Market terms are seen as imposed by the West, and adoption practice is seen as contaminated by the foreign market. Russian commentators generally believe that children became commodified with the emergence of international adoption. Adoption agencies are described as active dealers in this process: "There's a huge number of foreign agencies from most European countries operating here . . . and around 90 from the U.S.," said Vladimir Ustinov, the prosecutor general. "They're turning adoption into a market. Cases of inhuman treatment of Russian children by foreign citizens are frequent."[23] Stories about domestic adoptions describe children as individuals, detailing their talents, character, and expectations, as well as how they became separated from their biological parents, but never mentioning a price. In contrast, stories about Western adoptive parents often mention the price they paid for children. In *El Pais*'s "Generación Importada," every story begins with a price.[24] In some cases, the child's personal characteristics are explained in an attempt to prove that it was "worth spending money" on them.

The fact that a price is paid for children does not serve to protect their interests. This problem is evident in the case of Nadezhda Fratti, the Russian-Italian intermediary who organized "illegal" adoptions for a fee of around $2,500 per child. Fratti, aged forty-seven, formerly lived in the town of Volzhsky, close to the city of Volgograd in southern Russia. She returned to her hometown in 1993. Though she set herself up as a translator, she was in fact representing an Italian adoption agency, Arcobaleno, based in the northern Italian city of Padua. Over ten years in this business, Fratti sent several hundred children from the Volgograd region to Italy. Fratti has been charged with bribing officials and forging documents in order to accelerate the adoption of Russian children by foreigners.[25] The Fratti case was widely discussed in the Russian media as a criminal matter. Because "trafficking" does not have a synonym in Russian, she and the intermediaries were called "traders of children," but the terms "illegal adoption" and "illegal removal from Russia" predominated. Italians were quite reluctant to pursue the case and thought that Fratti had good intentions for orphaned children. *La Repubblica*, the Italian daily, reported that she herself was an orphan who was adopted and quoted her as saying that she knew "in her heart the best thing for abandoned children."[26] If Fratti had worked without payment, perhaps her charitable sentiments would have been appreciated. In some cases, foreign adoption is presented as a "gift of life" for Russian children with serious medical problems."[27] In the dominant discourse, however, adoptive parents are presented as "hunters for orphans" and their work to "save children" is not appreciated because of fears caused by connecting children and money.

The fate of many children remains unknown. The secrecy that surrounds adoptions, which offers opportunities to intermediaries, also creates uncertainty. In the wake of numerous stories of child abuse in the Russian media, people fear for the children. "A Russian television documentary on the Volgograd scandal . . . will demand to know what has happened to the 600 children, and imply that they have fallen into 'bad hands,' though there is no evidence of anything untoward happening to any of the 600-plus children involved in the Fratti case."²⁸ The language is curiously littered with "might" and "could be"; sometimes the process is described as a "lottery."

Rumors of Selling Children for Organs

The media circulates speculations about the mysterious fates of children after foreign adoption. Fears surrounded the Fratti case: "Nadezhda Fratti organised the export of over one thousand children from Russia to different countries of the world. The problem is that the majority of the children cannot be tracked down by police in different countries. It cannot be ruled out that some of the children were sent to San Remo establishments for rich pedophiles. The children could have been also used for transplantation operations."²⁹ These fantasies gained plausibility because there were cases in which adopted children were raped and exploited in pornography. "When one thinks about the scandalous case, one becomes terrified with the facts of the alleged adoptions. Nadezhda Fratti earned about $1.5 million from the illegal adoption of Russian children. Practically the same sum was spent for bribes to different officials, but, to tell the truth, no money can make up for the damaged children's fates. Often, the children were secretly transported abroad, even regardless of the fact that relatives in Russia wanted to adopt them."³⁰

The extreme case of "commodification" is the rumor that children are being stolen from poor countries and sold for their organs in rich ones. Doing research in Brazil in the 1980s, Nancy Scheper-Hughes found a persistent rumor circulating in impoverished shantytowns about babies being kidnapped and their organs taken for transplantation; later she discovered that the same rumor circulated elsewhere in South and Central America and in Africa. She explains that the rumor "confused the market in 'spare babies' for international adoption with the market in 'spare parts' for transplant surgery. Poor and semiliterate parents, tricked or intimidated into surrendering their babies for domestic and/or international adoption, imagined that their babies were wanted as fodder for transplant surgery. The rumour condensed the black markets for organs and babies into a single frightening story" (2000: 202).

This rumor was so powerful that it influenced attitudes toward international adoptions on a national level in Brazil. Allegations of "baby farms" and "fattening houses" in Guatemala, Honduras, Mexico, and Brazil, where newborns were said to be housed awaiting transport to the United States (sometimes via Paraguay) for use as organ donors, were investigated by various authorities and roundly denied (Sheper-Hughes 2000). But that did not prevent their wide circulation and the popular credence given to them. Along with her colleagues from Bellagio Task Force on Organ Transplantation, Bodily Integrity, and the International Traffic in Organs, Scheper-Hughes found the organ-stealing rumor circulating in China, South Africa, Brazil, and India and some verifications of it.

Scheper-Hughes interprets the rumor as an expression of the fear and resentment felt among poor people in the global South against rich nations in the global North, but the same interpretation might be applied to Russians in relation to Western Europeans and Americans. The rumor surfaced in Poland and Russia, where it was reported that poor children's organs were being sold to rich Arabs for spare parts. Rumors of stealing babies for spare parts circulate persistently in the Russian media. Scheper-Hughes's question can be asked in the Russian context: What does it mean when many people around the world begin to tell variants of the same bizarre story? How do we interpret the social imaginary of impoverished people in poor countries—and of Russians in relation to Western Europe and the United States?

In Russia, the organ-stealing rumor is often connected with international adoption. The majority of articles on international adoptions indicate that children might be used "for transplants." For example, the media reported that: "The investigation also has another version pertaining to Fratti's case but luckily it does not have any grounds yet. It is supposed Fratti sent several kids to Italy to be used as 'spare parts'—their internal organs were sold, so to speak. It should be stressed here again that this is only a version and nothing more—it has not been proven yet. Conclusions in this case can be drawn only after the fate of each adopted child is clear."[31] These reservations were hardly reassuring, especially as the children's fates could never be ascertained. In another article, the same journalist alleged that "the children could have been also used for transplantation operations. This conclusion comes from the fact that Nadezhda Fratti purposefully picked out mentally retarded but perfectly healthy children."[32] Adoptions of mentally ill or physically disabled children aroused particular suspicion because Russians can hardly imagine that anyone would choose to adopt a child with disabilities.

Stories about the murder of Alex Pavlis were accompanied by numerous details regarding organ trafficking. The headlines created confusion about whether the organs of this Russian child who was murdered by his adoptive American mother were taken from him after or before his death, which fueled the hysteria about trafficking adoptive children for organs. Scheper-Hughes notes that some confusion arises because of the ambiguity of "brain death" as a prerequisite for organ donation. The Russian media expresses suspicion about the harvesting of organs after brain death, especially when members of stigmatized groups are involved. In one case, doctors were charged with taking organs from a person who was still alive; the person had suffered brain death, but according to Russian law only "biological death" is acceptable for organ donation.[33] Under such headlines as "Organs of Alex Pavlis were used for business" and "Organs of Russian boy were taken for transplants," the articles explain that some of his organs were harvested, but do not specify when they were taken, which deepened the mystery. The presentation is deliberately ambiguous, suggesting that Alex may have died as a result of the removal of his organs.[34]   .

"Precious" or "Bad" Genes

Stories about biological mothers who cannot afford to keep their children and rich foreigners who can buy them present international adoption as an unequal transaction between the rich and poor. Unfortunately, patterns of international adoption are seldom reciprocal. In Russia, biological mothers are stigmatized and have fewer rights than their counterparts in Spain. On the other side, adoptive families are afraid of biological parents and international adoption is a comfortable way to avoid them. In a society where everything can be bought, children are becoming commodities that have price and are even advertised in catalogues.

Although in some countries children without parents are treated as "national treasures" (Yngvesson 2004), in Russia the dominant discourse is less economic and more nationalistic, or even biologized: children are seen as part of the genofund. During the 1990s, debates about international adoption were framed negatively by the problem of "losing genofund" and positively by the importance of a "family for a child" (Sargeant 1996). While the positive view emphasized the importance of parents, the negative view centered on the motherland, contending that it is better to die in one's own country than to live in "a country of enemies."[35] The history of the tense relationship between Russia and the United States must be taken into consideration, since the main receiving country from 1991 on was the United States.

Although the term genofund is often used in Russian public discourse, it does not have a fixed definition. A project that calls itself "Russian genofund" concentrates on studying Russians' DNA, but also includes investigations of typical Russian surnames and physiognomy. In public discourse, the term is used more loosely. One of the interpretations of "losing genofund" is the nationalist idea that precious Russian genes are going abroad. It is assumed that Russians have genius in their genes, as Russia has a great culture. If future Russian geniuses go abroad, the nation is diminished.[36] Those who have a positive attitude toward international adoptions criticize the notion of "losing genofund" as false patriotism or xenophobia. I suggest that in "genofund discourse" the figure of a mother is replaced by the "motherland" and the figure of a father is replaced by the state.

Potential Russian parents are preoccupied with genetics in a different sense. Adoption websites are full of supposedly genetic information about the children available for adoption. Potential parents are worried about "bad genes" or "bad inheritance." On a specialized website connected with *7ya* (*Family*), a popular TV program that carries information, debates, and recommendations about adoption, the medical information is exclusively devoted to genetic inheritance and what diseases could be passed on; only two articles discuss acquired conditions such as HIV, anemia, and skin problems.[37] While some explain that the "bad inheritance" usually associated with adopted children has no basis in reality, the other studies seek to show connections among genes, behavior, and intellect, for example, trying to prove the existence of genes for criminality or intelligence; some of them have taken adopted children as objects of research. In general, the accent is on parents' ability to create a "secure environment" for the child.[38]

The theme of "bad genes" is central to many national adoption stories. One woman who had a failed adoption advised others to think carefully before accepting a child for adoption because "you cannot divorce a child"; she "could not return" her adopted daughter Tatiana, who came to her at the age of nine. Under the headline of "Alien Genes," she explains Tatiana's "sexual pathology": first the girl complained that her adoptive father tried to rape her; then she organized a striptease show in the house; finally, she got pregnant at the age of fourteen. A doctor the mother contacted replied:

"What do you want? God only knows what kind of inheritance she has." It seems that biological children in these situations might be forgiven. Tatiana's adoptive mother "couldn't love her" and wanted to give her back, but she was already eighteen. When the article was written, the adoptive mother was living in fear of her adopted daughter because "her house is like a whorehouse now."[39] In order to avoid the problem with "genes," alternative forms of child placement, such as fosterage, are promoted.

The debate about international and national adoptions in Russia is not only medicalized but also geneticized. Negative attitudes toward international adoptions are articulated as "losing genofund," and negative attitudes toward intranational adoption are expressed by "bad inheritance." In relation to international adoptions, Russian children are seen as precious, irreplaceable, and full of potential for the "motherland." On a national level, the other genetic discourse emphasizes the possible inherited defects of adopted children and the connections between adoption and disease. Two different genetic discourses are used for the same children in two different contexts.

The Russian media treat international adoption negatively, as a "criminal deed" surrounded by people who want to make money on it. The market discourse undermines the positive image of international adoptions. Russians display a certain resistance to market terminology, which is seen as imposed by the West when children are commodified in international adoption practices. Their fates remain unknown, so they might be sold for their organs. In crossing the border, children lose their completeness and bodily integrity along with their motherland and become transformed into body parts and commodities. In national discourses, by contrast, these children are presented as "precious genofund." There is a clear contradiction between "genius genes" that are being lost, from one side, and the stigmatized "bad genes" inherited by the children of alcoholics and drug addicts, from the other side. Russian adopted children who are seen by Russian adoptive parents as ugly ducklings are magically turned into beautiful swans when they leave the country. However, not all became beautiful swans—surely not those who were "killed" or "returned." Some may feel like the adult adoptee interviewed by Judith Schachter Modell (2002), who saw herself as the ugly ducking growing up in a family of beautiful swans. In both market and genetic discourses, unfortunately, the child is objectified and the personal fates of children are not the central concern.

ACKNOWLEDGMENTS

This chapter was written with the support of the Project of the Ministry of Education and Science of Spain, MEC R&D project SEJ 2006–2009 15286, "Transnational Adoption: Familial and Social Integration of the Internationally Adopted Child. Interdisciplinary and Comparative Perspectives," whose principal investigator is Diana Marre.

NOTES

1. The term "genofund," which is common in Russia and the adjacent republics, was originally used to describe the reservoir of genetic information in a territory's native species of animals and plants and was later extended to its human population. The accent was initially on biodiversity, but the term can carry racialized notions of genetic superiority. Its application to international adoption points to the differential outcomes of the process, as the sending country's resources are diminished while those of the receiving country are enriched. See "Russian Genofund Project: Genogeographic Study of Genofund of Eurasia," at http://genofond. ru/about.asp?site_id=1582&part_id=1001&module_id=1051 (accessed 15 September 2005).

2. "Ministry of Education and Science Internet Project," at http://www. usynovite.ru/documents/federal/legislative/familycodex/ (accessed 15 September 2005). In Russia, as in many other countries, children who are legally classified as "orphans" may have living parents, but their parents have been unable to care for them.

3. D. Tokareva, "In Many Regions of the Russian Federation, Russian Citizens Adopt More Children Than Foreigners Do—First Official Data from the Ministry of Science," *ITAR-TASS*, 25 May 2006, at http://www.ami-tass.ru/article/9229.html (accessed 26 May 2006).

4. Russian Ministry of Education and Science 2005.

5. For details of these cases, see "Russian Adoption Murders," at http:// adoption.about.com/od/adoptionrights/p/russiancases.htm (accessed 20 September 2005). See also "Russian Orphan Killed in U.S. Adopted Illegally—Ministry of Education," 19 July 2005, *MosNews*, at http:///www.mosnews.com/2005/07/19/ ninavictoria.shtml (accessed 15 September 2005); "Russian Prosecutors Investigating Adoption Procedure of Boy Who Died in US from Starvation," *Newsfrom-Russia*, 5 August 2005, at http://newsfromrussia.com/accidents/2005/08/05/61058. html (accessed 15 September 2005).

6. "Adopted Russian Girl Sees Father Convicted in Child Porn Case," *Mos-News*, 24 August 2005, at http://www.mosnews.com/news/2005/08/24/childabuse. shtml (accessed 19 January 2006).

7. J. Dychovny, "Crackdown on Illicit Baby Trade," *MigNews*, 22 December 2005, at http://mignews.com.ua/en/article_print/190092/html (accessed 17 October 2006).

8. D. Butrin, "Russia's Orphans Sold to the Highest Bidders," *MosNews*, 18 April 2005, at http://www.mosnews.com/commentary/2005/04/18/adoption.shtml (accessed 19 January 2006).

9. I. Budarina, "Save Pushkin," *Mir Aeroflota* 13, no. 109: 12.

10. *Newsru*, 18 February 2001, at http://www.newsru.com/russia/18feb2001/d_n_print.html; 16 April 2001, at http://www.newsru.com/crime/16apr2001/fratti_print.html (all accessed 17 October 2005).

11. *RIA Novosti*, 15 April 2005, at http://newsfromrussia.com/world/2005/04/15/59153.html (accessed 24 January 2006).

12. I. Parfinenko, *Pravda*, 8 August 2005, at http://english.pravda.ru/printed.html?news_id=15939 (accessed 18 January 2006).

13. *MosNews*, 17 July 2005, at http://www.mosnews.com/news/2005/07/19/nina victoria.shtml (accessed 15 September 2005).

14. Ibid.

15. I. Belasheva, *Vremya Novostei*, 11 July 2005, at http://newsfromrussia.com/usa/2005/07/11/60568.html (accessed 24 January 2006).

16. Contrast Belasheva, *Vremya Novostei*, 11 July 2005, with *MosNews*, 19 July 2005, at http://www.mosnews.com/news/2005/07/19/ninavictoria.shtml, and 10 July 2005, at http://www.mosnews.2005/07/10/ninavictoria.shtml (accessed 15 and 24 September 2005).

17. *MosNews*, 24 May 2005, at http://www.mosnews.com/news/2005/05/24/adoptagents.shtml (accessed 24 January 2006).

18. *Rian*, 24 June 2005, at http://en.rian.ru/society/20050624/40758756.html (accessed 2 September 2005).

19. M. Lamcov, "Hunting for Orphans," *AIF* 14 (1119), 3 April 2002, at http://www.aif.ru/online/aif/1119/12_01 (accessed 17 October 2005).

20. J. Nikolaeva, "Children for Export," *AIF* 13, April 1999, at http://www.aif.ru:81/oldsite/968/art010.html (accessed 18 January 2006). This total included medical care and surgery, since many children had been relinquished because they needed medical attention.

21. T. Bonich, "Ah, Mama, Only If I Could Find You . . . ," *AIF* 9 (253), 15 May 2003, at http://www.aif.ru/online/dochki/253/16_01 (accessed 30 March 2006).

22. D. Butrin, "Russia's Orphans Sold to the Highest Bidders," 18 *MosNews*, April 2005, at http://www.mosnews.com/commentary/2005/04/18/adoption.shtml (accessed 19 January 2006).

23. I. Traynor and R. Carrol, "Police Raids Uncover 'Orphans for Sale' Racket," *Guardian Saturday*, 24 February 2001, at http://www.guardian.co.uk/Archive/Article/0,4273,4141449,00.html (accessed 17 October 2006).

24. L. Sanchez-Mellado, *El Pais*, 12 December 2004, at http://www.iespana.es/adoptaenrusia/elpais121204.html? (accessed 14 April 2005).

25. "The Attorney General's Office Investigates the Matter about the Illegal Removal of Orphans to Italy," *Newsru*, 27 March 2001, at http://www.newsru.com/crime/27mar2001/fratti_print.htm (accessed 17 September 2005); "Volgo-grad Law Court Transferred Hearings on the Case about the Removal of Rus-sian Children to Italy," *Newsru*, 16 December 2002, at http://www.newsru.com/russia/16dec2002/fratti_print.html (accessed 17 September 2005); "Defendants Plead Not Guilty of Illegal Kids Trafficking to Italy," *Newsru*, 30 December 2002, at http://all.newsfromrussia.com/society/2002/12/30/41537_.html (accessed 17 October 2006); "Italian Nadezhda Fratti Got a Sentence of 7 Years for Ille-gal Adoption of Russian Children," *Newsru*, 30 December 2002, at http://www.newsru.com/russia/30dec2002/sud_print.html (accessed 17 September 2005); "Italian Woman Guilty of Adoption Bribery," *Guardian*, 31 December 2002, at http://society.guardian.co.uk/intercountryadoption/story/0,8150,866994,00.html (accessed 15 September 2005); "The Supreme Court RF Refused to Overturn the Sentence of Nadezhda Fratti, Who Illegally Exported 558 Children from Russia," *Newsru*, 17 April 2003, at http://www.newsru.com/russia/17apr2003/fratti_print.html (accessed 17 September 2005).

26. Traynor and Carrol, "Police Raids Uncover 'Orphans for Sale' Racket," *Guardian Saturday*, 24 February 2001.

27. Lamcov, "Hunting for Orphans," *AIF* 14 (1119), 3 April 2002.

28. Traynor and Carrol, "Police Raids Uncover 'Orphans for Sale' Racket," *Guardian Saturday*, 24 February 2001.

29. A. Cherkasov, "Fratti-Shchelgacheva Case: Over a Thousand Russian Children Illegally Exported from Russia," *Pravda*, 15 July 2002, at http://english.pravda.ru/main/2002/07/15/32516.html (accessed 19 January 2006).

30. Ibid.

31. Ibid.

32. A. Cherkasov, "New Turns in Notorious Case of Nadezhda Fratti," *Pravda*, 9 June 2001, at http://english.pravda.ru/region/2001/09/06/14402.html (accessed 7 October 2005).

33. "Doctors Perform Organ Donation Surgeries on Living Patients," *Pravda*, 11 August 2004, at http://www.english.pravda.ru/print/hotspots/crimes/6513-organ-o (accessed 25 February 2006); *Eke*, 8 August 2005; H. White, "Four Russian Doc-tors to Be Re-Tried for Organ Stealing," *LifeSiteNews*, 11 April 2006, at http://www.lifesite.net/ldn/2006/apr/06041102.html (accessed 25 February 2006).

34. "Organs of Russian Boy Were Taken for Transplants," *Politru*, 4 April 2005, at http://www.polit.ru/news/2005/04/15/dfghdfg.html (accessed 17 Octo-ber 2005); "Organs of Six-Year-Old Alex Pavlis Used for Business," *Gazeta.ru*, 15 April 2005, at http://newsinfo.csm.ru/news/2005/04/news100674.php?id_r=10 (accessed 17 October 2005); "Russian Surgeons Removing Organs Saying Patients

Almost Dead Anyway," *LifeSiteNews*, 9 September 2003, at http://www.lifesite.net/ldn/2003/sep/030906.html (accessed 25 February 2006).

35. J. Nikolaeva, "Children for export," *AIF* 13, April 1999, at http://www.aif.ru:81/oldsite/968/art010.html (accessed 18 January 2006).

36. I. Bikkinin and D. Bikkinina, "Foreign Adoption from Russia: Myths, Cites, Data and Facts," *Tatar Gazette*, 2004, at http://tatar.yuldash.com/238.html (accessed 30 March 2006).

37. The website connected with the TV program *7ya* [*Family*] is at http://www.7ya.ru/pub/article.aspx?id=2524 (accessed 15 September 2005).

38. M. V. Alfimova and V. E. Golimbet, "Our Fate Is in Our Genes," *7ya*, 9 December 2003, at http://www/7ya.ru/pub/article.aspx?id=2735; A. Rudov, "Influence of Inheritance on Behaviour," *7ya*, 10 November 2003, at http://www.7ya.ru/pub/article.aspx?id=2589 (accessed 24 January 2006).

39. "You Cannot Divorce a Child," *AIF* 19 (1072), 8 May 2001, at http://www.aif.ru/online/aif/1072/15_01 (accessed 19 January 2006).

REFERENCES

Fonseca, Claudia. 2004. "Child Circulation in a Brazilian *Favela*." In *Cross-Cultural Approaches to Adoption*, ed. Fiona Bowie, 161–81. London: Routledge.

Leifsen, Esben. 2004. "Person, Relation and Value: The Economy of Circulating Ecuadorian Children in International Adoption." In *Cross-Cultural Approaches to Adoption*, ed. Fiona Bowie, 182–96. London: Routledge.

Marre, Diana. 2008. "'I Want Her to Learn Her Language and Maintain Her Culture': Transnational Adoptive Families' Views on 'Cultural Origins.'" In *Race, Ethnicity and Nation in Europe: Perspectives from Kinship and Genetics*, ed. Peter Wade. Oxford, UK: Berghahn Books.

Modell, Judith Schachter. 2002. *A Sealed and Secret Kinship: The Culture of Policies and Practices in American Adoption*. Oxford, UK: Berghahn Books.

Radin, Margaret Jane. 1996. *Contested Commodities*. Cambridge, MA: Harvard University Press.

Sargeant, Elena. 1996. "The 'Woman Question' and Problems of Maternity." In *Women in Russia and Ukraine*, ed. Rosalind J. March, 269–85. Cambridge: Cambridge University Press.

Scheper-Hughes, Nancy. 2000. "The Global Traffic of Human Organs." *Current Anthropology* 41, no. 2: 191–224.

Yngvesson, Barbara. 2004. "National Bodies and the Body of the Child: 'Completing' Families through International Adoption." In *Cross-Cultural Approaches to Adoption*, ed. Fiona Bowie, 211–26. London: Routledge.

Zelizer, Viviana A. 1994. *Pricing the Priceless Child: The Changing Social Value of Children*. Princeton, NJ: Princeton University Press.

Chapter 10

‖‖‖

The Medicalization of Adoption
in and from Peru

Jessaca B. Leinaweaver

In recent years anthropologists studying the gendered patterns of family-making, childrearing, and intimacy have come together around a focus on reproduction (Ginsburg and Rapp 1995). Kath Weston has distinguished between reproduction as "physical procreation and its sense as the perpetuation of society as a whole" (1991: 25)—in other words, between bodily and social reproduction. I present adoption as a crucial form of reproduction, not in the physical sense, since no new human beings are created through the process, but in the more socially significant sense of perpetuation and continuation. In adoption, as Nick Townsend has argued, "a social person is created by appropriation, and people become parents in every sense other than the genetic" (1997: 102).

The scholarly literature on fostering, child circulation, and informal adoption in many parts of the world reveals the considerable social significance of transferring children between houses or families (Bledsoe 1990, Brady 1976, Carroll 1970, Carsten 1991, Donner 1999, Fonseca 1986, Goody 1982, Kottak 1986, Soto 1987, Stack 1974). Adoption has the potential to complicate the dominant Euro-American ideology that physical procreation grounds social perpetuation, phrased as "blood is thicker than water" (Schneider 1968).[1] North American and European adoptive parents and adoptees often declare that their own relationships are just as real as birth relations. Yet the very terms of the claim reveal the way in which adoption is framed within Euro-American discursive constructions. Adoption cannot be discussed without invoking and reifying deeply held notions of biological relatedness (Modell 1994: 3, Schneider 1984: 55), even as adoptive families work to disengage the naturalized links between blood and love.

This chapter focuses on one prominent way in which understandings of the biological re-enter adoptive scenes: through the deployment of biomedical discourses and practices. The introduction of the biomedical into adoptive family relations is a historically and geographically specific process. Kaja Finkler, who has worked with adoptees searching for their birth parents in North America, argues that the understanding that disease is transmitted across generations has brought family relationships into the biomedical domain (2000: 3). In adoption, biomedicine is used to frame notions of appropriate and inappropriate families; it is a central way in which adoption's potential for radical transformation of Euro-American kinship ideologies is brought up short and re-integrated into the dominant paradigm. Analysis of the engagement of adoption and biomedicine reveals one critical way in which local and global understandings of biology and adoption are actually deeply intertwined.

Focusing on international adoption, which is a form of reproduction that draws explicitly upon international laws and conventions, I draw from my research in Peru, whose international adoption program is closely regulated and sends children to only ten designated countries.[2] The significance of the physical body in charting and enabling new relationships is bolstered by an increasingly globalized biomedical discourse in at least three ways. First, like public officials in many countries, Peruvian officials engage with international norms about mental health and malnutrition in order to justify finding children to be legally adoptable. Second, potential adoptive parents are deeply enmeshed in the biomedical, both in the attempts at assisted reproduction that commonly precede adoption and in the medical examinations required of persons seeking to adopt. Finally, biomedicine and adoption are linked in the discourse of nation: biomedicine is a clear anchor for North Americans' and Europeans' calculations of health risks and concerns when choosing a country from which to adopt. This chapter explores these three intersections of the biomedical and the adoptive in turn.

Kinship and Adoption in the Wake of War

My research has explored how urban highland Peruvians rely on kinship connections to survive in economically dire conditions. I spent over two years (2001–2003) studying children's circulation between households and families (Leinaweaver 2007, and in press), investigating whether and how people's ability to engage in these local and flexible kinship practices had been compromised by a relatively recent law, based in international conventions, that formalized adoptions and gave the Peruvian state more of an entry into ordinary people's lives.

During my fieldwork, I spent a great deal of time in a regional branch of the government adoption office, whose staff generously permitted me to read through one year's worth of files documenting fourteen adoptions, both domestic and international, from the region. The material upon which I draw for this chapter comes primarily from these files,[3] as well as from interviews with and observations of adoption officials and from government and NGO reports and public documents addressing adoption.

The home base of my research was the city of Ayacucho, a regional capital in the south-central Andes with a population of over 125,000 (Huber et al. 2003: 16). Within Peru, Ayacucho is synonymous with violence and terror. During the 1980s and 1990s, this region was the center of the internal war raging throughout the country. The violence left children orphaned and forced rural families to migrate to safer urban environments. Some families circulated their children among families, households, and communities in a practice resembling informal foster care. The war also deeply affected Ayacuchanos' relationship with the state, which is partially mediated through the adoption office and the state's interest in how families are reproduced (Kligman 1992). And as is so often the case, the violence also promoted the transfer of children from struggling Andean families to parents in the wealthier, more powerful global North via the unbalanced exchange of international adoption. Peru was one of the top three "sending countries" for adoptions to the United States in the early 1990s.

Significantly, the crucial revisions to Peru's adoption law were also passed in this period. In 1990, President Alberto Fujimori took over a country riven by internal war. Fujimori quickly put in place severe economic structural adjustments, helping to usher in an era of neoliberalism, and in 1992 he suspended the constitution and arrested the leader of Shining Path (*Sendero Luminoso*). Peru had to gain international respectability, and passing a new law on children in which Peru "makes its own the doctrine and principles of the UN Convention" on the Rights of the Child (Promudeh 2001: 8) was one way to accomplish that goal. In publicly invoking international norms, the Peruvian state was demonstrating its modernity. One effect was the immediate slowdown of adoptions from the country as the process was more closely scrutinized. However, the changes in the law also had an impact on Peruvian families' ability to raise their children. The impact was minor compared to that of the malignant combination of neoliberal policies, inflation, and underdevelopment that meant people were constantly struggling just to eke out a living and the violence and massive displacement caused by the civil war between Shining Path and government counterinsurgency forces. But the law's effects were not insignificant: it provided a new set of justifications for the removal of poor, indigenous children from their families. One of these key justifications relies upon biomedical measures.

Using Biomedical Measures to Assess Children's Natal Families as "Inappropriate"

I have outlined the Peruvian laws and international conventions that shape adoption within and from Peru elsewhere (Leinaweaver in press). Here, I emphasize that, following these cautious and duly delineated guidelines, children who have living kin cannot be adopted unless some objective yardstick is employed to demonstrate that they require protection. That yardstick must be one that resonates internationally, on the level at which these adoptions are conducted. In keeping with recent scholarship on migration and health, I view legally "abandoned" Peruvian children as premigrants whose bodies and psyches undergo a specific kind of mapping to prepare them for their journey to new families and new lands. For many infants and children who are processed in this fashion, the mapping peculiar to biomedicine becomes a tool with which officials can substantiate a declaration of abandonment.

Peruvian officials engage with international norms about mental health and malnutrition in order to justify legally declaring children adoptable. In this process, the globalized discourse of biomedicine is carefully deployed to assess both the mental health of birth mothers and the physical health of children. For the government officials, relying on biomedical measures proves that their work is lawful and their decisions rational rather than arbitrary. Under the new law, courts decide that certain children should be formally separated from their kin when any one of several conditions is met. A child's guardians are judged to be inappropriate primarily because they "do not comply with their corresponding obligations or duties" with regard to raising and educating the child, "or lack the moral or mental qualities necessary to assure a correct formation" (Congreso de la

República de Perú 2000: Article 248).[4] The Peruvian courts shore up this legal language with evidence from biomedicine to prove that parents or other kin are not capable of providing the child with an adequate standard of living. Biomedical discourse gives weight to what might otherwise be an ambiguous social policy: removing children from their homes in lieu of assisting their families.

As I read through the archives of children's abandonment and their pairing with adoptive parents, I was struck by how frequently biomedical criteria appear in the files as a way to declare families inadequate by measuring the unfitness of birth parents and the threats to children's well-being. By drawing attention to the way in which child abandonment is medicalized, I do not mean to cast doubt on the position that ill or malnourished children should receive better care, or that mentally ill mothers are hard-pressed to provide adequate care for their children. What I want to highlight in these cases is how the biomedical is used as an objective measure to deem individual guardians unacceptable, and how, through its use, other ways of understanding family life in Peru are obscured.

First, it is striking how frequently food is mentioned in the case files. Malnutrition is found in more than a quarter of Peruvian children, the vast majority of whom are not subject to removal from their families (Vásquez and Mendizabal 2002: 57, Leinaweaver 2007). Its presence in the files is a weighty one. In the archive of baby Tomás's legal abandonment, for example, we learn that after he was born, the nurses at the village health clinic took turns feeding his mother until they resigned themselves to notifying the hospital, whose social worker recommended that he be placed in a children's home. His mother lived off her village's generosity: "the people provide her food daily in different houses." The attention to food in Tomás's file is medicalized by the technical term "*desnutrición leve*" (mild malnutrition)—the only negative indicator, as his health is otherwise good.

A file defining the status of two siblings recounts that authorities in their town convinced the children's grandmother to place them in a local children's home. They had been living with their grandmother since their mother had been sent to Lima's mental hospital. Accompanying their grandmother to sell fruit in the market, the children came to the attention of the authorities, who exerted pressure to regularize their situation. Anxieties are expressed around food: with a fruit seller's income, their grandmother "will have a hard time meeting the children's support needs." The analysis of their health mentions below-average weight and minor illnesses. The record notes that their grandmother continued to visit them after they were sent to the children's home, bringing them fruit that she was unable to sell.

These children were institutionalized at the behest of medical and civil authorities. But it is also fairly common for working-class families in Ayacucho to use the region's orphanages as places to lodge children temporarily if they are hungry, ill, or in need of short-term child care. As long as the child is visited at least once every six months, he or she cannot be legally declared abandoned. Decisions to place a child with relatives or in an orphanage are not made lightly; these actions are usually motivated by extreme poverty. The risk of doing so is that, even though relatives visit, children may be declared abandoned—based not on the socially meaningful absence of kin in their lives, but rather on purportedly objective measurements of their health and well-being. Rather than addressing the conditions under which so many Peruvian children come to be malnourished, or the reasons why their parents cannot afford or obtain medical care, the state posits poor parenting as the cause of malnutrition and illness. To frame malnourishment as evidence of a parent's "moral abandonment" suggests a pathologization of poverty.

A second key strategy of medicalization used in defining children as abandoned and therefore adoptable is the reliance on psychiatry to prove that children's guardians are incapable of fulfilling their parental responsibilities. The siblings just mentioned were originally placed with their grandmother because their mentally ill mother had been institutionalized. In another case, Juan and Elena were determined to have come from a "disintegrated home." Their mother was a domestic worker in an economically marginal situation; her three older children were already living with relatives around the region.[5] When the children's father left to take up with another woman, the desperate mother suffered serious "mental alterations." The file notes that Juan and Elena were found wandering outside the bus station; neighbors reported their mother said she had burned them. Hospital psychologists pronounced this behavior an indicator of paranoid schizophrenia. The children were lodged in the local orphanage, and the case slowly worked its way through the courts. Two and a half years later, the courts declared the children to be legally abandoned.

The proceedings hit an obstacle when Juan and Elena's mother firmly stated that she did not want her children to be adopted. She appealed the decision and argued that she was recovering; her frequent visits to her children also spoke in her favor. A month after the declaration of abandonment, the courts accordingly declared the initial decree null and void, in part because the children's father had not yet been located and notified. However, the adoption office continued to push for the children to be declared abandoned. Nine months later the courts reinstated the declaration on the basis of two statements: one from a man who vehemently denied the children were his and one from doctors confirming the mother's diagnosis of paranoia. The mother appealed to the superior court, where staff for the adoption office argued that returning the children to their mother would threaten their "right to live in an appropriate family." At around the same time, the file notes that "the mother showed up naked and aggressive" at the orphanage, asking that the children be allowed to stay there until she recovered. Citing the mother's schizophrenia, the court finally declared the children legally abandoned a full three and a half years after they were sent to the orphanage, and three months after this, they were adopted.

Clearly, this mother's behavior—claiming she had burned her children, showing up naked and aggressive to beseech their caretakers that they not be relinquished for adoption—was deviant by most standards. Medical anthropologist João Biehl has approached a comparable case by asking how "novel conjunctions of kinship, public institutions, psychiatry, and medication work, if not to make people psychotic, then to give a certain form and value to their experience as psychotic, thus recasting subjectivity and mediating abandonment" (2005: 106). In analyzing the fragments of this mother's experience that are recorded in the legal documents charting her children's abandonment, I follow Biehl by looking to the layers of marginalization that give them meaning: abandoned by a man who says the children are not his progeny, working for meager "tips" as a domestic servant, separated from her other children, and embroiled in a three-year struggle to keep her two youngest from being permanently excised from her life.

What psychologists diagnosed as madness looks from another perspective like sheer desperation. To call it desperation would be to demand support and empathy from an interlocutor framed as humane. To call it madness is to locate blame within an individual, and even more deeply inside that individual's genetic or medical history, rather than to look to the conditions under which so many impoverished women come to be declared insane. Kathryn Oths argues that mental health is partly shaped by global relations; diagnoses of mental illnesses such as *debilidad* may serve as "a vehicle for the expression of a lifelong accumulation of bodily hardships. The life difficulties of Andeans, especially women, are rooted in the injustices and imbalance of power at many levels" (1999: 307; see also Stein 1995). Drawing attention to the medical situates the Peruvian state as scientifically advanced and progressive; unhitching the medical from power imbalance, social marginalization, and bodily hardship ensures that the state can be viewed as blameless, as well as modern.

The diagnosed mental illness of fully half of the birthmothers in the year's worth of files to which I had access is a troubling example of the process of medicalization. Kaja Finkler defines medicalization as a process whereby the biomedical interpretation of specific acts or behaviors precludes alternate interpretations (2000: 175). The official determination of who is mad and who is not is key in determining parental appropriateness. This determination is made with resort to biomedical authority, to psychologists enshrined within hospitals, even when causes are ascribed, in the files, to social events such as spousal abandonment.

Perhaps it is overly cynical to suggest that state authorities couple biomedical definitions of children as malnourished and ill with biomedical definitions of birthmothers as mentally unstable in order to provide an unassailable logic for removing poor and indigenous children from their natal families. Yet in several of the cases I reviewed, a child's consanguineal relative's stated wishes were denied because government officials had recourse to a higher standard. In these cases, global discourses of children's rights and of biomedicine as an objective standard are inextricably intertwined. In this process, which can be traced to the requirements of a transparent and deliberate adoption law, Peruvian kinship is being transformed.

International middle-class values have been so normalized in connection with children's welfare, health, and nutrition that those whose poverty prevents them from attaining those values are demonized. This strategy deflects attention from Peru's inability to provide basic social services for its citizens. By using a biomedical measure, the neoliberal state can criticize the family, and specific individuals within that family, rather than provide social support. Equally alarming, the reliance on the biomedical as an internationally accepted, objective standard dresses in sheep's clothing the predatory wolves of racism and class inequality that are embedded in the Peruvian state. While the law carefully asserts that "the lack of material resources in no way justifies the declaration of abandonment" (Congreso de la República de Perú 2000: Article 248), in practice, poverty is translated into malnutrition and ill health among children and psychological incapacity among parents. The adoption process is a potent tool through which the government can introduce medical measures into the lives of poor and indigenous people—administering a population and emphasizing static, physical, embodied markers rather than the agency visible in peasant and working-class Peruvians' strategies of child circulation and temporary use of the orphanage.

This justification for removing children from their families is especially alarming in a national context in which the indigenous poor are devalued to such an extent that a forced sterilization campaign ran rampant in the 1990s (Leinaweaver 2005). State discourse about health and fertility couples modernity with low birth rates, producing the conditions for adoptions to be facilitated through determinations about health. The Peruvian government's involvement in reproduction thus has the unseemly appearance of either preventing the reproduction of the poorest and most indigenous through sterilization or, if this is not possible, using biomedical claims to redefine those individuals as morally and physically flawed, systematically displacing their children into orphanages and ultimately channeling them into more socially appropriate families.

Using the Medical Model to Assess the Fitness of Potential Parents

Families seeking to adopt are also evaluated using a biomedical model. Having a clean bill of physical and psychological health is strongly associated with moral fitness for parenthood. It is instructive to compare the ways in which the biomedical model is used to assess birth families, who are found wanting, and adoptive families, who must prove their fitness. Although adoptive parents do not seem to resent the medical assessments of their potential children, they frequently express irritated resignation about having to undergo such invasive examinations themselves (Fonseca 2002). Potential adoptive parents engage with biomedicine in two major ways: first, the increasingly common fertility interventions that often precede a decision to adopt, and second, the medical reports they are required to provide as part of the adoption application.

Attempts at assisted reproduction are recounted within the adoption files in order to underscore applicants' sincere desire to become a parent and the arduous steps already taken in the service of that goal. The majority of people adopting internationally have suffered infertility, which social workers cite as the primary "motivation for adoption." Poignant accounts of struggles with fertility treatments are thus linked rhetorically to the development of an adoption plan. For example, one report read: "After the female applicant's initial diagnosis of blocked Fallopian tubes and the subsequent extraction of same, the applicants thought of adoption as an alternative to develop themselves as parents." Yet, as anthropologist Ashley Lebner has suggested, "the medicalization of infertility . . . encourages infertile couples to pursue the production of a genetically related child" (2000: 373). In this way, adoption becomes explicitly a second choice, yet paradoxically, these encounters with biomedicine ground the narrative that prospective adopters must produce of an intense desire to be a parent.[6] Because parenting is understood within the dominant Euro-American ideology of kinship as rooted in biology (Schneider 1968), undergoing such difficult procedures for the sake of a never-conceived child demonstrates the determination to be a parent even more clearly than would turning immediately to adoption.

Potential adoptive parents are required to submit medical reports as part of the adoption application. The contrast between birth mothers and adoptive parents is implicit in the coupling of a potential adoptive parent's dossier with a potential adopted child's abandonment report in a comprehensive file. Adoption officials contrast the two, comparing the kinds of parents, families, and households perceived to be "appropriate" for raising children to the negative construction of the image of the unsound parent. Although good health does not appear on the official list of characteristics required of prospective adopters,[7] medical certificates are one of the key features of these dossiers. The certificates must be less than three months old, produced by an authorized health center or institution, and document physical and mental health. Similar to the medical requirements for immigration, medical requisites for adoption include negative results of lab tests for HIV and Hepatitis B and lung X-rays of adopters and those who live with them.

Mental health is assessed by a psychologist through written autobiographies, semistructured interviews with the would-be parents both individually and as a couple, and a battery of psychological tests.[8] The psychologist reports on behavioral characteristics, such as cordiality, as well as more straightforwardly psychological characteristics, such as respect for social norms, a lifestyle suitable for a child's development, and intellectual capacity. In one file I reviewed, the adopting couple was reported to "conform reasonably to social codes and norms." Another couple was praised as "absolutely normal." The recurrent praise of conformity to social norms in these documents reveals the prevalent belief that parenting should occur in a normative context and highlights by implication the charge that the adoptive child's birth family is abnormal.

This attention to social norms takes place within a Euro-American dichotomy between birth families, seen as "natural" or "real," and adoptive families, seen by contrast as unnatural or inauthentic. As "self-conscious kinship" (Howell 2001), adoption must draw on other paradigms, separate from the all-defining model of nature versus law and birth versus rearing. Positioning adoptive parents as conforming to social norms and implicitly or explicitly contrasting them with birth families is one of these strategies through which adoptive parenthood becomes, if not naturalized, at least justified. That particular strategy is given disproportionate weight when it is framed within the context of biomedicine.

Some of the strategies that adoptive parents use to constitute their families in the face of intense cultural resistance, then, are mobilized at the expense of the poor and indigenous people who first produced the children in question. In itself, adoption is no better or worse a way of forming a family than any other. I hope that, as Judith Butler has written about her own critique of feminism, these arguments are taken "in the tradition of immanent critique that seeks to provide critical examination of the basic vocabulary of the movement of thought to which it belongs" (1999: vii). As a member of several adoptive families, I believe that it is imperative to consider critically the tools adoptive families mobilize in the service of their own formation.

Global Mapping of Health and Risk in the Discourse of the Nation

A third biomedical tool deployed by practitioners of adoption is not grounded in individual bodies of children or prospective parents but rather in a global mapping of health and risk. Analyzing the context and terrain of medicalization, which aids both in the breakup of natal families in Peru and in the constitution of adoptive families in the global North, brings this argument back to its origins in the recognition of international adoption as both reproducing global inequalities and profoundly dependent upon the biomedical.

Numerous authors have addressed specific health problems that arise after international adoptions (Sills Mitchel and Jenista 1997a, 1997b). On the world map of adoption, certain high-profile countries are associated with specific medical conditions. For example, "fetal alcohol syndrome is a particular concern to parents who adopt children from Eastern Europe and the former Soviet Union" (Quarles and Brodie 1998: 2003). According to Jane Aronson, a well-known pediatrician specializing in international adoption, "thirteen percent of Chinese adoptees had elevated blood lead levels on arrival."[9] For those considering domestic adoption, the 1990s media hysteria about crack babies continues to resonate (Ortiz and Briggs 2003). By contrast, Latin American infants, while still at risk for malnutrition and some of the health issues that come with institutionalization, are, according to Peruvian adoption officials, perceived as healthier and at lower risk for serious problems than children from elsewhere.

Prospective parents who were asked to explain why they chose Peru over other possible countries for adoption did not turn first to the links between health and nation. Many mentioned Peru's image abroad: colorful, scenic, mystical.[10] However, adoptive parents on a listserv dedicated to Peruvian adoption occasionally discussed health issues. The effects of malnutrition in a country with high food insecurity and accompanying food anxiety (Stein 1961: 77) and the unavailability of medical records were two common concerns. Significantly, the health issues associated with adoption from Peru were often cited to support, not a decision to adopt from another country, but rather a keen preference for babies over older children. The younger a child, the less likely that malnutrition has damaged his or her body or prospects, that institutionalization has taken its toll on the child's psyche, and that undocumented medical visits will present complications in future treatment. Related to this biomedically based desire to adopt an infant is the psychologically infused desire emerging from the idea that emotional bonding might not occur with an older child. Charlene Miall has suggested that this medicalization of sentiment penetrates the body itself: "the biological tie is [seen as] important for bonding and love and therefore bonding and love in adoption are second best" (1987: 36–37). This psychology of adoption, grounded in North American kinship ideology, undergirds a desire to adopt very young children who are both physically and psychologically unformed. A preference for one country over another in global geographies of adoption may thus reflect not only the presumed connections between particular health concerns and particular national identities but also the specific geopolitical context: what countries, because of war, poverty, or political agendas, have a readily available supply of infants?

Conclusion

Medical anthropologists have traced the development of medicalization, which was first identified in the 1960s, as an emerging criticism of the ways in which institutions labeled nonconforming behaviors as instances of "sickness" (Broom and Woodward 1996: 358). Contained within the broader rubric of medicalization is geneticization, or "the current drive to determine the genetic antecedents to illness, disease, and behaviors" (Lebner 2000: 372). Adoptive families are explicitly grounded in the social, in what Judith Schachter has labeled a "relation by arrangement, and not by nature" (Modell 1994: 4). Within the larger historical trend of medicalization, then, where do families formed by international adoption fit?

Medicalization infuses international adoption in at least three crucial areas. First, the biomedical model is central in the justification of abandonment and the production of an adoptable child. International conventions on adoption and children's rights provide the linkage between moral and material abandonment, but it is the adherence to biomedical authority that makes the declaration of abandonment indisputable. This form of medicalization is especially powerful when both physical health and mental health can be measured and evaluated to produce a double condemnation of the natal family's appropriateness.

Second, biomedical actions serve to constitute appropriate parents through both their attempts at assisted reproduction and their willingness to submit to medical examinations. The context for these actions on the part of potential adoptive parents is the larger trend toward medicalization in North America. Would-be parents undergo often uncomfortable and expensive assisted reproduction attempts, convincing both them and their peers of the desirability of producing a genetically related child. When this is not achieved, prospective adopters willingly, if sometimes grudgingly, submit to further medical tests that confirm, for them and for the international agencies, their suitability as parents.

Finally, the medicalization both of the adoptee's natal family's inappropriateness and of the adopters' moral suitability are situated in a global system where health and risk are mapped and charted in the discourse of international adoption. As Ashley Lebner has written, "We have been taught by our medical practitioners that if we really 'care' about our health, we should monitor our health as closely as we can and know our family histories, in order to help us (and them) maintain our health. But what happens when we don't know?" (2000: 371). The uncertainty and danger of not knowing are somewhat mitigated by the global mapping of risk —the notion that, even without the detailed medical family history that a "good" or "real" parent could provide, at the very least a child whose national provenance is known can be assessed by North American doctors based on previous experience with adopted children from the region. Furthermore, if adoption of an infant is likely, because of the specificities of the chosen country's sociopolitical landscape, real concerns about the uncertainties of adoption—clothed in reasonable preoccupations about physical health and the ability to "bond"—can be assuaged.

These three instances of the medicalization of the adoptive family suggest the potential for a rethinking of kinship and "nature." Each exemplifies the ways in which biomedical discourse and practice are mobilized to create and reify understandings of kinship. Providing good health to a child shows parental worthiness, while mental imbalance demonstrates inability to raise a child. Failed attempts at assisted reproduction and willingness to undergo invasive medical exams document the desire to become a parent. The global mapping of health and risk, finally, creates a framework in which these recourses to the biomedical model can be understood, legitimized, and validated.

In short, medicalization is a set of practices and discourses that together constitute family. Adoption office workers and adoptive parents deploy this dominant biomedical model in order to frame and give meaning to sentiment, connection, and belonging. The fact that all of this is occurring within the context of the adoptive family, which has historically been constituted as, at best, second best, and at worst, inferior, is particularly ironic, but at the same time makes the point quite powerfully. All family is "fictive," in the sense that it is built up by humans trying to make sense out of their relationships to one another, and in the sense that we make kinship into something "natural" through the discursive and embodied use of biomedical metaphors.

ACKNOWLEDGMENTS

Thanks to Fulbright IIE, the Wenner-Gren Foundation for Anthropological Research, a Doctoral Dissertation Improvement Grant from the National Science Foundation, a Jacob K. Javits Fellowship, and the University of Michigan for their support of this research. All translations from the Spanish are my own.

NOTES

1. This paradigm of relatedness has also long informed the scholarly study of kinship; see Schneider 1984.

2. These countries are Canada, the United States, Spain, Denmark, Luxembourg, Italy, Norway, Germany, France, and the Netherlands. Article 4 of the adoption law allows for adoptions to other countries to be considered in special cases.

3. Although I was not able to obtain consent from each family individually, the University of Michigan's Institutional Review Board approved my examination of the files under specific conditions of confidentiality. I reviewed the previous year's files while accompanying adoptive parents in the current year, deliberately not overlapping recorded information with direct observation. The key documents in each file include: a court document ordering that an investigation be opened; documents detailing the interviews and other aspects of this investigation; social, psychological, and medical reports on the child; and photographs.

4. The original Code of Children and Adolescents (Law 26102) was passed in late 1992. It has been revised several times since, and in this chapter I refer to Law 27337, passed in 2000, which was in force at the time of my research.

5. My extended research on child circulation in the region indicates that if a woman must work in a setting unsuitable for children, including a private home, she may address childcare responsibilities by placing the children temporarily with relatives or patrons elsewhere. The absence of her other children in itself does not indicate anomalous behavior.

6. The government's Guide to Adoptions explains that the only valid motivation for adoption is "when a person or couple wants to adopt a minor out of love." Invalid motivations include using the child as a pretext to keep the spouse, as a servant, as a balm for loneliness, to hide infertility, or to replace a spouse who has left or a child who has died; see Promudeh 2001: 8.

7. According to the Peruvian government adoption office's website, adoptive parents are evaluated based on "emotional stability, affective capacity, respect and acceptance towards the child. Moral solvency, normal intellectual resources (high school degree). Economic stability, a home that can meet the basic needs of the child. Preferably married, under age 55." See the website: http://www.mimdes.gob.pe/sna/faq.htm#3.

8. At the time of my research, required psychological tests included the Minnesota Multiphasic Personality Inventory, Rorschach, Karen Machover Human Figure Test, Eysenck and Eysenck Personality Inventory, and Raven Test of Progressive Matrices for Intellectual Capacity.

9. See her website, www.orphandoctor.com.

10. Christine Gailey has suggested that "race was a submerged motive" for

choosing private or international adoption over engagement with the U.S. government's child welfare system (2000: 44; also see Jacobson 2005 on discourses of race and health in international adoption). However, since Peruvian children are not likely to be as light-skinned as Eastern European children, race may not be such a salient factor for Peru.

REFERENCES

Biehl, João. G. 2005. *Vita: Life in a Zone of Social Abandonment.* Berkeley: University of California Press.

Bledsoe, Caroline H. 1990. " 'No Success without Struggle': Social Mobility and Hardship for Foster Children in Sierra Leone." *Man* 25: 70–88.

Brady, Ivan. 1976. "Adaptive Engineering: An Overview of Adoption in Oceania." In *Transactions in Kinship: Adoption and Fosterage in Oceania,* ed. Ivan Brady. Honolulu: University Press of Hawaii.

Broom, Dorothy H., and Roslyn V. Woodward. 1996. "Medicalisation Reconsidered: Toward a Collaborative Approach to Care." *Sociology of Health and Illness* 18: 357–78.

Butler, Judith. (1990) 1999. *Gender Trouble: Feminism and the Subversion of Identity.* New York: Routledge.

Carroll, Vern. 1970. "Introduction: What Does 'Adoption' Mean?" In *Adoption in Eastern Oceania,* ed. Vern Carroll. Honolulu: University Press of Hawaii.

Carsten, Janet. 1991. "Children in Between: Fostering and the Process of Kinship on Pulau Langkawi, Malaysia." *Man* 26, no. 3: 425–43.

Congreso de la República de Perú. 2000. Ley N° 27337 (Ley que aprueba el Nuevo Código de los Niños y Adolescentes). Lima, Peru.

Donner, William W. 1999. "Sharing and Compassion: Fosterage in a Polynesian Society." *Journal of Comparative Family Studies* 30: 703–22.

Finkler, Kaja. 2000. *Experiencing the New Genetics: Family and Kinship on the Medical Frontier.* Philadelphia: University of Pennsylvania Press.

Fonseca, Claudia. 1986. "Orphanages, Foundlings, and Foster Mothers: The System of Child Circulation in a Brazilian Squatter Settlement." *Anthropological Quarterly* 59: 15–27.

———. 2002. "An Unexpected Reversal: Charting the Course of International Adoption in Brazil." *Adoption and Fostering* 26: 28–39.

Gailey, Christine Ward. 2000. "Ideologies of Motherhood and Kinship in U.S. Adoption." In *Ideologies and Technologies of Motherhood: Race, Class, Sexuality, Nationalism,* ed. Helena Ragone and France Winddance Twine, 11–55. New York: Routledge.

Ginsburg, Faye D., and Rayna Rapp (eds.). 1995. *Conceiving the New World Order: The Global Politics of Reproduction.* Berkeley: University of California Press.

Goody, Esther N. 1982. *Parenthood and Social Reproduction: Fostering and Occupational Roles in West Africa*. Cambridge: Cambridge University Press.

Howell, Signe. 2001. "Self-Conscious Kinship: Some Contested Values in Norwegian Transnational Adoption." In *Relative Values: Reconfiguring Kinship Studies*, ed. Sarah Franklin and Susan McKinnon, 203–23. Durham, NC: Duke University Press.

Huber, Ludwig, Karin Apel, Jorge Iván A. Caro, Lenin Castillo, Enver Quinteros, and Hugo Rodriguez. 2003. "Centralismo y descentralización en Ayacucho." In *Ayacucho: Centralismo y descentralización*, ed. Ludwig Huber, 15–104. Lima: Instituto de Estudios Peruanos.

Jacobson, Heather. 2005. "Choosing Russia, Choosing China: An Analysis of Factors Involved in the Parental Choice of Adoptive Country." Paper presented at Reproductive Disruptions: Childlessness, Adoption, and Other Reproductive Complexities Conference, University of Michigan, Ann Arbor.

Kligman, Gail. 1992. "Abortion and International Adoption in Post-Ceauşescu Romania." *Feminist Studies* 18: 405–19.

Kottak, Conrad Phillip. 1986. "Kinship Modeling: Adaptation, Fosterage, and Fictive Kinship among the Betsileo." In *Madagascar: Society and History*, ed. Conrad Phillip Kottak, 392–414. Durham, NC: Carolina Academic Press.

Lebner, Ashley. 2000. "Genetic 'Mysteries' and International Adoption: The Cultural Impact of Biomedical Technologies on the Adoptive Family Experience." *Family Relations* 49: 371–77.

Leinaweaver, Jessaca B. 2005. "Mass Sterilizations and Child Circulations: Two Reproductive Responses to Poverty in Peru." *Anthropology News* 46, no. 1:13–18.

———. 2007. "On Moving Children: The Social Implications of Andean Child Circulation." *American Ethnologist* 34, no. 1: 163–80.

———. In press. *The Circulation of Children: Adoption, Kinship, and Morality in Andean Peru*. Durham, NC: Duke University Press.

Miall, Charlene E. 1987. "The Stigma of Adoptive Parent Status: Perceptions of Community Attitudes toward Adoption and the Experience of Informal Social Sanctioning." *Family Relations* 36: 34–39

Modell, Judith Schachter. 1994. *Kinship with Strangers: Adoption and Interpretations of Kinship in American Culture*. Berkeley: University of California Press.

Ortiz, Ana Teresa, and Laura Briggs. 2003. "Crack, Abortion, the Culture of Poverty, and Welfare Cheats: The Making of the 'Healthy White Baby Crisis.'" *Social Text* 75: 39–57.

Oths, Kathryn S. 1999. "Debilidad: A Biocultural Assessment of an Embodied Andean Illness." *Medical Anthropology Quarterly* 13: 286–315.

Promudeh (Ministerio de Promoción de la Mujer y del Desarrollo Humano). 2001. *Guida de Procedimiento Administrativo de Adopcion*. Lima, Peru.

Quarles, Christopher S., and Jeffrey H. Brodie. 1998. "Primary Care of International Adoptees." *American Family Physician* 58, no. 9: 2025–32.

Schneider, David M. 1968. *American Kinship: A Cultural Account.* Chicago: University of Chicago Press.

———. 1984. *A Critique of the Study of Kinship.* Ann Arbor: University of Michigan Press.

Sills Mitchel, Marie A., and Jerri Ann Jenista. 1997a. "Health Care of the Internationally Adopted Child, Part 1." *Journal of Pediatric Health Care* 11: 51–60.

———. 1997b. "Health Care of the Internationally Adopted Child, Part 2: Chronic Care and Long-Term Medical Issues." *Journal of Pediatric Health Care* 11: 117–26.

Soto, Isa Maria. 1987. West Indian Child Fostering: Its Role in Migrant Exchanges. In *Caribbean Life in New York City: Sociocultural Dimensions,* ed. Constance R. Sutton and Elsa M. Chaney. Staten Island: The Center for Migration Studies of New York.

Stack, Carol B. 1974. *All Our Kin: Strategies for Survival in a Black Community.* New York: Harper & Row.

Stein, William W. 1961. *Hualcan: Life in the Highlands of Peru.* Ithaca, NY: Cornell University Press.

———. 1995. *A Peruvian Psychiatric Hospital.* Lanham, MD: University Press of America.

Townsend, Nicholas W. 1997. "Reproduction in Anthropology and Demography." In *Anthropological Demography: Toward a New Synthesis,* ed. David I. Kertzer and Tom Fricke, 96–114. Chicago: University of Chicago Press.

Vásquez, Enrique, and Enrique Mendizabal (eds.). 2002. *Los niños . . . primero? El gasto público social focalizado en niños y niñas en el Perú 1990–2000.* Lima: Universidad del Pacífico Centro de Investigación and Save the Children Suecia.

Weston, Kath. 1991. *Families We Choose: Lesbians, Gays, Kinship.* New York: Columbia University Press.

‖‖

Chapter 11

Children, Individuality, Family

*Discussing Assisted Reproductive Technologies
and Adoption in Lithuania*

Auksuolė Čepaitienė

Advocating openness among adoptive parents and adopted children, a so-cial worker at a children's care center in Lithuania described adoption as a two-sided phenomenon, with a painful as well as a joyful side. A child abandoned by its parents finds a new family, and a couple who had been unable to conceive welcomes a child. This event is a great gift to both. But the process of adoption also involves sadness and losses. The long-lasting pain of a couple facing involuntary infertility does not end with the adop-tion of the child. The biological parents who relinquished the child endure a continuing loss. And the child feels a primordial pain: knowing "I was abandoned" and regretting that he or she is not the biological child of his or her adoptive parents—"I am sad because I wish I had been born from your belly, not from the other mummy's belly." It takes courage to face the two sides of adoption. This dramatic image of adoption is common in Lithuanian society. Birth signifies the central fact in the relationship be-tween parents and child. Adoption and assisted reproduction clarify and reinforce, as well as signify major exceptions to, the biological foundation for family formation that Western European kinship assumes.

This chapter analyzes similarities and differences in Lithuanian dis-courses related to assisted reproductive technologies (ART) and adoption and explores how people evaluate them as solutions for infertility. Eluci-dating the ways in which people express their preferences for either ART or adoption, it examines how they understand the relationship between a child and its parents. The conceptualization of the birth of the child, the negotiation of the social and juridical aspects of relatedness, and the idea that children have particular inborn traits signified by the terms "genes" and "inheritance" are the main subjects of this inquiry. Although the child establishes relatedness between parents in the family, popular conceptions of inherited characteristics lead to a perception that children who are adopted or conceived through ART are external to the family.

Children in Kuršėnai

The views of ordinary Lithuanians who have no particular connection with ART or adoption were surveyed as part of the international project, "Public Understanding of Genetics: A Cross-Cultural and Ethnographic Study of the 'New Genetics' and Social Identity" (2002–2004).[1] I had previously conducted research on kinship and social solidarity through the Lithuanian Institute of History and later examined normative aspects of kinship and family with support from the Lithuanian State Science and Study Foundation.[2] In 1999, 2002, and 2005, I investigated how people in Kuršėnai, a town located in the Šiauliai district of northwestern Lithuania, understand family and kinship. In 2002 I went there with a colleague, Darius Daukšas, to explore people's thinking about assisted reproductive technologies and genetics.

Kuršėnai is a small town that had 15,800 inhabitants in 1999. The majority had previously been employed in the pottery workshops, a brick factory, and a sugar refinery that flourished there from the interwar period through the Soviet era. However, the factories were gradually being shut down. Today, there are a few private and state-run enterprises, stores, a hospital, a technical college, a music school, a *gymnasium* preparing students for university, and three secondary schools. Kuršėnai is typical of contemporary Lithuania, with high rates of unemployment and out-migration, many elderly people, and many residents who commute to work elsewhere. People socialize mainly within the family circle and with a few friends and neighbors. What makes Kuršėnai special is its residents' awareness of children who need new parents.

Kuršėnai is known for its orphanage, which was established in 1938–1941. It was the first large institution in Lithuania constructed for this particular purpose. In the beginning children came there from smaller orphanages. Some had lost their parents during the war, and others were brought there after their parents' deaths in Siberia. Later Kuršėnai accepted children from all over Lithuania. Those children were abandoned

TABLE 11.1
Family Background of Children in Kuršėnai Orphanage

Year	Children	With living parents	Orphans
1941	100	—	—
1945	50	38	12
1950–1980	140–50	131–35	4–10
1990	115	113	2
1993	91	91	0
2000	91	—	—

Source: *Kuršėnų vaikų globos namų istorija* (*The history of Kuršėnai orphanage*) 1941–1993, 1994–2000, 1994, 2001; Kuršėnai, Lietuvos kraštotyros draugija, Šiaulių skyrius (manuscript).

by their biological parents, or their parents' rights were limited by the courts. At the end of the war, three-fourths of the children in the institution had living parents; between 1950 and 1980, about 95 percent did. By 1993, none were orphans. (See Table 11.1.) At present, the children have been taken into care because of alleged abuse and neglect.

The Kuršėnai orphanage is located in a suburb. It has a large house, a large vegetable garden, and a small farm. Children live there and go to school in the town. Their everyday lives seemed like that in an extended family, although Soviet childrearing practices had shaped the institution. Previously, under the policy of ignoring kinship ties, children were assigned to rooms strictly according to sex and age. Brothers and sisters had to stay in different rooms, and often in different orphanages. In the 1980s, the shift to family-type groupings of children and keeping siblings together represented a revolution in policy. A short history of the orphanage includes teachers' remarks about children's feelings of discomfort and being unwanted. The very fact that parents had neglected them was stigmatizing. Even today, the majority of children who are waiting to be adopted know that their biological parents are living in the same town.

In Kuršėnai I heard a story from the interwar period about the Venclauskiai family who earned a reputation by providing foster care. They lived in the city of Šiauliai, which is 20 km from Kuršėnai. The husband, Kazimieras Venclauskis, was a lawyer, a member of the Šiauliai Municipal Council, and a mayor of the city. The wife, Stanislava Jakševičiūtė-Venclauskienė, was an actress and an organizer of the first Lithuanian drama performance. They had two biological daughters. But during their lifetime they fostered almost a hundred children of various ages and backgrounds who came to the family in different ways. Some newborn babies were left on the steps of their house; mothers or fathers of the others asked the couple to take care of their children after their deaths. Some were taken to receive medical help or education. None was legally adopted. Most still carried the surnames of their birth parents, but a few were baptized under the Venclauskiai family name or the wife's maiden name. Fostering children was the wife's idea, and she assumed primary responsibility for their care. The husband's only request was that she limit the number of children at the dinner table to thirty. Citizens of Šiauliai used to call them "the great family." Residents still take pride in the Venclauskiai family's care for orphaned children and have established a museum in their house.[3]

I analyze the field research in Kuršėnai in relation to anthropological discussions of adoption, foster care, and assisted reproductive technologies (ART). Conventionally, this analysis is organized around questions of family and kinship (Alber 2003, Bestard 2004, Edwards, Franklin, Hirsch, Price, and Strathern 1993, Edwards 1999, Franklin and McKinnon 2001, Howell 2001, 2002, 2003, Orobitg and Salazar 2005, Strathern 1992a, 1992b, 1995). At present, ART attracts greater theoretical interest than adoption. In Lithuania, however, both subjects are under-researched.[4] Although many scholars have examined the interrelatedness of adoption, ART, family, and kinship, I look at the subject in a different way. The ethnographic question of how people understand ART and adoption encouraged me to focus my theoretical attention on the conceptualization of conception and birth and on the understanding of personhood and individuality (Fortes 1973, Strathern 1992a). Individuality is elaborated through social and cultural practices that are inseparable from the embodiment of personhood (Fortes 1973, Giddens 1997, Edwards 2005, Howell and Marre 2006). This concept describes a human being as singular and unique and acknowledges his or her "specificity" within a relational view (Strathern 1992a: 11–15). Taking these considerations into account, I examine Lithuanians' ideas about ART and adoption.

Emphasizing the Fact of Birth

The residents of Kuršėnai discuss ART within technological, moral, ideological, and social contexts. All their stories are framed by the idea that ART is a form of medical technology to help infertile couples have a child. It is an alternative to, yet analogous with, natural procreation and, in this sense, is similar to adoption (Melhuus and Howell 2008). This similarity between ART and adoption is exemplified in social practice and articulated in academic discussion. Jori Telfer describes adoption as a "second chance," a naturalized consequence of unsuccessful fertility treatments and a final hope for parenthood (2003, 73). Signe Howell (2001), Monica Bonaccorso (2004), and Ashley Lebner (2000) agree that ART and adoption are closely conjoined, as adoption often follows failed ART.

Kuršėnai residents, while acknowledging similarities between ART and adoption, immediately emphasize their differences. To them, the key differences lie in the technology of conception. People regard ART as "artificial" and "unnatural." For some it is not an acceptable way to get a child, and they advocate adoption as "natural." This way of thinking is related to cultural paradigms of conception and procreation and to the understanding of human nature through the dichotomy between "natural" and "artificial." Underlining the significance of the human body in reproduction (Mauss 1973) and rejecting the "dehumanized" clinic as its possible substitute, residents of Kuršėnai emphasize the fundamental distinction between human beings and animals (Fellous 2007) and compare ART with animal breeding rather than human procreation. In describing conceptualizations of personhood—its biological embodiment and its legal, moral, and ritual status—among the Tallensi of Ghana, Meyer Fortes speaks about the important rule that "to become a person one must be properly and normally born" (1973, 296). Lithuanians share this view. In a conversation between Daukšas and a retired couple, the wife began by commenting on the wish to have children, but the husband contended that ART is artificial and disregards human values, individual personality, and spirituality. As the conversation continued, the couple discussed the practice of donation as an "outsider" coming into the family, "blood" and "blood" connections, unknown paternity, a "first [genetic] mother" and a "second [adoptive] mother," sperm banks, and surrogate motherhood. Finally the talk returned to the matter of artificiality, and the husband deliberately concluded by referring to the nature of life and of human beings.

Most of the people we interviewed in Kuršėnai, like those whom Fortes observed in Ghana, emphasize the fact of birth and imbue the opposition between the "naturalness" of conception and the "artificiality" of ART with moral value. All our interviewees treated ART as a technological intervention into nature. However, some of them step over this fact, while others do not. Those who ignore the artificiality of ART mention examples of other curative medical technologies, such as heart transplantation.

The others advocate adoption: "it is a child who is already born and has no parents, and I accept him into a family." But in both cases conception and birth appears to be a significant "fact of life" for an individual, an event that defines a person's identity and belonging and is inscribed in their biography and personal knowledge about themselves.

Sociality and Relations of Dependency in a Family

The people we interviewed stated firmly that whether the conception is natural or artificial is a private family matter that concerns only the husband and wife. According to them, a child is the point of a family and a family without children is incomplete (Edwards et al. 1993, Edwards 1999, Ragone 1994, Bonaccorso 2004). The advent of a child justifies, motivates, and fixes the marital relationship. It establishes connectedness in a family and binds the parents together into kinship (Čepaitienė 2008). The child is what Martine Gross would call a "couple project" (in this volume). Signe Howell (2001) treats parents' desire for children as the emotional dimension of relatedness and sociality (cf. Orobitg and Salazar 2005, Salazar 1999, Yan 2001). Focusing on "the socially embedded individual," she speaks about the desire for children as a desire for substantive sociality, to be a family interacting with other families (Howell 2001: 208, 219–20). Kuršėnai residents agree. But there is one difference: our interviewees did not attribute sociality specifically to interaction between families. Instead, they situated the desire for a child inside the family and within fundamental human needs for interpersonal interaction.

This view is evident when they discuss the possibility of single women having a child through ART. In Kuršėnai I met an elderly woman, Irena, living with her divorced daughter and teenaged granddaughter. They are emotionally very close. The daughter's marriage ended in divorce. She is the only one in the family who is earning an income. Irena helps her daughter by looking after her granddaughter. Although she is a lifelong resident of Kuršėnai, the three are enclosed within a very small social circle, with few relatives and neighbors. When we began to discuss ART, Irena spontaneously (and, to me, surprisingly) explained her positive attitude toward single women wanting to conceive a child without a male partner. Her opinion was very different from that of other interviewees. Irena said that these days, when it's difficult to find a husband, single motherhood is quite normal. "Why bother with some sort of a man, when it's better to raise a child? Someone who'll be a friend to you." Her opinion is grounded on the premise that people feel lonely. She believes that a child brings happiness and vitality to everybody. "I very much wanted to have many children, but have only the two daughters. I used to dislike people who had many children; I was simply green with envy. Life is bustling and stimulating when there are children." She pities her neighbor whose children have moved to another town. "She's all right during the summer, but the fall and winter send her into depression. But when the children and grandchildren come to visit, the house is full of them and leave her no time for depression." This story is echoed by the other interviewees, particularly men, who say that ART is good for single women because in their old age a child would be a source of consolation and satisfaction.

In these stories, the child is expected to participate in interpersonal relationships and bring life and vitality to a family or an individual. The desire to have a child is a desire to have somebody who will be close to you, a *friend*. But a parent-child relationship is by nature asymmetrical: a child is a dependent person in need of adult care and socialization. As Jenny Hockey and Allison James (1993) argue, children's physical, economic, and social dependency is grounded in power relations and defined through thinking about the child as the other. This aspect of dependency makes adoption an ambiguous matter (Telfer 2003). On the one hand, the abandoned child needs care, which guarantees its socialization and the development of its personality. On the other hand, the process of adoption —and the very fact that the child was abandoned—challenges its original belonging and identity and reinforces its otherness and dependency. This ambivalence resembles the dramatic two-sidedness presented by the Lithuanian social worker. The residents of Kuršėnai emphasize that the adopted child in the adoptive family remains the "other," and many prefer ART to adoption. But the question of the "otherness" and dependency that follows any child in their stories stays open.

Legal Interpretations of Family Relatedness

The child's relatedness to parents, as well as relationships between family members, the child's identity, its care, and adoption are defined legally (Howell 2002). The legal construction of family relationships has a long tradition, although its forms have changed over time.

Until 1998 the adoption of children, which in a legal and cultural sense means the juridical kinning of a child, was a form of care that predominated in Lithuania along with institutional care and care in the families of relatives. At that time half of neglected children were living in orphanages; the rest were fostered by relatives or were adopted. During the last decade, policies and practices in education and social work have been transformed. The protection of children's rights became regulated by a variety of international conventions as Lithuania became a signatory to international laws (Bankauskiene and Staskeviciene 2005). The Child Care Law (1998) and the Civil Code (2000) were formulated and came into force, legally acknowledging a range of forms of children's care. Alongside adoption and institutions such as orphanages and boarding schools appeared such new forms as care in a foster family and short-term care. This trend inspired the development of a system of work with foster families, selecting and training parents, educating professional social workers, and setting up agencies. Foster families as well as orphanages and boarding schools were provided with allowances for children's care. The money came from the government, and various groups competed for public resources (Bankauskiene and Staskeviciene 2005).

Historically, the legal and institutional governance of children's care and a variety of its forms is not a recent innovation in Lithuania, as some scholars mistakenly assume (Bankauskiene and Staskeviciene 2005). The Statutes of Lithuania (*Statuta Lituaniae*) of 1529, 1566, and 1588 have separate chapters on the law of wardship dealing with the protection of wards, the rights and obligations of guardians, and how to administer care (*Lietuvos Statutas* 2002, Andriulis 2003). The law defines the categories of persons who should take care of an orphan whose parents are dead: according to the parents' wishes, as expressed in a will; through the kinship lines of father and mother and degrees of closeness; or appointed by the state, mainly in court. There are special requirements to become a guardian. Women had to be married, and men had to be of a particular age; guardians had to live in the same district as the child, be of good character, and manage the household well. Those principles remained unchanged until the end of the eighteenth century. Significantly, the legal institutions of care at that time were related to the administration of an orphan's property (Andriulis 2003).

Today the legal and institutional management of children's care is comparable to the juridical definition of ART (Melhuus and Howell 2008), which was established in Lithuania during the late 1990s. Both sets of laws govern social relations and persons. There is one difference between them: ART draws not only on individual identity but also on the biotechnological origin of a person and adds prenatal dimensions to human relatedness and personhood. For example, the draft of the Law on Artificial Insemination (2002) speaks about types of donorship of gametes and the right to choose them according to the phenotype of a donor; about kinship and relatives, and about ova donation by sisters, cousins, aunts, and nieces. It states the principles for defining maternity, paternity, and kin relationship of a child; the protection of rights of donors and children; biological parents' exemption from duties to their children; and the confidentiality of donors and recipients.

The legal governance of persons, conception, and care, and of relatedness and family represents the management of social relations and identities. Individuality, human physicality, and the emotional dimensions of belonging and mutual interaction are included in articles of law, court procedures, competition for funding, official lists, files, and records. Government appears to constitute an ordered reality of its own, which is not directly related to an individual person and his or her everyday interactions. But government has the power to intervene in any person's life while constructing relations and identities anew. When I asked Antanas, who works in the Kuršėnai orphanage, about the bureaucratic obstacles people have to surmount if they want to adopt a child, he presented an example of eight siblings living in the orphanage. The eldest brother has reached the age of majority, a sister is seventeen, the next brother is sixteen, and the others are younger. Their newborn sister is in the orphanage for infants, and a couple wishes to adopt her. The elder brothers and sisters insist that they not be separated. They all wrote a letter of protest against adoption of their baby sister, arguing that they are family and the elder children can take responsibility for her. But the court decided in favor of the couple. Antanas said, "you know what will happen in the future —longing for relatives, quarrels, searches [for relatives], and so on" (cf. Carsten 2000).

The view that institutional and personal realities are different worlds shapes the Venclauskiais' daughter's narrative as well. Comparing the life of children in the Kuršėnai orphanage with that in their family, she begins by saying that the state built that orphanage. "The director who was hired was a nice woman. The orphanage was very well ordered. But there was no family there. To my mother, children came naturally. There was a bed full of children. In the morning everybody who wished jumped into mother's bed. There was no order, but children loved my mother. There was really home there."

The interviewees' stories return to the matter of subjectivity and the emotional dimensions of relationships, which many regard as quite different from the governmental ordering of children. They think that cases absorbed into legal and institutional contexts lose their "natural" intersubjectivity based on personal attachments. Nevertheless, legal interpretations of family relations and the identity of a child remain an influential "fact of life," forming the principles of his or her existence and making or re-making the family.

Prenatal Dimensions of Individuality

Describing the relatedness of a child born through ART, people negotiate belonging, closeness, and subjectivity within physical, social, and emotional dimensions (Edwards and Strathern 2000, Orobitg and Salazar 2005, Howell and Marre 2006). They speak about the personality of a child and the properties of its character that would guarantee its good relationship with parents. A middle-aged man, Mindaugas, said: "I would take [a child] from orphanage, and I would not know [the parents]. And you take that donor, for example, a man whom you know. It suits me. For example, my friend would fertilize my wife, of course . . . maybe. But if I go to the orphanage, maybe a child for me is beautiful, but its descent is not clear, for example, his parents were alcoholics, or there might be some genetically inherited diseases. You do not know its kin, descent, nothing."

Many interviewees think that a child has inborn "properties of a father or a mother," or other relatives, that are "inherited" as "a particular gene." They say that children from orphanages might inherit their biological parents' behavior and fate: alcoholism, drug addiction, laziness, and other negative habits. They give examples that illustrate how a "good family" adopted and educated a child, only to find that he or she became like the biological mother who had abandoned him or her. People generalize, saying that a child is "born to be a priest or a thief." No doubt this attribution of a child's personality to genetic inheritance is an attempt to make the child feel simultaneously "the other" and related. The narratives people use to describe genetic inheritance are filled with information, expressions, and examples borrowed from TV and newspapers (Lebner 2000) and recall folklore stories instead of actual cases. Mainly those narratives

assist in establishing the child's otherness. They function as an explanatory model that shows the child's character and individuality and either
creates or erases the boundaries between the child and its biological and
adoptive parents (Lebner 2000, Howell 2002).

The emphasis on inborn qualities conceives of the child as not a *tabula
rasa*; no newborn is a "blank slate," whether adopted, conceived naturally
or through ART, whether one's own or that of a stranger. Sharon Stephens
has pointed out that "children are not empty vessels waiting to be filled"
(Stephens 1995: 23, quoted in Telfer 2003: 79). According to residents of
Kuršėnai, a child has essential traits that are inherited. People use the
word "genes," but they define those inborn features not through biological substances or processes but through something that it is impossible to
grasp. They call it "*pradas*," an original element.

Antanas, drawing on his working experience at Kuršėnai orphanage,
reports that the adoptive parents want to know everything about an adoptee and his or her biological parents. In that context, he mentions genetics. To our question, "why genetics?" he gives another example from his
experience: "At first [when a child comes] the staff at the orphanage think,
what a good child we have . . . And suddenly some time has passed, and
the child becomes cruel or another feature appears. And then we look at
his life story, and find out that his parents did the same." Staff customar-
ily interpret the child's behavior in relation to inborn properties that are
found in a child's file archived at the orphanage. He says "it is more about
us [the staff], because actually this life story [and our thinking about in-
heritance] is nonsense. Among normal biological families whose genetic
tendencies are normal, and among those of the upper class, there are also
children born to be a priest or a thief. What we see is that it is difficult
to suppress some negative experience or some negative inborn feature."
Antanas' story begins with discussion about genetics but shifts to a story
about experience that is equated with the inborn characteristics.

The idea that inborn properties are produced through experience and
behavior is traditional in Lithuanian culture. Lithuanians consider that
the character and features of a child—physical, psychological, moral, and
social—are determined by the behavior of a pregnant mother as well as
by the behavior of others with her. Rasa Paukštytė has suggested that
in Lithuanian villages the system of norms, beliefs, and prohibitions was
oriented toward forming the body, emotions, moral agency, working capacities, and talents of a future child during pregnancy (Paukštytė 1999).
Thus the proverb "born to be a priest or a thief" speaks not about genes

or the biological aspects of inheritance but about the child bred and born in a particular social and cultural setting (Edwards 1999, 2005). But mainly it speaks about prenatal dimensions of its individuality developed through specificity of experiences that persons, couples, families, and communities present. The understanding that a child is a unique creature is confirmed by the Venclauskiais' daughter when she tells about her mother's fostered children: "Everyone came with their own story. There was no secret."

Conclusion

Both ART and adoption remain controversial. People in Kuršėnai speak of a child as the greatest wealth for a couple, but say that it is given by nature, fate, or God; that it might be planned, yet is received naturally; and that it is born from love, or with the assistance of technology. They say that it is good to adopt, but at the same time they think that it is better to conceive, carry, and deliver a child of one's own through ART. They present cases of adoption that are successful, but at the same time say that ART might be better because it enables parents to have their own child. They conclude that it is difficult to tell what is best: "There is a huge risk. To raise one's own child is also a risk. Maybe you, or maybe [the child] later makes his or her life whatever it becomes."

People's emphasis on the desire to have a child places a child in a central position in a family, which coincides with its dependent status. Significantly, the centrality of a child speaks not about the child but about a man and a woman and their relationship. As a man working in orphanage put it, by "going for adoption parents often solve their own problems, but not the children's problems." However, the child, whether adopted or borne, is a new person in a family who comes with his or her "inborn features" and life history constructed through certainties of belonging, social, legal, and morally evaluated "facts of life," and lived experiences that are held to be cumulative (Telfer 2003). The child participates in the interrelationship between the husband and wife, and the three are the influential actors in their shared social reality (Simpson 1998). They experience both subjectivity and intersubjectivity (Berger and Luckmann 1999). In the intertwining of their relationships, they create a new reality in which, over time, the development of the experience supersedes the child's dependency on the parents and makes the three into individuals.

ACKNOWLEDGMENTS

I am grateful to Darius Dauksas and my colleagues from the project "Public Understanding of Genetics" for their help, comments, and discussion.

NOTES

1. "The Public Understanding of Genetics: A cross-cultural and ethnographic study of the 'new genetics' and social identity" is sponsored by the European Commission Fifth Framework Programme: Quality of Life and Management of Living Resources, contract number QLG7-CT-2001-01668.

2. The research project, "Normative and Folk Understanding of Kinship and Ethnicity," was sponsored by the Lithuanian State Science and Study Foundation, grant number T-05201, T-04/05.

3. While staying in Šiauliai in 2005, I visited the Venclauskiai family's former house, now a museum, and talked with their youngest daughter, a lawyer in her nineties. I looked over many letters that her mother had received from the fostered children and read the children's published memoirs. See L. Peleckis, *Namuose ant Pasadnos ulyčios* (*At home on Pasadna street*) (Vilnius: Valstybinis leidybos centras, 1991); I. Nekrašienė (ed.), *Kazimieras Venclauskis* (Šiauliai: Šiauliai "Aušros" Muziejus, 2000). I thank Irena Nekrašienė, the curator of Šiauliai "Aušra" museum, for her assistance in enabling me to see the materials related to the Venclauskiai family.

4. Gendrė Kaniušaitė has shown that, although the subject of orphans attracts considerable attention in contemporary society, Lithuanian ethnographic studies neglect this theme. In the few instances in which orphans are discussed, they are related to the themes of being outside or inside of community and of legal interpretations of family relationships. See Gendrė Kaniušaitė, "An Orphan in Lithuanian Society: The Analysis of Ethnological Literature" (Vilnius University, 2006).

REFERENCES

Alber, Erdmute. 2003. "Denying Biological Parenthood: Fosterage in Northern Benin." *Ethnos* 68, no. 4: 487–506.

Andriulis, V. 2003. *Lietuvos Statutų (1529, 1566, 1588 m.) šeimos teisė (Family Law Statute of Lithuania 1529, 1566, 1588)*. Vilnius: Teisinės informacijos centras.

Bankauskiene, N., and V. Staskeviciene. 2005. "A Case Study of a Lithuanian Foster Family." *European Educational Research Journal* 4, no. 2: 121–31.

Berger, Peter L., and Thomas Luckmann. (1967) 1999. *The Social Construction of Reality: A Treatise in the Sociology of Knowledge*. New York: Doubleday.

Bestard, Joan. 2004. "Kinship and the New Genetics: The Changing Meaning of Biogenetic Substance." *Social Anthropology* 12, no. 3: 253–63.

Bonaccorso, Monica. 2004. "Making Connections: Family and Relatedness in Clinics of Assisted Conception in Italy." *Modern Italy* 9, no. 1: 59–68.

Carsten, Janet. 2000. "'Knowing Where You've Come From': Ruptures and Continuities of Time and Kinship in Narratives of Adoption Reunions." *Journal of the Royal Anthropological Institute* 6: 687–703.

Čepaitienė, Auksuolė. 2008. "Imagining Assisted Reproductive Technologies: Family, Kinship, and 'Local Thinking' in Lithuania." In *Kinship Matters: European Cultures of Kinship in the Age of Biotechnology*, ed. Jeanette Edwards and Carles Salazar. Oxford, UK: Berghahn Books.

Edwards, Jeanette. 1999. *Born and Bred: Idioms of Kinship and New Reproductive Technologies in England*. Oxford: Oxford University Press.

———. 2005. "'Make-up': Personhood through the Lens of Biotechnology." *Ethnos* 70, no. 3: 413–31.

Edwards, Jeanette, Sarah Franklin, Eric Hirsch, Frances Price, and Marilyn Strathern. 1993. *Technologies of Procreation: Kinship in the Age of Assisted Conception*. Manchester: Manchester University Press.

Edwards, Jeanette, and Marilyn Strathern. 2000. "Including Our Own." In *Cultures of Relatedness: New Approaches to the Study of Kinship*, ed. Janet Carsten, 149–66. Cambridge: Cambridge University Press.

Fellous, M. 2007. "Identity-Related and Socio-anthropological Implications of a Techno-industrial and Medical Innovation (Concerning the Project of Animal Transplantation in Humans)." Paper presented at the international conference Anthropology, Ethnography and Biotechnology, 12–14 September, Vilnius.

Fortes, Meyer. 1973. "On the Concept of the Person among the Tallensi." In *La Notion de Personne en Afrique Noire: Colloques Internationaux du C.N.R.S.* 544: 283–320.

Franklin, Sarah, and Susan McKinnon. 2001. Introduction to *Relative Values: Reconfiguring Kinship Studies*, ed. Sarah Franklin and Susan McKinnon, 1–25. Durham, NC: Duke University Press.

Giddens, Anthony. 1997. *Modernity and Self-Identity: Self and Society in the Late Modern Age*. Cambridge, UK: Polity Press.

Hockey, Jenny, and Allison James. 1993. *Growing Up and Growing Old: Ageing and Dependency in the Life Course*. London: Sage.

Howell, Signe. 2001. "Self-Conscious Kinship: Some Contested Values in Norwegian Transnational Adoption." In *Relative Values: Reconfiguring Kinship Studies*, ed. S. Franklin and S. McKinnon, 203–23. Durham, NC: Duke University Press.

———. 2002. "Community beyond Place: Adoptive Families in Norway." In *Realising Community: Concepts, Social Relationships and Sentiments*, ed. Vered Amit, 84–103. London: Routledge.

Howell, Signe. 2003. "Kinning: The Creation of Life Trajectories in Transnational Adoptive Families." *Journal of Royal Anthropological Institute* 9, no. 3: 465–84.

Howell, Signe, and Diana Marre. 2006. "To Kin a Transnationally Adopted Child in Norway and Spain: The Achievement of Resemblances and Belonging." *Ethnos* 71, no. 3: 293–316.

Lebner, Ashley. 2000. "Genetic 'Mysteries' and International Adoption: The Cultural Impact of Biomedical Technologies on the Adoptive Family Experience." *Family Relations* 49, no. 4: 371–77.

Lietuvos Statutas. The Statute of Lithuania. Statuta Lituaniae: 1529. 2002. Vilnius: Artlora.

Mauss, Marcel. (1934) 1973. "Techniques of the Body." *Economy and Society* 2, no. 1: 70–88.

Melhuus, Marit, and Signe Howell. 2008. "Adoption and Assisted Conception: One Universe of Unnatural Procreation. An Examination of Norwegian Legislation." In *Kinship Matters: European Cultures of Kinship in the Age of Biotechnology*, ed. Jeanette Edwards and Carles Salazar. Oxford, UK: Berghahn Books.

Orobitg, Gemma, and Carles Salazar. 2005. "The Gift of Motherhood: Egg Donation in a Barcelona Infertility Clinic." *Ethnos* 70, no. 1: 31–52.

Paukštytė, Rasa. 1999. *Gimtuvės ir krikštynos Lietuvos kaimo gyvenime (XIX a. pabaigoje–XX a. pirmoje pusėje) (Child birth and baptism in Lithuanian village life [the end of 19th and the first half of 20th centuries]).* Vilnius: Diemedžio leidykla.

Ragone, Helena. 1994. *Surrogate Motherhood: Conception in the Heart.* Boulder, CO: Westview Press.

Salazar, Carles. 1999. "On Blood and Its Alternatives: An Irish History." *Social Anthropology* 7, no. 2: 155–67.

Simpson, Bob. 1998. *Changing Families: An Ethnographic Approach to Divorce and Separation.* Oxford, UK: Berg.

Strathern, Marilyn. 1992a. *After Nature: English Kinship in the Late Twentieth Century.* Cambridge: Cambridge University Press.

———. 1992b. *Reproducing the Future: Anthropology, Kinship and the New Reproductive Technologies.* Manchester: Manchester University Press.

———. 1995. "Displacing Knowledge: Technology and the Consequences for Kinship." In *Conceiving the New World Order: The Global Politics of Reproduction*, ed. Faye Ginsburg and Rayna Rapp, 346–63. Berkeley: University of California Press.

Telfer, Jori. 2003. "The Imagined Child: Ambiguity and Agency in Australian Intercountry Adoption." *Australian Journal of Anthropology* 14, no. 2: 72–80.

Yan, Yunxiang. 2001. "Practising Kinship in Rural North China." In *Relative Values: Reconfiguring Kinship Studies*, ed. Sarah Franklin and Susan McKinnon, 224–245. Durham, NC: Duke University Press.

Part III

||||||||||||||||||||||||||||||||||||||||||||||||||||||

Experiences in Receiving Countries

What do emergent trends among transnationally adopted youth and their families in receiving countries suggest about issues of identity formation and social acceptance that develop as children mature? In Western Europe and North America, most internationally adopted children are visibly different from their adoptive parents, making it impossible not to deal directly with transracial adoption. What happens when adopted children of native-born parents who are culturally European or American resemble immigrants and the children of immigrants and may be mistaken for "foreigners"? What are the implications of the searches for siblings and return journeys to discover national or cultural "roots" in which some adoptees and their families engage? What do parents mean when they say they want their children to preserve the culture of their county of origin, yet be fully accepted within their new nation? Older notions of racial characteristics lurk within some notions of "culture," just as they do in popular conceptions of "genetic heritage."

Today Spain receives more transnationally adopted children than any other country besides the United States and leads the European Union in both international adoptions and immigration. Diana Marre explores the implications for international adoptees and for Spanish society of the fact that here, as in the rest of Europe, immigrants and international adoptees come from the same regions, yet international adoption is not treated as an international migration processes. For example, a teacher at a prominent primary school in Barcelona said "we do not have immigrant children, we have children adopted internationally." Social and legal regulations vis-à-vis non-European immigrants and adoptees differ enormously, as do the attitudes of the native-born population. Marre examines the complex and ambivalent meanings of "cultural origins" that are articulated by adoptive parents regarding children who do not look like them. The possibility that adopted children might be stigmatized and marginalized as immigrants is the underside of Spanish attitudes toward difference as it binds race to culture.

Caroline Legrand explores how the search for ancestral "roots" differs between transnational adoptees and the descendants of immigrants. Reclaiming the culture of origin does not hold the same meanings for members of each group, and the two groups construct distinct relationships to genealogical memory and knowledge. Legrand examines what hides behind these "routes to the roots" projects by exploring questions of who owns the rights to investigate their ancestry. Drawing on ethnographic data collected in France, Ireland, and Québec, this chapter begins to construct an anthropology of genealogical practices.

Signe Howell reconsiders the questions that adoption raises about the European-American distinction between biological and social kinship. When adoption takes place between different countries—especially when the children look different from their new parents and kin, as they do when they are moved from countries in Asia, Africa, Latin America to Europe and North America—questions of identity, belonging, race, ethnicity, and culture are on the agenda. It is impossible for transnationally adopted persons and their parents to avoid confronting them and the contradictions to which they often give rise. Offering a theoretical framework that elucidates the transformations involved in transnational, transcultural, transracial adoption, Howell illuminates the meanings of adoption for the social construction of kinship.

Adoption often overlaps with assisted reproduction, as gay and lesbian adults conceive children through in vitro fertilization and various forms of surrogacy. Many men, and some women, must legally adopt the children for whose conception they are responsible. Focusing on France, where gay male parents are forced to differentiate between those who gestate and those who raise the child, Anne Cadoret considers how parents address the problem of filiation. Are the women who donate an egg and/or carry a fetus "mothers"? Are they kin, or is surrogacy merely a business contract? The cultural logic that governs the decisions gay men in France make regarding whom to recognize as parents yields insight into changing social norms and practices of parenthood, just as adoptive families shed light on normative forms of reproduction.

Finally, Toby Alice Volkman explores the recent preoccupation among the U.S. American families of girls adopted from China with "seeking sisters," biological siblings from whom they were separated by placement in foster care, orphanages, and adoptive families. An impossible longing for birth mothers may be transposed onto a search for siblings that is simpler, both practically and emotionally, given the availability of DNA testing and Internet connections. Successful sibling searches lend themselves to cheerful media coverage. Reporters and readers take pleasure in stories of twins running into each other's arms or jumping for joy as they reclaim their kinship. While less fraught with ambivalence than searches for and reunions with birth parents, sibling searches and reunions raise troubling new questions. Adoptive families struggle to deal with loss, while negotiating tensions between kinship imagined as biogenetic and kinship imagined as actively created, over time, on the basis of other ties.

Chapter 12

"We Do Not Have Immigrant Children at This School, We Just Have Children Adopted from Abroad"

Flexible Understandings of Children's "Origins"

Diana Marre

An adoptive mother of two teenage girls born in Asia was explaining to her colleagues her objections to the clothing style one of her daughters preferred. To convince the young woman that her appearance was a problem, she told her, "one day you'll fall off the Ramblas [promenade in Barcelona] and people will take you for an immigrant." Why would that happen? And why would it be a problem for an adopted girl to be taken for an immigrant?

In this chapter, I explore the blurring of "race" with "culture" and "ethnicity" that pervades the narratives of professionals, bureaucrats, and parents with adopted children born in Asia, Africa, and Latin America who do not look like them. Today, culture and/or ethnicity often stand in as euphemisms for race, since that term is hardly ever used in Spain (del Olmo 2004, Stolcke 1992, 1995). Significantly, this conflation means that culture appears to be heritable, not simply the result of socialization. I examine Spanish adoptive parents' construction of difference and contrast this discourse with discourses about immigrants and their children. Despite the salience of narratives of "integration" for internationally adopted children, their place of origin is still used as the basis for social and cultural ascription as well as the basis for social and economic discrimination against immigrants because it seems that "there are better [. . .] places to live or to be born in" (del Olmo 2004: 15).

I carried out ethnographic research in Barcelona from 2001, interviewing adoptive families—married and unmarried couples, single mothers and fathers, and gay and lesbian couples—living in Catalonia.[1] The interviews were complemented by participant observation in discussion groups of adoptive families and associations of adoptive families in Catalonia. I also monitored the Internet listservs of two associations of adoptive families as well as two listservs on post-adoption issues that represent a broader Spanish population.

As Peter Selman (in this volume) shows, since 2004 Spain has received more internationally adopted children than any other country in the world after the United States. Spain has also received more international immigrants than any other country except the United States. In Spain, immigration from outside Western Europe and international adoptions are increasing at the same time. Immigrants and adopted children come from the same regions: the impoverished South and the countries of the former Soviet Union. Both trends became socially significant during the late 1990s, but their connections remain problematic.

On October 7, 2007, the security video camera on a train near Barcelona captured images of an incident that has aroused wide interest and considerable controversy. A twenty-year-old man cast racial and xenophobic slurs followed by the word "immigrant" at a sixteen-year-old girl of Ecuadorian origin, while slapping her, groping and pinching her breast, and kicking her brutally in the face. Meanwhile, with his free hand, the man held a mobile phone and told someone elsewhere about how he had repeatedly assaulted other people of North or sub-Saharan African origin. The videotape of this incident was widely broadcast by the mass media and available on the Internet.[2]

Contentious public debates about the assault on the girl raged during October and November 2007. Concern centered on the fact that the young assailant was released after questioning by law enforcement agents. It was said, perhaps as an exonerating factor, that he came from a broken home and was brought up by his grandmother and he was drunk. It was pointed out that while the victim entered the court to testify in broad daylight with her face uncovered; the assailant entered through a side door, with his face covered, and surrounded by security. Much discussion focused on the attitude of the one visible witness, who did nothing to intervene. The president of the Autonomous Community of Madrid,[3] from the most right-wing party in Spain, branded this behavior "scandalous," remarking that "This is the way Nazism started, because everyone looked the other way."[4] The young man who witnessed the assault was tempted with large sums of money by various television networks, but he spoke voluntarily on the morning show of the main Catalonian TV network. This youth, whom some media have called "the second train victim," said that he is gay; he left Salta, a small Catholic town in Argentina, a year and a half ago when he fell in love with a man from Olesa de Montserrat, a small Catalan city. He said he did not do anything because he was afraid, since he himself is an "immigrant" and has "darker" skin. He asked for protection because the widely broadcast video shows his face clearly, while the faces of the assailant and the assaulted girl were deliberately blurred. Finally, he stated something everyone knew but nobody had mentioned: that two other men in the car, who were Catalan or at least Spanish, also did nothing, but nobody said anything about them.

In Spain, as in most other European countries, social and legal regulations relative to non-European immigrants and adoptees differ enormously; as does the general attitude of the population. A teacher at a Barcelona primary school in an upper-class neighborhood told me, "we do not have immigrant children, we have children adopted internationally." This statement confirms an idea a colleague suggested: "when people see 'different' children in Barcelona's lower-class neighborhoods, they think that they are immigrant children. However, when these children are in middle- and upper-class neighborhoods, people think that they are children adopted internationally." Although attitudes toward immigrants vary widely and the subject is increasingly controversial, opinion toward children being adopted from other countries is generally positive. In Spain, intercountry adoptions are not considered as involving international migration. Parents who adopted internationally are aware that many immigrants and immigrants' children have "integration" difficulties (del Olmo 2007). Nevertheless, most say that they want their adopted children to preserve their "cultural origins" at the same time that, paradoxically, they are among those who tend to deny any possible similarities between immigrants and their internationally adopted children.

International Immigration in Spain

In Spain as a whole, international immigration began in the mid-1990s. Until then, Spain had a long history of very high levels of emigration to its former colonial empire and of internal migration between Autonomous Communities, which some of them also consider immigration. In 1995, Spain had 38 million inhabitants; foreign residents represented just 1 percent of the population, while Spanish emigrants abroad were more than triple that number. In January 2008, Spain had 46 million inhabitants; immigrants represented 11.3 percent of the Spanish population, and 14.5 of that in Catalonia. Moroccans are the largest single immigrant group. However, 40.2 percent of immigrants come from the 27 countries of the European Union, and Romanians had the highest rate of increase in 2007.[5]

Situated on the northern coast of the Mediterranean, Spain is a growing site of entry for immigrants from North and Central Africa. Old colonial ties with Equatorial Guinea and Morocco and the geographical proximity of the Spanish Autonomous Cities of Ceuta and Melilla, located in Moroccan territory, and of the Canary Islands off the coast of Africa have made Spain the initial and, more recently, the final destination of many Africans. Spain also attracts immigrants from South and Central America and the Philippines, all former colonies. Some of these countries were the main destinations of Spanish emigrants from the late nineteenth through the early twentieth centuries and again during the Spanish civil war in the 1930s. Immigrants from Latin America share a common language and religion with most of the Autonomous Communities of Spain, which contributes to a belief in their cultural similarity. Preferential status continues to be accorded to citizens of countries with former colonial ties, allowing Latin Americans, people from the Philippines, and Equatorial Guineans to claim Spanish nationality after a legal residency of two years. Legal residency is also granted to people with work contracts.

In social terms, immigrants and their children retain their status as foreigners even after they become naturalized citizens because of their accent, physical appearance, and/or religion. A social worker born in Latin America who has been living for the last twenty years in Catalonia with her Catalan husband and three Catalan children and who speaks perfect Catalan (which politicians regard as the main sign of integration) but has some "Latin American physical traits" asked herself rhetorically why people could not stop seeing her as a Latin American immigrant. A young writer born in Morocco but raised in Catalonia from infancy, who recently received an award for a book written in Catalan, said that she would like to take part in her neighborhood association, not only in the association of Moroccan or North African women, the place designated for her as a daughter of a Moroccan immigrant family because Spanish and Catalan people recognize immediately that she has North African physical traits.[6] Although the matter is seldom openly discussed, persons identifiable as of foreign origin suffer from social exclusion and discrimination.[7] In Spain, as in other Western European and North American countries, most immigrants have more education than the average Spaniard and are overqualified for the unskilled jobs they hold.[8]

International Adoption in Spain

Why do so many people in Spain adopt from abroad? While there is neither a unique cause nor sufficient research to draw definitive conclusions, we can point to several factors with some confidence.

Firstly, there is a severe shortage of local children available for adoption. The scarcity of native-born children in Spain occurred rather recently, after the end of Franco's dictatorship in 1975 and the transition to democracy brought changes in family life, particularly for women. Contraception was allowed in 1978, divorce approved in 1981, voluntary sterilization surgery permitted in 1983, and abortion legalized in 1985. What took decades to develop in other countries happened in less than ten years in Spain. The social welfare system was restructured, while feminism promoted the right of Spanish women to choose not to marry, to delay childbirth, or to remain childless.[9]

Secondly, family law in Spain tends to preserve genitors' rights, unless they themselves renounce them. The 1987 law considered be the starting point for the current regulation of adoption recognized that one cause of the rarity of domestic adoption in Spain was legislation that is excessively protective of biological parents' rights.[10] Spain, with around 46 million inhabitants, has more that 30,000 children and youth under state protection, but it has the second-largest number of international adoptions, including adoptions of children with special needs.

Thirdly, women's incorporation into the labor market remains incomplete and women workers do not enjoy the same wage rates and working conditions as men. Female employment and fertility rates are closely connected. While Spain had the EU's highest birth rate in 1975, with 2.8 children per woman, it had the lowest rate when international adoption began in 1995, with 1.17 children per woman. In 2007, however, the birth rate was higher than it had been during the previous fourteen years, with 1.37 children per woman, and 18 percent of the children were born to an immigrant mother.[11] A study of fertility found that 60 percent of women interviewed thought that becoming pregnant and having children are serious obstacles to a professional career.[12] In 2007, just 36 percent of Catalan families who apply for an international adoption had done an infertility treatment (Font Lletjòs 2008). These facts are suggesting an "outsourcing" of some reproductive functions, following the trend to shift some productive functions from the global North and West to the global East and South and/or to immigrant women.

In Spain, as elsewhere, the initial motivation to adopt was humanitarian. Many officials and adoptive parents link international adoption with the repeated broadcasting of a 1995 British television program, "The Rooms of Death," about orphanages in China, which still circulates on the Internet.[13] For many adoptive families, the desire "to give to a child a better future" is as valid as the desire to become parents. Recently, when the new law on international adoption was sent to Parliament, the vice president, Maria Teresa Fernandez de la Vega, emphasized the fact that, in proportion to its population, Spain has the highest rate of adoption in the world. "Almost everyone knows someone who cares for a child adopted in China, Russia, or Ukraine." The Ministry of Justice explained that the new law represented a response to a newly globalized world where "there is inequality of opportunity and a lot of people are abandoned to their fate"; "Spain has developed a strong sense of solidarity."[14] As Ana Berástegui Pedro Viejo (forthcoming) points out, it seems that a "culture of adoption" has developed, articulated in such statements as: "Why, if there are so many children suffering from injustice, could I not get, quickly and without personal physical cost, the youngest and healthiest child whom I need?"

In 1995 and 1996, Spain's birth rate reached its nadir, and the administrations in charge of adoption matters in the Autonomous Communities of Catalonia and Madrid did not carry forward more applications to domestic adoption because no children were available.[15] At that time, international adoption began to acquire a public profile. Single women and single men have been able to adopt from the beginning. In July 2005, the Spanish Parliament approved a modification of the civil code to allow same-sex marriages and, as a direct consequence, adoption by same-sex couples. Previously, when gay and lesbian couples were not allowed to adopt, they did so as single parents. International adoption, like international immigration, is a ten-year-old phenomenon.[16]

Parents' Decisions in International Adoption

Most parents feel that, after the decision to adopt a child, the selection of the country where they will adopt is the most important decision they make. From the parents' perspective, this choice determines the children's skin color and physical features. The adoption law prohibits discrimination, but some parents try to avoid this legal impediment by choosing a specific country. Most parents know what their daughters will look like if they adopt from China. Children from Ethiopia, Haiti, or the Congo will look African. Those from Russia and Eastern Europe are usually European in appearance. Latin America, where many Spanish families adopted initially but whose relative importance as a sending region has decreased, involves more uncertainty. Although most parents adopting there said that their child would probably be "very ethnic," the mixture of indigenous, European, and African ancestry generates a wide range.

China is the country of origin chosen by the largest number of Catalan adoptive parents. A single mother, who worked as a volunteer at an association of adopting families while waiting for the assignment of a girl from China, pointed out: "Many parents, once they solve their race problem"—referring to the racial prejudices they must overcome—"choose to adopt from China because the process is legal, transparent and 'clean.'" The issue of corruption in countries of origin is a frequent subject of discussion among families adopting from Eastern Europe, Latin America, and Africa, but is exceptional in relation to Asian countries and seldom arises in relation to China. Tellingly, corruption is always attributed to the persons or institutions that receive or ask for the bribe and never to those who offer or give it (Marre 2007).[17]

Russia and Eastern Europe is the second most popular sending region among Spanish families. According to those who have adopted from those countries and to professionals who work in adoption services, the process is quite variable; both waiting periods and total costs are unpredictable. The former director of Catalan Institute of Fosterage and Adoption (ICAA) explained that in Russia the "process is not easy," but people choose to adopt there for "ethnic reasons," because the "children are white (*blanquitos*) and more similar to us."[18] Many parents adopting in Russia justify their decision in terms of "cultural or ethnic similarities," which often, according to the former ICAA director, are in fact "physical resemblances." There were some cases in which a family adopting in Russia rejected the child assigned to them because or his or her "Asian" traits, saying that they needed a physical resemblance with the baby in order to identify themselves as parents.

Parents who adopted from Haiti, Ethiopia, and China feel that when they walk around with their daughter it is as if she were wearing a T-shirt that reads "I'm adopted." Parents who adopted in Russia and Eastern Europe often want to keep the adoption a secret, or at least to be able to decide with whom to share this intimate fact. For many parents, the origins question is related to having to talk about it not only with their children—when, how, and under what circumstances they were adopted—but also with strangers. Many do not want to be compelled to explain their family relationships to people whom they do not know. As Lilia Khabibullina (in this volume) says, "it seems that children adopted in Russia are 'invisible' because of their 'European looks.'" The popularity of Russian children might in some cases be explained by the racial preferences of adoptive parents. On the other hand, parents who adopted in Russia say that people who adopt in Asia or Africa do it to try to seem "open-minded."

Significantly, Spanish adoptive parents have not only an ethnic or racialized construction of their adopted children but also an ethnic or racialized construction of themselves. Adoptive parents are commonly considered ethnically homogeneous and racially white. In Spain, the definition of national identities as fundamentally white and racially similar to other Europeans developed relatively recently. During Franco's dictatorship it was said ironically that Africa begins in the Pyrenees, which made Spain African. Since the 1980s, as part of its effort to join Europe and the European Union, Spain embarked on a process of "modernization" and "civilization" that includes establishing its "whiteness." An adoptive grandmother born and bred in the United Kingdom who has lived in Spain for the last forty years found this sense of whiteness excessive. "If they [adoptive parents] think that no one would notice the difference in a Russian, Ukrainian, Romanian child . . . because even though they are not that noticeable, they can notice that it's a blonder child with facial features that don't look that Spanish."

To Maintain Adopted Children's "Cultural Origins"

The desirability of keeping some connection with their child's country of origin is rarely questioned by adoptive parents. This principle is included in the Hague Convention on Intercountry Adoption, as Barbara Yngvesson has pointed out (2000, 2003, and in this volume), so it is widely disseminated and incorporated in national legal codes. The professionals whom Signe Howell (in this volume) calls psycho-technocrats unanimously recommend the maintenance of bonds with the child's native land. Recent trends in thinking about adoption encourage a child to embrace his or her "two cultures." When older children are adopted, however, the main objective is to help them gradually adapt to the family and feel included in society. In Spain, parents are adamant about their adopted child not losing touch with the culture of origin. Every home I have visited for an interview with an adoptive family has some visible sign of the child's country of origin. The main exceptions are probably parents who adopted in Eastern Europe, which they regard as being adopted "into the same culture" rather than moving from one culture into another.

When the visible differences between internationally adopted children and their parents cross lines of race, the community created around them, especially through associations of international adoptive families, become more "visible and vocal," to use Toby Volkman's terms (2003: 30). In Spain, as in United States, families adopting from China are often organized into associations. So are Spanish families adopting in Ethiopia, Haiti, or elsewhere. The association of families adopting in Russian and Eastern Europe was the last to be formed and remains the least active, although this region is now one of the most popular source of children.

Some parents associate the culture of origin with a language, even if the child was adopted as a baby. Some associations of adoptive families with daughters from China offer Chinese language classes. An adoptive mother said that she would be happy if, when "some ill-humored classmate called her Chinese, or told her 'go back to your country,'" the girl "would answer with a string of insults in Chinese, even if they were made up." In contrast, a mother with children adopted in Russia said that, although her children had a map of Russia in their room with a thumbtack on the cities where they had been born, she was not educating them about Russian culture. She could not help laughing in the Russian consul's face when, at the time she registered her children, he recommended that she renew their passports every five years so that the children could have

Russian nationality when they grew up. She concluded: "My children are rightfully Spanish, children of a Spanish mother, me, and I think it's quite silly to believe that they will choose, when they turn eighteen, to renounce their Spanish nationality for Russian nationality."

Families pass around recipes from the country or region and incorporate new foods into their diets. They buy children's books, music, and artifacts and go see movies from the country of origin. From the moment the decision is made, they explore the culture through its literature, music, language, and cuisine. "I love Chinese culture in many respects and I deeply respect the country. I owe them my girl's life and I feel very sorry for the woman who carried her for nine months and I don't even want to think what she was going through," another mother said. "I need to know the culture of the nation that gave her life." With certain distress, one adoptive mother asked, "Is it good to idealize an unknown mother they cannot get to know? Is it advisable that in the mental universe of our girls there be a mother who is good and ideal while we turn into the witches because we don't let them go out at night?" This overlapping of origins and the biological mother is also evident in the words of a young Catalonian woman born in India, who said, "For me, going to my country in search of my origins meant being able to understand certain attitudes that had come up and were related to my genetic inheritance" (Martínez 2004). For her, as for the mother of a Chinese girl adopted when she was three months old who emphasized that she would make sure her child did not "lose" her culture, culture of origin seems to refer to a biological or genetic inheritance.

Most internationally adopted children do not look like their parents. To the outsider's eye they represent an enigma, a challenge to the normal order of things. Their very presence in the family demands an explanation. Most adopters say they are aware that their children are "different." Culture and country of origin both refer to this difference. Although "racial difference" is never mentioned, race remains present behind the scenes, spoken of obliquely as "different traits" or "ethnically different." As an adoptive mother from the Autonomous Community of Galicia pointed out, referring to her China-born daughter, "Of course I want to be able to talk to my child about her cultural origins. She'll be aware of the difference whenever she looks at herself in the mirror."

The categories employed to classify people based on their physical appearance are a legacy of the past. For example, people in Spain, official and informally, still use the term "Caucasian," which is derived from a century-old racial classification system, as a euphemism for "white" and/ or "European" as distinct from "African" or "Asian." As Wade put it, "only some aspects of phenotype are worked into racial signifiers and they are the aspects that were originally seen to be ways of distinguishing between Europeans and those they encountered in their colonial explorations. 'Phenotype' is thus linked to a particular history" (Wade 2002).

From the parents' point of view, it seems better to acknowledge, or even emphasize, differences than attempt to deny or never to speak about something that is self-evident and might be stigmatizing. Adoptive parents devote considerable effort to highlighting the differences between themselves and their children. But, at the same time, they feel that attachment transcends difference confirming the value and importance of their task. "Imagine how much 'ours' we feel her, that we don't even see her as black anymore. I'm not kidding. You don't see the color, it's just love," says a professor with an adopted little girl of Ethiopian origin and two biological sons. The journalist who interviewed this mother understood her comment as expressing a positive attitude toward ostensibly racial differences. Evidently, this adoptive mother had solved her "race problem." Nevertheless, she articulates her love for her girl by saying that her parents "don't see the color." What would happen if they saw her blackness? Would they be unable to love her in the same way?

Many parents with adopted children who are visibly different from themselves blur the culture, or even the customs, of their child's country of origin with child's attitudes. The parents of girls from China usually spoke of their birthplace's thousand-year-old culture as the reason for their girls' "natural" meekness and intelligence—though these qualities are reinforced by the Spanish parents from the first encounter. Some parents embody these qualities in their daughters' names. An adoptive mother of a Chinese and a Congolese girl told me she had called them Honey and Forest in reference to their "nature," a term also used to refer to racial differences. Mothers of African-born daughters say that it is best to take the girls to a hair salon "for black people." "You have to go to one of these hair salons . . . run by immigrants, because not only do they know how to deal with the hair, but they also have the adequate products. One can look at how they do it, but we will never be able to do it as they do it because for them it's natural." An adoptive mother advised others to make contact with black women when they take their children to the park because it is the only way of learning how to handle kinky hair.

"Natural" is also the adjective used to describe the inner rhythm that parents perceive in their daughters, as Katherine Tyler also found (2005). The father of a girl who was almost two when she was adopted in Central Africa mentioned that he and others on the trip were very surprised by the way his daughter received him at the airport, with an African dance full of "natural" rhythm. Parents describe the "natural" ability of their daughters from Africa to eat delicately with their hands, forming a sort of bowl with them, instead of using a plate. References to the tastes, rhythmic and musical skills, and abundant energy of children adopted in Africa or Haiti are constructed as 'natural' while references to the meekness, intelligence, and serenity of girls adopted from China are understood as related to their ancient culture. Traits and behaviours are regarded as inherited from the children's place of origin in both cases.

In sum, even children adopted as infants, before they learnt language or were socialized, are regarded as manifesting the characteristics of the culture of their country of origin; culture is regarded as inherited, as if it were biological. Culture is clearly standing in for race in these discourses. Most adoptive parents talk about the adoption of a child with "different origins," "very ethnic," or "ethnically different" when they are referring to an interracial adoption. Indeed, the notion of race is replaced by the notion of ethnicity (del Olmo 2004, Stolcke 1992, 1995, Wade 2002).

At the same time, adoptive parents are all very confident of their capacity to ensure that their racially different children will be integrated into their families and nation. As an adoptive father who founded one of the oldest associations of adoptive parents in Catalonia put it, "their race doesn't matter because they'll end up being Catalan." The integration of adoptees into their adoptive families attracted the attention of Catalan politicians in their endeavor to cope with the question of immigration. At a 2003 international conference on adoption in Catalonia, the former president of the Catalan government observed that international adoption in Catalonia was twice as frequent as in the rest of Spain and underlined both the open-mindedness of Catalans and the openness of Catalan identity compared to other cultures, including the Spanish. In a village where a racist, anti-immigration political group had appeared, he had met a Catalan mother with a Chinese child speaking Catalan, the main symbol of national integration. Similar sentiments were voiced by a mother born and bred in Galicia with one biological daughter who was waiting to adopt a girl from China. She acknowledged her future daughter's Chinese origins, but emphasized her cultural integration. "She is going to be aware that her cultural origins are different every time she looks at herself in the mirror. But my daughter is going to be GALICIAN!!!!!! She is going to live here, speak our language—mine, my daughter's, my family's, learn the *muiñeira* and dress up as *antroido varredoiro* for carnival, eat *filloas* and *clado* and *robaliza ao forno* (Mmmmm!) and so on. . . . My daughter's past is going to be the Civil War her grandfather lived through, her great-grandfather's "cultural" barbershop, her great-grandmother's wisdom, the oral stories of her grandmother, the killing of the pig for San Martiño."

At present, when most adoptees are young children, international adoption creates a multiracial society that is not really multicultural, as the adoptees are supposed to become fully Catalan or Galician and/or Spaniards. Although there are mutual interests in transnational adoption,[19] the relation is nevertheless an unequal one. From the parents' point of view, the country of origin is always inferior to their own. In the parents' retelling of the story of their journey to get the children, they never describe the place as pleasant, or even interesting. Rather, they mention its lack of resources, its problems, its poverty, its corruption, and its stifling hot or freezing cold weather. They experience and then systematically retell the moment of taking the plane back home as a relief.[20] The pervasive undervaluation of a place or culture which they keep saying they want to keep alive for their children seems paradoxical—until we realize that it is part of a "kinning" process (Howell 2003, and in this volume) in an adoption process and that presents particular characteristics in an interracial adoption.

Immigrant Children and Internationally Adopted Children

Parents think that their internationally adopted children are quite different from immigrants and their children. Consider this comparison offered by an adoptive mother:

> Integration problems in our society are bigger for them than for our adopted children even if they come from the same countries, because our environment rapidly accepts our children and does not impose that many barriers on them. . . . As for the neighborhoods, I think . . . it's an attempt to feel safer and more protected. If a family of immigrants arrives in a town they will probably seek help among the people from their country and settle in that area. . . . I would establish a distinction between adopted children and immigrant children because our children's behavior and

culture is ours; they're integrated into this country. Regardless of what the child is like . . . it is our child . . . but the immigrants . . . are at a disadvantage, not because they're bad (though some are really bad) [but because] they don't know our behavior, attitude, manners, and culture, and the conflict arises because of lack of understanding, they're suspicious of us and we're suspicious of them . . . they annoy us . . . there are differences that arise and we all feel awful. My daughter has nothing to do with the daughter of a woman who has just arrived in Madrid from another country . . . and I'm not criticizing this woman. What I say is that my daughter perceives the atmosphere that surrounds her through the education given to her by her Spanish parents, who live here and don't yearn for another country and who don't have other cultures or any difficulties. Even though the Turkish pastries, the *mousaca*, the Greek yogurt, and the Arabic mathematics might be great, what happened to some French people in France doesn't happen to me.

Immigrants do not constitute a single, homogeneous category (Howell and Melhuus 2007). Those immigrants who are kinned and incorporated into a Spanish family are viewed by the authorities and the rest of the native-born population as quite different from those who arrive in order to find work, escape from a restrictive political system, or seek a better future (Howell and Marre 2006). But as internationally adopted children are growing up, the situation is changing. Although there is no open conversation or public discourse on race in contemporary Spain, there are racist articulations and concomitant accusations of racism. Until now only immigrants have suffered from racist actions. However, in 2006 a member of a city government near Madrid with a daughter adopted from China was threatened, saying "your girl will follow the same way as your mother" —a very old woman who had just died.[21] Coincidently or casually, this year some plastic surgeons have reported that adoptive parents have asked for eye surgery for their daughters born in China. Some adoptive parents have reported discriminatory attitudes toward their adolescent children on the part of the police because their Latin American appearance gives rise to suspicion that they belong to urban gangs. International adoptees and immigrants more often develop relationships in adolescence. Some adoptive parents say that their adolescent children began to make contact with immigrants from their country of origin, looking for "their people" or seeking a sense of belonging, speaking like them and adopting their mode of dress. This attitude often includes a sense of solidarity similar to that experienced by their parents in the past. Adoptive parents and adoption professionals, psychologists, social scientists are beginning to realize that international adoption and immigration in Spain have more similarities and points of contact than we had previously assumed.

NOTES

1. Today, the Autonomous Community of Catalonia has the world's highest rate of international adoptions per capita, and the number of adoptees per inhabitant in Catalonia is double that of Norway and Spain as a whole. See Selman, in this volume.

2. For the video shown by the media, see http://es.youtube.com/results?search_query=agresi%C3%B3n+xenofoba+tren+barcelona&search_type=&aq=f (accessed 27 May 2008).

3. Spain is organized in seventeen Autonomous Communities and two Autonomous Cities (both in Moroccan territory) with their own legislative and executive governments and with autonomy in most aspects of citizens' daily life, including education, health, transport, and security. Three of the Autonomous Communities—Galicia, Catalonia, and the Basque Country—are considered historic communities with their own languages (Galician, Catalan, and Euskera), legal codes, policy making bodies, and security forces. Everything concerning adoption in Spain is decentralized; each Autonomous Community has its own regulations. The former Ministry of Labour and Social Affairs and the current Ministry of Education, Social Affairs, and Sport of Spain facilitates communication between the autonomous authorities.

4. Available at http://www.laopinion.es/secciones/noticia.jsp?pRef=2934_1_110 388__Portada-Tenerife-Esperanza-Aguirre-actitud-pasajero-presencio-agresion-racista-propia-nazismo (accessed 27 May 2008).

5. *La Vanguardia*, 20 June 2008.

6. At the beginning of 2008, the Council of Education of the Catalan government (a coalition of three left-wing parties) proposed a new regulation regarding the incorporation of immigrant children in public schools. They must enter school through "transitional classrooms," a segregated space where they are to become fluent in Catalan and Spanish, before joining a common classroom. A person in charge of education in a medium-sized Catalan city asked with regard to immigrants' children: "Until when must we consider them immigrants, and why should we consider them as pupils with special educational needs?" *El País*, 17 February 2007.

7. The 2008 report from Amnesty International, called *Spain: Between Unwillingness and Invisibility*, pointed out that Spain is one of the five countries in European Union that never publish official data on racism or discrimination (AI

2008: 4). Similarly, the 2008 annual report of SOS Racism states that "in addition to institutional racism, 2007 has also been characterized by a high level of societal racism in Spain," with discrimination in access to education, employment, and housing (SOS Racism 2008).

8. In 2002, 35 percent of the immigrants in Barcelona had studied at university, while only 31 percent of natives had done so. *El País Cataluña*, 19 February 2002.

9. The marriage rate declined from 7.6 percent in 1975 to 5 percent in 2004 and is currently at the average rate for the EU. At 31, the average age at first maternity is the highest in the EU.

10. This situation has also deterred some parents from adopting Spanish children who are available. In 2007 there were 7,000 children under government protection in Catalonia, an Autonomous Community with 7,000,000 inhabitants. A policy "that makes national children remain institutionalized until they reach adult age" should be considered a failure, said the former President of the Catalonia Autonomous Community in his keynote address to the conference on "Adoption in Catalonia and International Adoption: Complexities and New Horizons," held 29–31 May 2003.

11. *La Vanguardia*, 25 October 2005. The EU average is 1.5 children per woman.

12. *El Periódico*, 16 March 2007.

13. In fact, statistics on international adoption only cover the period since 1997.

14. *La Vanguardia*, 10 February 2007.

15. In 2003, the Autonomous Communities of Madrid and Catalonia reopened domestic adoption because some children from the immigrant population are available for adoption.

16. According to the information given by the Ministry of Labour and Social Affairs during the first months of 2005, Spain, with 5,541 international adoptions in 2004, has the second largest number of international adoptions in the world. The United States has the largest, with 22,884 children adopted in 2004. See Selman, in this volume.

17. In 2006 a Spanish Collaborative Entity in International Adoption (ECAI) lost its authorization to work in Russia and Bolivia. In both cases, corruption was attributed to the chaos in the country of origin. The Spanish Organic Law 1/1996 established that the ECAIs, formalized as NGOs and audited by the state, would be the authorized entities to act as intermediaries in international adoptions.

18. Quoted in a report carried by *Efe*, Spain's state-owned news agency, 22 March 2006.

19. In 2003 the Catalonian government organized a conference on international adoption, called "New Horizons," to which it invited officials in charge of international adoption in several countries of Asia, Africa, and Eastern Europe in

order to initiate contact with them so as to cater to the demands of adoptive families. Significantly, some workshop coordinators belonged to the Foreign Chamber of Commerce of Catalonia.

20. This feeling is expressed in two films related to international adoption: John Sayles's *Casa de los Babys* (The House of the Babies) (2003), set in Latin America, and Benard Tavernier's *Holy Lola* (2005), set in Cambodia. Both films also raise the issue of corruption in the adoption process.

21. *El País*, 21 April 2006.

REFERENCES

Amnistía Internacional. 2008. *España: Entre la desgana y la invisibilidad; Políticas del estado español en la lucha contra el racismo.* Available online at http://www.elpais.com/elpaismedia/ultimahora/media/200804/10/sociedad/2008 0410elpepusoc_1_Pes_PDF.pdf (accessed 27 May 2008).

Berástegui Pedro-Viejo, Ana. Forthcoming. "Adopción internacional: ¿Solidaridad con la infancia o reproducción asistida?" In *La adopción internacional entre el "aquí" y el "allá": Miradas diversas,* ed. Diana Marre. Barcelona.

del Olmo, Margarita. 2004. "Trading with Differences: Racism from Race to Culture." *Cuadernos del Sur. Historia* 33: 9–23.

———. 2007. "The Challenge of Understanding Racism beyond Violence, Fear and Immigration." In *New Perspectives and Problems in Anthropology,* ed. Éva B. Bodzsàr and Annamária Zsákai, 31–36. Newcastle, UK: Cambridge Scholars Publishing.

Font Lletjòs, E. 2008. "Perfil de les families adoptants a Catalunya." *Infancia: Butlletí dels professionals de la infància i la adolescencia* 16 (March-April).

Generalitat de Catalunya (Government of Catalonia). 2008 *Les adopcions internacionals s'estabilitzen.* Barcelona: Departament d'Acció Social i Ciutadania (Department of Social Action and Citizenship), Oficina de Premsa.

Howell, Signe. 2003. "Kinning: The Creation of Life Trajectories in Transnational Adoptive Families." *Journal of the Royal Anthropological Institute* 9, no. 3: 465–84.

Howell, Signe, and Diana Marre. 2006. "To Kin a Transnationally Adopted Child in Norway and Spain: The Achievement of Resemblances and Belonging." *Ethnos* 71, no. 3: 293–317.

Howell, Signe, and Marit Melhuus. 2007. "Race, Biology and Culture in Contemporary Norway: Identity and Belonging in Adoption, Donor Gametes and Immigration." In *Race, Ethnicity and Nation: Perspectives from Kinship and Genetics,* ed. Peter Wade, 53–72. Oxford, UK: Berghahn Books.

Marre, Diana 2007. "'I Want Her to Learn Her Language and Maintain Her Culture': Transnational Adoptive Families' Views on 'Cultural Origins.'" In *Race,*

Ethnicity and Nation: Perspectives from Kinship and Genetics, ed. Peter Wade, 73–95. Oxford, UK: Berghahn Books.

Marre, Diana, and Joan Bestard, eds. 2004. *La adopción y el acogimiento: Presente y perspectivas*. Barcelona: Ediciones de la Universidad de Barcelona.

Marre, Diana, and Joan Bestard. 2008. "The Family Body: Person, Body and Resemblance." In *Kinship Matters: European Cultures of Kinship in the Age of Biotechnology*, ed. Jeanette Edwards and Carles Salazar. Oxford, UK: Berghahn Books.

Martínez, Ana. 2004. "El largo y costoso proceso de la adopción." *Expansión*, 23 February.

Sayles, John. 2003. *La Casa de los Babys* (*The House of the Babies*). Film.

SOS Racismo 2008. *Annual Report on Racism in Spain 2008*. Barcelona: Icaria.

Stolcke, Verena. 1992. "¿El sexo es para el género como la raza es para la etnicidad?" *Mientras tanto* 48.

———. 1995. "Talking Culture: New Boundaries, New Rhetorics of Exclusion in Europe." *Current Anthropology* 36, no. 1: 1–23.

Tavernier, Bernard. 2005. *Holy Lola*. Film.

Tyler, Katharine. 2005. "The Genealogical Imagination: The Inheritance of Interracial Identities." *Sociological Review* 53, no. 3: 476–94.

Volkman, Toby Alice. 2003/2005. "Embodying Chinese Culture. Transnational Adoption in North America." *Social Text* 74 (vol. 21, no. 1): 29–55. Reprinted in *Cultures of Transnational Adoption*, ed. Toby Alice Volkman, 81–115. Durham, NC: Duke University Press.

Wade, Peter. 2002. *Race, Nature and Culture: An Anthropological Perspective*. London: Pluto Press.

———. 2007. "Race, Ethnicity and Nation: Perspectives from Kinship and Genetics." Introduction to *Race, Ethnicity and Nation: Perspectives from Kinship and Genetics*, ed. Peter Wade. Oxford, UK: Berghahn Books.

Yngvesson, Barbara. 2003. "'Going 'Home': Adoption, Loss of Bearings, and the Mythology of Roots." *Social Text* 74 (vol. 21, no. 1): 8–27. Reprinted in *Cultures of Transnational Adoption*, ed. Toby Alice Volkman, 25–48. Durham, NC: Duke University Press.

Yngvesson, Barbara, and Maureen A. Mahoney. 2000. "'As One Should, Ought and Wants to Be.' Belonging and Authenticity in Identity Narratives." *Theory, Culture & Society* 17, no. 6: 77–110.

Chapter 13

IIIIIIIIIIIIIIIIIIIIIIIIIIIIIIIIIIIIIIIIIIIIIIIIIIIII

Routes to the Roots

Toward an Anthropology of
Genealogical Practices

Caroline Legrand

Does ancestry research belong to anyone? Is the search for roots the property of any social or cultural group? Is this practice more legitimate in some cases than in others? These questions may sound a bit curious. Yet they invite us to consider the search for roots in a comparative way, to examine the discourses, habits, and activities of people who investigate their family and personal histories. The question is whether the qualities and issues that arise in the search for roots depend on the identity of the individuals who carry out this exploration.

This chapter considers two categories of people in particular: adopted people, and descendants of immigrants. My aim is not only to identify what searching for roots means for these two sets of people but also to compare their ways of doing research and their relations to genealogical memory and knowledge. This analysis illuminates what hides behind these properties and contributes to an anthropology of genealogical practices.

For that purpose, I refer mainly to empirical data that I have collected over the last ten years. From 1998 to 2004, I interviewed people who were seeking their roots and tracing close or distant relatives in Ireland, some of whom were adoptees. From 2005 to 2006, I met descendants of French and Irish immigrants, who were involved in genealogy in Québec. During those periods, I also debated the meanings of roots within non-biological families as part of research on foster care and adoption in France. Critical readings on adoption and genealogy inform my analysis.

I begin by examining the challenges involved by constituting this subject as an anthropological field. Despite recent attempts to explore the market for genealogy, the study of this activity suffers from a major ethnographic split. I suggest that this divide needs to be filled by situating adoptees and the descendants of immigrants within the same theoretical frame. The second part of the chapter shows that these two sets of persons actually often view and utilize genealogical research in similar ways. I conclude by speculating about the benefits of their investigations.

Uses of and Approaches to Genealogy in Social Anthropology

Social anthropologists first used genealogy as a means to collect kinship terminologies and life stories, which were then used to analyze the ways cultural groups constitute social bonds through marriages, naming, and inheritance practices. This approach, inherited from W. H. Rivers, has since then undergone serious criticism (Schneider 1984). Yet, genealogy is still mainly understood as a tool for investigation and analysis.

At the end of the 1970s, after the search for origins had been popularized by the work of journalist Alex Haley,[1] several sociologists and anthropologists realized that genealogy could also become a research topic in itself. Tamara Hareven (1978) undertook to capture the reason why so many Americans had recently begun doing genealogical research. She observed that the shaping of family trees had been spreading from the white middle class to racial-ethnic minority groups. She suggested that this trend revealed something new about the shaping of individual identities and collective memories. Among other things, it provides a symbolic route for rediscovery of a past and, with it, a specific historic identity. It became clear that the discovery of ethnic origins has obvious value for other people besides African Americans. In this age of multiculturalism, genealogy enables people to demonstrate that they come from a family with a long history. By this means, they can highlight both their own singularity and their sense of belonging.

Hareven's research gave rise to further research in North America (Jacobson 1986, Caron 2002, Harvey 2005, and to some extent Finkler 2005) and in some Western European countries. Studies of French practices by Martine Segalen and Claude Michelat (1991) and by Sylvie Sagnes (1995, 2000) show that genealogical research has been appropriated by people who are neither aristocrats nor bourgeois. In Ireland, too, genealogy has been democratized and is no longer restricted to Dublin's Protestant gentry. Indeed, the search for Irish roots extends beyond Ireland to involve

Irish communities abroad (Hood 2002, Nash 2002, Legrand 2002, 2006). Scholars have started to pay particular attention both to the reasons why people get involved in the search for roots and to the way people recreate a line of ancestors and sense of history by means of kin selections and narrative reinterpretations. Yet, few of these studies take adoptees' stories into account. The discussion proceeds as though adoptees' search for roots had nothing to do with the genealogical fever that is spreading worldwide.

This idea is shared by adoptees and adoptive families as well. Most reject the notion that they are doing genealogy and speak of their investigations in terms of a "search for origins." They see the process in which they are engaged as seeking their identity, while they regard genealogical activity as a hobby for persons who grew up with their birth parents. These ways of thinking and speaking indirectly assert that adoptees' routes to their roots are unique and not comparable. This contention is strengthened by the clear differences in the approaches and attitudes toward genealogy held by adoptees on one side, and by descendants of immigrants on the other. Adoptees lack very basic knowledge concerning their birth and their genitors. The revelations they experience while searching for their roots involve the confrontation and reconciliation of two distinct forms of kinship, biological and social, which is a specific feature of their identity.

Why not consider both practices as arising from the same drive to find ancestors and information—even concrete evidence and proofs—about who you really are and to whom you belong? For those scholars who emphasize the singularity of adoption,[2] suggesting any equivalence between adoptees and non-adopted people is highly suspect. As an anthropologist, I think we should not isolate adoptees' choices and practices any further. Comparison seems all the more imperative now that tracing ancestors has become a social obligation whereby people express loyalty to their forbears and find comfort in the idea that descent creates solidarity. American society puts pressure on people to dig up their pasts and identify more precisely who they are. The fact that so many adoptees feel the need to trace their ancestors is part of this phenomenon.

Genealogy as a Kind of Knowledge

Genealogy can be defined as a kind of empirical knowledge dealing with kinship, place, and history. People say that genealogy is about "roots," which is to say the ways familial ties and people's sense of belonging have been drawn up and consolidated through history. In some cultures, genealogical knowledge and discourses are profoundly essentialist, for they place "blood" and "land" at the core of personal identity. Men and women commonly view themselves as made of blood, and they think that their geographic and socio-cultural environment shapes their identity and gives it a spatial base. The significance accorded to "blood" and "land" explains why the search for origins includes the search for both biological relationships and the places people and families once called "home." As a kind of knowledge, genealogy can also be defined as inherited from the past and received from a close or a distant relative. This knowledge is supposed to be passed on from parents to children, but geographical dislocation or familial ruptures may stand in the way of this transmission.

Adoptees and migrants are often viewed as victims of significant disruptions. Many people consider adoptees to be suffering from blood dislocation and genealogical bewilderment, while spatial remoteness and deterritorialization are blamed for migrants' identity disorders. These groups' separation from blood and land make them archetypal representatives of so-called roots detectives. Of course, many people engage in genealogy whose backgrounds do not include such ruptures, although the fear of the loss that accompanies forgetting may motivate people to do genealogy as well as to engage in local history (Sagnes 2000). Similarly, the fact of having moved from one country to another does not necessarily prompt migrants to do genealogical research (Byron 1998). Yet, another cultural factor contributes to turning people into family tree-makers. In North America, and to a lesser degree in Europe, genealogy has become a kind of imperative. People are compelled to see genealogy as a duty, a tribute that everyone should pay to their ancestors and forbears. The media participate in this process by publicly encouraging people to search for their roots.

But the fact remains that adoptees and the descendants of immigrants are viewed as the main practitioners of genealogical research. This representation deserves exploration. More critical attention should be paid to the ways these two sets of persons deal with their lack or loss of roots in daily life. How do they experience separations from blood and land, and do their visions undergo change over time? Does maternity, paternity, or aging stimulate their searches for roots and identity?

Moreover, the extension of international adoptions shows how these two categories are porous. Children are removed not only from their biological kin but also from their native country and become part of transnational migration flows. The efforts they make to identify a genitor, to recover from their broken narratives and from their feelings of alienation, need to be thoroughly explored and compared with the experiences and perspectives of other populations of migrants. I call for a cross-cultural typology of genealogy-makers and roots-related behaviors (for a beginning, see Legrand 2002).

Martine Segalen and Claude Michelat (1991) state that there is something very narcissistic in the search for roots. Genealogists are trying not only to gain ancestry, prestige, or answers about their identity but also to become part of the memories of their children and descendants. The desire for transmission is common among the descendants of immigrants who explore their family trees. The need to connect the past with the present and the future is shared by adopted people, who often begin searching for origins after having given birth to their own child. Genealogical investigation relates in some way to rites of passage.

Parenthood and retirement appear as privileged moments for people to start questioning "who they are" and "where they come from." Giving birth materializes a kind of continuity between generations and at the same time increases the sense of rupture for people who have been separated from their genitors. Similarly, retirement, which deprives people of an active status within society, is often viewed a last chance to renew memories before dying. Moments of transition stimulate genealogical pursuits.

Genealogy as a Complex and Sensitive Investigation Process

In addition to being subject to breakdowns in transmission, genealogical knowledge could be defined as a continuously perfectible product. It can be reviewed, augmented, and transformed through the collection of primary documents, circumstantial evidence, and the exploration of a vast range of sources, including civil or parish records, private testimonies, and institutional or personal accounts. Let me provide concrete examples of how both adoptees and descendants of migrants proceed while engaging in genealogical activities.

The tracing of familial and personal histories is frequently experienced as a visceral need. People act as if a force deep within their bodies urges them to identify parents, siblings, and close cousins or to trace distant ancestors. They view kinship—especially biological kinship—as a network of indelible ties that must be reconstructed when facing dislocations or attenuation through remoteness. Most of the time, adoptees and migrants refer to blood as a magnet that draws them to certify and confirm their relationships. It attests to the fact that their representation of family is biologically oriented. The salience of this presumption is visible in the current fashion for DNA tests, which are commonly used by adoptees and others to trace their ancestry.

Adoptees and the descendants of immigrants frequently describe genealogy as a very complex activity in which every type of document and memory should be mobilized, questioned, and critically evaluated. Drawing analogies with other activities, they describe their search as solving a "jigsaw puzzle" or pursuing a "hunt." The quest for roots is presented as a construction set which requires step-by-step progress. The logo chosen by the Irish Adopted People society, set up in 1989, is a nine-piece puzzle. Six of these pieces represent the Irish flag while three words appear on the remaining pieces. These words—Dignity, History and Equality—refer to the inalienable right to gain access to personal information including the ways one is related to another. Adoptees and descendants of immigrants share the idea that genealogical knowledge is a right you may have to fight for.

Since the mid-1990s, a council of genealogical societies has provided several recommendations to the Irish government to complete the information given on death certificates and to facilitate the access to civil records. By doing so, it has extended the suggestions made in 1984 by a local society whose members urged the government to computerize biographical data in order to protect the archives. Every year, similar requests are sent by adoptees' networks. Their battle appears even more complex because it is opposed by advocates for mothers who anonymously gave their children for adoption.

The genealogical universe is alive with questions of identity, family, and history. These campaigns for transparency are conducted by roots-hunters who gather in order to progress in their own investigations and to defend their rights, as collective action makes these claims more powerful. "Interconnectedness" is another key word among roots-hunters. Most have joined adoptee, genealogical, or surname societies. These organized groups, which radiate influence worldwide rather than locally, have mushroomed impressively during recent decades. Their attractiveness lies in the fact that they act as intermediaries between one family tree-maker, his past, his birthplace, his culture, and his people. They offer searchers both a kind of platform for publicly advocating reforms and a space to exchange information on the way to identify relatives (Modell 2002, Howell 2003, Volkman 2005). This cooperation is essential, for genealogical research is often described as a very difficult and uncertain task. No matter why you want to trace your genitors, your siblings, or your ancestors, the process demands time, patience, and organization. Some say that a bit of luck is the magic ingredient that helps people succeed in tracing their roots and locating family members, but both adoptees and descendants of immigrants consider that it is more a matter of knowledge than mere chance.

The search for close and distant relatives requires very specialized knowledge. The searcher must learn how to conduct research, the kinds of information available in different types of records, and the places, state agencies, and institutions that hold relevant files. Learning from people who have done similar searches helps people to become familiar with these data and processes, as well as with the fact that genealogy often gives rise to annoying or upsetting situations. Genealogical investigations are not always successful. They are often accompanied by disillusionments or disappointments. Family reunions may turn a kinship network upside down and upset other family members close to the newly found relative.

The quest for roots arouses a myriad of feelings and emotions. Not only do genealogical searches respond to the "call of the land," the "call of a name," or the "call of blood," but connecting to place, people, and history deeply moves roots-hunters. According to the people I met, all senses seem to be intensified while decoding a name on a birth record or walking on ground trodden by ancestors. As an Irish American put it, "I felt like I had come home. It was a very real, physical feeling, not just a sentimental emotion, although it did make me cry. I felt like my soul belonged there." From that point of view, nothing differentiates the narratives produced by descendants of immigrants and by adoptees. The stories both write or tell about their search for roots are filled with the senses of touch, smell, sight, and hearing. Each time they discover something new about their forebears, each time they travel to their homeland or speak with someone they have been looking for, adoptees and descendants of immigrants reach a higher degree of comprehension of who they are.

Genealogy as an Institutionally Framed Practice

Open to personal interpretations and even more to contestations, the making of family trees and narratives is subject to expert evaluations and institutional controls. I suggest looking not only at the ways in which adoptees and the descendants of immigrants dig up close or distant relatives to build personal narratives of who they are and where they come from but also at the authorities that regulate the production and circulation of genealogical knowledge. Who holds the records? Who decides which sources should be open to the public, and which should remain sealed and secret? Is access to these materials free, or must individuals pay for it? Are individuals allowed to track their relatives down to the places they live? Do some countries prohibit some practices that are part of genealogical research? What major institutions and experts supervise and validate the making of family trees and genealogical knowledge? Are these institutions or people engaged in a competitive process?

The Hague Convention on Intercountry Adoption stipulates that children have the right to know their parents. Everyone should be given free access to relevant information about his or her birth and genitors. Nevertheless, the state's power to regulate the transmission of this information is considered prior to this right, as Françoise-Romaine Ouellette demonstrates (in this volume). She points out that Québec has adopted very strong confidentiality rules in this matter. Not only does the law forbid biological siblings from seeking reunion without the consent of their birth mother, but it still allows mothers who gave their child up for adoption to remain anonymous. Another relevant point about Québec is the absence of professional genealogy groups, which exist in France (Candau 1997), Ireland, and the United States.

Differences in the regulations governing DNA testing and information contribute to the variety of shapes assumed by individual memories across cultures and nation states. Adoptees are allowed to buy DNA kits via the Internet in Belgium and Canada, but this is strictly forbidden in countries such as France. French citizens might face a 15,000 Euro fine if they order paternity tests without the consent of a judge. Institutions do not remain passive in the face of genealogical activities. Political and legal bodies lay down rules that specify conditions under which people can or cannot gain access to particular types of private information.

Information that non-adopted people consider valuable for reconstructing their family histories is also restricted by law. Irish law states that many records must remain sealed; for example, under the hundred-year rule, which is designed to ensure that information about living people is not revealed, the 1921 civil census will not be opened to the public until 2021. The Irish state managed to centralize genealogical information so that people of Irish descent living abroad might be encouraged to travel to specific places whereby they could access relevant data, including parish records and passenger lists (Legrand 2006).

Whose Research? Who Benefits?

Ethnography focuses on the very personal and private dimension of genealogical activity. People find real benefits in tracing their own roots. The clarification and confirmation of descent is the primary goal of genealogists. Self-knowledge is at stake, although this quest could be seen as a necessary stage for the claiming of civil rights or property and the earning of social recognition.

Yet, genealogy's aims go far beyond the case of so-called uprooted people. People and institutions surrounding the person tracing his or her origins become involved in the process. Indeed, adoptive parents may be more invested in the tracing of their child's roots than the child him- or herself. Parents of adolescents often view the search for origins as a way to solve their teenager's troubles, to gain recognition of their parental role, or to cope with neighbors' curiosity (Legrand 2002, Yngvesson 2005, Volkman 2005). Genealogical practice involves more than the person in quest of his or her origins; the kin-group and community to they belong are also concerned.

Countries that sent children into adoption or lost people to emigration might consider the search for roots a potentially valuable market. The histories of Ireland, Greece, and Poland are characterized by several centuries of transnational and transcontinental emigration. Each of these countries has received funds from the European Community to set up tourist programs that suit the needs and expectations of people in its diaspora (Legrand 2002, 2006). In Ireland, the government realized that it could develop roots tourism in order to boost its economy. People of Irish descent have been asked to visit their ancestral homeland, and considerable efforts have been made to facilitate access to vital records and professional genealogists. Politicians pride themselves on transforming Ireland into a Mecca for genealogists. By the end of 2004, 8 percent of visiting

Americans and Australians declared that they were visiting Ireland to dig up their roots and see their ancestors' homeland. These visitors consume a lot of roots-related artifacts, such as familial coats of arms. Beyond its economic value, genealogy is a means to change Ireland's image. Weary of being considered a poor, agrarian, and post-colonial country, Ireland has sought to move closer to its diasporic population in order to display its openness and postmodernity (Legrand 2006).

Regaining prestige is also a goal of the government of South Korea. Both Eleana Kim (2005) and Elise Prebin (2006) explain that Korea was blamed for sending children away at the time when the country organized the Olympic Games in 1988. It was accused of taking financial advantage of transnational adoptions and of showing no concern about adoptees' later lives. Policy changes have been made to reduce the number of children given to adoption in Western countries, and the government sponsored adoptees returning to their motherland. By this means, the Korean government intends both to assert its concern with adoption and make sure everything adoptees do and see when visiting their birth country is well under control.

In sum, genealogical activity can be instrumentalized by state institutions, which means that search for roots, origins, and belonging initiated by adopted persons and descendants of emigrants is liable to be inflected with political value.

ACKNOWLEDGMENTS

I thank Natacha Collomb and Tim Neil for helpful comments on an earlier version of this essay.

NOTES

1. Alex Haley's *Roots: The Saga of an American Family* (1976), the Pulitzer Prize–winning book in which he details his search for his African ancestor, Kunta Kinte, who was kidnapped and enslaved, was presented as "truth" on a popular television series, but has been proven to be a fictionalized account of his family's history.

2. Adoption has often been used to illustrate both the diversity of familial constellations and historical trends in parenthood patterns; see Goody 1971, Fine 1998, and Leblic 2004. Along with debates about the evolution of adoption's legal and ethical framework, tensions between social and biological kinship appear of

major concern to anthropologists, sociologists, and psychologists. The dualism of biology and society has given rise to many questions about adoptees' becoming and about the ways they deal with identity, their new family, and, in some cases, their new country; see Carsten 2000, Volkman 2005.

REFERENCES

Byron, Reginald. 1998. "Ethnicity and Generation: Feeling 'Irish' in Contemporary America." *Ethnologia Europaea* 8, no. 1: 27–36.

Candau, Joël. 1997. "Quête mémorielle et nouveaux marchés de la généalogie." In *La généalogie entre sciences et passion*, ed. Tiphane Barthelemy and Marie-Claude Pingaud, 119–29. Paris: Editions du CTHS.

Caron, Caroline-Isabelle. 2002. "La narration généalogique en Amérique du Nord francophone: Un moteur de la construction identitaire." *Ethnologie Com-parées* 4. Accessed 10 January 2006 from http://alor.univ-montp3.fr/cerce/r4/c.i.c.doc.

Carsten, Janet. 2000. "Knowing Where You've Come From: Rupture and Conti-nuities of Time and Kinship in Narratives of Adoption Reunions." *Journal of the Royal Anthropological Institute Institute* 6, no. 4: 687–703.

Fine, Agnès (ed.). 1998. *Adoptions: Ethnologie des parentés choisies*. Paris: Editions de la Maison des sciences de l'homme.

Finkler, K. 2005. "Family, Kinship, Memory and Temporality in the Age of the New Genetics." *Social Science and Medicine* 61, no. 5: 1059–71.

Goody, Esther. 1971. "Forms of Proto-Parenthood: The Sharing and Substitution of Parental Roles." In *Kinship: Selected Readings*, ed. Jack Goody, 331–45. Mid-dlesex, UK: Penguin Books.

Haley, Alex. 1976. *Roots: The Saga of an American Family*. Garden City, NY: Dou-bleday.

Hareven, Tamara. 1978. "The Search for Generational Memory: Tribal Rites in In-dustrial Society." *Daedalus* 107, no. 4: 270–83.

Harvey, F. 2005. "La généalogie et la transmission de la culture: Une approche sociologique." *Les cahiers des dix* 59: 285–305.

Hood, Susan. 2002. *Royal Roots, Republican Inheritance: The Survival of the Office of Arms*. Dublin: Woodfield Press.

Howell, Signe. 2003. "Kinning: The Creation of Life Trajectories in Transnational Adoptive Families." *Journal of the Royal Anthropological Institute* 9, no. 3: 465–84.

Jacobson, Cardell K. 1986. "Social Dislocations and the Search for Genealogical Roots." *Human Relations* 39, no. 4: 347–58.

Kim, Eleana. (2003) 2005. "Wedding Citizenship and Culture: Korean Adoptees and the Global Family of Korea." *Social Text* 74 (vol. 21, no. 1): 67–81. Reprinted in *Cultures of Transnational Adoption*, ed. Toby Alice Volkman, 49–80. Durham, NC: Duke University Press.

Leblic, Isabelle (ed.). 2004. *De l'adoption: Des pratiques de filiation différentes.* Clermont-Ferrand, France: Presses Universitaires Blaise Pascal.

Legrand, Caroline. 2002. "L'Adoption en Seine-Saint-Denis: Modalités de prise en charge et devenir des usagers de l'Aide Sociale à l'Enfance sortis du service entre 1980 et 2000." Rapport d'études, Bobigny, Conseil Général de Seine-Saint-Denis.

———. 2006. *La quête de parenté: Pratiques et enjeux de la généalogie en Irlande.* Québec: Presses de l'Université Laval.

Modell, Judith Schachter. 2002. *A Sealed and Secret Kinship: The Culture of Policies and Practices in American Adoption.* Oxford, UK: Berghahn Books.

Nash, Catherine. 2002. "Genealogical Identities." *Environment and Planning D: Society and Space* 20: 27–52.

Ouellette, Françoise-Romaine (ed.). 2005. *Les ajustements du droit aux nouvelles réalités de l'adoption internationale.* Montréal: INRS.

Prébin, Elise. 2006. *Adoption Internationale: Les revenants de Corée.* Thèse de doctorat en ethnologie, Nanterre, Université Paris X.

Sagnes, Sylvie. 1995. "De terre et de sang: La passion généalogique." *Terrain* 25: 125–45.

———. 2000. *Racines et enracinement: Parenté et localité dans la France contemporaine.* Thèse de doctorat en anthropologie sociale et historique, Toulouse: Ecole des Hautes Etudes en Sciences Sociales.

Schneider, David. M. 1984. *A Critique of the Study of Kinship.* Ann Arbor: University of Michigan Press.

Segalen, Martine, and Claude Michelat. 1991. "L'amour de la généalogie." In *Jeux de Familles*, ed. Martine Segalen, 193–208. Paris: Presses du CNRS.

Volkman, Toby Alice (ed.). 2005. *Cultures of Transnational Adoption.* Durham, NC: Duke University Press.

Yngvesson, Barbara. 2005. "Going 'Home': Adoption, Loss of Bearings, and the Mythology of Roots." In *Cultures of Transnational Adoption*, ed. Toby Alice Volkman, 25–48. Durham, NC: Duke University Press.

Chapter 14

||||||||||||||||||||||||||||||||||||||||||||||||||||||||

Return Journeys and the Search for Roots
Contradictory Values Concerning Identity

Signe Howell

Discussions about adoption invariably give rise to issues that spring out of the Euro-American distinction between biological and social kinship. When adoption takes place between different countries, questions of identity, belonging, ethnicity, race, and culture are immediately placed on the agenda—especially when the children look different from their new parents and kin, as they do when they are moved from countries in Asia, Africa, Latin America, and the former Soviet bloc to Europe and North America. Today it is impossible for transnationally adopted persons in Western Europe and North America to avoid confronting these issues. Drawing primarily upon my research on transnational adoption in Norway, this chapter explores some dominant values of people involved in transnational adoption and considers how adoptees handle the challenges inherent in the practice.

I begin with the Second International Gathering of Adult Korean Adoptees held in Oslo in August 2001. A total of 137 persons between the ages of eighteen and their late forties who were born in Korea and adopted by non-Korean parents in Europe and North America met in Oslo in order to share experiences, discuss common problems, and establish an international network of Korean adoptees. Given that the only common bond between the participants is the fact of having been born in Korea and growing up in a non-Korean adoptive family in a different country, the event raises questions about the significance of biology and country of origin. In this analysis, I contrast the situation of transnationally adopted persons with that of other immigrants in Norway and other countries that adopt from overseas. I suggest that whereas the diaspora communities of transnational migrants are replete with significant others in their new country of residence, their country of origin, and many corners of the world, the significant others of adoptees are their adoptive family and their kin. By and large, the adoptees are "socially naked" in relation to their country of origin. For this reason transnationally adopted persons are anomalous within the diaspora community of their birth country. I suggest that to characterize international organizations of transnationally adopted persons as a manifestation of diaspora would be to extend the meaning of that concept beyond the limits of its usefulness.

Flesh, Blood, and Place as Identity Constructors

During the gathering of Korean adoptees, an "open mike" session was arranged in which the participants were encouraged to write a story, a poem, or some other text to share with the group. The Korean American who took the initiative, a man of about thirty who was practiced in this kind of exercise, read a piece he had written on a previous occasion in order to show the rest what kind of text he envisaged. In emotionally laden, poetic language, he described his imagination of the day he was born. He detailed his birth mother's imagined looks (she was very beautiful, with long black hair), her imagined behavior and utterances and those of imagined other people present, the imagined village from which he came, and the imagined landscape nearby. There was no mention of being abandoned—a significant silence, given his later experience. His reading was charged with feeling, and the audience—all of whom, with the exception of myself, were adopted—was very quiet afterwards. This text and its context encapsulated much of what puzzled me about transnational adoption, the many paradoxes that I had observed with regard to the meanings of kinship, family, identity, origins, ethnicity, nationality, roots, and place.

This gathering of Korean adoptees frames my reflections on ideas about identity and meaningful relatedness, not just in terms of kinship, but of belonging more generally, especially as it is focused upon place of origin. The place in this case is the adoptees' country of birth, a place that they left, usually as infants, to be adopted anonymously into a new country. It is an unknown place, populated by unknown people. Most do not know the details of their origins or the identity of any biological relatives, although the place where they were found, or the orphanage where they lived before being adopted, is usually known. And yet, for some, the birth country is a place to which they attribute profound significance. They make it an integral part of their identity and fill it with imagined people of deep significance: their mother, father, and siblings. This powerful discourse essentializes kinship and place of origin and makes them integral to a genealogy which can only be based on biology.

The adoptees who adhere to this understanding of kinship constitute a vocal minority that reflects a widespread understanding in contemporary Europe and North America about identity and belonging that is expressed most graphically in the common sayings that "blood is thicker than water" and that kin are "of the same flesh and blood." This understanding has been reinforced during the past decade by an increasing biocentrism in discourses about personhood and identity. Arguably, it is a consequence of recent research in medicine, biotechnology, and genetics. In particular, DNA testing that confirms whether a person is a "real" relative or not (Franklin and McKinnon 2001, Melhuus 2003) encourages a view that treats biogenetic connectedness as the mainstay of kinship. The conviction that relatedness is predicated upon blood, genes, and DNA poses a serious epistemological challenge for families formed through adoption. Elsewhere (Howell 2003) I have shown how adoptive parents deny an either/or attitude to the relationship with their children, but fluctuate between different explanatory models for kinship according to context.

The tendency today in Scandinavia and elsewhere in Western Europe, manifested most clearly in legislation about adoption and new reproductive technology,[1] is to insist that knowledge about biological origins is necessary for a person's harmonious development and sense of self. Social workers, educators, therapists, and medical personnel, a group of experts I term psycho-technocrats because their professional attitudes are drawn from a globalizing academic psychology, propagate what pertains to correct knowledge at any given time. Their views affect both adoptive parents and transnationally adopted persons as they reach adulthood and, no doubt, contribute to the recent popularity of searching for "roots" and the desire for return visits to the country of origin (Howell 2003, 2006). However, my research in Norway shows that, contrary to popular expectations, it is most often the adoptive parents who take the initiative to make such journeys. Most adoptees are indifferent, quite happy to participate, but with few personal expectations. However, those adoptees who harbor a desire to see their county of origin and their biological relatives —and those rare few who actually succeed in meeting them—confirm these popular expectations. The enthusiastic media attention paid to their experiences contributes to keeping the scenario alive.

The importance accorded to origins, descent, and genealogy is growing in various discourses on personhood and identity in Norway, as well as elsewhere in Europe and North America. Never before has private genealogical research been so popular. While similar scenarios are observable in all the countries that receive children for adoption, some indications point to a difference in this regard between Norwegian and American adoptees. Americans seem to be more preoccupied with their roots than are Norwegians, and issues pertaining to race are much higher on the agenda in America than they are in Norway, perhaps because Americans are generally more aware of their racial-ethnic identity. The presence in the United States of large communities of immigrants from the countries from which children are adopted gives rise to ethnic categories such as Korean American, Chinese American or, more loosely, Hispanic or Latino. Many American adoptees categorize themselves along similar lines and experience an affinity with immigrants who originate from the same country as themselves. Adoptees often seek out these communities, an American adoption worker told me. They also seek out other adoptees from the same country. Strikingly, this is not the case in Norway.[2] Norwegian transnationally adopted young people tend not to identify with other transnational adoptees, whether from the same country of origin or not. Rather, they distance themselves from them as well as from other immigrants (Howell 2002, Howell and Melhuus 2007).

Return Journeys and the Search for Roots

An increasing preoccupation with return visits to their birth country and reunions with biological relatives is noticeable in all countries that adopt transnationally. The American documentary *Daughter from Danang* has been shown several times on American public television. Its central character is a woman who was adopted to the United States from Viet Nam at the age of seven following the war.[3] Her father was an American soldier, and her mother was Vietnamese. Years later, as a married woman with children of her own, she wanted to visit Viet Nam to meet her biological relatives. The film traces her journey. Expectations on both sides are very high. The meeting between biological mother and daughter is very emotional, as are those with her various half-siblings. At an early stage of the visit she says: "I just hope that they understand I have been a hundred and one percent Americanized. I have no earthly idea of their expectations." However, her worst fears are confirmed when she is leaving and everything goes wrong. As would be expected from a well-to-do daughter in Viet Nam, she is asked to contribute to the financial support of her aged mother as well as to give substantial support to her poor sister who has been looking after the mother all these years. The adopted woman reacts very strongly against what she regards as attempts to exploit her. She feels repelled by mixing money and love in a relationship of this kind. Much to the consternation of her Vietnamese relatives, she begins to cry and she is heard to exclaim: "Don't know what to do! I just don't know. I wish this did not happen . . . I wish the trip did not happen now, because I'm gonna leave with all these bad memories and all this bad feeling, and it's not how I wanted it to be." After returning to the United States, she tells the interviewer she does not know if she will contact her birth family again.

The story is a graphic example of conflicting cultural understandings of the meaning and responsibilities of kin relatedness. Similar stories are told in Norway. The reunions of transnationally adopted children and their biological relatives frequently result in tension and disappointment on both sides, and yet the adoptees' expectations of a meaningful relationship continue to be fueled by the world at large and, until recently, by the psycho-technocrats. Today the experts are more cautious in supporting such quests, but this view is not reflected in the media.

The majority of Norwegian transnationally adopted people I have studied have no desire to visit the place they were born. One young Norwegian man who was adopted from Korea at the age of two and a half has little interest in the country. Pointing out that he knows nothing about South Korea, does not speak the language, has no memories of ever having been there, knows nobody there, and knows nothing of its history or culture, he asks why he would wish to visit it more than any other country. He resents being asked by well-meaning people: "When are you going back to Korea? When are you going to find your biological parents?" (Follevåg 2002: 23)[4] Similar sentiments were expressed by a twenty-nine-year-old woman adopted from Bangladesh who demands the right to "be just a happy Norwegian" (Flydal 2003: 10). She objects to what she characterizes as everybody's self-appointed right to ask transnationally adopted persons about return visits, what they know about biological parents, and if their adoptive parents have been kind to them. She declares that "personally,

I am not interested in biological roots," but throughout her life she has found "that people I hardly know are very concerned about them on my behalf" (Flydal 2003: 11). The sentiments expressed by Follevåg and Flydal are quite common among persons adopted transnationally.[5] Their voices are seldom heard, however, and when they speak listeners tend to ignore what they have to say.

The Ontological Status of the Individual in Euro-American Culture

Two major components of contemporary Western thinking that emphasize the constituting significance of the biological link help us understand the prevalence of this model of personhood. First, the metaphoric statement that "blood is thicker than water" that Schneider (1968) argued is central to American kinship similarly constitutes kinship in Northern European societies. Second, the autonomous individual is a dominant value in Western traditions of identity and personhood. Ever since Kant "threw new light on the understanding of human nature by insisting on man being autonomous, i.e., self-regulating" (Svendsen 2004: 145), Western philosophical and ideological traditions have maintained the ontological and moral centrality of the autonomous individual. Twentieth-century discourses about identity and personhood occurred within a cultural climate which "has come to celebrate the values of autonomy and self-realization" (Rose 1999: xv), which in turn gave rise to the prevalence of "psy-discourse." These viewpoints have had profound effects upon how we think of what it means to be a human being, a child, and a gendered person, as well as what significance we attribute to biogenetic factors (nature) on the one hand and to social and environmental circumstances (nurture) on the other. A discourse of rights in which universal rights are anchored in the autonomous individual is well established and articulated in laws and international conventions. Everything social and cultural is regarded as epiphenomenal to the existential centrality of the individual. The individual becomes his or her own reference point, the bearer of his or her destiny. Paradoxically, at the same time, individual identity is perceived as inseparable from connections to others in his or her biologically based genealogical chart. The ultimate relevance of genealogy for the individual lies in the relationships displayed in family trees. In them he or she is connected through descent to other individuals, affirming individuality and relatedness simultaneously. However, most Norwegian adoptees are given a place in their adoptive parents' family trees and feel comfortable there.

While we place moral emphasis on the autonomous individual, we also recognize that individuals are "made by" others who are highly significant to the person. The question arises as to what significance these various others are thought to have for the individual and what being made by them actually entails. The point for many at the gathering of Korean adoptees seemed to be to know the "truth" about those who made them and to be acknowledged by them as a relative, regardless of what had happened subsequently. Several of the Norwegian adoptees who attended the gathering in Oslo expressed surprise to me at the importance attributed to biological kin by a number of the foreign delegates.

The head of the section in the Norwegian Ministry of Family and Children that approves all applications for transnational adoptions, himself a trained psychologist, shares the prevalent opinion about identity. In an interview conducted by a journalist who was adopted from Korea, he admonished her when she argued that she was not interested in biology or her country of birth and thinks that most of the other transnationally adopted persons in Norway feel as she does. "Don't you feel a sense of community when you meet other adopted persons?" he asked. When she denied this, he insisted that she must feel that Korea represents an anchorage for her. She denied this. Undeterred, he maintained that without a sense of anchorage people become rootless, and that he feels sad when adoptees reject the chance to find out about their roots (Andersen 2003: 6). The journalist, on the other hand, argued that it is the quality of personal relationships that determines the quality of an individual's sense of personal identity and satisfaction, and that the majority of transnational adoptees in Norway would agree. Her sentiments are reflected in a book entitled *Adopted Identity* (*Adoptert Identitet*) written by Follevåg, who says, "children adopted from overseas are virtually indoctrinated and 'culture terrorized' into believing that they must learn about their 'original culture' in order to become 'complete human beings' with a complete identity" (2002: 18). Despite these and many similar sentiments expressed by transnationally adopted people in Norway, an explanatory focus upon the biological aspect of individual identity rather than on the sociality of individuals continues to predominate.

I want to contrast such assumptions with recent research in developmental psychology which demonstrates that humans are innately social.

Within hours of birth, newborns strive to engage in meaningful communication with whomever takes an interest in them (Bråten 1998, Trevarthen and Logotheti 1986). From this perspective, identity ceases to be a matter of bounded individuality and becomes relational. Sociality becomes central, not epiphenomenal to social life. Too often we forget that humans live, not in isolation, but in social worlds and that meaningful communication takes place within "interpretative communities" (Fish 1980). Failure to appreciate the constitutive significance of intersubjectivity, sociality, emotionality, and shared semantic and moral universes leads to narrow and static models of child development and personhood that, ultimately, fail to take account of the power of kinning (Howell 2003). Identity and self-perception are dependent upon the quality of the relationships that a child establishes with significant others during the process of growing up, as well as the values and practices of the wider social world. Naked biology is not enough. This may explain the frequent failure to establish a lasting rapport—beyond the emotionality of first meeting—between biological relatives and transnationally adopted persons.

The Power of Kinning the Socially Naked Child

The anthropological study of kinship has taught us to study relations, not individuals. Adoption both challenges and confirms commonsense notions about kinship and leads us to take analytical account of the parameters for actual relationships. I have argued elsewhere (Howell 2003) for a previously unexplored phenomenon that I call "kinning" through which a person—usually a newborn child—is brought into a significant and permanent relationship with a group of people where the connection is expressed in an idiom of kinship. Kinning transforms the autonomous, non-social individual into a relational person. Henceforth the person is clearly anchored in necessary and stable relations. We may identify three aspects of kinning: to kin by nature, to kin by nurture, and to kin by law. Contemporary Euro-American adoption involves only the two last aspects, although the first constitutes the model.

A dominant ideology in Western Europe and North America regards kinned relatedness as epiphenomenal to the individual. In the many countries in Africa, Asia, and Latin America from which Europeans and Americans adopt, by contrast, personhood is perceived as being constituted through relations with significant others. Part of the answer to why transnational adoption is as successful a practice as it is may be found in my suggestion that the abandoned child becomes a socially naked child, a child denuded of all kinship. By abandoning a child anonymously—for whatever reason—the biological parents are in effect de-kinning him or her. The abandoned child is the example *par excellence* of the autonomous individual so central in contemporary Western thinking. But, paradoxically, this social nakedness renders the child a non-person, even in a sense non-human, in its birth country. Given the ontological and moral privileging of the autonomous individual in contemporary Euro-American society, this social nakedness does not devalue the child as a human being, while in Asian and African societies the value that these societies attribute to the autonomous individual finds little or no resonance. There, to have no relatives removes the child's social identity and hence its value. By entering the anonymous non-kin world of an institution, usually an orphanage, the abandoned child who is earmarked for adoption overseas enters a liminal world, awaiting a new set of kin.

This social nakedness makes adoption across national borders possible, turning it into a morally acceptable act for donors as well as receivers. The birth country allows people from an alien country to remove such non-persons and to kin them to themselves. The child's de-kinned condition enables the state to relinquish a citizen and the new state to accept her because she will not be naked in her new country; she enters it fully clothed in new relatives. In this case, biology is rendered insignificant, sociality becomes all-important. So, according to my argument, the children stripped of biological kinned relatedness are being socially and emotionally kinned by their new parents and family in their new country.

Imagining the Place of Origin

Although the popularity of return visits is increasing in Norway, only a small proportion of adoptees have actually undertaken such a journey.[6] By contrast, about two-thirds of the Korean adoptees at the gathering in Oslo had been to Korea.[7] More than half had actively searched for biological relatives. A few had met them. Although these people are at one end of the spectrum regarding a concern with roots, they represent a general trend. My findings show, however, that the majority of Norwegian adoptees who undertake a return journey are more interested in seeing the place from which they came than in looking for relatives (Howell 2003,

2004). However, it is usually a naked place, devoid of known kin. Values attributed to what I term "relational place" are common in Norway. Norwegians put a lot of symbolic store by their place of origin, usually a farm in the countryside, and they inscribe it with a genealogical temporality that they pass on to their children. Being predicated upon the metaphor of shared flesh and blood, this scenario may create a problem for adoptive families. Whether consciously or not, many adoptive parents seek to remedy this lack of a shared relational place. A common strategy is to plant their adopted children symbolically in their own ancestral land by photographing them there dressed in the traditional regional costume. Nevertheless, in contrast to Norwegian-born children's imaginings of their kinned past, the imaginings of transnationally adopted children must necessarily be less concrete, or at least more confused, which may account for the desire to identify a place of origin that some adoptees experience. To see their country of origin, even if the actual place where they were born is unknown, is a common motivation for undertaking a return journey. Interestingly, the majority of those interviewed expressed a sense of disorientation following a visit and insisted that they felt more Norwegian than before they left.

Naked Places and Diasporas

The situation of transnationally adopted children from the same country contrasts sharply with that of groups of people who have voluntarily migrated from the same country and settled in different countries, forming what is commonly called diasporic communities. In an essay on migrating and mobile populations from the Caribbean island of Nevis, Karen Olwig concludes that the West Indians living outside Nevis are not preoccupied primarily with their current places of residence but are engaged in maintaining social relations with people from Nevis in many different parts of the world. Their attention is focused on "a specific place which plays a central role as a common source of identity in their global network of relations" (1997: 35)—namely their village of origin on Nevis where identifiable relatives are still living. We may discern what may be called a "globalizing place," a place located geographically but also virtually, for all those who live in other places but are connected to the place through descent. They continue to focus upon it as a source of personal and ethnic identity. This phenomenon is common among diasporic communities.

Can we understand transitionally adopted persons' preoccupation with their country of birth in a similar manner? Is the gathering in Oslo to be understood in terms of a diaspora? I seriously doubt it. Their situation is the inverse of that of diasporic communities. The adoptees focus on place devoid of identifiable people, while diasporic communities focus on place rendered meaningful by being linked through identifiable people.

The adoptees who left as infants without any information about their personal situation—and this is still the majority—are caught in a paradox. In the context of migration, it is people located in a specific place who make a relationship, not the place by itself. To descendents of emigrants from Nevis, place of origin takes on significance because of the people who either live there now or have lived there in the past: not just anyone, but identifiable kin with whom they have some kind of meaningful (imagined or actual) relationship—in the present context, people who may be placed within some kind of reciprocal kinship vocabulary. In this way, a place becomes infused with sentimental value. A similar process is manifest in Norwegian attitudes toward the family farm, however modest it might have been. Even though they, or even their parents, have not lived there, their sense of self is intertwined with what they regard as their place of origin. On special occasions they wear the traditional costume from the region where it is located, not from where they happen to be living. These costumes are becoming increasingly popular among middle-class urbanites, and transnationally adopted children are often dressed in one that is linked to one parent's place of origin.

If we accept the view that children sent abroad for adoption were, by virtue of being abandoned, de-kinned and severed from their place of birth and early residence, the situation of adoptees takes on a very different tenor. It is not so hard for the nation to let them go because it is only through other people that that a person is connected to a place and to the nation. Transnationally adopted persons' relationship with their country of origin is not analogous to that of other migrants. Their places of origin are not a globalizing space, as Olwig shows among those descended from Nevis, because for the adoptees their country of origin is a naked place. If you cannot identify the place you were born and where your birth parents lived, if you cannot name your birth parents or other relatives, then what do "roots" tours that "return" to the "motherland" mean? Just as biology on its own (naked biology) is not enough to make persons feel connected to other persons, place on its own (naked place) is not enough either. I suggest that this is the reason why the majority of Norwegian transnationally adopted persons are satisfied with seeing the country of their birth, but harbor no desire to return and refrain from searching for biological relatives. The Korean American who wrote about his imagined day of birth sought to infuse an unidentified place with imagined scenery and imagined people. His quest was driven by an apparent longing to connect to a place and to make his birth a meaningful event, but it was doomed to fail because the place and the people remain beyond a world of social relationships. Other Korean-born adoptees at the gathering seemed to share his longings as they publicly expressed a profound sense of disorientation and disappointment in their lives. They might establish meaningful relations with one another, but their sociality is of a fundamentally different kind than that of diasporic communities.

In Conclusion

By accepting in effect that "blood is thicker than water," those transnationally adopted persons who seek personal fulfillment through their country and people of origin often render themselves deeply unhappy. The mutual incomprehension that arises when people from radically different cultural understandings of the practice of kinship confront one another can cause personal havoc. The people who trace their origins to Nevis know one another, or at least know of one another, via kin networks. They may have been born in London, Manchester, or Cape Town, but their parents or grandparents were born on Nevis and many relatives still live there. Children step into this moving line of relations and find a place for themselves without difficulty, continuing the reality of the diaspora. Appadurai calls the understandings of reality shared by geographically mobile cultural groups "ethnoscapes" (1996). Why do transnationally adopted persons not inhabit an ethnoscape? My answer is that they do not form a diaspora because they were de-kinned and re-kinned when they were abandoned and adopted. They are not knowingly party to any histories linked to persons in the country of origin. Although their country of birth is populated by millions of people who look more like them than do their adoptive parents and the majority of the population in the country in which they live, they otherwise have nothing in common with those people. So what is going on when the adoptees "seek their roots," as the expression goes? They may be "creating an essentialized place which they hope will serve as a window through which they view the world," as a colleague put it in conversation.[8]

However, this essentialized place exists only in the adoptees' imagination. It is not grounded in a real social world populated by real people with whom the adoptees can claim meaningful relationship. These adoptees create for themselves imagined kinship anchored in an imagined place, granting themselves imagined belonging. Even if they succeed in meeting biological relatives, neither the adoptees nor their biological relatives are prepared for the huge gap in values and experiences that separate them after the first euphoric encounter. Most adoptees do not think about the effect that their sudden appearance will have on their birth family, or realize that they may have to abandon the focus upon their own individuality and agency and enter into a community of relations with demands that extend far beyond those experienced in their adopted family. Naked biology, devoid of embodied emotions and cultural commonality, usually turns out to be insufficient for a meaningful and lasting kin relationship; a fact that the "daughter from Danang" and her Vietnamese biological relatives both failed to appreciate.

ACKNOWLEDGMENTS

This chapter is a shortened and revised version of "Imagined Kin, Place and Community: Some Paradoxes in the Transnational Movement of Children in Adoption," in Holding Worlds Together: Ethnography of Truth and Belonging, ed. Marianne Elisabeth Lien and Marit Melhuus, 17–36 (Oxford, UK: Berghahn Books, 2006). Research on transnational adoption has been made possible through a grant from the Norwegian Social Science Research Council program Globalisation and Development (2001–2004) and the EU-funded project Public Understanding of Genetics: A Cross-cultural and Ethnographic Study of the "New Genetics" (2002–2004) under Framework 5, the Quality of Life and Management of Living Resources.

NOTES

1. These principles are confirmed by the international charters and conventions that deal with children's rights and transnational adoption. The proliferation of bilateral and multilateral aid organizations and NGOs whose work is directed at children contributes to the dissemination of these ideas.

2. Non-Western immigrant communities are of recent origin, and most are not made up of people from countries from which Norwegians adopt. The largest

immigrant communities in Norway are made up of Pakistanis, Turks, North Africans, Somalis and, more recently, Eastern Europeans. Few adoptees come from these countries.

3. In 1975, a controversial evacuation program called Operation Babylift sent large numbers of Vietnamese infants and young children to American couples for adoption.

4. G. Follevåg, speech given on the occasion of the fiftieth anniversary of Verdens, *Verdens Barn* 15, no. 3 (2003): 20–22.

5. See *Dagbladet Magasinet*, 7 June 2003.

6. This generalization applies mainly to adoptees from Korea, India, and the Philippines whom I have interviewed. It is possible that people who originate from Latin American countries may have different experiences.

7. Children of the World used to arrange one return visit to South Korea a year. Since 2000 they have arranged three a year, as demand has risen. Adopsjonsforum previously arranged a trip to India once every two or three years, but more recently they are arranged once or twice a year.

8. Sarah Lund made this point following my presentation of an earlier version of this essay.

REFERENCES

Andersen, H. 2003. "Ukjent opphave" [Unknown origin.] *Magasinet Dagbladet*, 4 June: 1–9.

Appadurai, Arjun. 1996. *Modernity at Large: Cultural Dimensions of Globalization.* Minneapolis: University of Minnesota Press.

Bråten, Stein (ed.). 1998. *Intersubjective Communication and Emotion in Early Ontogeny.* Cambridge: Cambridge University Press.

Fish, S. 1980. *Is There a Test in This Class? The Authority of Interpretive Communities.* Cambridge, MA: Harvard University Press.

Flydal, Hanna. 2003. "Retten til bare å være en lykkelig nordmann." *Adopsjonsforum* 28, no. 5: 10–11.

Follevåg, Geir. 2002. *Adoptert Identitet.* Oslo: Spartacus.

Franklin, Sarah, and Susan McKinnon (eds.). 2001. *Relative Values: Reconfiguring Kinship Studies.* Durham, NC: Duke University Press.

Goody, Jack. 1969. "Adoption in Cross-Cultural Perspective." *Comparative Studies in Sociology and History* 11, no. 1: 55–78.

Howell, Signe. 1986. " 'Reading Culture': Or, How Anthropological Texts Create Fieldwork Expectations and Shape Future Texts." In *Exploring the Written: Anthropology and the Multiplicity of Writing*, ed. Eduardo P. Archetti, 317–36. Oslo: Scandinavian University Press.

Howell, Signe. 2001. "Self-Conscious Kinship: Some Contested Values in Norwegian Transnational Adoption." In *Relative Values: Reconfiguring Kinship Studies*, ed. Sarah Franklin and Susan McKinnon, 203–23. Durham, NC: Duke University Press.

———. 2002. "Community beyond Place: Adoptive Families in Norway." In *Realizing Community: Concepts, Social Relationships and Sentiments*, ed. Vered Amit, 84–104. London: Routledge.

———. 2003. "Kinning: Creating Life-Trajectories in Adoptive Families." *Journal of the Royal Anthropological Institute* (N.S.) 9, no. 3: 465–84.

———. 2004. "The Backpackers That Come to Stay: New Challenges to Norwegian Transnational Families." In *Cross-Cultural Approaches to Adoption*, ed. Fiona Bowie, 227–41. London: Routledge.

———. 2006. *The Kinning of Foreigners: Transnational Adoption in a Global Perspective*. Oxford, UK: Berghahn Books.

Howell, Signe, and Marit Melhuus. 2007. "Race, Biology and Identity in Contemporary Norway: Adoption, Donor Gametes, and Immigration." In *Race, Ethnicity and Nation: Perspectives form Kinship and Genetics*, ed. Peter Wade, 53–72. Oxford, UK: Berghahn Books.

Melhuus, Marit. 2003. "Exchange Matters: Issues of Law and the Flow of Human Substances." In *Globalisation: Studies in Anthropology*, ed. T. Hylland Eriksen, 170–97. London: Pluto Press.

Olwig, Karen Fog, and Kirsten Hastrup (eds.). 1997. *Siting Culture: The Shifting Anthropological Object*. London: Routledge.

Rose, Nikolas S. 1999. *Governing the Soul: The Shaping of the Private Self*. London: Free Association Books.

Schneider, David M. (1968) 1980. *American Kinship: A Cultural* Account. Chicago: University of Chicago Press.

Svendsen, L. F. H. 2004. "Kineseren fra Königsberg—Immanuel Kant (1724–1804)." In *P2-akademiet/Kulturredaksjonen NRK P2*, 145–55. Oslo: Transit Forlag.

Trevarthen, Colwyn, and Katherina Logotheti. 1986. "Child in Society and Society in Children: The Nature of Basic Trust." In *Societies at Peace: Anthropological Perspectives*, ed. Signe Howell and Roy Willis, 165–86. London: Routledge.

||||||||||||||||||||||||||||||||||||||||||||||||||||||

Chapter 15

Mothers for Others
Between Friendship and the Market

Anne Cadoret
Translated by Margaret Dunham

Filiation, or descent, is established through three elements that the sociologist Florence Weber (2006) calls "le sang, le nom, le quotidien"—blood, a name, and daily life. These three elements refer to the domains of biology, law, and family organization respectively. Although these elements may combine in hetero-parental families, where the genetic mother and the genetic father of children may live and raise their children together, this combination is not usual in families where the parents are gay or lesbian. Same-sex couples must rely on one of these three elements in order to become parents and find the right distance from the excluded link.

This chapter reflects on the role played by biology in the construction of family and social relationships by focusing on a tie that is considered essentially biological: genetic and gestational motherhood. I present two families who had recourse to another mother. The first family is that of two lesbians, Amélie and Françoise; the woman whose child they adopted is their friend who became pregnant unintentionally and chose not to abort but to give the baby to them. The second family is that of a gay man, José, who made an agreement with a surrogate mother—that is, a woman who carried a child conceived with his sperm and her own egg and then relinquished her parental rights. After briefly sketching the manner in which these people became parents, I explore the logic each chose in order to make a family, giving special prominence to the words they use to designate the "actors" in their parenthood. I then examine how social links are created by introducing the question of commercial transactions that may grant a certain role to mothers for others, between "*filia et fobia*," friendship and the market.

Amélie and Françoise

Amélie and Françoise met in the United States, where Amélie had gone in search of an accepted lesbian culture in the mid-1980s. Because Amélie was unable to obtain an immigrant visa, they came to her native France. When they had just moved to the countryside in Bourgogne close to Amélie's family, an American friend, Sarah, called them to propose giving them her fourth child. She was pregnant and did not want to raise the child herself, but she was aware of her friends' desire for a child and absolutely refused to abort. My informants accepted her offer and, with the help of Amélie's brother and sister-in-law, made a legal arrangement that gave them custody of the child. Sarah came to France to give birth, giving the child her name but renouncing her maternal rights. Amélie's brother, the married father of two children, recognized the child as his own, born out of wedlock, and gave the child to the care of his sister. During her seventh month of pregnancy, Sarah settled herself in Bourgogne, where her own family—her first three children and her male partner—joined her just before the birth of the child, a boy named Claude. Several years later, a simple adoption ruling confirmed Amélie's parental role and made her Claude's legal mother. However, her partner, Françoise, who shared the daily tasks of mothering equally with Amélie, had no legal ties to this child.

Later a second child was born to the family. A few years after Claude's arrival, Françoise gave birth to a child, Dominique, with the help of a man who agreed (through a private arrangement) to donate his sperm on condition of complete anonymity. Françoise legally became his single mother.

This lesbian couple's claim to being a family can be charted relative to the three elements: blood, a name, and daily life. On the biological level, Claude has identified biological parents (Sarah and her partner), and Dominique has an identified mother (Françoise) and a non-anonymous donor father. Both children know the identities of their "genitors." On the juridical level, both children have a mother: Amélie became Claude's mother through the process of simple adoption, and Françoise gave birth to Dominique. As for legal fathers (Cadoret 2006), Dominique has none, and in Claude's case the father is personified by Amélie's brother. On the level of daily life, both of the children have two parents. As Amélie put it: "We are two women for two children. Each one of them considers both of us as their mothers. We are in that sort of set-up, and it is very clear for the children. They don't have any favorites." In daily life, neither child has a father.

José

José wants to be a single father. He does not want a matrimonial alliance, or an affective relationship marked by the vagaries of love. He explained: "I consider relationships in general and particularly homosexual relationships as short-term contracts which can sometimes be renewed; they last for a certain time, every once in a while they are renewed for a little while." This time-frame is "contrary to father/child or mother/child relationships, which of course are eternal, even when things go badly." He makes a sharp distinction between ephemeral alliance relationships and eternal filiation relationships and points out that "one cannot divorce one's children."

Filiation is much stronger when it is reinforced by the biological link of birth. However, a biological link based on a "natural" fact is necessary but insufficient for establishing filiation. José sought a form of filiation that was total, unique, indivisible, and non-reproducible. He even went so far as to marry a lesbian woman in order to ensure an undivided filiation. We must keep in mind that only marriage establishes an undivided filiation, a cognatic one. If the child's parents are not married and the parents choose a parental agreement, we have a bilateral filiation, a maternal one and a paternal one; the mother's filiation established by the birth of the child would not entail the father's, as it would have done in the case of a wedded couple. So José rejected this duplication of filiation and decided to use the services of a "mother for others" for his two children.

Biological Mothers

What role do our informants allow the woman who gave her own genes and bore the child? The child comes from the woman, whether she is called a "surrogate mother," "mother for others," "mère-porteuse" (literally, "carrying mother"), "biological mother," or "madre de alquiler" ("rented mother").[1] All three of our informants used the expression "biological mother" to designate this woman, depriving her of the label of genitor. Amélie and Françoise even refused to refer to her by the simple term "mother." This decision is based both on the recognition of her specific role in creating and carrying the child, thus the use of the term "mother" rather than "genitor," and on the desire to limit her to this specific role and exclude her from being a parent or caregiver. In this schema, there is no possibility of creating family ties.

My informants were perfectly willing to accept an individual link between the child and the biological mother; but thought that this link should be limited to the interest and affection that two people may have for one another without the child being incorporated into another family. "I don't want to be subjected to any blackmail from anyone, whether a heterosexual or a lesbian mother in a co-parenting agreement," José declared in one of our early interviews. The lesbian couple compared their situation to adoption, "which is to say a child's transfer from one family to another," and they imposed this position upon their friend Sarah, who had "given" them her child, refusing her idea of an extended family. For Sarah, they acknowledged, "there would have been her own parents and children. Then, well, that would have been the source of very blurry family ties. When we realized this we said, 'ah no, we adopted Claude, we didn't adopt the whole family.'"

The role that my informants allow the other woman, the "mother for others," is that of a body. The biological side is clearly recognized, and no one rejects that inheritance. For example, the parents commented on the resemblances between the child and its biological mother or father. Marc "has his mother's lower face and his father's upper face," José asserted. Amélie reported: "Claude is very near-sighted, so we say it comes from his biological father, who is very near-sighted; he inherited those genes. But he doesn't look like his biological mother; his hair is a bit like hers, his hair and his mouth." "His hands too, with very long fingers," Françoise added. "And then his height; she is tall too," Amélie concluded.

Do our three parents, Amélie and Françoise on one hand and José on the other, have the same views and behavior regarding the biological mother? The whole question of the mother, a genitor who is known and recognized, should be looked at in the light of two areas of analysis: first, the biological field with the definition of motherhood; second, the social processes as manifested through the link that binds the two units, the biological mother and the legal or actual parents. This link should be defined in terms of how it was established, the manner in which the parties met and agreed to embark on this project.

Definitions of Motherhood

While recognizing the biological link between mother and child, my informants did not want the genetic side of things to dictate society's behavior, under the pretext of being a natural fact. According to Françoise Héritier: "Alongside filiation [descent] that can be determined through the character of legitimacy, through will power or the fact of possession, French law henceforth recognizes the criterion of genetic truth for establishing filiation and opposes it to the three others, thereby introducing dual preeminence, on one hand of an individual's variable desire over the collective interest (and by the revocability of the filiation previously established by other means), that of the adult's interests over those of the child, on the other hand, of genes over laws, which is to say a so-called natural fact because it is biological over the rules instituted by society (which is a form of barbarity)" (2002: 217).[2] My informants are up against this ideology and are very careful in their choice of words, fearing the implicit meanings these words refer to.

Amélie refuses to have Sarah introduced to her acquaintances as the "mother" or even as the "biological mother" to those ignorant of her history. Amélie and Françoise want to avoid any possible shift of the biological link toward a parental link, such as instituting sibling relations or recognizing grandparents. Amélie was distressed by a gesture in that direction: "One has to be very careful, and not get everything mixed up! Sarah's mother, after Claude's birth, sent us a present signed Grandma and Grandpa or something—it was in English—with a ridiculous piece of clothing for Claude. We were really upset. We wrote to Sarah telling her, 'whoa, your mother really went too far.'" The link between Claude and Sarah must remain one between individuals, without any other family members entering into the picture, because Amélie's family must not be swallowed up by Sarah's. Amélie is well aware of the ideological strength of biology in our society. She explained: Sarah "is on a terrain that can only be slippery for her, but also for us, which is maybe also why it's so hard. Especially in France, the 'real' parents in adoption are the biological parents and not the. . . . People, Claude's friends; on TV, everywhere, we hear people say 'the real, the bios'; if one stresses the bio side, she is the real mother in the end." Both Amélie and Françoise want to be mothers and they value Sarah's motherhood as much as their own desire for maternity. They must therefore justify to others as well as to themselves why the mother-child tie between Sarah and Claude was severed.

In fact, Amélie and Françoise share the incomprehension of abandonment and the refusal of motherhood noted by Cecile Ensellem (2007). Comparing the expectations of the Conseil National d'Accès aux Origines Personnelles (CNAOP) (National Council for Personal Origins Access), created in 2002 to facilitate possible reunions between mothers and the children to whom they gave birth, and the second bioethics laws discussed two years later, which reinforced the anonymity of the gamete donors and questioned this difference in position on anonymity, Ensellem contends that the primary reason for this difference is that there is a rejection of the refusal of motherhood. This trend exemplifies the increasing power of what Marcela Iacub (2004) calls the "mother's belly," the effects of which my informants wish to circumscribe.

José has nothing to fear from competition between two maternal figures. The existence of the biological mother is not a threat to his paternity and does not endanger the building of his family. He has no need to deconstruct the societal image of motherhood, but rather must construct it for his children. When the biological mother announced that she was putting together a photo album of the children she bore for him, he was delighted because "she is the mother, and will remain the mother to the end of time. Of course, she doesn't take care of them, of course she has no rights, but the fact remains that she is the mother. And, in fact, that she should put this album together, that she regularly asks how things are going, etc., proves that there is still a link, and that fills me with joy. For me, and especially for the kids, because obviously later they will start wondering." However, this link must remain a bare recognition of her role as a "mother for others" without entailing any particular affective interest, without tipping over into an increase in the value of motherhood. When Marc sees her, José is delighted that "there is absolutely no attraction whatsoever, either for Marc or for the mother; she's just a lady, like the ladies one sees in the park, like one sees . . ." I wonder whether, at the current stage in the building of families, a personal link between the mother and the child could be a threat to his paternal power by referring to a maternal spirit conceived as inevitable.

Social Ties

In *Transformations of Kinship*, Godelier and his co-authors concluded that "the family will continue to be a focus of anthropological study in the foreseeable future, but what has made anthropological kinship analysis distinctive—and different from sociological, historical or social-psychological studies of the family—is that kinship has always been something more than the family. In the classic societies, that 'something more' has been the whole of social organization articulated by kinship-based structures such as clans, castes, moieties, or marriage classes. However, such kin-based structures appear to be disappearing before the forces making for large-scale integration, leading one to think that in the future families (and their fragments) may find themselves articulated with one another not by kinship structures but by quite different principles" (1998: 4). I explore the role of these other principles in contemporary European and North American society by considering the question of mothers for others in the light of the market economy.

For our lesbian informants, the phrase "mother for others" must be rejected when payment is involved, because they refuse the commodification of motherhood, the economic link between the "receiving" and the "giving" parents. They liken it to the open adoption processes current in the United States and Canada. They remain within an ideology of giving. But this ideology of giving presupposes carefully working out the roles that will be attributed to the donor and the recipient because, as is well known from the work of Marcel Mauss (1990), any gift without a counter-gift gives the donor excessive power over the receiver. However, this power may be limited by kinship ties, such as those of first cousins, or even descent.

In "Strategic Naturalization: Kinship in an Infertility Clinic," Charis Thompson describes six cases of oocyte donations or gestation for others and defines the kinship ties between the people taking part in the processes. She notes the arguments of the intended mothers, whether gestators or oocyte donors, in order to clarify and specify each person's place within the construction of filiation. "In non-commercial gestational surrogacy, an emotional or familial commitment takes the place of a financial transaction" (2001: 179). She remarks that the role played by the intended mother, whether it be in giving her genes or bearing the child, will be allotted the same importance in the same way by both women, gestators and oocyte donors, for instituting the maternal relation as involving just one woman, thereafter called the mother, and limiting the role of the other to that of procreational assistant. Let us also assume that the male partner of the intended mother is the one who gives the sperm for fertilizing the oocyte.

The situation we are faced with in the case of Amélie and Françoise is not a case of "gestational surrogacy," where one or both of the gametes comes from the intended parents, the gestational mother having carried the pregnancy after the transfer of the embryo, but that of a woman who conceived a child with her own partner and carried it for nine months before giving it to her friends. Moreover, the intention of giving was not present before conceiving, as for the other "mothers for others," but as an alternative to abortion. In the situations described by Thompson, "Patients, practitioners, and third party reproducers (egg and sperm donors and surrogates), with the help of medical techniques, lab standards, body parts, psychological screening, and rapidly evolving laws, all take on part of this work." Amélie and Françoise were alone, without medical and judicial intermediaries to help them find their place. This difference explains their insistence on avoiding any use of the word "mother" and their carefulness in using "biological mother" so as to distance any possible attribution of the status of motherhood to Sarah.

Other studies of gestational surrogacy outside of the family circle (Delaisi de Parseval and Collard 2007) and first-person testimonies[3] show that the intended mother and the gestator sometimes refer to each other as being "like sisters." My informants refer to this closeness when they tell me: "to carry a baby for another woman, you have to be unbelievably generous, or else it has to be for someone really close, like two sisters." However, Amélie and Sarah are not sisters, or two people who do not know each other who could say, when sharing the conception of the child, that they are "like sisters"; instead, they are friends of long standing. Are they then too close to be able to say they are "like sisters" but too far apart to be "two sisters"? Since they had no family ties or mediating institutions, such as a medical clinic, to define their roles, nothing prevented Sarah from claiming a maternal link with Claude. However, when the parenting role is not defined by giving birth and must not be limited to the body, some distance has to be established between the symbolic and judicial system that defines parenthood and the material body. When these two statuses are not aligned, as in the cases presented here, each actor's role must be explicated and recognized in order to become established. It is this task of becoming recognized that my two informants were undertaking in reminding Sarah that she is a "mother for others" and not "just" a mother.

José is at the same crossroads between two cultural systems in constructing motherhood. In one system, the woman who gives birth to the child is automatically the mother; in the other, the role of mother is not kept but given to "others." However, while these three informants concur that the establishment of family ties goes beyond the bodily creation of the child, they differ as to the manner in which the child circulates. The lesbian couple wants to consider themselves outside any commercial transactions and base their practice on the analogy with open adoption in order to settle their entrance into motherhood. In this adoption process, "the biological and adoptive parents communicate with each other before and/or after the child's adoption" (Doumeng 2000: 147). José became part of an economic system that arranges contacts and separations between the donor and the father. Do these circuits belong to such radically different cultural conceptions as it would at first appear?

When Amélie and Françoise speak of open adoption as a children's circuit that lies outside the market economy, they erase three elements. First, adoption, even if it is open, is based on a system of supply and demand: a supply of adoptable children and a demand for children to adopt. The more open the adoption, the more the parties to the contract must find ways to make themselves known, to publicize their offers and their demands. Valérie Doumeng reminds us that "the definitions of open adoptions are based on the concept of communication between the parties involved in the adoption process" (2000: 147). Finally, there must be an official third party to guarantee the transaction and to state each person's role, that of the birth mother who renounces her parental rights and that of the adopters who acquire them. The protection of the child, that "priceless" commodity (Zelizer 1965), no longer allows the free circulation of children within a direct exchange system between two women or two family units as in non-Western societies.

José's request to become a father and the offer of the women who agreed to pregnancy but gave up motherhood[4] are part of a transactional system centered on children. He looked on the Internet, selected an agency that accepted homosexual fathers and guaranteed aspects of the transaction, such as monitoring the mother's pregnancy or aiding in establishing a contract, and then chose a "mother for others" among those proposed by the agency, who also had to consent to José as a father.

The Child's Circuit: Between Market and Money

The issue that differentiates these mothers from this father might not be the market as much as money. How to organize a transaction between takers and givers without the child or the mother being turned into merchandise? One path is to look at how gestational surrogacy is organized in the countries where it exists[5] and to note that in certain countries, such as Great Britain and Canada, surrogacy is permitted but payment is prohibited beyond the reimbursement of fees for prenatal care and childbirth. In the light of Philippe Steiner's (2006) study of organ donors, which observes that economic reasons are increasingly important, we must look into the organization of the transaction itself so as to avoid the elaboration of a black market. This analogy suggests setting the medical profession at the center of the process. Perhaps organizations other than medical ones could play the role of intermediaries between parents and procreational assistants by assigning clear, recognizable, explicable roles to each of the participants in parenthood. Just as the Conseil National d'Accès aux Origines Personnelles helps reunite mothers who gave birth anonymously with the children they bore, in the same way the centers that preserve oocytes and sperm (CECOS) could open their files to children who want to know where they came from and to the gamete donors who wish to become known without necessarily becoming parents to the children born from their sperm. Similarly, an organization might define the roles of "mothers for others" and the intended parents, as well as supervising the circulation of the child between them.

NOTES

1. When surrogacy began, these terms were synonymous: surrogate mother, mère-porteuse, and madre de alquiler included both genetic and gestational motherhood. Today, the surrogate mother is not always the genetic mother, but may be implanted with an embryo whose genetic material comes from others. In French, the terms surrogate and mère-porteuse are no longer used; a woman who carries a child whose genes she does not share is called "gestatrice pour autrui."

2. The original text reads: "Outre la filiation qui peut être déterminée par le caractère de légitimité, par la volonté et par la possession d'état, le droit français reconnaît désormais pour établir la filiation le critère de vérité génétique et l'a rendu opposable aux trois autres, introduisant la double prééminence, d'une part,

du désir variable de l'individu sur l'intérêt collectif (et par la révocabilité de la fili-ation préalablement établie par les autres modes), celle de l'intérêt de l'adulte sur celui de l'enfant, d'autre part, du gène sur la loi, c'est-à-dire d'une vérité soi-disant naturelle parce que biologique sur la règle qui institue la société (ce qui est une forme de barbarie)."

3. For example, a "mother for others" spoke of her experiences during the Gestators for Others Day organized by the Maïa Association on 1 December 2006 in Paris.

4. Some women enjoy being pregnant, but do not want to be mothers. See, for example, the report of the child psychiatrist, Daniel Marcelli, during a forum on new form of kinship organized by the Adoption Mission of the Médecins du Monde on 18 January 2007.

5. The list (which is not exhaustive) includes South Africa, Great Britain, Greece, Israel, some states in Canada, and the United States.

REFERENCES

Cadoret, Anne. 2006. "Vous avez dit 'père' . . . qui est le père?" *Dialogue* 173, no. 3: 45–57.

Delaisi de Parseval, Geneviève, and Chantal Collard. 2007. "La gestation pour autrui: Un bricolage des représentations de la paternité et maternité euro-américaines." *L'Homme* 183: 29–53.

Doumeng, Valérie. 2000. "Etude comparative de l'adoption française et de l'adoption ouverte aux Etats-Unis." In *Parents de sang, parents adoptifs: Approches juridiques et anthropologiques de l'adoption—France, Europe, USA, Canada*, ed. Agnès Fine and Claire Neirinck, 147–67. Paris: Maison des Sciences de l'Homme and Librairie générale de droit et de jurisprudence, coll. Droit et société no 29.

Ensellem, Cecile. 2007. "Accouchement sous X et assistance médicale à la procréation." *Recherches Familiales* 4: 111–22.

Godelier, Maurice, Thomas R. Trautmann, and Franklin E. Tjon Sie Fat (eds.). 1998. *Transformations of Kinship*. Washington, DC: Smithsonian Institution Press.

Héritier, Françoise. 2002. *Masculin/Féminin II: Dissoudre la hiérarchie*. Paris: Odile Jacob.

Iacub. Marcela. 2004. *L'empire du ventre: Pour une autre histoire de la maternité*. Paris: Fayard.

Mauss, Marcel. 1990. *The Gift: The Form and Reason for Exchange in Archaic Societies*. London: Routledge.

Steiner, Philippe. 2006. "Le don d'organes: Une typologie analytique." *Revue Française de Sociologie* 47, no. 3: 479–506.

Thompson, Charis. 2001. "Strategic Naturalization: Kinship in an Infertility Clinic." In *Relative Values: Reconfiguring Kinship Studies*, ed. Sarah Franklin and Susan McKinnon, 175–202. Durham, NC: Duke University Press.

Weber, F. 2006. *Le sang, le nom, le quotidien: Une sociologie de la parenté practique.* Paris: Aux lieux d'être.

Zelizer, Viviana. 1965. *Pricing the Priceless Child: The Changing Social Value of Children.* Princeton, NJ: Princeton University Press.

Chapter 16

|||||||||||||||||||||||||||||||||||||||||||||||||||||||

Seeking Sisters
Twinship and Kinship in an Age of Internet Miracles and DNA Technologies

Toby Alice Volkman

The acquisition of certain kinds of knowledge can produce a kinship tie where none existed before, because
knowledge itself can make kinship appear.
—Sarah Franklin, 2001

In the summer of 2005, I was sitting in a dentist's waiting room in New
York City and leafing through *Good Housekeeping* magazine when a full-
page color photograph of two beautiful Chinese girls caught my eye.
Wearing identical red and white checked dresses, the girls looked out
at the camera, dark eyes smiling dreamily under luxuriant black bangs.
The caption read: "a perfect melding." "Lost and Found: A Story of Mystery and Miracles" recounted the tale of how two American families, one
in Illinois, the other in Alabama, discovered that their adopted Chinese
daughters are, most likely, biologically related sisters.[1]

Until that chance encounter with *Good Housekeeping*, I had been aware
that some adoptive parents with Chinese children had been interested in
pursuing sibling connections with other adoptive families. I had not realized, however, that a new world of possibilities seemed to be opening
up that would entice some parents to search actively for their daughters'
sisters, while raising questions and concerns for others. The thrill of seeking and, perhaps, finding siblings must be understood in light of cultural
preoccupations with genetics and biology, on the one hand, and roots
and identity, on the other. The increasing sophistication and availability
of DNA testing, the emergence of "recreational genomics," the continuing

role of the Internet as a global connective tissue, and the appeal of "miracle" tales such as "Lost and Found" have all contributed to a flurry of sibling searching in the adoptive community. This phenomenon, in turn, has generated a myriad of quandaries and questions about ways of framing and imagining relatedness and about sisterhood and kinship more broadly.

The adoption of children from China to countries in the West has grown steadily since it began during the early 1990s. By late 2006, over 60,000 children, mostly girls, had been adopted to the United States alone. When I conducted research in 2001, I was interested in the many ways adoptive parents of Chinese children in North America deployed notions of culture in their attempts to deal with the visible fact of difference embodied by their families. Although many other factors, especially American attitudes toward race and an embrace of multiculturalism, underlie the tremendous interest in enacting culture, I suggested that this phenomenon could be understood, in part, in relationship to longing, especially longing for birth mothers. The entire birth family was part of these discussions, but for the most part the figure of the birth mother dominated the landscape of longing and desire. Parents' preoccupations with Chinese culture and with creating connections to China represented, I speculated, a displacement of those longings and desires (Volkman 2005).

This chapter explores the implications of the preoccupation with "seeking sisters." Longing for virtually impossible-to-find Chinese birth mothers, I suggest, may be transposed onto a search for siblings, a search that is both practically and emotionally simpler. Sibling searches certainly lend themselves to more cheerful, upbeat media coverage. In contrast to the tropes of tears, tragedy, and wordless embraces that characterize media representations of reunions between children and birth parents, reporters take evident pleasure in stories of separated toddler or school-age twins running into each other's arms or jumping for joy as they reclaim their kinship. Although there may be differences, the disparities in class or culture are not so glaring, and there are no awkward silences without a common language. While less fraught with ambivalence than reunions with birth parents—after all, siblings did not abandon one another, and indeed they share the common experience of abandonment or relinquishment —sibling searches and reunions raise new questions. A closer examination of "sib-search" and "sib-find," as the adoption community dubs this phenomenon, helps us to understand how adoptive families attempt to deal with loss, while negotiating tensions between kinship imagined as biogenetic and kinship imagined as actively created over time on the basis of other ties.

In the first part of this chapter, I discuss the theme of longing for birth mothers: why it has assumed such centrality, and how it is expressed in the practices of Chinese adoption in the United States. I then turn to the sibling search movement, drawing largely on popular media coverage and Internet discussions. Finally, I situate sibling-searching in the context of contemporary fascination with genetic genealogy, the rise of search and reunion among sperm donor siblings, and new reproductive technologies that disrupt older understandings of biological and social ties.

Longing for Birth Mothers

At the beginning of the adoption process, some parents say that they prefer to adopt in a distant place, such as China, to avoid the complexities of dealing with birth parents. Over time, however, adoptive parents often express sadness about their lack of any knowledge of, or possible contact with, the birth family of their child. As parents come to feel more secure in their attachment with their child, the reality of another set of parents seems less threatening. This sadness is also an effect of the contemporary discourse of adoption that not only acknowledges birth parents but asserts a universal need to know genetic origins, to heal what some have called "genealogical bewilderment" or "the broken narrative" of the self (Lifton 1994). Sociologist Sara Dorow writes of "ghosts of unsettled pasts, foreclosed relationships, and excluded others that haunt the present" (2006: 25). The rise of open adoption, the movement to unseal birth records, and widespread media coverage of birth parent search and reunion stories have contributed to a very positive view of searching. Searching is often encouraged by adoption professionals, usually with the caveat that the search should be initiated by the adoptee, not the parents; the question of agency is considered crucial. The outcome may be painful, yet searching is seen as a valuable healing process.

Although many factors contribute to contemporary fascination with what the adoptive community has named "birth culture," I have argued that some of that interest stems from parents' sadness in relation to the absent mother. The longing for origins may be displaced onto the body of the nation and its imagined culture, which can be studied, celebrated, performed, and embodied. A sense of longing pervades the recent literature on Chinese adoption. In her book, *The Lost Daughters of China*, Karin Evans imagines in sensuous detail the scene of a marketplace, crawling with buckets of squirming shrimp and eels, her three-month-old baby found tucked among bundles of bok choy and long beans, oranges and winter melons. She then conjures "all the possible identities" for the baby's "elusive mother" (Evans 2000: 85). In other accounts, it is hard to disentangle place, culture, and biology. In *Wuhu Diary*, Emily Prager recounts her journey back to China with her five-year-old daughter Lulu in search of Lulu's history. A note found with the baby when she was abandoned sparks this musing: "I consider this note in her first mother's handwriting to be almost magical. It is Lu's and my only link to the people who created her, that and the genes she carries. We know they were musical. They were expansive. They had great, strong voices, lovely long legs, and remarkable hands. They were eternally cheerful, smart, and good-looking. They had wills of iron and were awfully good-hearted." Prager adds: "Lulu is now part of our heritages, in the kinship charts. Yet the mysteries of her genetic code, how old it is . . . what characteristics it wrought in those now dead, are lost to her, probably forever. So anything we can find, any tiny nugget that we can find, we will take and store. If paleontologists can build a race from just a jawbone, surely we can glimpse a mother and father from an entire town" (2001: 40).

The mysteries that are part of any adoption are compounded in China by the absence of a narrative about a child's birth and by a political, social, and economic situation that seems to preclude the possibility of ever learning more. In many rural areas, China's population policies permit couples who already have a firstborn daughter, but want to have a son, to try for a second child. Although many couples desire both a boy and a girl, preference for sons remains strong, and a female infant who is a second daughter may be abandoned. Because there is no legal way to relinquish a child in China, babies are typically abandoned at a place where they would be found, taken to safety, and then brought to an orphanage unaccompanied by any birth parent information (Johnson, Banghang and Liao 1998). This situation is quite different from that in South Korea, where adopting parents are often provided with some information at the time of a child's referral, and adoptees who subsequently return to search for birth family members may learn more details about the circumstances of their adoption, or even the birth parents' names, from orphanage files.

The Chinese adoptive community has invented many ways of attempting to fill these absences, including an array of efforts to create "Chinese culture" at home and return journeys to China. "Culture" takes the form of Chinese dance and language study, or dress and dumplings, "Culture Days," and Lunar New Year celebrations. As the first cohort of adoptees is on the cusp of adolescence, some are expressing this cultural connection in other ways, such as the thirteen-year-old who decided on a Chinese red and gold theme and Chinese food for her bat mitzvah.[2] Journeys to China take many forms: from providing a child with an experience of her birthplace and of looking like the majority through more organized "culture camps," "homeland," "heritage," "motherland," or "roots" tours, orphanage visits, and teen leadership programs. In 2006 the first Chinese government-sponsored tour took place, as more than 40 adoptees and their families from the United States were hosted by Chinese officials, a trip reminiscent of South Korea's embrace of adoptees as "overseas Koreans."[3]

Miracles and DNA

In spite of all this culture-making and journeying, relationships with birth mothers are, and in the case of China may always remain, fantasies. What has changed during the last few years is the apparent potential for finding biologically related siblings of adopted children who have been adopted to other families outside of China. This potential suggests a new locus for longings that may produce unanticipated results.

It is likely that quite a few of the girls who have been adopted from China have biological sisters, born to couples who kept their first born female child but abandoned the second and subsequent infant girls in order to try for a boy. Many adoptive parents are aware of the possibility that their daughter may have siblings in China. What is less commonly considered is that, in addition to an older sister or younger brother in China, some adopted girls may have one or more sisters who, like themselves, were abandoned and subsequently adopted to families somewhere in the world of receiving countries, most likely in North America, Europe, or Australia. The web of kinship linking families with children from China spins out into unpredictable, global patterns.

As early as 2001, the media warmed to the story of siblings found, with a story in *Health Magazine* about two single mothers in California who adopted from the same orphanage in 1997, traveled in the same adoption group to China, and became friends. As their daughters grew and began to look and sound increasingly alike, the mothers decided to do

DNA testing. They found that the girls were indeed fraternal twins (Evans 2001). A second story appeared in 2002, when a Seattle newspaper reported on an American couple who sent a disposable camera to the foster home in China where their soon-to-be adopted daughter had lived for over a year, thinking that this would be a way of learning more about their daughter's pre-adoption life. When they returned from China with their child and developed the film, they were astonished to see her photograph with another toddler who appeared to be her identical twin. DNA testing confirmed the genetic link. Although the second child had already been referred to a different American family, she was still in China, and the Seattle couple eventually received permission to adopt her too. Nine months later, the toddlers reportedly met at the Seattle airport and gave each other a "big hug." The reporter pronounced the story "a miracle made possible only by a photograph."[4]

In these stories we find elements that recur in subsequent accounts of sibling reunions: the chance revelation of biological kinship; the role of visual media, especially resemblances spotted in photos on the Web; the radical transformations of lives that ensue; and the coexistence of the language of hard science—DNA testing, genetic markers, lab results, and probabilities—with the language of miracles.

While most depictions in the popular media tend to gloss over the nature of the scientific claims, concerns about the tests' reliability are actively discussed among adoptive parents. DNA testing has been used for many years to establish relatedness between parents and children in birth parent searches. This practice, long familiar to the Korean adoption community, is being used in other contexts as well, including the matching of parents in El Salvador with children who were separated from them during that country's civil war and in some cases adopted to the United States, France, and Italy.[5] The use of testing to identify siblings where there is no parental DNA is relatively new, developed only in the aftermath of 9/11.[6] It is also, by all accounts, far less reliable. The tests examine alleles, or genetic markers, that are found at specific locations on the chromosome. Typically, sibling tests assess 15 or more markers and, "based on the number and location of matching alleles in two samples, geneticists deliver a result in the form of a percentage of probability of a biological relation" (Liberman 2005: 4). The ambiguity of the results stems from the fact that since children inherit different combinations of their parents' genes, biological siblings may have either a very high or a very low percentage of matching alleles. While most fall somewhere in the middle, there is no way to be certain. Some critics argue that even a high frequency of shared markers may reveal nothing more than the probability that two individuals are from the same region of China. The only certainty is in the case of identical twins, who share the same DNA.

In "Embodying Chinese Culture" (2005), I wrote of two families who had their daughters' DNA tested, only to be disappointed that there appeared to be no genetic connection. The parents, one set in the United States and the other in Europe, wondered if their daughters, fifteen months apart and adopted from the same orphanage, might be biological sisters. The girls look so much alike, wrote one mother, "that their photos could easily be mistaken for one another's. It's really astonishing. Even if they aren't siblings . . . it will be very cool to know somebody who looks that much like them." The families met, the girls' DNA was tested, and after six weeks of anxious waiting, the results were inconclusive. Both families were deeply disappointed. Responding to this disappointment, social worker Jane Brown mused: "In a world where one is genetically all alone, it is a rare thing to have even a chance at making a connection."[7]

In the *Good Housekeeping* story, the parents of a four-year-old girl named Meredith had been browsing an orphanage Web site and were intrigued by the odd coincidence that another family had a four-year-old also named Meredith. Struck by similarities in their photos, one of the fathers mixed up the images and showed them to friends and relatives of both families, who could not distinguish the girls. Further conversations led the parents to identify all sorts of similarities, ranging from the tilt of their heads to the fact that both Merediths had expressed a longing, from the time they were very young, for a sister. Eventually the families decided to have the girls' DNA tested. Following lab results that indicated that it was probable that Meredith Grace and Meredith Ellen were fraternal twins, the families arranged a series of reunions in Chicago and Birmingham, Alabama. The reunions fulfilled everyone's hopes: the girls were thrilled with one another and the idea of their sisterhood, and the parents all got along remarkably well. The separations, however, were wrenching for the girls and difficult for both families, who had not figured out how to deal with a 700-mile distance and the girls' apparently intense desire to be together. The Chicago dad wrote in his online journal: "All parties are aware that this is a weird situation, and that there is nothing in the rulebooks to tell us what to do. . . . Our best guess is that they will have the same sort of relationship with each other that MG [Meredith Grace] has with her South Dakota cousins, but . . . we don't want *anything* to screw this up" (J. Rittenhouse 2006).[8]

Shortly after the Merediths met, Susan Rittenhouse, the Chicago mother, started a listserv, Sister Far, for "parents of internationally adopted children who have found (or suspect that they have found) a biological sibling or twin" (SisterFar@yahoo.com). In the summer of 2006, the listserv had 137 members, whose children included 15 sets of presumed twins and seven sets of siblings, most from China but a few from Cambodia, Russia, Guatemala, and Nepal.[9] Members find their way to Sister Far because a girl in their adoption travel group looks like their daughter, they happened to come across a photo, or they found some other "weird coincidences or resemblances." The topics most commonly discussed include DNA testing: how to do it, what lab to choose, how to interpret the results. Discussions also cover effects on other siblings and dealing with a biological sibling when the adopted child has been told that biological relationships do not define family. Once parents do the DNA testing, they must decide what makes sense. In spite of all the publicity around her own family, Rittenhouse, who is a biologist, is cautious about the scientific and social uncertainties. One reason she started Sister Far is to provide a forum for parents to think carefully about the implications of doing any of this. The hardest part, she told me, "comes after you've had the DNA tests. Then what do you do?"[10]

The tale of the two Merediths coincided with and may, in part, have inspired a flurry of other sib-search activity, including a growing number of Internet "sib-find" lists that are specific to particular provinces in China. Adoptive parents have started several organizations to pursue sibling matches. Kinsearch Registry is the first DNA bank for internationally adopted children. It collects cheek swabs from adopted Chinese children, and attempts to match them through the DNA profiles. Given that the large number of adopted Chinese children in the United States, Kinsearch expected a flood of cheek swabs when it opened for operation in 2004. Instead, applications trickled in.[11] The slower than anticipated response may reflect a lack of knowledge or enthusiasm on the part of the wider community, an unwillingness to consider contact with members of the child's birth family, or a deep opposition to the whole idea. It may also reflect the caution that characterizes a second organization, the a-China DNA Project. Founded at around the same time as Kinsearch, a-China DNA is focused primarily on education and on developing more powerful tests.

Mary Coolbaugh Murphy, a geneticist and one of the group's founders, argues that a convincing assay requires testing at least 50 loci, or specific sites on the chromosome, whereas most labs now look at only 15. Such tests would be very expensive. Moreover, most labs lack large Chinese databases; several thousand genetic profiles would constitute, in Coolbaugh Murphy's view, a reasonable base. More than 2,100 parents with children from China responded to the online survey set up by a-China DNA to gauge level of interest and knowledge.[12]

The two organizations' approaches reflect some of the differences within the wider community of parents: Kinsearch, eager to proceed and reasonably confident of tests' accuracy, building on parental enthusiasm; and a-China DNA, more wary about the reliability of the science and concerned to link its mission to a set of wider research and policy objectives. In spite of these differences, both groups share a vision of their work as pioneering. Kinsearch describes itself as "ground breaking," and the co-director of a-China DNA wrote: "This is new territory for all of us. At this stage I am in listening mode, as parents within the Chinese adoption community express both their reservations about and continued commitment to uniting their children with biological family here and abroad. . . . I am firmly in the action mode, however, when it comes to getting behind the initial steps of establishing the DNA database. Within our children's DNA lies the answer to a question that will very likely at one time or another . . . need to be answered: 'Who is my biological family?'" (Ebejer 2005).

Beyond concerns about the potential unreliability and uncertain results of genetic testing, many parents worry about the question of agency. Simply put, who is making decisions for whom? Should parents intervene to seek out biological siblings for their young children, after years of espousing the common wisdom that birth parent searches should be initiated by adoptees themselves? What is in the best interest of the children, who are too young to understand the implications of this kind of relationship?

The founders of these organizations acknowledge this quandary. Some argue that establishing a databank and furthering the science simply lays the necessary groundwork for future searching. Susan Rittenhouse argues that "we make decisions that affect our children's lives all the time." One mother who inadvertently discovered her daughter's twin wrote that both sets of parents agreed not to discuss the situation publicly, or with researchers, until the girls were young adults, old enough to decide themselves how they wished to handle their story. Another mother explained that her five-year-old daughter's twin more or less fell into her lap: she and the other family had traveled to China together and became good friends before they decided to do the DNA testing. It would have been fine, she said, if the tests had revealed that the girls were not related and were simply "China sisters." Now that that testing has confirmed the genetic relationship, however, the daughter has "taken ownership" of this relationship and integrated it into her life. If her daughter chooses to share her experience with others, or chooses not to do so, when she is older, that will be up to her. Meanwhile the mother is busy explaining to the kindergarten teacher that the girl her daughter talks about is not an imaginary friend, but a real five-year-old sister who happens to live elsewhere with her family.

Social worker Jane Brown, who has voiced her sympathy for those who are "genetically all alone," is among the adoption professionals questioning the current wave of DNA testing, asserting that it is clearly not in the best interest of the children. Brown is dismayed by parents who rush to find "pseudo sibs," "as though this is some sort of game or contest: broadcasting their child's photo everywhere, imagining that every child who was found in the same province looks JUST like their child, trying to persuade five or six other families at a time to do the DNA testing, and who never even seem to . . . have any thoughts at all about how their CHILD might think about all of this."[13]

The Kin in the Gene?

However these questions are approached, it is clear that sib-search is part of a wider phenomenon that grows out of our current fascination with genetics and builds on new technologies in biomedicine. Genetic tests, which used to cost thousands of dollars and were used almost entirely by research scientists, are now relatively cheap. The New York Times reports that, thanks largely to the Human Genome Project, "a cottage industry of commercial test companies has sprung up." The Genographic Project, a study of human migration launched by the National Geographic Society, IBM, and a company known as Family Tree DNA, has already tested the DNA of thousands of Americans who, at a cost of $99.95, can send a cheek swab to the project and in return "find out where they fit on the resulting map."[14] In early 2006, Newsweek magazine ran a cover story, "In Our Blood," which quoted the head of Family Tree DNA as saying: "Six years ago the term genetic genealogy was meaningless. . . . Now the interest is huge."[15] Around the same time the *New Yorker* published "The Tree of Me" in which reporter John Seabrook, cites a poll showing that "a hundred and twenty million Americans are interested in family history" and asserts that, after gardening, family history is the second most popular hobby in the United States, while genealogy is second only to pornography as the most searched-for subject on the web. A database maintained by the Mormons, FamilySearch.com, had more than five billion hits during the first two years after its launch. China sib-search is tiny, but well within mainstream popular culture. Seabrook envisions a "controlling structure for the family" that "seems to be evolving from a tree into something more like a root system, hairy with adoptive parents, two-mommy families, sperm-bank daddies, and other kinds of family appendages that don't fit onto trunks and branches."[16]

The exploration of these root systems using DNA has captured the interest of diverse groups of Americans. The excitement of establishing ancestry and reinventing identity seems initially to have overpowered whatever scientific reservations sociologists like Troy Duster and the scientists themselves may have. As genetic testing becomes increasingly affordable, its uses proliferate beyond criminology and medical research into "roots" or heritage mapping. As Duster points out, "This is not just somebody's desire to go find out whether their grandfather is Polish. . . . It's about access to money and power."[17] Prospective immigrants to the United States pay for DNA tests to prove relatedness to American citizens or permanent residents in order to speed up their applications,[18] while middle-class Americans use DNA tests to establish "minority" ancestry—for their adopted as well as their biological children—to boost their chances of college admission, financial aid, or employment. Although scientists are cautious about what exactly the tests reveal, *New York Times* reporter Amy Harmon points out that "that has not stopped many test-takers from adopting new DNA-based ethnicities—and a sense of entitlement to the privileges reserved for them."[19]

Adoptive families who use DNA testing to try to identify siblings are moving in tandem with families created through new reproductive technologies. As a growing number of children conceived with donor sperm and by in vitro fertilization come of age, these young adults, like earlier generations of adopted persons, have decided that they too want to find, and have the right to know, the missing pieces in their genetic histories. In recent years, some sperm banks in the United States have begun to offer "known" donors who have agreed to let their identity be revealed if their offspring wish to contact them once they turn eighteen. More important, the Internet has facilitated searching for half-siblings of offspring conceived by donor insemination. Donor Sibling Registry, a website founded in 2000 by a Colorado mother and her son, "is helping to open a new chapter in the oldest form of assisted reproductive technology," writes *New York Times* reporter Amy Harmon. The site allows parents and their offspring to search for relatives using sperm bank information and donor numbers that the bank provided when the sperm was purchased. By March 2006, Donor Sibling Registry had 7,000 members and had already matched 1,600 family members, mostly half-siblings. The site's popularity, Harmon suggests, "speaks to the sustained power of biological ties at a time when it is becoming almost routine for women to bear children who do not share a partner's DNA, or even their own."[20] In the United States, potential users form a large group: some 30,000 children are born annually to mothers after donor insemination (DI);[21] by 1995, an estimated one million babies had been conceived by donor insemination since World War II.[22]

Donor sibling matches do not necessarily depend on DNA tests. In the United States, individuals can match sperm donor numbers, as suggested in the snappy title of one of Amy Harmon's articles: "Hello, I'm Your Sister. Our Father Is Donor 150."[23] In the United Kingdom, DNA plays a more crucial role, since until last year it was illegal for IVF offspring to trace their genetic parents. In a sign of changing times, a voluntary database known as UK Donorlink, for donors and DI offspring, has been funded by the Department of Health. People interested in participating send any information they have along with a cheek swab for DNA tests. The first successful Donorlink match was celebrated in May 2006 in an article in *The Daily Mail*: "The two young women running towards each other across a Cambridge park and then embracing like long-lost friends should have little [in] common. Indeed, they live on opposite sides of the globe and until now they have never met." Keeley, from Perth, Australia, and Elizabeth, from Cambridge, are half-siblings, conceived with sperm from a man they know only as Donor X. Like the Chinese sib-find stories, this story draws on familiar tropes: instant recognition and embrace, uncanny resemblances that include not only physical features but also a love of Italy and the piano, and conversion to Catholicism in the same year. Both women sensed their whole lives that something in their family history was amiss. Their meeting, said Elizabeth, is "like the weirdest blind date."[24]

Unlike adoptees, donor half-siblings are usually genetically related to one of the parents who raised them; they are not "genetically all alone." Although, like adoptees, they are searching for siblings, they have some chance of finding a genetic parent if the donor decides to shed his anonymity. What is distinctly different here is the possibility of meeting a large number of half-siblings. Rather than locating a single sister who shares a set of unknown birth parents in a distant land and a similar history of abandonment and adoption, these donor siblings may find themselves in a large crowd of age-mates linked only by a sperm donor's genes and the fact that their mothers, for one reason or another, conceived using assisted reproductive technologies. These newly discovered half-siblings and their families are embarking on a path whose rules are not yet written and emerging social groups are linked in new ways: by a number, an imagined anonymous donor, and some DNA; by a search for physical resemblances; and by a sense of the uncanny. A new, transnational form of donor siblingship is emerging, since sperm itself now moves in transnational circuits: one of the leaders in this vast global market is a Danish firm that, by 2002, was exporting its product to more than fifty countries (Spar 2006: 38).[25]

All of these emerging formations constitute creative reconfigurations of the boundaries between nature and culture. Even mothers whose only connection is that they conceived with sperm from the same anonymous donor may seek one another out on the Donor Registry. Harmon describes seven mothers, "eager to create a patchwork family for themselves and their children," who "feel bonded by the half-blood relations of their children" and "perhaps by the vaguely biological urge that led them all to choose Fairfax Cryobank's Donor 401."[26]

The social and emotional uncertainties involved in thinking through and navigating these relationships are captured in an adoptive mother's email note:

> We adopted our dear daughter from China. We weren't trying to avoid birth family contact but assumed that this wouldn't be a part of our journey. . . . Through a series of amazing miracles, we found ourselves looking at a picture of someone who appeared to be our four year old dear daughter's IDENTICAL TWIN. We had NO CLUE before this.
>
> We struggled mightily with every decision along the way. We asked ourselves questions to which there are no answers. "How would Dear Daughter feel as an adult if we didn't pursue a DNA test and relationship

with the then potential twin? Would she feel we 'cheated' her? How would she feel if we did pursue it? Would she feel we took away her choice in this? Maybe we could pursue a relationship without the DNA test? But would we be willing to invest the time, money, and emotional energy as parents and as a family to pursue a relationship with a 'maybe' twin?" . . . There were no easy answers and it felt that no path was without risk. (19 March 2003)

Anthropologist Kaya Finkler observed that adoptees without family medical histories feel like non-persons in the doctor's office, missing knowledge of the "kin in the gene" that defines identity (Finkler 2001). Yet, as Charis Thompson writes in her essay on a California infertility clinic, the genetic basis of kinship is hardly straightforward in an era of sophisticated assisted reproduction. Thompson shows how the "overlapping idioms of shared bodily substance and genes come apart" in the clinic. In cases of in vitro fertilization with ovum donation, motherhood is traced through substance: the mother carries the fetus created with another woman's genetic material. In gestational surrogacy, the reverse is true, as motherhood is traced through genes: the mother is the woman who provides the genetic material for the fetus carried in and nurtured by another woman's body. Nature and culture are co-produced in the clinic, Thompson writes, where "the facts and practices of biomedicine and the social meanings of kinship are used to generate and substantiate each other" (2001: 176).

The sibling search phenomenon complicates fundamental questions about relatedness. Where does the new kinship, based on DNA-tested, sought-for sisters, fall on the spectrum from "made" to grounded in "biology"? What does sister searching mean in a community in which the legitimation of socially constructed kinship is crucial? This is a world in which parents abhor the stranger's question "are they really sisters?" and spend hours sharing rejoinders to this and other comments that imply that adoptive sisterhood is somehow less desirable or less real than its genetic counterpart. What is the impact of the discovery of a DNA sister, or of a possible, but not quite certain, sister? Or, of what Jane Brown provocatively calls a "pseudo sib"? Of twins who live in Norway and California, Brussels and South Carolina? Of a sister who speaks a language other than English or Chinese? Is sibling searching yet another vector for middle-class anxiety, as one mother suggested, like dance lessons or admission to Yale? Or is the fascination with these ties a return to genetic essentialism?

One mother put it bluntly: "I think the whole thing is the biggest scam to hit the adoption community." The problem, she explained, is that this "sends a clear message to adopted siblings that being sisters by adoption is not as 'real' or 'special' or whatever other descriptor you want to use, as being biologically sisters. And I think that devalues all the work that adoptive families do in convincing society that adoptive families are on par with biological families. . . . We, and the adoptive community as a whole, have been struggling to get people to understand that siblings by adoption = siblings by shared genetic code. What damage would we do if we had the testing done?"[27]

For social workers such as Jane Brown, the damage is clear, the truth claims flawed. In Brown's view, as testing companies rush to exploit a lucrative market, parents caught up in their own desires to fill in missing blanks or give their family a special status neglect what their children really need: "straight talk about loss, perceived rejection, and race." Brown argues that the discovery of supposed siblings might be an easy "feel-good experience" at age five, but as children grow, so will their confusion and anger at their parents for creating relationships built on uncertainties, a lack of everyday interaction, and on a valuation of genetic ties that undermines the non-genetic relationships of adoptive families.

Alternatively, might sibling searching be a new and more expansive way of viewing family, or extending the ties that shape creative kinship? One of the two California mothers I mentioned earlier moved to a different part of the state, so that their families could be closer. The mothers compare notes on how they are raising their daughters, and sometimes share parenting tasks. One of the grandmothers, who carries photographs of both girls in her wallet, was reportedly considering moving too: "The sense of family is so strong, there are no boundaries here," she said. "I want to be close to my two granddaughters and watch their progress in this adventure" (Evans 2001).

If one can have multiple mothers, or fathers (adoptive, birth, step, god, gay, the anthropologists' fictive, and perhaps others), and one might already have assorted siblings (step, half, or otherwise linked by new reproductive technologies, and including those adoptive families call "orphanage sisters") why not embrace new kinds of siblings too? Are these not other steps in the dance that Thompson calls the flexible "choreography"

of innovative kinship practices? Long-distance kinship seems impracti-
cal to some, but in an increasingly globalized world, where people move
around the planet, why limit the imagination to a bilateral connection between the United States and China? Why not have sisters in South Dakota
and Scandinavia, California and Brazil, Birmingham and Chicago, as well
as China?

As I was finishing this chapter, I met a woman who introduced me to
her children, mentioning that one was informally adopted. "She's part of
our DNA," she declared, explaining that she had become a sort of surrogate mother for the girl. Puzzled for a moment, I realized that the woman
had flipped the usual trope of adoptive families on its head. Instead of
affirming the kin-ness of children who do not share parents' genetic heritage, she asserted the DNA-ness of such a child. DNA had become a metaphor for socially constructed kinship, for relationships based on social,
cultural, and affective bonds in which genes were irrelevant.[28]

This anecdote, like the stories of DNA-linked twins, likely sisters, per-
haps-sisters, or "pseudo-sibs," suggests that variations on the complex and
fluid choreography of the infertility lab go well beyond that specialized
setting. The intense interest that some adoptive parents have in finding
their Chinese daughters' siblings reflects both their desire to heal the multiple losses of adoption and the power of genetic discourses in the world
of contemporary quotidian, DNA-inflected kinship. Geneticist Mary
Coolbaugh Murphy expressed this point forcefully:

> We can't find a birth parent but there's an ancient Chinese tradition of
> connection with the ancestors. In everybody's cells are bits and pieces of
> every ancestor they have ever had. I'm trying to help my daughter under-
> stand that she carries this within her, everywhere she goes. It connects
> her to a bigger community, something outside herself; it adds another
> layer of connection. It's not that adoption trumps blood, or that blood
> trumps adoption.

The strong negative reactions of other parents remind us that there are
myriad approaches to grief and loss, and that genetic discourses remain
contested. How do we understand the presumed universal need to know
genetic origins? Is this longing specific to a cultural moment, in which
American kinship privileges biology and the nuclear family over other
sorts of affiliation and other models of family? Do we need genetics, as

anthropologist Ann Anagnost has asked, to "tether our identity in a world that is becoming increasingly mixed up?"[29]

Adoptive parents are listening to these emerging debates, observing intimate family dramas as they unfold in public media, and feeling unsure of their implications. In the early years of Chinese adoption just a decade ago, many in the Chinese adoptive community enthusiastically took up the challenge of thinking about culture and race. In the last few years, the Internet and DNA technologies have pressed us to attend as well to our conceptions of genetics, science, and how knowledge itself may make kinship appear.

NOTES

1. Abigail Pogebrin, "Lost and Found: A Story of Mystery and Miracles," *Good Housekeeping*, June 2005.

2. Sarah Price Brown, "Dual Identity, Double the Questions," *Jewish Journal of Greater Los Angeles*, 14 July 2007.

3. The trip was organized by a well-connected Chinese American importer of Tiger Balm who is also the adoptive father of a thirteen-year-old Chinese girl in California. See L. A. Chung, "China Declares Welcome Home," *San Jose Mercury News*, 22 July 2006, and Janine DeFao, "Children Adopted from China to Visit as Government Guests," *San Francisco Chronicle*, 23 July 2006. *Found in China*, a film by Carolyn Stanek (2007), follows another "homeland" tour, exploring the diverse experiences and reflections of a group of parents and their adopted girls, ranging from nine to thirteen years of age. On the complex issues raised by South Korea's official embrace of Korean adoptees, see Eleana Kim 2005.

4. David Eggert, "After Nine Month Separation, Chinese Twins Are Reunited," 4 April 2002, and Eggert, "By Sheer Chance, Chinese Twin Toddlers Are Reunited," 14 April 2002, *Seattle Post-Intelligencer*. See also "Against All Odds, Twin Girls Reunited," *The Early Show*, CBS News, 12 April 2006; Sheila Jacoby, "Two Hearts, One Family," posted in 2006 on her website: www.fulingkids.org/twins/htm.

5. Lonny Shalveson, "DNA Reuniting Salvadoran War Orphans with Parents," *Morning Edition*, National Public Radio, 5 July 2006.

6. After 9/11, government funding permitted expensive tests to determine the siblingship of victims. The tests examined 87 loci as well as mitochondrial DNA (mDNA) that establish whether there is a common maternal ancestor. Funding also allowed the development of sophisticated software to analyze the test results. Mary Coolbaugh Murphy recalls that the owner of the company that developed

that software anticipated how matching siblings would be a more enjoyable and uplifting use for these tests (2006, personal communication).

7. Jane Brown 2002. See listserv: InternationalAdoptTalk@yahoogroups.com.

8. See also Jim Rittenhouse's online journal www.marmotgraphics.com/jim/journal/2004/02/journal_andnowitcanbetold.html (accessed January 8, 2008).

9. Susan Rittenhouse, personal communication, 2006.

10. Ibid.

11. Barbara Rappaport, personal communication, 2006.

12. In December 2007, a-China DNA disbanded, discouraged by the difficulty of obtaining funding to create a databank that could be used for purposes other than sibling searches, especially for medical and epidemiological research. Pogebrin, "Lost and Found," 142.

13. Jane Brown, personal communication, 2006.

14. Amy Harmon, "Seeking Ancestry, and Privilege, in DNA Ties Uncovered by Tests," *New York Times*, 12 April 2006; Harmon, "Love You, K2a2a, Whoever You Are," *New York Times*, News of the Week in Review, 26 January 2006.

15. Claudia Kalb, "In Our Blood," *Newsweek*, 6 February 2006, 47–55, quotation on 48.

16. John Seabrook, "The Tree of Me," *New Yorker*, 26 March 2006, 58–71.

17. Duster quoted in Harmon, "Seeking Ancestry, and Privilege, in DNA Ties Uncovered by Tests."

18. "DNA Testing Is Becoming More Common in Immigration," *New York Times*, 30 July 2006.

19. Harmon, "Seeking Ancestry, and Privilege, in DNA Ties Uncovered by Tests."

20. Amy Harmon, "Hello, I'm Your Sister. Our Father Is Donor 150," *New York Times*, 20 November 2005.

21. "Sperm Donor Siblings Find Family Ties," *CBS News*, 18 March 2006.

22. Peggy Orenstein, "Looking for a Donor to Call Dad," *New York Times Magazine*, 18 June 1995.

23. Harmon, "Hello, I'm Your Sister."

24. Diana Gloger and Elizabeth Sanderson, "Day the Daughters of Donor X Finally Met," *Daily Mail* (London), May 2006.

25. Although Danish sperm is widely exported and considered high quality, Denmark does not allow any identifying information other than hair and eye color, height and weight, and Danish law does not allow donors' identity to be revealed (Spar 2006: 38). Global inconsistencies pervade this market, however. In Sweden, for example, sperm donors must reveal their names (Spar 2006: xiv).

26. Harmon, "Hello, I'm Your Sister."

27. Lisa Forrey, personal communication, 2006.

28. Another example of the prevalence of DNA metaphors is this comment by an adoptive mother in response to a discussion about being Jewish and Chinese:

"It seems to me that ethnicity, race, religion, and gender are helixically wrapped around people and that while at any given moment one may dominate there should be fluidity between the strands."

29. Ann Anagnost, personal communication, 2007.

REFERENCES

Dorow, Sara K. 2006. *Transnational Adoption: A Cultural Economy of Race, Gender, and Kinship*. New York: New York University Press.

Duster, Troy. 2006. "Deep Roots and Tangled Branches." *Chronicle Review, Chronicle of Higher Education*, February 3.

Ebejer, Mary. 2005. "Two Different Journeys: Searching and DNA Collection." *China Connection* 11, no. 2: 8.

Evans, Karin. 2000. *The Lost Daughters of China: Abandoned Girls, Their Journey to America, and the Search for a Missing Past*. New York: Putnam.

———. 2001. "Sister Act." *Health* (December): 74–118.

Finkler, Kaya. 2001. "The Kin in the Gene: The Medicalization of Family and Kinship in American Society." *Current Anthropology* 42: 235–63.

Johnson, Kay, with Huang Banghang and Wang Liao. 1998. "Infant Abandonment and Adoption in China." *Population and Development Review* 24: 469–510.

Kim, Eleana. 2005. "Wedding Citizenship and Culture." In *Cultures of Transnational Adoption*, ed. Toby Alice Volkman, 49–80. Durham, NC: Duke University Press.

Liberman, Ellen. 2005. "The Search for Siblings: Seeing, Searching, Testing and Finding." *China Connection* 11, no. 2: 4–7.

Lifton, Betty Jean. 1994. *Journey of the Adopted Self: A Quest for Wholeness*. New York: Basic Books.

Prager, Emily. 2001. *Wuhu Diary: On Taking My Adopted Daughter Back to Her Hometown in China*. New York: Random House.

Rittenhouse, Jim. 2006. "When Meredith Found Her Biological Sister, Meredith, 700 Miles Away." *China Connection* 11, no. 2: 19–24.

Spar, Debora L. 2006. *The Baby Business: How Money, Science, and Politics Drive the Commerce of Conception*. Boston: Harvard Business School Press.

Stanek, Carolyn. 2007. *Found in China*. Film. Tai-Kai Productions.

Thompson, Charis. 2001. "Strategic Naturalizing: Kinship in an Infertility Clinic." In *Relative Values: Reconfiguring Kinship Studies*, ed. Sarah Franklin and Susan McKinnon, 175–202. Durham, NC: Duke University Press.

Volkman, Toby Alice. 2005. "Embodying Chinese Culture." In *Cultures of Transnational Adoption*, ed. Toby Alice Volkman, 81–113. Durham, NC: Duke University Press.

About the Contributors

Domingos Abreu is Professor and Researcher at the Universidade Federal do Ceará, Brazil. During 2004–2005 he taught and did research at University of Virginia and University of Lunière (France). His books and articles on childhood, adoption, and international adoption include *No bico da cegonha: Histórias de adoçao e da adoçao internacional no Brasil* (Relume Dumará, 2002), "Adoções no Brasil: Entre o illegal e o socialmente aceito." and "Récits et representations d'adotion internacional: Les logiques du don et de la dette."

Laura Briggs, who coedited this volume, is Associate Professor and Head of Women's Studies and holds affiliate appointments in History, Anthropology, and Latin American Studies at the University of Arizona. Her areas of specialization are sexuality and reproduction, race and colonialism, and transnational U.S. history. Her first book is *Reproducing Empire: Race, Sex, Science, and U.S. Imperialism in Puerto Rico* (University of California Press, 2002); she is currently completing a monograph on transnational and transracial adoption. Her articles and book chapters illuminating the connections between adoption and imperialism include "Making 'American' Families: Transnational Adoption and U.S. Latin America Policy," in *Haunted by Empire: Geographies of Intimacy in North American Empire*, ed. Ann Stoler (Duke University Press, 2006); "Adopción transnacional: Robo de criaturas, familias homoparentales y neoliberalismo," translated by Gloria Elena Bernal, *Debate Feminista* 17:33 (Abril 2006): 46–68; "Orphaning the Children of Welfare Mothers: 'Crack Babies,' Race, and Adoption Reform," in *Outsiders Within: Racial Crossings and Adoption Politics*, edited by Jane Jeong Trenka, Chinyere Oparah, and Sun Yung Shin (South End Press, 2006); and "Mother, Child, Race, Nation: Visual Iconography of Rescue and the Politics of Transnational and Transracial Adoption in the 1950s," *Gender & History* 15 (August 2003): 179–200.

Anne Cadoret is Researcher at the Centre National de la Recherche Scientifique (CNRS) in Paris, France. Her books include *Des parents comme les autres: Parenté et homosexualité* (Editions Odile Jacob, 2002) and *Parenté Plurielle: Anthropologie du Placement Familial* (L'Harmattan, 1995). She coedited *Homoparentalités: Approches Scientifiques et Politiques* with Caroline Mécary, Martine Gross, and Bruno Perreau (Puf, 2006).

Auksuolė Čepaitienė is Senior Research Fellow at the Department of Ethnology in the Lithuanian Institute of History and a Lecturer at Vilnius University in Lithuania. Trained as historian, she studied ethnology at the Kaunas Vytautas Magnus University, where she earned a Ph.D. in 1997. She has done research on identity and local conceptions of family and kinship in the context of social and cultural change. In 2002–2004 she participated in an international research project funded by the European Commission, "Public Understanding of Genetics: a Cross-Cultural and Ethnographic Study of the 'New Genetics' and 'Social Identity.' "

Chantal Collard is Professor of Anthropology at Concordia University in Montréal, Québec, Canada. Her research interests include issues related to kinship, gender, intercountry adoption from Haiti, intrafamilial adoption, and embryo donation/adoption in North America. She is author of *Une Famille, Un Village, Une Nation: La Parenté dans le Comté de Charlevoix, 1900–1960* (Éditions du Boréal, 1999).

Claudia Fonseca is Professor of Social Anthropology at the Universidad Federal do Rio Grande do Sul (Porto Alegre) and at the Universidad de San Martin (Buenos Aires). Her research interests include legal anthropology, family organization, and gender relations, with special focus on human rights and international adoption. Among her recent works are *Caminhos de Adoçao* (Cortez 1995). Her recent English-language publications include chapters in *Cross-Cultural Approaches to Adoption*, edited by Fiona Bowie (Routledge, 2004), and in *Cultures of Transnational Adoption*, edited by Toby Alice Volkman (Duke University Press, 2005).

Martine Gross is Social Sciences Research Fellow at the Centre d'Études Interdisciplinaires des faits religieux (Centre National de la Recherche Scientifique, Ecole des Hautes Études en Sciences Socials), France. She is the editor of *Homoparentalités, Etat des lieux* (Eres, 2005), coauthor with Mathieu Peyceré and Dominique Strauss-Kahn of *Fonder une famille homoparentale* (J'ai lu, 2007), and coauthor with Edwige Antier of *Deux papas, deux mamans, qu'en penser?* (Calmann-Lévy, 2007). She has published numerous articles on lesbian and gay parenting and on Christian and Jewish identities among lesbians and gay men.

Signe Howell is Professor of Social Anthropology at the University of Oslo, Norway. Her book, *The Kinning of Foreigners: Transnational Adoption in a Global Perspective* (Berghahn Books, 2006), situates transnational adoption in Norway in global perspective. She has published many articles and book chapters on adoption laws and international conventions, relationships between donor and receiving countries, questions of identity and roots, and the experiences of adoptive parents. Her previous ethnographic research focused on religion, ritual, and kinship in Malaysia and Indonesia; she has also written on the cultural bases of peace and of social ethics.

Lilia Khabibullina is currently completing her Ph.D. in Social and Cultural Anthropology at the University of Barcelona, Spain. She also collaborates with the Autonomous University of Barcelona and the Institute of Childhood and Urban World (CIIMU) by participating in two research projects about adoption and immigration financed by the Ministry of Education and Science of Spain. Her research interests focus on kinship, children, adoption, reproduction, immigration, intercultural mediation, and gender.

Caroline Legrand, who holds a Ph.D. in Social Anthropology from the École des Hautes Études en Sciences Sociales, is associated with the Laboratoire d'Anthropologie Sociale in Paris, France. She has authored *La quête de parenté: Pratiques et enjeux de la généalogie en Irlande* (Presses de l'Université Laval, Québec, 2006), and coedited *Patrimoines des migrations, migrations des Patrimoines* (Presses de l'Université Laval, Québec, 2008) with Marie-Blanche Fourcade.

Jessaca B. Leinaweaver is Assistant Professor of Anthropology at Brown University in Providence, Rhode Island, where she is also affiliated with the Population Studies and Training Center and the Center for Latin American Studies. She recently published *The Circulation of Children: Adoption, Kinship and Morality in Andean Peru* (Duke University Press, 2008). Her research interests include children, families, aging, gender, and migration.

Diana Marre, who coedited this volume, is Senior Researcher in Social Anthropology at the Autonomous University of Barcelona and the Institute of Childhood and Urban World of Barcelona (CIIMU), Spain. Among her recent works in English are a chapter in *Race, Ethnicity and Nation in Europe: Perspectives from Kinship and Genetics,* edited by Peter Wade (Berghahn Books, 2007), and a chapter coauthored with Joan Bestard in *Kinship Matters: European Cultures of Kinship in the Age of Biotechnology,* edited by Jeanette Edwards and Carles Salazar (Berghahn Books, 2008). She coedited *La Adopción y el Acogimiento: Presente y Perspectivas* (Universitat de Barcelona 2004) with Joan Bestard.

Françoise-Romaine Ouellette is Professor at the Institute National de la Recherche Scientifique, Centre Urbanisation, Culture et Société, in Montréal, Québec, Canada. She serves as the scientific director of Familles en Mouvance et Dynamiques Intergénérationnelles, a research partnership composed of university researchers, public officials, and community groups. She has published articles and books on cultural, legal, and ethical issues related to adoption, foster care, and children's rights. Her research focuses on adoption in the context of changing family norms and values. Her other interests include naming practices, identification papers, transcultural approaches to clinical intervention, and family meals. She is also a trained psychoanalyst.

Judith Schachter is Professor of Anthropology, History, and Art at Carnegie Mellon University in Pittsburgh. Her main research interests are child adoption, foster care, kinship, and family. Previously publishing under the surname Modell, she is author of *Kinship with Strangers: Adoption and Interpretations of Kinship in American Culture* (University of California Press, 1994) and *A Sealed and Secret Kinship: The Culture of Policies and Practices in American Adoption* (Berghahn, 2002), as well as numerous articles. Schachter is currently completing a book on the influence of state and federal policies on Native Hawaiian interpretations of kinship and family. Her interests include visual anthropology, narratives and life stories, and the history of anthropology. She is also known for her interviews with residents of the declined industrial town of Homestead, Pennsylvania, and her biography of Ruth Benedict.

Peter Selman is Visiting Fellow in the School of Geography, Politics, and Sociology at Newcastle University, United Kingdom. His main areas of interest are child adoption, teenage pregnancy, and demographic change and public policy. He currently chairs the Network for Inter-country Adoption (NICA) and serves on the board of trustees of the British Association for Adoption and Fostering (BAAF), the leading UK charity working for children separated from their birth families. He is author of *Intercountry Adoption: Developments, Trends and Perspectives* (BAAF, 2000) and has written many articles and chapters on adoption policy.

Toby Alice Volkman, a cultural anthropologist, recently edited *Cultures of Transnational Adoption* (Duke University Press, 2005). Her forthcoming edited volume is *Origins, Journeys, and Returns: Social Justice and International Higher Education* (Social Science Research Council). Currently Director of Special Projects at the Ford Foundation International Fellowships Program in New York, she has also served as deputy provost at The New School, program officer at the Ford Foundation, and program director for South and Southeast Asia at the Social Science Research Council. She previously published a book and numerous articles on ritual and social change in Indonesia.

Barbara Yngvesson is Professor of Anthropology in the School of Social Science at Hampshire College in Amherst, Massachusetts. For the past ten years she has studied the transnational market in children, funded by grants from the National Science Foundation. Her focus has been on the flow of adoptable children from Asia and Latin America to Sweden and the United States, on return journeys by adult adoptees to visit their birth families and nations, and on adult adoptees' experiences of identity and belonging. She has published widely on transracial/transnational adoption in anthropology and law journals, as well as in edited volumes on globalization, adoption, and motherhood. Her previous work focused on the uses that ordinary citizens make of the legal process.

Index